Josephine Butler

Josephine Butler

JANE JORDAN

JOHN MURRAY
Albemarle Street, London

First published in 2001
by John Murray (Publishers) Ltd,
50 Albemarle Street, London W1S 4BD

A catalogue record for this book is available from the British Library

ISBN 0-7195-5584-1

Typeset in 12.25/13.5 Monotype Garamond by
Servis Filmsetting Ltd, Manchester

Printed and bound in Great Britain by
St Edmundsbury Press Ltd
Bury St Edmunds, Suffolk

For Margaret Simey

Contents

Illustrations

(between pages 176 and 177)

The author and the publisher would like to thank the following for permission to reproduce illustrations: Plates 1, 9, 12, 13, 15, 16, 29, Northumberland Record Office; 2, 5, 6, 7, 8, Beverley Grey; 10, by courtesy of the University of Liverpool Library, Special Collections and Archives, Josephine Butler Collection; 11, 24, 26, 28, Mary Evans Picture Library; 17, 18, 19, 20, 21, 23, 25, 27, 30, 31, The Women's Library (formerly the Fawcett Library). Plates 3 and 14 are taken from A. S. G. Butler, *Portrait of Josephine Butler*, London: Faber & Faber, 1954. Plate 22 is taken from Elizabeth Longford, *Eminent Victorian Women*, London: Weidenfeld & Nicolson, 1981

Acknowledgements

There is one person whom I must acknowledge before all others, without whose practical help, fine judgement, loving encouragement and support, this book would never have been written. Timothy Jordan has read countless versions of the manuscript and has given me invaluable advice. Cathy Wells-Cole, who also read the manuscript, expertly suggested cuts and revisions. I am fortunate to have such a pair to lean on. I thank Simon Trewin for his support, and Caroline Knox for her warm encouragement. I am also grateful to the following at John Murray: Beth Humphries, Gail Pirkis, Caroline Westmore and Hazel Wood. My thanks too to my mother, Mary Tucker, for willing me on, for her pride in me, and for her ability to find out information about the most curious subjects. Matthew Jordan, Tom Jordan, and Andrew Tucker have, in their different ways, encouraged me and humoured me. My special thanks go to Susanna Jordan. She is this book's good angel.

David Doughan, who, for myself and many others, simply *was* the Fawcett Library until his retirement in 1999, has been of inestimable help to me. His knowledge of the period is astounding: there was not a question to which he did not know the answer. I have had warm and generous assistance from all the staff at the Fawcett Library, now the National Library of Women: in particular, I must single out Vera Di Campli San Vito and Penny Martin.

Katy Hooper, who meticulously re-catalogued the Josephine Butler Collection at the Sydney Jones Library, Liverpool University, has been of great help to me, as has Adrian Allan, University Archivist at Liverpool University, who gave me very helpful information and advice when I was beginning my research. I also wish to thank Jane Collings and Eleanor Gawne at the Royal Institute of British Architects, staff at the British Library, the Northumberland Record Office, the University of St Andrews Library, and the Brotherton Collection, Leeds University Library, J. Bennett, Assistant Curator of the Walker Gallery, Liverpool, and Kristin Doern for sharing information about Catherine Booth, to Gordon Taylor at the Salvation Army International Heritage Centre, Stella Brecknell, curator of the Oxford University Museum Archives, and Simon Hughes for kindly tracking down material in the Oxford University Archives relating to Butler Hall. Joyce Goodman generously sent me information about the Canon Street House of Rest in Winchester, and Dr Jean Hugh-Jones, Hon. Secretary of the Liverpool Medical History Society, kindly took the trouble to offer diagnoses of Josephine's various ailments. For some years now, Elizabeth Crawford has kept me supplied with books by and about Josephine.

Beverley Grey, Josephine's great-niece, whom I met towards the end of my research, has been wonderfully generous to me and let me loose on her remarkable collection of family mementoes. Beverley has lent me books and has allowed me to reproduce many family photographs. I also wish to thank James Butler, Josephine's great-grandson, for his help, in particular for the information he provided me during our delightful telephone conversations.

Margaret Simey has been an inspiration to me while I have been researching and writing this book, and from the very first impressed upon me Josephine Butler's passion for justice. My visits to her in Liverpool, although few, have meant a great deal to me. It is to Margaret that I dedicate this book.

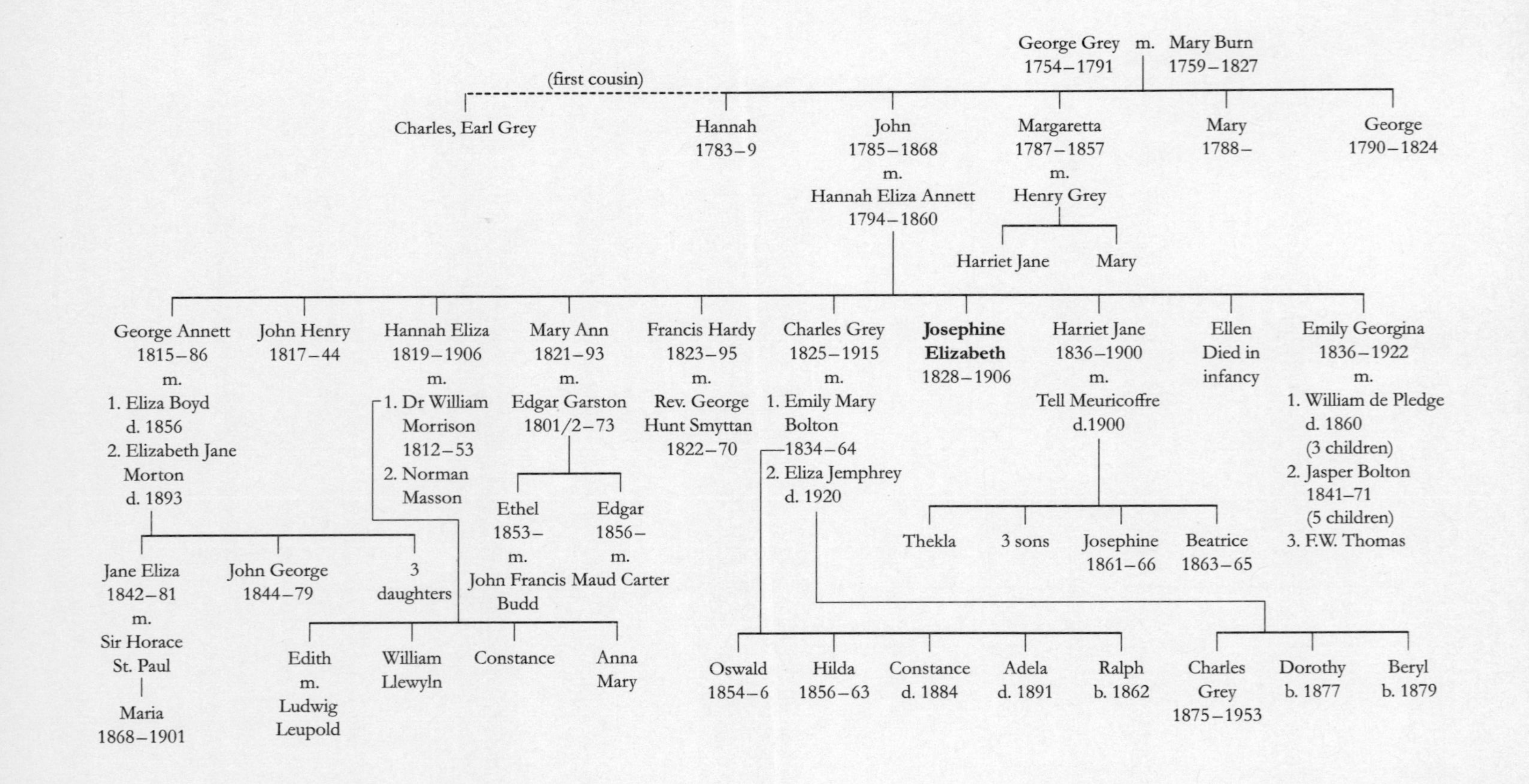
George Grey m. Mary Burn
1754–1791 1759–1827
(first cousin)
Charles, Earl Grey
Hannah
1783–9
John
1785–1868
m.
Hannah Eliza Annett
1794–1860
Margaretta
1787–1857
m.
Henry Grey
Mary
1788–
George
1790–1824
Harriet Jane
Mary
George Annett
1815–86
m.
1. Eliza Boyd
d. 1856
2. Elizabeth Jane
Morton
d. 1893
John Henry
1817–44
Hannah Eliza
1819–1906
m.
1. Dr William
Morrison
1812–53
2. Norman
Masson
Mary Ann
1821–93
m.
Edgar Garston
1801/2–73
Francis Hardy
1823–95
m.
Rev. George
Hunt Smyttan
1822–70
Charles Grey
1825–1915
m.
1. Emily Mary
Bolton
1834–64
2. Eliza Jemphrey
d. 1920
Josephine
Elizabeth
1828–1906
Harriet Jane
1836–1900
m.
Tell Meuricoffre
d.1900
Ellen
Died in
infancy
Emily Georgina
1836–1922
m.
1. William de Pledge
d. 1860
(3 children)
2. Jasper Bolton
1841–71
(5 children)
3. F.W. Thomas
Ethel
1853–
m.
John Francis
Budd
Edgar
1856–
m.
Maud Carter
Thekla
3 sons
Josephine
1861–66
Beatrice
1863–65
Jane Eliza
1842–81
m.
Sir Horace
St. Paul
Maria
1868–1901
John George
1844–79
3
daughters
Edith
m.
Ludwig
Leupold
William
Llewyln
Constance
Anna
Mary
Oswald
1854–6
Hilda
1856–63
Constance
d. 1884
Adela
d. 1891
Ralph
b. 1862
Charles
Grey
1875–1953
Dorothy
b. 1877
Beryl
b. 1879

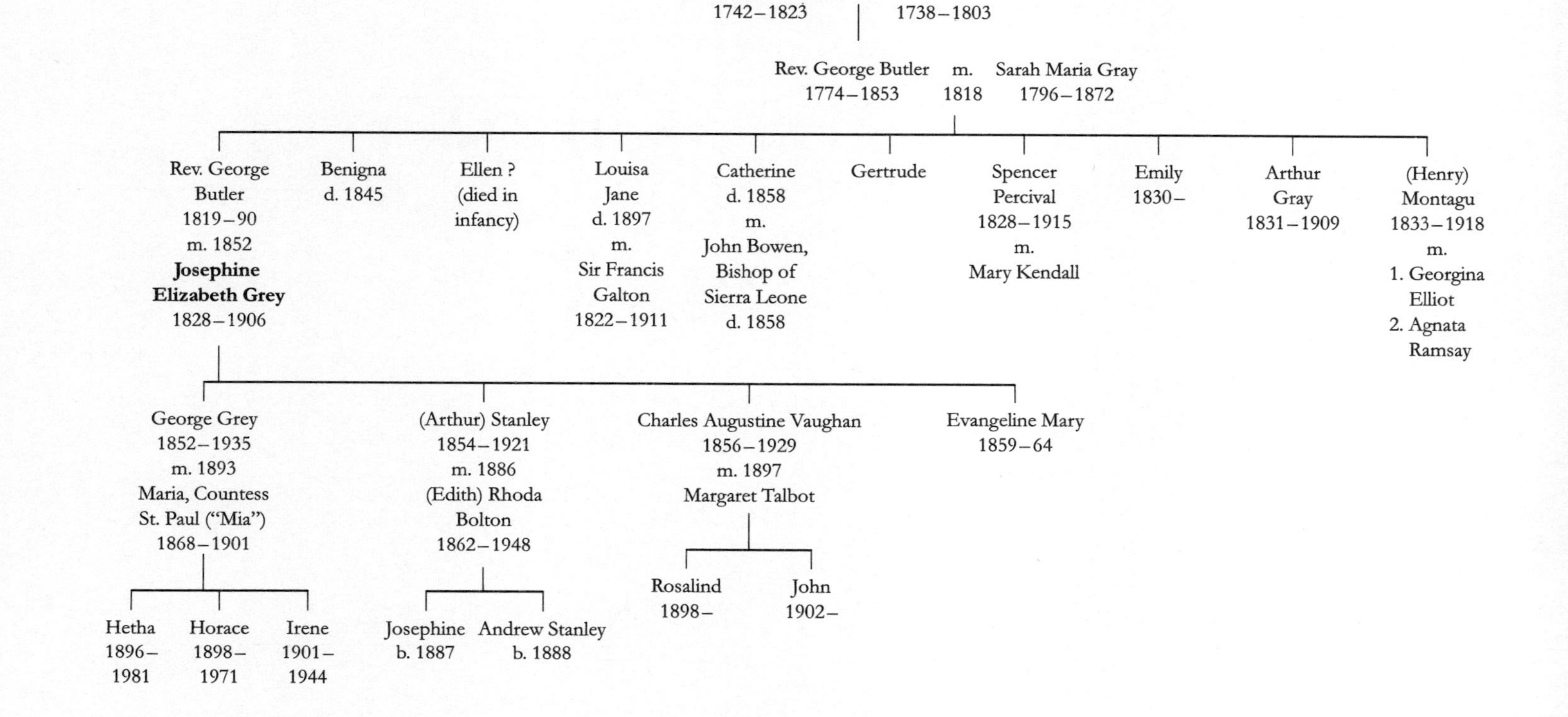
Rev. Weeden Butler m. Anne Giberne
1742–1823
1738–1803
Rev. George Butler m. Sarah Maria Gray
1774–1853 1818 1796–1872
Rev. George Butler
1819–90
m. 1852
Josephine Elizabeth Grey
1828–1906
Benigna
d. 1845
Ellen ?
(died in infancy)
Louisa Jane
d. 1897
m.
Sir Francis Galton
1822–1911
Catherine
d. 1858
m.
John Bowen, Bishop of Sierra Leone
d. 1858
Gertrude
Spencer Percival
1828–1915
m.
Mary Kendall
Emily
1830–
Arthur Gray
1831–1909
(Henry) Montagu
1833–1918
m.
1. Georgina Elliot
2. Agnata Ramsay
George Grey
1852–1935
m. 1893
Maria, Countess St. Paul ("Mia")
1868–1901
(Arthur) Stanley
1854–1921
m. 1886
(Edith) Rhoda Bolton
1862–1948
Charles Augustine Vaughan
1856–1929
m. 1897
Margaret Talbot
Evangeline Mary
1859–64
Hetha
1896–1981
Horace
1898–1971
Irene
1901–1944
Josephine
b. 1887
Andrew Stanley
b. 1888
Rosalind
1898–
John
1902–

Introduction

IN PROFESSOR JAMES Stuart's tribute to Josephine Butler after her death he said of her: 'Mrs Butler was one of the great people of the world. In character, in work done, in influence on others, she was among that few great people who have moulded the course of things. The world is different because she lived . . . She was a great leader of men and women'.[1] Similarly, Millicent Fawcett described Josephine Butler as 'the most distinguished woman of the Nineteenth Century'.[2] These judgements would have been confidently made at the time they were expressed, and yet today Josephine Butler is not widely known.

Even at the first meeting of the Ladies' National Association to be held after Josephine's death, Charlotte Wilson, one of Josephine Butler's oldest friends and colleagues, felt the need to remind the younger generation among the assembled ladies 'What Mrs Butler saved England from'.[3] For sixteen years, Josephine Butler had led the campaign to repeal the Contagious Diseases Acts, legislation instituted in the 1860s to control the spread of syphilis in Britain's armed forces through the enforced inspection of suspected prostitutes and the detention of infected women. The vague terms of the Acts meant that *any* woman residing in certain garrison towns or ports was potentially a suspect. Moreover, since the Acts were first conceived, certain bodies of medical men and politicians were of the view that the legislation should be extended to cover the whole of the civil population. Indeed, the Home Secretary, Henry Austin Bruce, proposed such a bill in 1872 which would have stripped every woman in the kingdom of her civil rights in order that men might 'sin with impunity'. To her Quaker friend, Joseph Edmondson, Josephine observed, 'It is coming to be more & more a deadly fight on the part of us women for *our bodies*'.[4]

The sexual double standard embodied in the Acts was abhorrent to Josephine Butler. To her they meant that the state regarded prostitution as a necessity, and not only condoned male vice but encouraged it. Yet only women were forced to undergo the degrading examination, and only women were denied their civil rights until they were proved to be free from disease. She refused to countenance what she saw as an assumption that God had created a class of women solely for the use of profligate men, and further, that working-class women were created to minister to the sexual needs of gentlemen.

When she answered what she saw as a divine call to take up the cause of poor women, Josephine was actively involved in a number of campaigns to elevate the social position of, largely, women of her own class: the higher education of women, the protection of married women's property and earnings, and the extension of the suffrage. What distinguished Josephine Butler was her decision to step aside from these movements to defend the seemingly indefensible: to identify herself with, and speak for, women who were regarded as the sewers of society. In order to campaign for the repeal of the Contagious Diseases Acts and to protest against the principles embodied in this legislation, Josephine not only had to speak in public, but speak about a subject unmentionable among women of her class. She braved the personal obloquy of being called 'indecent, prurient, shameless', and encouraged her less courageous sisters by reminding them that however painful such attacks were, 'we are not going to die of these wounds'.[5] She never ceased to urge women to take their place in the 'foremost ranks' in this campaign, and was convinced that women were 'called to exercise a certain bold self-assertion. This expression may startle some, but I believe it is one of the most sacred duties . . . We do not do it for ourselves as individuals, but we do it for the whole of a degraded class'.[6] She denounced women's silence on such legislation as 'a crime', and declared herself 'ready to say that it is a subject which *only* women can rightfully deal with'.[7]

Her own approach to rescue work was highly unconventional. She began by taking prostitutes into her own family home, and regarded them as victims of social and economic circumstances rather than as guilty women. When, at the very beginning of the repeal campaign, Josephine was asked to read a paper on 'The Moral Reclaimability of Prostitutes', she was 'so surprised' at the request, 'that I could scarcely regain my breath for a moment'. She answered that it was more in her line 'to read a paper before two or three hundred prostitutes on "the reclaimability of profligate men"'.[8] To the 'outcasts' of society ('*never* use the word "prostitute" if you can help it', was her advice to one colleague),[9] Josephine offered food, shelter and tender nursing, as well as training and employment. She never spoke to them of their sin, never asked them about their past life, but instead offered them the possibility of a new life.

Josephine Butler's feminism and her radical politics in general were driven by her Christian faith, which animated her support for the abolition of slavery, her anti-imperialist attitudes, her concern for the socially disadvantaged and her calls for the extension of the franchise, in particular to women. It was from Christ's teachings that she learned 'the equality of all human beings', and asked by a Parliamentary Select Committee whether the motives for her action against the Acts were 'founded upon moral and religious considerations?', she asserted that they were based 'also very strongly upon constitutional and legal considerations'.[10] In her eyes, religion and social justice were one.[11] This is reflected in a stained-glass window in St Olave's Church in the City of London, which was installed when the church was restored in the early 1950s from the bomb damage it suffered in the Second World War. This window was itself inspired by the early twentieth-century window commemorating Josephine Butler and other prominent Victorian women in Liverpool's Anglican Cathedral. In the St Olave's window, Josephine stands between Elizabeth Fry, Florence Nightingale and Edith Cavell, a bible in her right hand and in her left a rolled petition to Parliament.[12]

The impact of the campaigns led by Josephine Butler upon national and international politics, and upon the feminist movement in particular, was immense. She travelled all over the country, and over much of Europe, inspiring individuals, stimulating local organizations into action, inaugurating international conferences throughout Europe, and addressing meetings, sometimes small gatherings of women, sometimes audiences of hundreds. She would often speak in different towns and cities, night after night, yet rarely repeating the same speech. James Stuart said that, 'As an orator she touched the hearts of her hearers as no one else has done to whom I have listened', and another colleague, Benjamin Scott, wrote of audiences of working men 'spellbound by the passionate eloquence of a gentle sweet-voiced woman'.[13] Her influence on the politics of protest cannot be overstated.

On her death, Josephine was called 'the Mary Wollstonecraft of the Victorian Era'.[14] During her lifetime she was more often compared to Joan of Arc, a saintly warrior.[15] One of her own heroines was the fourteenth-century St Catherine. She published her biography *Catherine of Siena* in 1878, consciously determined to provide an account of 'the real woman', rather than the 'superhuman' portrait left by medieval hagiographers which, she argued, as little resembled the real woman 'as the figures on the painted windows of old churches resemble the flesh and blood original'.[16] There is little doubt that in writing of St Catherine, she was reflecting on aspects of her own life, and certainly there are difficulties for a modern biographer attempting to portray the real woman who was Josephine Butler. One such difficulty is that the main source of information is Josephine herself. In her speeches, her pamphlets, her biographies of members of her family, and her histories of her campaigns, she is perpetually writing her public life for public consumption. 'What more than this could anyone desire?' she would ask, in discouraging any attempt to write her biography, or to persuade her to write her own life story. Thus, much of her personal life is excluded, and can only be pieced together by reference to her correspondence. Her biographies of her father, her husband and her sister, as well as her official history of the repeal campaign, all carry an apologetic statement that she had been urged by others to take up her pen, and she further wrote of her *Personal Reminiscences of a Great Crusade* (1896), that she had 'tried to make myself as little prominent as possible'.[17] Such an apology is a familiar feature of women's autobiographical writing, but Josephine entertained a specific disgust for the present 'shouting age' which demanded 'shouting' biographies, books which revealed their subject's inner life: 'I cannot help feeling that it is above all unseemly to endeavour to probe and to expose to the public the *spiritual life and experience* of those who are gone'.[18] W. T. Stead, editor of the *Review of Reviews*, offered Josephine '*a large sum of money*' to publish her autobiography, but she declined, telling her friends privately, 'I hate the very appearance of egotism, and I feel almost a *disgust* of speaking of myself'.[19]

Just before her seventy-fifth birthday, Josephine wrote to one of her closest colleagues, Miss Fanny Forsaith, forbidding her to allow anyone to write her biography after her death, or to hand over any material for such a book. She had already given her sons the same instruction. Her prohibition is not, though, simply protective of her personal life. Interestingly, she shows an awareness that a record of her public life 'and *nothing else*' would be incomplete, one-sided, and an insult to her children. The letter to Fanny was dictated to an amanuensis, and says, 'We have had so much bright family life, so many incidents occurring in our joint lives both tragic and joyful that the Abolitionist crusade seems to become, in comparison, quite secondary'. Then in her own hand Josephine adds, 'to *us*'.[20] I think that addition is crucial, for it cements her allegiance to her husband and her three sons, and puts her role as wife and mother above that of her leadership of a political campaign. Certainly her public life depended on the ungrudging support given her by George Butler and their marriage, which she described as a united life. Throughout her life, that balance between Josephine's private and public worlds was constantly being negotiated. It has been my endeavour in this biography to reflect that difficult balance, and to represent the 'real woman', 'the flesh and blood original'.

I

Early Life and Influences

'A fiery hatred of all injustices'

JOSEPHINE ELIZABETH GREY was born on 13 April 1828 at Milfield, her father's estate in Glendale, Northumberland. The Greys had long been a prominent border family, with three branches, the most notable of which were the Earls Grey of Howick, of whom Charles, the second Earl Grey was the Whig Prime Minister (1831–34). The other branches were the Greys of Falloden and the Greys of Milfield.

Josephine was the seventh of ten children born to John and Hannah Grey. Their births spanned more than twenty years. Josephine's eldest brother, George Annett, thirteen years her senior, was born in 1815. Next came John Henry (1817), and then Hannah Eliza (1819), named after her mother, but always known as Eliza or 'Lee', and Mary Ann (1821) known by the nickname 'Tully'. Fanny Hardy, named after her mother's sister, was born in 1823, Charles Grey in 1825, and Josephine Elizabeth in 1828: 'I came into the world prematurely, and was a weak, wretched infant, hard to rear at all'.[1] Two years after Josephine came Harriet Jane, or Hatty, who became her special friend. The next daughter, Ellen, died in infancy, and the last child, Emily Georgina, was born in 1836, eight years after Josephine.[2]

Josephine was born into a family of strong-minded women. Her father had been greatly influenced by his mother, Mary Grey, who had brought up John, his brother and his two surviving sisters, after his father died when he was just six years old. Mary Grey appears to have been a remarkably independent woman. A widow at the age of thirty-two, with four young children, she took it upon herself to manage the extensive Milfield estate for twelve years until handing these duties over to John when he reached eighteen.

Mary Grey brought up her children to abhor injustice and thrilled them with extracts read from Thomas Clarkson's *History of the Abolition of the Slave Trade* (1808). She was determined to provide her daughters with a good education, and sent them away to a school in London. The eldest daughter, Margaretta, was a legend in the family for her unconventional, independent ways. One family story told of how in the days before a Ladies' Gallery had been established in the House of Commons, she had dressed as a young man in order to listen to a debate. She would discuss politics in letters to her brother John, and she had strong views about the situation of women, albeit 'women in the upper classes of society', which she recorded in a private diary:

> What I remonstrate against is the negative forms of employment: the wasting of energy, the crippling of talent under false ideas of station, propriety, and refinement, that seems to shut up a large portion of the women of our generation from proper spheres of occupation and adequate exercise of power . . . The education of girls also comes to an end at the time when the serious work of self-improvement properly begins . . . Life is too often divested of any real and important purpose.[3]

The example of John Grey's mother and of his sister, to whom he was very close, would have had a good deal to do with his moral influence over his children and, particularly, with the encouragement he gave his wife and daughters to take an interest in the political life of the country. He would 'confer with them on all matters of interest and importance, political, social, and professional, as well as domestic'. He was proud of his eldest daughter Eliza's 'superiority of mental qualities',[4] and seems to have supported the wishes of women for equal access to education and to public office. Indeed, 'that they should ever be indifferent to anything that concerned their country's good was to him the only marvel', remarked Josephine.[5]

Josephine's mother was another strong woman. Born Hannah Eliza Annett, she was 'a notable housekeeper and a woman of taste', wrote Josephine's brother, Charles.[6] Hannah's parents were descendants of an exiled Huguenot family (originally spelt Annette) who settled in Alnwick, and were, according to Josephine, saintly people and humble in rank.[7] Hannah was brought up in the Moravian Church, a Protestant sect which influenced many aspects of Methodist worship, including the practice of lay preaching. Family legend had it that Hannah had been blessed as a child by John Wesley, while he was a guest in her parents' house: 'he took on his knee a little golden-haired baby (*my mother*) & leaning over her with his *white* hair, for he was a very old man then, he prayed and *blest* her. The blessing clung to her thro' life, poor darling mother'.[8] In fact, John Wesley died in 1791 and Hannah was not born until 1794, but the story had a powerful influence in the family and upon Hannah, who took it upon herself to provide her children with a strong moral education.

> Living in the country, far from any town, and, if I may say so, in the pre-educational era (for women at least), we had none of the advantages which girls of the present day have. But we owed much to our dear mother, who was very firm in requiring from us that whatever we did should be thoroughly done, and that in taking up any study we should aim at becoming as perfect as we could in it, without external aid. This was a moral discipline which perhaps compensated in value for the lack of a great store of knowledge. She would assemble us daily for the reading aloud of some solid book, and by a kind of examination following the reading, assure herself that we had mastered the subject. She urged us to aim at excellence, if not perfection, in at least one thing.[9]

Josephine's 'one thing' was the piano. As a young woman, Hannah had been taught by 'the eminent La Trobe', a composer of Moravian hymns and choral music.[10] Presumably all her daughters played a little, but Josephine was a talented pianist and it seems to have been her mother's special wish that Josephine make the piano a serious study. She was 'very firm' about wanting her to be a good musician, getting her to practise far beyond the conventional requirements of a young lady's accomplishments.[11] Her mother gave her two bound volumes of Beethoven sonatas which she treasured to the end of her life, and Hatty would later recall her pleasure in her sister's playing, 'when we used to sit in the drawing-room at Dilston watching those beautiful sunsets over Hexham and the Tyne Valley, and you used to play Beethoven to us on your splendid grand piano. I remember, especially, the magic of the Moonlight Sonata'.[12] For all her natural shyness in childhood, Josephine seems not to have been unnerved at the prospect of playing in front of an audience, but she was never vain of her talent, maintaining that she had 'not half so much *execution* as many amateurs. People liked my playing I think because my *soul* went into it, & I forgot everything else'.[13]

Her sister Fanny remembered that it was to their mother that they always turned, 'even in failing health, as the centre from which the active household life and interests diverged'.[14] As well as supervising the household and the education of her large family, Hannah Grey was gifted artistically. It was a trait that she passed down to her daughters: Fanny was an accomplished watercolourist, Josephine so to a lesser extent, and Hatty a brilliant cartoonist.

John Grey was a very much loved father, for which we have the testimony of his wife who, on one of her rare absences from home, when she was visiting a sick uncle at Alnwick, wrote to her husband, 'I often think of you all, and think I see the little party round the oak table at tea when papa's day's work is over . . . I am sure there never was a father whose presence was more joyfully hailed, or whose smiles and approval were more valued, than yourself'.[15] Hannah found the peace and order of her former home disturbing, and began to long for the domestic chaos of Milfield: 'It would be quite a treat to see Charlie come in and throw his hat in a wrong place, and leave his books in a litter, as that would give life to the scene'. Charlie himself had an even earlier memory of life at Milfield, when their servant, Alec, 'rigged up a little carriage and trained a Newfoundland dog and a goat to drag it'. Alec would take out the infant Charles and his sister Fanny in this contraption and the children would race the London to Edinburgh coach, 'amid cheers from the outside passengers'![16] During one severe winter's snowstorm, this coach became stranded near Milfield and John Grey opened his house to the passengers. Charles remembered that his father 'had to kill his own cattle and sheep and poultry, and my Mother made bread, etc. for them'.[17] The party stayed a fortnight!

Josephine wrote of the austere simplicity of her father's life, of his 'sparsely furnished bed room', like that of a soldier accustomed to sudden orders to pack up and leave. Her sister Hatty added, 'It is rather the oneness and well-proportioned simplicity of his whole character which strikes one – goodness, justice, benevolence, kind persuasive manners'.[18] She recalled that he never preached to them, but that 'in daily intercourse, his truth, purity, and nobility of mind shone out in all he said, and still more in what he did'.[19] John Grey's kind persuasive manners were in evidence whether he was in conversation with his daughters, the tenant farmers on his estate, or his female servants, to whom he used to read novels by Sir Walter Scott while they sewed. He made provision of winter schooling for the local children, and night schools for the working men, and by the time the family left Milfield, every tenant on the estate, every labourer and shepherd could read and write. The neighbourhood was noted for its sobriety and for the low incidence of crime.

John Grey was a strong moral force as a prominent landowner and land manager, and as a justice of the peace, but he was also a man of great political influence nationally, and his political views and activities were important influences upon his children, especially Josephine. 'What an education I had under my noble father – an anti-slavery man, a Liberal, a *true* lover of Liberty, a *free* Churchman of wide sympathies, & called to constant crusades against tyranny'.[20] She wrote of his passion for justice, and his 'deeply rooted, fiery hatred of all injustices' as something she had inherited from him, adding, 'My dear mother felt with him, and seconded all his efforts'.[21]

Josephine's earliest acquaintance with the political questions of the day was as a toddling two-year-old. In June 1830 George IV died, and by November that year the Duke of Wellington had resigned as Prime Minister. The new king, William IV, called Earl Grey to the palace to ask him to form a government. The most pressing legislation to be brought in by the new Whig administration was the Reform Bill. John Grey, who had long been a political confidant of the new Prime Minister, was in a rare position to offer his cousin guidance and support in these crucial first months of office. Josephine recalled how, at Milfield Hill, her mother with the children would go every day to the end of the lane, where the mail-bags were thrown off the London express, to get news of the general election or the progress of the Bill. Good news was hailed with shouts of joy from the children who were too young to know what it meant, and even baby Hatty, who could scarcely talk, would, when asked her name, add to it enthusiastically, '*good fig*' (presumably 'good Whig').[22] Among the many portraits of Earl Grey and other eminent politicians of the day hanging on the walls at Dilston, John Grey also possessed an engraving of the passing of the Reform Bill.

One political victory that affected Josephine deeply and was to have a powerful influence upon her was that of the emancipation of slaves throughout the British Empire. To the end of her life, she could recall clearly how her father spoke about slavery to his children: 'I have felt his powerful frame to tremble, and his voice would break'. She remembered distressing first-hand reports 'of the hideous wrongs inflicted on negro men and women'.[23] In particular, it was the sexual slavery endured by female slaves that shocked the young Josephine: 'I think their lot was peculiarly horrible, for they were almost invariably forced to minister to the worst passions of their masters'.

John Grey became the personal friend of the philanthropist

Thomas Clarkson (1760–1846) who, together with William Wilberforce (1759–1833), led the Abolition movement in Britain, and his correspondence with Clarkson went to Josephine on her father's death. Grey was active in the campaign as a member of the Anti-Slavery Society of Northumberland, organizing petitions and haranguing electoral candidates who were known to hold pro-slavery sympathies; one of her older brother Charles's earliest memories was of attending Anti-Slavery meetings, during Wilberforce's campaign, 'and hearing my father and others make eloquent speeches'.[24] In Josephine's memoir of her father, she recalls his pointing out that it was easy enough to organize petitions and make speeches, but that nationally and internationally true progress would only come from 'a regard for the true welfare of our fellow-creatures, and a ready spirit of self-sacrifice towards that end'.[25] To John Grey, slavery was 'a system in my mind repugnant to every principle of justice and to every feeling of humanity', and he saw it as his duty to do his utmost to remove the 'foul stain' on his country's character for abetting it for so long.[26]

The Abolition of Slavery Act was carried by Earl Grey's administration in 1833. Initial provision of compensation to slave owners and former slaves' right to 'buy' their children's freedom shocked John Grey, and he wrote to the Prime Minister, attacking the fact that slave owners were compensated for giving up a property which no human legislature could give them rights to, while the liberated slaves had to 'labour under hard task-masters to buy the freedom which they [had] been so unjustly deprived of,' with no such compensation.[27] The Bill was revised, partly owing to his influence, and its provisions made considerably more, yet not wholly, humanitarian.

In 1833, when Josephine was five years old, her father was appointed manager of the Greenwich Hospital Estates in Northumberland, which were spread as far as Carlisle, Berwick and Newcastle. The land had a romantic past. It had originally belonged to the Earls of Derwentwater, the last of whom, James Radcliffe, was brought up as the companion of James Edward Stuart, the Old Pretender, and was beheaded at the age of twenty-seven for his part in the Stuart Rebellion of 1715. John and Hannah Grey chose to erect their new house at Dilston, near Corbridge. Dilston, or Devil's Stone, derives from the name of the mountain stream Devil's Water, which leads into the Tyne. It was a well-chosen position, roughly in the middle of the vast property, and it was also a fairly isolated site, which they selected for its extraordinary natural beauty. Josephine loved deeply 'the wild informal beauty all round its doors'.[28] The house overlooked the ruins of Radcliffe Castle and the little chapel in which the last Earl, according to legend, was buried with his head under his arm and his embalmed heart sealed in a box. Charlie was allowed to lay the foundation stone of the house, in which the children had embedded coins and newspapers of the day.

Josephine remembered the excitement of being taken as a child to see the limestone quarries, collieries and brickworks on the estates, and in particular the lead mines at Alston Moor with their 'clever mechanical contrivances for making use of the mountain streams for washing the ore, and the process of smelting, and separating of the shining silver from the lead'.[29] Likewise, Hatty had vivid memories of accompanying their father, 'sometimes going in and out of the little gates about stack-yards and farmsteads, where young beasts were stretching their necks horizontally to prevent the slippery bits of sliced turnips from falling out of their soft wet mouths'.[30] She recalled the kindness and consideration with which John Grey told the tenants what needed to be done, recognizing their difficulties, but dealing with them straightforwardly and making his tenants feel 'that they and he must *work together to do what is right*'.[31]

John Grey's responsibility to the estate tenants extended far beyond the improvement of their living conditions, the raising of wages, and the institution of grants to assist in the cultivation of the soil. He managed to persuade the Governors of Greenwich Hospital to subsidize every school in the area which admitted pupils from the estate, and saw to it that education was provided for every single child, and adult too if necessary, through night-school. In time, he founded a club and a library for farmers, for the dissemination of new agricultural theories, and he started up various agricultural societies to encourage the improvement of livestock. 'He was the personal friend and adviser of, one may say, the population of a province,' wrote a journalist for the *Agricultural Gazette*.[32]

A condition of John Grey's appointment to the management of Greenwich Hospital Estates was that he abstain from taking an active part in politics, which was to him, a gifted orator and a man whose keen intelligence had had so much influence in both local and national political life, a bitter frustration. Nineteen years on, in 1852, the year his daughter Josephine was married, John Grey sent Eliza, her sister, a local newspaper giving election news, complaining that he could only 'watch and advise. I am like a bull in a net, or a bear in a cage, growling at the wretches whom I can't reach!'[33]

The Greys moved into Dilston Hall in 1835, but, as Hannah saw it, they had been a 'broken' family for two years. While John Grey supervised the construction of their new home, Hannah stayed on at Milfield with the younger children. Josephine, Hatty, and their little sister Ellen all went down with scarlet fever; the two older girls pulled through, but baby Ellie's fever developed into typhus, and she died while her father was away at Dilston. She was a pretty little girl. Her parents liked to call her Flossie because of her soft fine hair, and to her father she was 'the sweetest child that ever was'. Although Josephine's and Hatty's childhood memories begin at Dilston, their mother looked back to Milfield 'as the home of happy recollections, when you *all* grew together side by side, and filled one house with glee'.[34] The Greys' eldest son, George, now became the master of Milfield, and married in 1839.

Mrs Grey, at the age of forty-two, was now pregnant with her tenth and last child, Emily Georgina, who was born on 26 May 1836. That autumn their eldest daughter, Eliza, aged just seventeen, married a young Welsh surgeon, William Morrison, who had arrived in Newcastle to take up his post as the first licensed Lecturer in Anatomy and Psychology at the School of Medicine there. In the first few years of marriage Morrison also maintained a local practice, which took in the pit villages on the outskirts of Newcastle. He no doubt took a concerned interest in his wife's younger sister, Josephine, who continued to suffer from weakness throughout her childhood: 'I was always weak about the heart – not organic disease, I believe – but I used to get faint if I ran about much'.[35]

At Dilston, the Greys were missing the company of the two eldest children as well as mourning the death of Flossie, yet, even so, the new house and its wild romantic grounds were filled with the voices of the seven remaining children. In family letters of the period the chatter, the merry laughter and games of the young people are constantly heard. The Greys continued to make holiday visits to Milfield. Josephine recalled her father's delight as he bundled his remaining children into the old 'large open carriage, traversing almost the length of Northumberland from south to north, in regions where no railways existed', over the 'rabbity rocks' to their old home, the children taking it in turns to sit up on the box with Papa.[36]

The house at Dilston was big enough to accommodate not only the

Greys' children, from baby Emily up to nineteen-year-old John, but also a constant coming and going of house guests, such as Sir George and Lady Grey.[37] As well as family members and friends, their guests included many foreign visitors from France, Sweden and Russia, interested to see the agricultural reforms carried out by Josephine's father. 'It was,' wrote Josephine, 'a house the door of which stood wide open, as if to welcome all comers, through the livelong summer day'.[38] When some friends of Josephine visited Dilston in 1890, they reported the innovations of the new owners. Josephine was not impressed: 'we had *no* peacocks in our time, & our door was always open!'[39] It was an upbringing which brought her into contact with the society of Northumberland gentry, as well as the society of tenant farmers and agricultural labourers, engineers and navvies, and no doubt it helped form the ease of manner with people from all classes which is so characteristic of her adult life and work.

Josephine's father was an equally delightful character in a domestic setting. 'The tying of a neck-tie was a mystery he never could compass,' she wrote. 'It always ended with the appearance of a piece of crumpled hemp.'[40] At a yell from his dressing-room, his daughters would scramble across the upstairs hall, on to which all their bedrooms opened: 'six daughters used to come out of their six doors, all anxious to help the old Dad . . . But he was so tall. Some of us had to get on to a stool!!'[41]

Her sister Fanny later observed that after their mother had died John Grey seemed to feel it his duty to become father and mother both to his family, even though all were now grown-up and married. When Fanny, newly widowed, was ill at Dilston, her father, taking care not to wake her, would slip open her bedroom door and place a great bunch of sweet-smelling flowers on a chair by the bed: 'sometimes the most incongruous flowers, but all showing the intention of the large, loving heart, where nothing was considered too small to give pleasure: he looked such a large man to think of such little things'.[42]

Her father's influence upon Josephine's political thinking and her life's work is clear, but her most important familial relationship was with her younger sister, Harriet Jane: 'We were a *pair* . . . We were never separated, except perhaps for a few days occasionally . . . we were one in heart and soul, and one in all our pursuits. We walked, rode, played, and learned our lessons together. When one was scolded, both wept; when one was praised, both were pleased.'[43] As they grew older, their separateness from their sisters grew more marked, and the two little girls shared a love of outdoor life, of nature, and of animals: they had their own horses; they caught ferrets, wildcats and owls; and their brother John brought them back a tortoise apiece from his voyages. Hatty was the more reckless of the two, the wilder and more tomboyish. It was Hatty who collected so many jam-jars full of newts and frogs that the shelf in their bedroom collapsed, flooding her bed; and although all the Greys learned to ride almost as soon as they could walk, it was Hatty who dared to stand upright on the saddle, and who wanted to run away to the circus. Hatty was also her father's favourite riding partner when he visited his tenants. His raven-haired little daughter must have been a useful ambassador as he made his cottage rounds, enabling him to get into easy conversation with the farmers' wives by first begging a cup of tea for his little companion. As she grew older and hardier Hatty might stay out all day with her father to observe some work in progress only to return home with him in a driving storm, 'bending our heads nearly to the horse's mane, to receive the sharp pelting hail on our hats, the horses laying back their ears, and bounding at the stinging of the hail on their flanks, and coming in with a heavy clinging skirt, and veil frozen into a mask the shape of one's nose, revealing very rosy cheeks when it was peeled off'.[44] Both Josephine and Hatty developed into capable horsewomen ('My sister and I have often had to undo bad training for Papa with horses he bought'),[45] and when the girls were older they would enjoy visiting their brother George at Milfield for the hunting. On one occasion, an elderly guest remarked upon the presence of the young ladies in the hunting field, but when he was told that they were George's sisters, he replied, 'Oh, then, it's in the blood. They can't help it!'[46]

Josephine and Hatty finished their education with two years spent together at a school in Newcastle. Their time there served to strengthen the ties between the two sisters. Their kindly and sympathetic headmistress was 'not a good disciplinarian, and gave us much liberty (which we appreciated)'. Lessons were learned imperfectly, according to Josephine, although she was an excellent linguist, becoming fluent in French and Italian. Hatty, who hated lessons, seems to have spent too much time filling her copybooks and the margins of textbooks with pen and ink drawings.[47]

Josephine's early religious experiences, and the religious instruction she received from her mother, proved of far deeper influence than any formal ladies' education. Theirs was a Dissenting neighbourhood and there were many Wesleyans and Presbyterian farmers in the district.

The Greys' family church was the Anglican St Andrew's Church in Corbridge, 'to which we trudged dutifully every Sunday, and where an honest man in the pulpit taught us loyally all that he probably knew himself about God'.[48] Josephine and her sisters were married at St Andrew's Church, and their parents were buried there. John Grey was a man of wide religious tolerance, and had campaigned publicly in favour of the Catholic Emancipation (Relief) Act of 1829. He had declared at one meeting, 'I claim for every man political freedom; I assert that his religious opinions should be left to himself, his conscience, and his God'.[49] He himself showed strong sympathies with Methodism, and when the Grey family were at Milfield, Hannah allowed the children's governess to take Josephine and Hatty to the small Methodist chapel which her husband had erected for his tenants.[50] When, as a married woman, Josephine revisited her birthplace, the people of Milfield sought her out 'to come and give them an address in the same little Methodist Chapel . . . O! how they crowded in & round the doors'.[51] In her later life, it was a great surprise to Josephine to realize that some of her closest friends believed that she had been brought up in the established Church:

> I thought everyone knew that I am *not* of the Church of England & never was. I go to the Church once a Sunday out of a feeling of loyalty to my husband – that is all. I was brought up a Wesleyan . . . I imbibed from childhood the widest ideas of vital Christianity, only it *was* Christianity. I have not much sympathy with the *Church*.[52]

Josephine described the Scottish borders at the beginning of the century as 'a barren wilderness, so far as spiritual life was concerned'. Then Edward Irving, a follower and friend of John Wesley, came to the region. He had a large following in Scotland and in London, and here, too, he brought about a spiritual revival.[53] His preaching was of 'imminent judgement and the glory that was to be revealed', and was associated with cases of miraculous healing and with speaking in tongues.[54] Josephine and Hatty were instructed by their governess that 'the "Second Advent" meant that Christ would come *personally* & suddenly, some day, in the clouds of heaven, to judge the world, & to reign as King'.[55]

It was a time of revivalist fervour, and Josephine remembered well being taken to the camp meetings to which the shepherds of the Cheviots travelled long distances. Later, at Dilston, she was spellbound by the visits to their home of a wealthy land-owning neighbour,

Mr Sitwell of Barmoor Castle, who had been struck from his saddle one day, and fell to his knees in prayer, repenting of his idle existence. Sitwell became one of the first ministers or 'angels' of the Irvingites: 'I can never forget some of his words, which seemed to speak of a heaven at hand on earth'.[56] They would go with their governess 'in a cart, with straw in it and a sack to sit on' to the Irvingite church at Barmoor to listen to their 'prophecyings'. Their preference, though, was for simple Methodist worship.

This governess, Josephine believed, saved her mother's life when one night Mrs Grey, who had been ill, woke up in pain and got up to look for her medicine. In the dark, she drank instead a strong dose of prussic acid, cyanide, then staggered to that governess, who calmly repeated to her the words, 'and if they drink any deadly thing it shall not hurt them', from Christ's words to his disciples when he reappeared to them just before his ascension, and promised that 'these signs shall follow them that believe' (Mark 16: 17–18). Immediately Hannah began to vomit up the poison, and apparently suffered no consequences. Josephine grew up in an atmosphere of miraculous cures and conversions and retained her conviction in the power of belief.

When she was eighteen or nineteen, Josephine underwent a revolution in her relations with God, which she referred to as 'my soul's deep discontent',[57] an experience which appears to reflect the influence upon her of Methodist worship. She would later claim that she had mourned for the oppressed since she was a child. Certainly, she was deeply affected by one particular experience she had as a young woman, during a visit she made to Ireland in 1847 at the height of the potato famine. The Irish question had been a concern of her father's, and in 1839 he had considerable correspondence with Earl Grey about the mounting crisis there.[58] Josephine and Hatty went to Ireland as the guests of their brother Charles, who had decided to spend the autumn holidaying in Leix, or Laois, known then as Queen's County, before starting work as a land surveyor for his father.

The memory of that visit that stayed with Josephine was of the starving peasantry. It was so painful to her that she kept it suppressed until 1887, when she felt moved to publish a pamphlet in support of Home Rule for Ireland. It is unlikely that Josephine had witnessed acute distress amongst the poor until she came to Ireland. She said herself that there was no real poverty amongst the cottagers at

Milfield or at Dilston. What she saw in Ireland would remain with her for life.

> A young girl, I had no conception of the full meaning of the misery I saw around me, yet it printed itself upon my brain and memory. I can recollect being awakened in the early morning by a strange sound like the croaking or chattering of many birds. Some of the voices were hoarse and almost extinguished by the faintness of famine; and on looking out of my window I recollect seeing the garden and fields in front of the house completely darkened with a population of men, women, and children, squatting, in rags; uncovered skeleton limbs protruding everywhere from their wretched clothing, and clamorous, though faint voices uplifted for food . . . I recollect, too, when walking through lanes and villages, the strange morbid famine smell in the air, the sign of approaching death even in those who were still dragging out a wretched existence. Nor can I forget the occasional shrill wail which was sighed out by some poor creature sending her last cry of despair to heaven before falling down in a state of collapse by the wayside.[59]

Her father's tales of atrocities committed upon slaves, her own experience of having seen the starving peasants in Ireland, and indeed, the prejudices of society 'on the root question' of sexual inequality, contributed to what she called the '*travail* of soul' she experienced as a young woman.[60] To the young Josephine, the world seemed 'out of joint'.[61] In 1905, in a letter to intimate friends, Josephine revealed for the first time her religious crisis:

> There were extensive and pathless woods near the house. So great was the burden on my soul about the inequalities & injustices & cruelties in the world that I used to run away into these far woods, where no one followed me, & kneeling on the ground, for hours, I used to *shriek* to God to come & deliver!! This is awfully true. My sisters thought I was a little mad. Perhaps I was; but God turned the madness to a purpose He had.[62]

She had many urgent questions to ask, yet, by her own account a very reserved young woman, she felt unable to consult her mother and father on such intimate matters: 'my dear parents might have helped me a little & yet I was shy'.[63] She also distrusted the ability of ministers of religion to provide adequate answers, and felt that she could not stake her soul's destiny 'upon a faith received at second-hand'. It became 'a matter of life and death' with her to know something with certainty of God, and of her relations to Him: '"Give me light or slay me" was the cry of my heart'.[64] And so she began to speak directly to God. This was a practice that would never leave her.

> I spoke to Him in solitude, as a person who could answer. I sometimes gave whole nights to prayer, because the day was not sufficiently my own. Do not imagine that on these occasions I worked myself up into any excitement; there was much pain in such an effort, and dogged determination required. Nor was it a devotional sentiment which urged me on. It was the desire to know God and my relation to Him.[65]

Life at Dilston did have its lighter, social, side, of course, and Aunt Margaretta may well have fretted over her nieces' upbringing, preoccupied as the Grey girls were with horse-riding and dancing. For all their mother's moral discipline, and their father's extreme sensitivity to all matters sexual, Josephine and her sisters enjoyed mingling with the young men and women of the neighbourhood, and the young people do appear to have been left unchaperoned a good deal. They were a handsome family. When Mary Ann ('Tully') was newly settled as a young wife in Liverpool, their father wrote of his feelings as he looked at her empty chair: 'I very often bring you up to my mind's eye, at times in your hat and habit, looking stylish, and managing your curb with masterly hand; at others gliding smoothly into the drawing-room with bright ringlets and smiling face'.[66] Josephine recalled Fanny as a young woman as 'a very graceful dancer', 'with her brilliantly flashing black eyes, and soft black hair and rosy cheeks'.[67] Little Emmy, who, Josephine believed, would beat them all at schoolwork, was also a pretty dancer. Josephine described her at fifteen, growing very tall and elegant, 'her golden hair dressed like a crown' whenever they went out in the evenings.[68]

There were opportunities for all the girls to go to dances. At the great annual County Ball at Alnwick, 'Fanny, Hatty and I were great *belles*, in our snowy book-muslin* frocks, and natural flowers wreathed on our heads & waists & skirts'.[69] John Grey drove his daughters over from Dilston to Milfield, and for the night of the ball they would take rooms at the Swan at Alnwick. As Josephine later explained to one of her sons, the balls of the 1840s were 'stately affairs and, in fact, political gatherings':

*A very fine, and thus expensive, muslin, so-named because it was folded like a book when sold.

> I recollect grandpapa Grey & old Lord Grey, & Lord Howick & Lord Durham all standing in a group in the very middle of the ballroom floor, regardless of the dancers all round them, deep in some Liberal political intrigue. Then the Duke and Duchess and all the Castle party would arrive, and the Tankervilles, who were Conservatives, and the Liberal group would break up. I used to dance with . . . the present Lord Tankerville, tho' my father did not quite like my dancing with a Tory!![70]

Tully was the second Grey sister to marry and leave home, in 1842. At the age of twenty-one, she married Edgar Garston, a man twenty or so years her senior. He was a prosperous tradesman, based in Liverpool, who became Director of the Union Bank there. A fascinating character, he had as a young man acted as interpreter for the Italian witnesses at Queen Caroline's trial for adultery in 1820, and then in 1825 was a volunteer in the Greek War of Independence. Charles Grey recalled that Edgar was 'a skilful fencer and taught me the use of the foil'.[71] The Garstons' first child, Ethel, was not born until 1853, conceived after eleven years of marriage, and a brother, Edgar, followed in 1856.

Apart from the death of little Ellie, the only tragedy to touch Josephine's early life was the death at sea of her elder brother, John Henry, when she was sixteen. The sole surviving memento of John is a watercolour by J. H. Mole, who was commissioned to paint portraits of all the Grey children.[72] It shows him as a country gentleman, fly-fishing with his dog, and looking a handsome replica of their father. On a warm June night in 1844, Mr Grey observed the scene as his children excitedly took turns with his telescope to view an eclipse of the moon. Amongst the chatter he heard them express the wish that their absent brother was observing the very same phenomenon from his ship in the Pacific. The next day, word was received that their brother John had been dead for several weeks. From the ship's captain came the stark message, 'All well, except Mr Grey, who died off the Cape.' A barely literate sailor-boy who had acted as John's servant thought to send the family a fuller account, telling how in the final hours John Grey had 'talked much about his brother George, and thought he was coming to him', and how, 'At midnight (giving the latitude and longitude exactly, in the sailor fashion), Mr Grey sang out for his mother'.[73]

In 1847 Eliza's husband was offered the post of Senior Surgeon of Hong Kong, and set off with Eliza and their four little children. He apparently said of Josephine, then nineteen, 'I shall never see *her* again. She's doomed.' Years later, Josephine told a friend that she had broken a blood vessel in her lungs when she was eighteen, '& everybody gave me up & said I wd die – but I did not!'[74] A year after Eliza's departure for Hong Kong, their sister Fanny married the Reverend George Hunt Smyttan in June 1848. That year he had taken his BA at Corpus Christi Cambridge, and a fortnight after the wedding was ordained a deacon at Durham. For the first two years of marriage, Fanny and her husband lived at his elegant home, Charlton Hall, where George was first curate and then rector of the living of Ellingham-with-Alnwick.

Josephine's brother Charles recalled that in the year of Fanny's marriage, his father drove himself, Josephine and Hatty down to Durham. It seems likely that they attended George Smyttan's ordination, and likely too that Charles showed his sisters around the university. Charles had gone up to Durham in 1842 and stated that he was in the 'Engineer class', although he made the change from Engineering to Classics.[75] He eventually graduated in 1846 with a second-class degree in Mathematics, then a branch of classical study, and he stayed on at Durham to take his MA. Charles's graduate studies coincided with the arrival at Durham University of the new classics master, George Butler. Charles may well have introduced his sisters to Butler on their family visit to Durham, and there would have been a second opportunity for Josephine to meet George when she and Hatty returned to Durham for the conferment of Charles's MA on 6 February 1849. George Butler was twenty-nine, Josephine just twenty. Within a year he was writing her love poems.

2

Courtship and Marriage

'The Rose of Dilston'

LIKE JOSEPHINE, GEORGE Butler came from a large family, yet his background was rather different, one remarkable for academic achievement. As Josephine later put it, George's ancestors 'were of less aristocratic origin than the Greys; they were chiefly distinguished by *learning* and *goodness*'.[1] George's father, the Dean of Peterborough, had been a senior wrangler at Cambridge, and was headmaster of Harrow from 1805 to 1829, a post in which he was eventually succeeded by his youngest son, Henry Montagu. George and his brothers were all at school there. An awestruck Hatty informed Eliza that Monty Butler, as he was known, had swept all the prizes in the Harrow examination, and he went on to become a senior classic, fellow and later Master of Trinity College, Cambridge. Of George's other two brothers, Spencer Percival became a lawyer, and Arthur became headmaster of Haileybury and later Dean of Oriel College, Oxford, while Spencer's three sons had distinguished careers at Cambridge and in the Indian Civil Service. There were also four surviving sisters, two of whom made prominent marriages: Catherine married the Bishop of Sierra Leone, and Louisa Jane married Francis Galton, who was a cousin of Charles Darwin and became the leading exponent of the science of heredity, although he is perhaps more popularly known for discovering the uniqueness of fingerprints, which led to the forensic use of fingerprinting. Galton's ground-breaking *Hereditary Genius* was published in 1869. He was, naturally, fascinated by the long line of outstanding academic achievement which manifested itself in the Butler family, remarking that they 'well deserve study as an instance of hereditary gifts'.[2]

After a first year at Trinity College, Cambridge, which he did not take entirely seriously, but which was not without examination success, George Butler switched to Exeter College, Oxford, at his father's prompting, no doubt, to study Classics. There he renewed his studies in earnest. In 1841 George came to the notice of the prestigious debating society, the Decade, and was invited by Benjamin Jowett, fellow and later Master of Balliol, to join their select number. John Blackett, an old friend from Harrow days, was also a member, as were Matthew Arnold and Arthur Stanley (son of the Bishop of Norwich, and the future Dean of Westminster): in all 'an excellent set', as George proudly noted to his father.[3] A year later he received the honour of being made a fellow of Exeter College while still an undergraduate. A first-class degree followed in 1843, and he took his MA in 1846. In 1848 he took a post as Classics lecturer at Durham University. Josephine remains quiet on the subject of how they met. We know that she visited the university twice in the company of her brother Charles, and it seems likely that George's Oxford friend John Blackett, who came from Northumberland, was their mutual friend at this time and that they may have met through him. Certainly, by the time of her sister's wedding Hatty refers to John and his brother as old friends.

Josephine wrote that George was attracted 'by the liberal traditions and unconventional habits of life which prevailed in our family and in the society around us',[4] but the outdoor life at Dilston must also have had its appeal. George was no dried-up academic, but, to use his friend Anthony Froude's choice phrase, 'he was first-rate in all manly exercises'.[5] He was a striking-looking man, large-framed and athletic in build, with frank and handsome eyes, a mass of dark curls, and, in later years, sporting a considerable moustache and beard. George shared Josephine's love of horse-riding, but he was also a keen player of racquets and royal tennis, had a reputation as a fine batsman, he swam and went hill-walking, hunted and fished. He liked to start the day with a cold bath and morning walk and could clear a five-bar gate with ease. When they settled in Oxford, Josephine would often have people coming to the door asking when Mr Butler was coming out to skate, because crowds would gather to watch him. There is a rather alarming anecdote about George's getting over a very severe headache one morning at Dilston. In the time it took for the doctor to be sent for from Hexham, George had stepped out with his gun and brought down six pheasants and two and a half brace of partridges![6]

In the autumn of 1850 George was appointed Public Examiner in the Schools at Oxford University. As he prepared himself for his return to Oxford and the beginning of a new career, he decided to read through all his old letters, and in doing so reviewed his life to date. From his room at Durham he wrote to Josephine, 'I am here amidst a wilderness of letters, which I have brought into something like order and management. I read a great number last night before burning them, and this kept me till nearly three a.m. To-day I feel rather like an extinct volcano'. Some of the letters were from his father, remonstrating with him, he said, 'for idleness and extravagance while I was at Cambridge'.[7] Before he went to bed, George re-read a couple of Josephine's letters to him which, coming after the reminders of what appears to have been a period of religious doubt, were like holy balm: 'I felt as if I had been walking about in the Catacombs and suddenly emerged into fresh air'.

George and Josephine, whom George would soon be calling by her family nickname of 'Josey',[8] kept up a correspondence after he left Durham, somewhat persistently, it seems, on George's side. A steady flow of love poems arrived at Dilston, poems that suggest Josephine did rather more than 'hold him at bay', as she later wrote to her eldest sister Eliza. A rebuff is clear in one poem George composed on 13 October 1850, on his farewell visit to Dilston before his return to Oxford, in which he asks forgiveness for 'thy just reproof', and steels himself for 'The path of duty – harsh and stern'. 'O! leave me not to blank despair', he pleads, for by now he realizes that Josephine Grey, his 'Rose of Dilston', is the woman he must share his life with.

> No more can nature give relief,
> Nor are her treasures ope to me,
> For all my joy and all my grief
> Is centred, Josephine, in thee.[9]

It may be that George's ardour was rebuffed until he made a formal proposal of marriage. Any hesitation on his part may have been owing to his anxiety, or more crucially his parents' anxiety, that he was in no position yet to provide a home for a wife and young family. George liked to joke about his parents' melodramatic fears that he would meet a sorry end, but the joking barely conceals the very real pressure upon George from home. He was relieved that Josephine took his father's view of things, and wrote to her that, 'whatever delay may be interposed between us and our wishes will only have the effect of making us love each other more, and we shall know each other better'.[10]

George was even able to joke that a certain ladies' man, a Mr Neave, who was on his way out to China, and who had shown a decided interest in Hatty, might beat them to the altar, and whisk Hatty off down the Rhine for her honeymoon while he and Josephine continued to languish in England. Hatty was in no danger of surrendering to Mr Neave's charms, but the joke suggests that George was sensitive to the awkwardness of his position in relation to the Greys.

George and Josephine appear to have become engaged on 8 January 1851, exactly a year before they would marry,[11] but Josephine's attempts to hold George in check may have had rather greater effect than she imagined. She complained privately to Eliza that of late George's letters were 'not very much in the common run of love letters'. This is quite an understatement if the few examples of courtship correspondence she chose to reprint in her husband's biography are typical. George was fond of discoursing on the wonders of the Greek philosophers, and he set his fiancée to read Ruskin's recent study, *The Seven Lamps of Architecture.* Josephine rose to the challenge and bravely announced to George that she was going to embark on a course of Greek, but he did not recommend it. These letters show that at first Josephine looked to her future husband as her moral guide. George was only nine years her senior, but she seems to have regarded the age gap as nearly that of a generation, and she offered him almost daughterly veneration. However flattering this may have been, George gently sought to make her see sense. He was not, he assured her, her earthly master, and feared that she had formed too high an estimate of his character, one that he would not be able to live up to. He asked instead that she accept his vision of what a marriage should be: 'namely, a perfectly equal union, with absolute freedom on both sides for personal initiative in thought and action and for individual development'.[12] Again, he stressed that he had no authority to make decisions for her: 'I am more content to leave you to walk by yourself in the path you shall choose; but I know that I do not leave you alone and unsupported, for *His* arm will guide, strengthen, and protect you'.[13]

It is interesting that at this important moment in her life, Josephine did not turn to a female confidante within her large family circle at home. It is perhaps understandable that she did not approach her mother, but she had sisters aplenty: Tully and Fanny were newly married, but both continued to visit Dilston regularly; Hatty, her soulmate, was unmarried and perhaps not appropriate to the task; and little Emmy was still a child. It was to her eldest sister, the remotely situated Eliza, living in Hong Kong with her young family, that she chose to open her heart. Perhaps significantly, Eliza was thirty-one, the same age as George.

On 13 February 1851 Josephine copied out extracts from George's family's letters of congratulations on their engagement to send to Eliza. A month later she wrote again, saying,

> It is quite overwhelming to be the recipient of so many congratulations, and testimonies to his talents and goodness from all sides, as I have been for the last few weeks – by all kinds of curious ways direct & indirect I hear that I am a most fortunate person, and that he is a concentration of every desirable quality. I am, in fact, bound to believe that he did me an honour by asking me to marry him.[14]

Josephine Grey was not to be outdone, however, thinking that as she had 'quite cleared the debt by paying him the compliment of accepting him, I don't feel at all overpowered by the honour done to me'. Her letters, confessionals really, are lengthy and surprisingly intimate, as Josephine tells Eliza her innermost worries about the engagement and about her future life with George. One wonders at the practical sense of seeking advice on intimate matters from a sister living halfway round the world, given the weeks it would have taken for letters to sail to and from Hong Kong. (When Eliza's husband died in 1853, her letter to her mother and father took seven weeks to reach England.) It may have been enough for Josephine merely to articulate and commit to paper her fears, which we may understand to be in part sexual, and she may have been emboldened by Eliza's distance. The correspondence offers a rare insight into the mind of a young Victorian woman about to be married.

Her chief worry was not that she might not be worthy of George, but 'whether we shall exactly *do for each other*'. She explained that they got on 'capitally' in letters, writing to each other a great deal, 'and in No. 1 style', though, as we have seen, not in the style of love letters.[15] It was quite another thing to relax in George's company, and her natural awkwardness was made all the worse by his reproaches.

> Since the compact was made, he has only been 7 days at different times in the house, or in my society, I should say. So that although I feel perfectly at my ease in writing to him, I don't when he comes – there is always some ice to be broken every time. And I think he feels the same, for the last

> time he was here, he asked me if I was the same Josephine who wrote him such nice letters . . . and he thinks I look too much the same as I used to when I used to hold him at bay.[16]

Josephine was distracted with anxiety, which the twists and turns of her letters well convey, but she held to her feeling that the fault lay with George: 'he seems to me (I don't say *he is*, for I may be mistaken) *too* little impulsive. I think I should feel a greater sympathy with him, and it would open up easier intercourse between us, if he did not seem to be very guarded always – I think he has always accustomed himself to the exercise of a most rigid self-control'. 'The feeling may be there,' she argued, 'but he puts such bolts and bars and iron doors upon himself that nobody can find it out'. She was wounded by his suggestion that she was unnaturally frigid with him:

> I don't see why he should not *come out* with his feelings to me sometimes. If I did not exercise a *childlike* faith in the existence and strength of his affection for me, I might sometimes doubt it . . . however, there *is* a reserve between us, and I won't be the first to demonstrate a desire to shake it off – as he ought to do it . . . if he did not care a great deal about me, why was he so doggedly persevering about it.[17]

At such times the nine years between them seemed insurmountable: 'He is 32 nearly – you wanted to know how old he is – rather too old I think. If he is made a professor he will look quite old and owlish'. Josephine put on a show of being sanguine about George's awaited visit to Dilston for a stay of some weeks, overseeing the arrangements to have the west dressing-room turned into a study for him ('he is going to read hard while he is here'), but she confessed, 'He comes on Wednesday, and I feel a sort of trepidation at the thought of it'. Most of all, she regretted that Hatty, who was shrewdly packed off to Milfield by her parents, was deserting her: 'I feel so friendless without her, and need her to back me up'.

The letter Josephine wrote to Eliza after George had been at Dilston for one month is just a fraction of the length of the earlier anxious correspondence, and this alone is enough to suggest how perfectly happy she and George were when they were at last left alone together: 'I am so glad of this visit, for we did not know each other well enough before'.[18] Josephine's parents discreetly let the young people have the run of the house: Mrs Grey feigned indisposition and stayed in her bedroom, while John Grey kept out of the house altogether for much of the time, preoccupied with estate business. Such was their solitude that 'George and I have had to keep house together – and I do so admire and like the domestic part of his character which has been thus drawn out'. It is touching to read of her amazement that a fiancé who was all of two-and-thirty could still be 'playful and merry': 'He has a great deal of quiet fun about him. I never knew anybody of his years so young in health and feelings . . . He is just like a boy, and confesses in such funny innocent ways how overhead and toes in love he is – but he is not *the least* spooney . . . There is the most perfect affection and confidence between us'. During his stay, George took Josephine into Newcastle to be measured for her wedding ring, even though the wedding date was still uncertain.

It had long been his father's dearest wish that George, his eldest son, should join the ministry, and he hoped that his ordination would take place before his marriage. From the safe distance of Durham, George had written to his father to say that he had 'no internal call to, no inclination for, the Church', and could not see his way to getting over 'the scruples I have against such a step as you advise . . . I feel, at present, no attraction towards the study of dogmatical Theology, or any branch of study in which a clergyman should be versed'.[19] This was in part a reaction to the Oxford Movement, the 'Tractarians' who responded to challenges to faith and to the Anglican Church with an increased emphasis on ritualism, an investment of symbolic meaning in ceremony that was close to Roman Catholicism. As Josephine understood it, George 'had lived at Oxford through all the fever of the Tractarian controversy', and yet had remained untouched.[20] It was at Durham that George's antipathy to the priesthood hardened, where he observed what he felt to be a 'feeble imitation' of Oxford ritualism, and he resolved to put an end to the matter. As he explained to Josephine,

> You know that I don't like parsons, but that is not to the point. If I should ever take orders, I don't mean to be a mere parson; for if I were like some of them whom I know, I should cease to be a *man*. I shall never wear straight waistcoats, long coats, and stiff collars! I think all dressing up and official manner are an affectation; while great strictness in outward appearances interferes with the devotion of the heart.[21]

He had come to the conclusion that to be a good clergyman was much the same as being a good man, and that he fully resolved to be.

Before George and Josephine were married, the Greys commissioned George Richmond to paint their daughter's portrait, for which

Josephine most reluctantly travelled down to London in June 1851. 'I cannot bear the idea of going – I detest London,' she told Eliza.[22] Richmond's biographer claims that at this time the demand for his portraits was so great that the artist would sometimes have three, or even four, sitters in a day.[23] From Josephine's account, Richmond had time enough to put his young subject at ease, and she plainly relished her visits to his studio: 'Our sittings are very pleasant . . . he is a capital talker, & very witty & amusing, & knows all the great nobs, having taken their likenesses'.[24] In 1850 Richmond had painted Charlotte Brontë's portrait, and in 1851 that of Elizabeth Gaskell, as well as Josephine's. Each portrait cost £31 10*s*. The three studies are remarkably similar. Josephine was finally permitted to see the finished portrait on 21 June, and was pleased to pronounce it 'very like': 'I was quite startled at first to see such a beautiful picture, but Richmond has a way of taking people at their very best without exactly flattering them. He has made it look so graceful'. Whether flattering or no, Richmond's portrait of Josephine is a handsome study: the full and sensuous Pre-Raphaelite lips, the beautiful frank eyes, the strong straight nose and the fine cheekbones are all details confirmed by subsequent photographs. The rapt, self-possessed expression of a woman in love, caught by Richmond, fits exactly Hatty's description of her sister: 'Josey looks so pretty just now. She gets a kind of rich glowing colour, and her eyes look lustrous, with light dancing in them'.[25]

Later that summer Josephine was visited by two of George's sisters, Catherine and Emily, the latter being the same age as Hatty. From Exeter College, George was pining to be there too: 'How I wish I were with them! I think when I am in London I shall feel strongly tempted to put myself on the train and fly away to the North Countrie. Only I am afraid then my anxious parents' doubts on the subject of my economical powers wd be changed to a certain conviction that I should end my days in prison'.[26] Josephine's earlier complaint that he did not write very loving letters was now a thing of the past: George closed this letter with the words, 'Goodbye my own sweet love. Every day, as it brings me a fresh proof of your love, makes you dearer to me, and makes me feel what a treasure I am possessed of.'

The Grey and Butler girls hit it off instantly, partly thanks to a shared passion for horse-riding. Josephine described to George how she and Hatty organized a pony ride over towards Hexham, with Bobby as 'our sumpter-horse, carrying a basket of provisions and several shawls'. Leaving the ponies at a farmhouse, they scrambled down a steep ravine to the legendary Queen Margaret's Cave, where Margaret of Anjou, the wife of Henry VI, was believed to have sheltered when she fled north with her son Edward after Henry had been captured at the outbreak of the Wars of the Roses. Josephine later recalled that she and Hatty used to be told off for taking visitors through the woods to this cave.[27] In her letter to George she described how they had 'brought a candle which Hatty lighted, crawling in first herself. We all followed; the entrance is very low, but it is roomy inside. We sat on pieces of damp rock, our one candle making darkness visible, and tried to think it a pleasant, cool retreat. Cool it certainly was. We could find no traces of Queen Margaret; no bits of ermine, or fragments of the crown with which pictures represent her scouring about these woods with the little prince'.[28] There is a change of tone in Josephine's letters, too, with, here, the playful Miltonic reference and the comic recollection of history book representations of Queen Margaret. Another day the girls planned to make a similar expedition to Hadrian's Wall.

George, meanwhile, was tied to his summer work as an examiner. In one delightful letter he described to Josephine the effect upon him of the arrival of one of her communications: 'Your last letter was brought to me while I was in the Schools. I did not do what you did with your schoolchildren when you received mine, and say "Begone, rebel army; and don't kick up a row", and then jump out of the window and run along the walk under the pine trees; because my brother Examiners would have stared, and the windows were too high. But I did something of the same kind mentally'.[29] One wonders who these pupils were, although Hatty referred at this time to her sister's talent for teaching French and piano, saying that 'she seems to know by instinct what difficulties a pupil will feel, even when they hardly know enough about it to ask; and she meets it with such a clear explanation'.[30] That Josephine was instructing them in her own home seems borne out by the closeness of George's description of the gardens to her own account of Dilston as a place where 'one could glide out of a lower window and be hidden for a moment, plunging straight among wild wood paths and beds of ferns, or find oneself quickly in some cool concealment, beneath slender birch trees, or by the bed of a mountain stream'.[31]

George's letter brought some good news about an article he had been commissioned to write by the Oxford publisher, Parker. It was to be a review of the foremost translations of Dante. George was expected at Dilston on Christmas Eve, and he looked forward to working on it together with Josephine: 'We will read Dante together and talk about it, and put together the results of our conversation'.

Just then, Josephine was engaged in rather less sedentary pursuits. Before she saw George again, she was caught up in a flurry of last-minute preparations for the wedding, and a daze of parties in which she made the most of her last days of maidenhood. The Greys seem to have shown no concern that Josephine was attending dances in town without her fiancé, and Hatty certainly had no qualms about accompanying her sister. She became quite a connoisseur of balls, recording in her diary for Thursday, 20 November 1851 a dance at Newtown Hall, Durham ('Josey the belle'), and yet another the next night: 'a very jolly ball, kept up with great spirit: enjoyed it very much'.[32] On the following Monday the girls met their mother in Newcastle to shop for the wedding, ordering bridesmaids' bonnets and suchlike. This lasted two whole days – and they were back there the following week. At Dilston, too, there was constant entertaining, with more visits from assorted Butlers, and from Fanny and her husband.

It was not one endless round of gaiety, however, and both sisters showed signs of anxiety as the wedding date approached. Hatty registered surprise that her dear Josey was 'as little dreamy and absorbed in her own feelings as any engaged girl I ever saw'.[33] She was equally concerned about how her own position at Dilston would be affected by Josephine's marriage: 'I really don't know what we are going to do without her, sweet little body. As the time draws near, I live in a worse and worse state of fear. I am perfectly unfit to fill up even half the gap her departure will make, and I am so sorry for all of them losing her, putting aside my own selfish broken-in-two feelings; for I don't think I can ever grow like her'. All her hopes rested on fifteen-year-old Emmy: 'she is growing such a fine girl, with a calm just way of looking at things, and an uprightness that can't be turned aside, and so much good feeling'.

A rather more solemn detail was the marriage settlement which was drawn up on 19 December 1851. It is not known what provision John Grey made for his daughter on her marriage, but George's father agreed to transfer £2,500 at 3 per cent in consolidated bank annuities, and £2,655 at 3 per cent in reduced annuities, which would provide George and Josephine with an annual income of some £150. The settlement was, however, designed primarily to provide against their early deaths, and towards 'the placing out or advancement in the world' of their orphan children. Brothers of both bride and groom, Charles Grey Grey and Spencer Percival Butler, were to be trustees, and the indenture was witnessed by Josephine's father, and by her brother-in-law, Edgar Garston.[34]

Josephine was married from the parish church of St Andrew's at nearby Corbridge. We are fortunate to have Hatty's account of her sister's wedding day, although, as is quite natural in a lively unattached woman of twenty-one, Hatty was more conscientious about recording her own romantic conquests. Sightings of 'the bride' are few and far between. Hatty had her fair share of beaux among the wedding guests: groom's men, John and Monty Blackett and Spencer Butler, were all on hand to take her in to dinner, or to engage her in a 'nice long chat', of which she enjoyed many. After dinner on the eve of the wedding, Hatty stayed up to make favours for the menfolk, and then came the day itself.

> *Thursday 8 January 1852*
> Dear Josey's wedding day – breakfasted with Mama and bride, pinned favours on the gentlemen; Ormy Walker came; brought camelias. Groom's men – John Blackett, Bolland, Spencer, and Charley [Grey]. Maids – Meggy Carr, Emily Butler, Emmy and me. Flags all about the lawn – pretty wedding procession – 5 carriages – church very full. Josey looked lovely, in white, orange wreath, and long veil, behaved very well. I went in the carriage with Papa and her; came back with bride's maids and Spencer . . . Breakfast at one o'clock. Went in with John Blackett; Charley, Emmy and Spencer made jokes. Dressed the bride to go away at three. Old shoes, and broom thrown after her, dear sweet bride.[35]

It is not known where George and Josephine spent their honeymoon: from George's jest about Hatty getting to the altar before her sister and honeymooning down the Rhine, it is possible that this was their destination.

A dizzying number of friends and neighbours continued to call in at Dilston as the afternoon went on, and a sizeable party came up by the 5 p.m. train. Tea was served at 7 p.m., there was a bonfire and fireworks in the castle ruins, and by 7.30 p.m. the dancing had commenced. Hatty recorded,

> M. Blackett took me in . . . all danced very merrily – had a delightful gallop with Edgar [Garston] – nice quadrille with John and M. Blackett.

> Supper at 11 – some singing – then dancing again, 'grave and gay' with Bolland, great fun – dear Papa hurt his foot in it. People went away about 2. Delicious moonlight walk with M.B. – bathed Papa's foot etc. – to bed half past 3.

The festivities continued throughout the week, with a daily bustle of house guests to and from the station. There were charades in the dining room ('Spencer did the unprotected female, & [Willy] Bell the young heiress, splendidly'), 'scrambling dinners', much gossiping and 'merry games in the window'; and, despite the wind and snow flurries, there were pony rides along the banks of the swollen Tyne, walking expeditions to Aydon Castle, visits to neighbours, and on the Tuesday, Mr Grey carried off all the gentlemen to the Farmers' Dinner at Hexham. Nor were the servants neglected: they had a ball of their own the day after the wedding, at which Charles, Tully and Emmy danced ('Edgar and Emmy dressed *en Grec*'), and a tea party on the Monday. Hatty's amusing new brother-in-law, Spencer, just two years her elder, seems to have inspired a serious crush: the two went off riding together on the Monday after the wedding, and on the Tuesday she made a point of recording in her diary how they searched for costumes for fireside games. Hatty saw off Emily Butler and Spencer at the station the next day, and reported, then, that all was 'wet and cold and dreary'.

3

Oxford

'The great wall of prejudice'

WHEN THE BUTLERS returned from their honeymoon they set up house together in Oxford, at 124 High Street ('The High'). An early watercolour sketch of the drawing room done by Josephine records an as yet sparsely furnished room of somewhat formal grandeur: a marble mantelpiece topped with a gilt clock under a glass dome, a few pictures on the walls 'rather high up', two little armchairs and 'one very stiff sofa' with 'hard cushions worked with beads'.[1] George's younger brother, Arty, at University College, later spoke of the effect of Josephine's entrance into Oxford society: 'I can never forget the charm of her first appearance in Oxford. She took everyone by storm'; she was ever, he said, his ideal of 'domestic personal charm'.[2] Hatty visited her sister almost at once, and Arty was on hand (every day!) to chaperon her on tours of the colleges and to take her to Oxford parties. She was certainly on her best behaviour, solemnly recording, four days after her arrival, that she 'Went to George's lecture at night on Scripture: very interesting'.[3]

The Butlers began their married life in some uncertainty as to George's prospects: he clearly regarded his position as examiner a temporary one and continued to apply for academic posts, but without success. When George brought his young bride to Oxford he seems to have made a decided effort to involve her in his work. In the quiet of evenings in their lodgings, they studied Italian together; they prepared a new unexpurgated edition of Chaucer's poems for publication, studying early 'old black letter' editions side by side in the Bodleian; they made copies of the views of Oxford by Turner in the Taylor Gallery; and drew up large wall maps to illustrate George's geographical lectures. The study of Art and Geography was among the liberalizing influences George Butler sought to introduce to Oxford. He lectured on Greek sculpture and architecture, as well as on Christian painters before Raphael, drawing attention to their intensity and power of imagination. He also became involved in cataloguing for the Taylor Gallery their original drawings by Michelangelo and Raphael. His Geography lectures, given in the face of a certain aloofness in Oxford opinion towards 'so elementary a study', sought to establish it as a serious scientific undertaking.[4]

Josephine became pregnant soon after her marriage, and Hatty was required to return to Oxford in October 1852 to assist with the birth of the Butlers' first baby, George Grey Butler, who was born in the early hours of the morning of 15 November. At Josephine's insistence, there was no physician in attendance, which was in part her 'protest against wicked customs' that denied professional status to female midwives. She preferred, as she said, to trust in God: 'My beloved mother had twelve children and never had a doctor near her. I followed her example and was carried safely through every confinement. [Hatty] was the same.'[5] The account of the birth in Hatty's diary makes no mention at all of the happy father.

> *Monday 15 November 1852.* Little Master George Butler born at 3.30 a.m. Darling Josey getting on well; nice little baby that can open its eyes & has curly dark hair, & only cries a little bit.
> *Tuesday 16 November.* Wrote heaps of letters . . . Josey & baby flourishing.
> *Saturday 20 November.* Dear Josey got on to the sofa in her own room; I read to her, & she had a capital night after the change.
> *Saturday 27 November.* Josey and Baby out.[6]

Shortly after the birth, both sisters began cutting wisdom teeth and Josephine had to nurse her baby while suffering from 'bad face-ache'. Their eldest brother, George Annett Grey, made a rare appearance in order to visit his new nephew, and then there were preparations to be made for the christening. This was conducted at St Mary Magdalene's on Saturday, 18 December. Hatty was godmother (noting with pride that little George 'behaved very well'), and Spencer Butler and William Henry Lyttleton, a friend of George's from Trinity College Cambridge, stood as godfathers. Hatty remained with the Butlers over Christmas and the New Year, and proved herself an excellent godmother, as Josephine noted to her Butler brothers-in-law: 'Hatty is so kind to my little chap, & gives him long lectures, wh he listens to, looking up in her face all the time'.[7] She illustrated the letter with a cartoon of baby George staring up at his aunt, wide-eyed and open-mouthed.

Hatty and Emily Grey would often come to stay with them in Oxford, 'bringing a new and lively element into Oxford society'. It was a feminine element much appreciated by George's friends, William Thomson and Max Müller, the German orientalist and philologist who had recently come to Oxford as Professor of Modern European Languages, and who became a special friend of Josephine's. In the summer of 1853 these two called on Josephine with a request that, as the day was so fine, she would allow the girls to join their party to Newnham Park: 'It is Mr Thomson's party, and some ladies – friends of his – are going. He had a barge fitted up for them. The inducement was so great that I could not refuse, and I was amused at the children's glee'.[8] George and Josephine would also take the girls on long rambles or take them horse-riding with parties of dons. Horse-riding was as ever one of Josephine's pleasures, and she and George would often ride out to Bagley Woods or Abingdon Park on summer evenings to hear the nightingales: 'We sometimes rode from five in the afternoon, till the sun set and the dew fell, on grassy paths between the thick undergrowths of woods'.[9] Josephine boasted that, when the phrenologist Sir William Hamilton first set eyes on her in Oxford, he declared that he could tell she was a good rider: 'She has firmness . . . a general sense of harmony! And a light figure!'[10]

Max Müller recalled that there were at that time in Oxford 'very few houses outside the circle of Heads of Houses, where there was a lady and a certain amount of social life'.[11] The Butlers' home was one such household, the Thomsons' another. Josephine's piano didn't arrive in Oxford until 9 October 1852, by which time she was eight months pregnant with Georgie. It was a splendid instrument, which had won first prize in its category at the Great Exhibition in 1851, 'and its price was *200* guineas!', a costly wedding present. 'Dear old piano,' she would later write, 'I could bring music out of it wh I could never bring out of any other piano. It seemed to *talk to me*'.[12] Two years before her death, Josephine still recalled the thrill of performing in Oxford: 'I think I seldom enjoyed anything more than the musical evenings we had in Oxford'; Mozart and Beethoven quartets, she said, 'still haunt my ears . . . Many men came to listen – for Oxford was nearly all men then – and no one spoke or even coughed'.

She was, though, prohibited from playing the piano whenever

George's friend Arthur Stanley called (a future professor of ecclesiastical history at Oxford). She was told that he was deficient in all the five senses and could not appreciate music. 'What will my dear mother say when I tell her he hates music?' she asked.[13] Arthur Stanley had a sparkling intellect and his sermons were full of original thought, but Josephine thought him a social oddity with his simple childlike ways. Friends like Stanley would often descend upon their old friend Butler. At such times Josephine would sit demurely in a corner, silently absorbing the masculine talk which, as she acknowledged, was often brilliant. Oxford men were a different species, and as yet she hardly knew how to converse with them, or they with Josephine.

She had particular difficulty with Benjamin Jowett, the celebrated Professor of Greek at Balliol. She tells of a large picnic party to the ancient Wychwood forest, arranged by Jowett and Max Müller during her second summer at Oxford. Emily Grey, aged seventeen, was then on a visit. Emmy took the reins of a light dogcart with Jowett as her passenger. 'We did not fancy these two could have many subjects in common to furnish conversation; and after our return we asked her how they got on. "Oh, very well", she replied. "I asked him questions, and if he was long in replying I drove the dogcart over some bumps on the roadside, and this joggled the answers out of him".'[14] Josephine had a rather different experience with Jowett. In the evening she set off to walk a little of the way back on foot, and after a time sat down to wait for the others by a dry ditch at the roadside. 'Not very romantic, but it was pleasant – a complete solitude and silence, a very gentle evening breeze blowing, bringing sweet scents from the fields and woods, and stars coming out one by one'. Her solitude was at last disturbed by a fellow walker: 'It was Mr Jowett, who took a seat by my side, with his feet also in the dry ditch. Then I thought, "What shall I say?"' They listened to the sounds of cockchafers and frogs, and after trying several topics of conversation, the pair sat on in embarrassed silence.

Much of the Butlers' early married life in Oxford was very happy and productive, although these years were not untouched by personal sorrow. George's father died suddenly at the end of April 1853. Josephine happened to be on a visit with five-month-old Georgie. Before luncheon, she took a turn in the garden with the Dean, but he had to rest against a tree and began breathing heavily. At luncheon,

> I felt, rather than saw him throw himself back in his chair: there was a sigh, a sudden movement, and in a moment all the guests had fled. He was

> laid on a couch, still and motionless . . . I telegraphed to George (all the brothers were absent), and he came off at once. I had only said that the Dean was ill. I met him at the door, and he asked: 'What account of my father?' I replied: 'Your father is gone!' I am sorry I said it so abruptly; for he trembled and became very pale.[15]

Josephine seems also to have blamed herself for permitting her father-in-law to carry Georgie in his arms, his first grandson of whom he was so proud. Georgie grew up in the belief that Grandfather Butler 'had strained his heart that way', and that this had hastened his death.[16]

At the end of the year, there was an exchange of letters between Josephine and her father about the death from hepatitis of Eliza's husband in Hong Kong, and concern, too, for Eliza herself. In her same letter Josephine had confided to her father, 'We find housekeeping hard work, with small means and prices so high. I pay 22 shillings a ton for coals'.[17] Revealingly, on the problems of housekeeping, she was to write to a young Oxford friend, Zoe Skene, who was about to be married, that 'a comparatively small house when it must be sustained by small means may crush a poor wife', and she advised, 'I find it is not cleverness or courage so much as humility, which helps one to rise again after discouragement'.[18] Yet domestic economy was as nothing compared to the joys of observing the funny ways of their growing prodigy. Georgie, or Bunty, as they called him, now a year old, was 'getting very knowing and old fashioned'. When he felt sleepy and wanted to be 'hushed off', he would warm his blanket in front of the fire: 'He is very fond of a toasted blanket (which indeed few people would object to in this frosty weather), and when laid down in it, he keeps on with a low chuckling laugh of pleasure, till he falls asleep'.[19]

George was finally ordained by the Bishop of Oxford in the spring of 1854. It was a matter George considered 'gravely for a long time', but since his career seemed likely to continue to be in education, 'the desire arose in his mind to be able to stand towards the younger men or boys . . . in the position of their pastor as well as their teacher'.[20] Josephine sent her mother a delightful account of the ordination ceremony, which lasted nearly four hours: 'George and I are so accustomed to do everything together, that . . . when the bishop's hands rested on his shining curls I felt as if I was being ordained too'.[21] Thereafter, George assisted the vicar of St Giles's in Oxford and he would take over the parish of Dilston in the summer holidays.

Until George had finished his examining duties, he would stay on alone in Oxford, while Josephine would travel ahead to Dilston for the summer visit. Although she and George wrote to each other every day, very few of these letters have survived. One of July 1854 describes a holiday at Tynemouth. Josephine's second son, Arthur Stanley, was born earlier that year; named after George's Oxford friend, Arthur Penrhyn Stanley, he was known variously as Stanley, Catty, Cat or Kit. Tully and Edgar arrived from Dilston with a picnic, bringing with them their own baby daughter, Ethel, and Eliza's daughters, Edith and Constance. Josephine described how she rode down to the beach on the back of a donkey, holding Georgie and Stanley in her arms, the maid Mary leading, and how she let Georgie sit in the saddle by himself, 'not bad for a baby of 20 months'. She also took Georgie into the sea with her: 'He did not cry when bathed himself, but when he saw me take a header from the machine, and disappear in the water, he screamed, and seemed in a terrible fright, and held out his little arms to save me'.[22] Her letter to George concludes with some housewifely advice, the only instance of its kind in the whole of her preserved correspondence of a lifetime, telling him, 'When you leave you had better put her (Cook) on board wages as before – 10*s*. a week'.[23]

Josephine was still at Dilston for her sister Hatty's wedding later that summer. Hatty had fallen in love with Chevalier Tell Meuricoffre, a Swiss banker who appears to have visited her father at Dilston in 1852, and who was also known to Tully's husband, Edgar. They were married at Corbridge on 24 August 1854, and set off at once for Naples, where Tell's business was established. Back in Oxford, Josephine was shocked to realize her loss: 'It made me feel that you were gone indeed, that a wide space is between me and one who had been a dear companion and confidential friend'.[24] When Hatty had her first baby, so great was her need to see her sister that she made Tell take her across Europe in deepest winter to spend Christmas in a snowbound Oxford 'with my little Southern baby in a white lace robe'.[25] In future years, it was the frequency with which the Butlers packed up and headed for European climes, especially from the late 1860s onwards, when they felt the need of 'a breathing space' from the 'brick and stone walls' of Liverpool,[26] that ensured that the two families met often, either at the Meuricoffres' palatial home overlooking the Bay of Naples, Capo di Monte, a house mentioned in Baedeker's Guide as 'one of the "sights" of Naples,'[27] or at their Swiss home, La Gordanne, in the Canton Vaud.

Meanwhile, George's reputation grew quickly, and he took on extra summer work as an examiner for the East India Company's Civil Service, and for the Royal Artillery and the Royal Engineers, from 1855 to 1857, which required him to travel to London and Woolwich, and which could earn him a salary of £100 for a month's work. Such an offer was not to be turned down, even if it meant separation from Josephine and the boys: 'we shall have August and September to play,' he urged.[28] One summer's evening in 1855, while George was up in London, Josephine put the boys to bed, and, feeling lonely and dissatisfied with herself, stepped out and took a stroll through the beautiful St John's Gardens, only to be seized upon by a high-spirited group of young women. It was Zoe Skene and her bridesmaids. She was to be married the next day to George's friend, William Thomson. It must have been a rare vision that wedding eve, a party of excited young women chatting in a moonlit garden amongst banks of gleaming bridal-white lilies, flowers that Josephine fancied bloomed for her alone, now that the vacation had begun and the colleges were deserted. Indeed, the college gardeners often weighed down pretty Mrs Butler with bouquets when she took her babies out for exercise.

Since their first years together at Oxford, George had been involved in the building of the controversial Museum for the Sciences, now the Oxford University Museum of Natural History, and in February 1854 he was asked to serve as Honorary Secretary of the museum delegacy, in which capacity he attended several meetings a month. The controversies over the museum were major and various, many of them aroused by the question of evolution, or, in the words of Sir Henry Acland, a moving spirit behind the museum, 'the true genesis of the earth'. Sir Charles Lyell, whose *Principles of Geology* (1830–33) had done much to begin the debate about evolution, had attacked the university for its neglect of the sciences, but it was still questioned whether there was a place for scientific study in Oxford. For George and Josephine, the scientific discoveries of recent years were not 'the Enemies of God'; rather, she said, they 'have helped us to a revelation of a wider universe, a larger purpose and a greater God than we had before realised'.[29]

Characteristically, one of George's first concerns was for the museum workmen, who were provided with two mess rooms as well as a reading room. George consulted with them to ensure that their working conditions and living quarters were satisfactory, attended daily prayers with them in their work sheds, and even read them the church service on Sundays. They also received visits from Ruskin who came to canvass support for the Working Men's College in Oxford, now Ruskin College, where he gave evening classes, and to speak to them about the pride of medieval workmen.

The original estimate for the construction of the museum did not include the cost of ornamentation, and a public appeal to fund decorative stonework was launched on 1 June 1855. It was hoped that individual patrons would pay for the marble pillar shafts, representing different rocks from the British Isles, which were to be topped by carved stone capitals representing indigenous flora and fauna. George Butler, for example, subscribed one marble shaft and one capital at £5 each, and Josephine put forward a design, incorporating the lilies in St John's Gardens, for the decoration of the capital.[30]

It fell to George to see to the needs of the sculptor commissioned to execute, for a total payment of £420, a series of six life-size statues of scientific men for the museum. This was a young Scotsman, Alexander Munro, who shared a London studio with the painter Arthur Hughes. In Oxford, Munro lodged with the Butlers, and he was able to work on his clay models of portrait busts from their house, the first of which, representing Galileo, was completed by April 1856. The young couple must have been refreshingly congenial company. George Butler was an authority on classical and Renaissance art and a talented watercolourist admired by Ruskin, and his beautiful wife, although perhaps an inferior artist, was learning a great deal under George's instruction.

Alex Munro produced two distinctive marble busts of Josephine, and a plaster relief. The first bust, which bears the date 1855, is in the possession of the first women's university college, Girton College, Cambridge, yet the pose is a most incongruous one for Girton, or indeed for Josephine. The gaze is resolute, and recognizable, but the long hair is unbound, flowing loosely down her back, and she is wearing nothing but the simplest drapery, a plain chemise which reveals one naked shoulder. A thin band in her hair, dotted with stars, has the appearance of a halo.

The starry headband may be explained by Josephine's allusion to a visit she and George made to Dante Gabriel Rossetti's studio in Chelsea. Rossetti knew the article George had written on the foremost translations of Dante, and had sent some of his translations of sonnets for George's comment. He also invited the Butlers to visit his studio. Rossetti's Dantesque poem, 'The Blessed Damozel', was published in the Pre-Raphaelite Brotherhood's journal, the *Germ*, in February 1850.[31] In the poem, the 'damozel', or damsel, leans over the golden bar of heaven to look down upon her mortal lover, and wishes for his speedy death so that they may become lovers in death as they were in life. Her appearance accords with several of Munro's details: 'Her robe, ungirt from clasp to hem', 'Her hair that lay along her back', and 'the stars in her hair were seven'.[32] Munro would have known of the poem, and it is likely that he was a frequent visitor at the Chelsea house; his friend, Arthur Hughes, although not one of the original seven members of the Pre-Raphaelite Brotherhood, was certainly of its circle. Hughes's influence upon Munro's work shows itself in the demure pose of Munro's second bust of Josephine.

In the later bust, which Munro called his 'Beatrice marble',[33] presumably inspired by Dante's Beatrice, Josephine wears a plain chemise drawn up to the neck, over which hangs a simple antique yoked dress. The eyes are lowered, the gaze introspective and solemn, even grave. Munro has achieved a wonderful sense of unity by the careful echoing of certain details in the dress through the gathering of the individual strands of hair, and the Pre-Raphaelite style is evident in an impossibly long plait of hair down her back which hangs in heavy and lazy serpentine coils, and which looks as though it is about to tumble down. Josephine herself grew to prefer photographs of this bust to the portraits taken of herself in photographic studios, writing to a friend, 'I have tried in vain three times to get a decent one of myself. They are somehow never the least like. But I have at last got one done of Munro's bust of me, wh is nice I think'.[34]

The bas-relief of Josephine appears to be taken from one of Munro's early sketches for the second bust. We recognize the extraordinary hair-style, but the sitter's gaze is straight ahead in this version. The base of the neck is set in a profusion of Morning Glory flowers: the erotic play of the wide-open flowers and irrepressible tendrils does not quite accord with the plain directness of the sitter's gaze.

All three studies are undeniably beautiful, yet none is strictly speaking a portrait of Josephine Butler. None captures the Josephine that George Richmond saw. Munro's rival, the sculptor Thomas Woolner, who knew of Josephine, was critical of the second of the busts, saying, 'there are some points of merit in it, but he has lost her eyes by dropping the lids; those wonderful sad eyes! how on earth he could shut up those "magic casements" when he could have had them open and looking out upon this sad world of ours'.[35]

The Butlers' social life in Oxford had what Josephine termed 'its shadow side'.[36] It is in her response to what was less appealing about Oxford that we see early signs of the attitudes and convictions which drove the much more public life that was to be hers. 'Monastic' was how Josephine described Oxford in term time, 'a society of celibates', and she often had to bear narrowly conventional and often wounding views of women. In her father's house, Josephine and her sisters had been treated as the intellectual equals of their father and brothers. Her own husband 'recognised the right of women, equally with men, to minister in the church, or to plead openly for justice & truth', a fact that Josephine attributed to the influence of George's mother, Sarah Butler, who had been brought up a Quaker.[37] George had a high regard for his wife's intellect, and Josephine recalled that 'from my earliest married life, my dear husband used to say, if there was any difficult political problem or crisis before the world, "I must ask my dear wife, she is such a politician"'.[38] When she did eventually speak up in Oxford society, however, she was made to feel that hers was a jarring voice, and her opinions ill-judged. Josephine's memories of early married life in Oxford are largely of occasions on which she refused to remain silent when individual women, or women as a sex, were slandered. One day a painting of Raphael was being discussed and she criticized the artist's representation of one of his female figures, posed in an attitude of prayer, as insipid.

> 'Insipid! Of course it must be', said a distinguished college tutor; 'a woman's face when engaged in prayer could never wear any other expression than that of insipidity'. 'What!' I asked, 'when one converses with a man of high intelligence and noble soul, if there be any answering chord in one's own mind, does one's expression immediately become insipid? Does it not rather beam with increased intelligence and exalted thought? And how much more if one converses face to face with the highest Intelligence of all! Then every faculty of the mind and emotion of the soul is called to its highest exercise!'. No one made any remark, and the silence seemed to rebuke my audacity.[39]

This was not to be her last word on the subject. The 'distinguished college tutor' turns out to have been Benjamin Jowett. Some years later she wrote a long letter to Jowett, giving him a detailed account of her own faith. The letter is undated, but a reference to the instruction she gives her boys seems to indicate that it was written some time after the Butlers moved from Oxford in 1857. Yet the letter begins where her account of the discussion about Raphael leaves off. In what becomes an exposition of her faith, she begins by correcting Jowett's assumption that women's faith is by nature insipid and non-intellectual.

> I think there prevails among clever men who do not know intimately the hearts of many women, an idea that women generally accept Christianity without a thought or a difficulty; that they are in a measure instinctively pious, and that religion is rather an indulgence of the feelings with them, than anything else . . . For myself I can say that to be guided by feeling would be simply dangerous; that I am obliged to give feeling a subordinate place, and to be guided by a stern sense of *right* throughout a life which involves daily and hourly self denial. I believe there are few honest women knowing anything of religion, who would not confess the same.[40]

It took some time before Josephine could admit to herself that the wisdom of Oxford was undermined by many areas of deplorable ignorance which resulted in dangerous prejudices and bigoted judgements. Writing of her sister Hatty, Josephine explained that she had, 'like myself, at that time an exaggerated idea of the profound wisdom of the learned men and professors who used to come to our drawing-room every evening, in an easy and friendly way'. Affecting great awe at the thought of meeting these wise men, Hatty vowed to her sister that she would get up early every morning to learn passages from Bacon's essays, in the hope of equipping herself to enter into their talk. Josephine never gives any indication that she was overcome by a sense of her own intellectual inadequacy in such learned company, but Hatty's cheery presence in Oxford was no doubt a comfort to her sister in her early married life. In time, the two of them overcame their awe of learned men by producing irreverent sketches of the gowned dons, clergy and undergraduates.

Josephine was also angered by the prejudice among these Oxford intellectuals in relation to questions of women and sexuality, or, more properly, the question of the sexual double standard which characterized Victorian thinking on sexuality, and which judged sexual experience in a man a natural, biological need, but in a woman an unnatural, irremediable loss of womanhood. 'Every instinct of womanhood within me was already in revolt against certain accepted theories in Society, and I suffered as only God and the faithful companion of my life could ever know,' she wrote.[41] There may have been monastic aspects to Oxford in the early 1850s, but it was hardly the celibate shrine of masculine learning that male dons would have had her believe. A case came to light of 'a very young girl' who, it was strongly rumoured, had been seduced by an Oxford don and had borne his child. Josephine described how she ventured to speak to one of the supposedly wisest men in the university, in the hope that he would suggest some means of bringing to a sense of his crime the man who had wronged the girl. She was strongly advised that it was best to do nothing: 'It could only do harm to open up in any way such a question as this; it was dangerous to arouse a sleeping lion'.[42]

Such a response was astonishing to Josephine, and deeply discouraging, but she quickly understood that her counsellor only spoke the received Oxford opinion, which she had come up against in January 1853, when Elizabeth Gaskell's novel *Ruth* was published. The novel tells of the seduction and abandonment of an orphaned, unworldly seamstress of remarkable beauty, by a gentleman whose mother removes him from further moral contamination by his 'vicious companion'. Ruth, still a pure woman in Gaskell's view, is left to bear their child alone. Gaskell's intention is clearly to question the sexual double standard, and to raise the matter of a father's responsibility for his illegitimate offspring. The shame of illegitimacy is discussed frankly in the novel. Josephine read *Ruth* as Gaskell intended, and thought it 'a book which seemed to me to have a very wholesome tendency, though dealing with a painful subject', but the male intellectuals with whom she discussed the novel viewed a moral lapse as much worse in a woman than in a man: 'A pure woman, it was reiterated, should be absolutely ignorant of a certain class of evils in the world, albeit those evils bore with murderous cruelty on other women . . . Silence was thought to be the great duty of all on such subjects'.[43]

Such injustices and the blind eye turned to them appear to have borne more and more heavily upon Josephine. She tells of an incident in which, sitting before her open window on a close summer's night, she heard a cry that she seems to have taken for a sign:

> It was a woman's cry – a woman aspiring to heaven and dragged back to hell – and my heart was pierced with pain . . . I cannot explain the nature of the impression, which remains with me to this day; but . . . when the day dawned it seemed to show me again more plainly than ever the great wall of prejudice, built up on a foundation of lies, which surrounded a whole world of sorrows, griefs, injustices, and crimes which must not be spoken of.[44]

It is possible to detect in this unease the beginnings of her battle for both legal and moral justice for women and for the poor, and there are suggestions that during her time at Oxford Josephine had begun to see her way forward. She and George saw Christ's actions as revolutionary, and regarded themselves as Christian revolutionaries.[45] Josephine was, in fact, developing very precise ideas about the sort of active work she wished to undertake, writing in her spiritual diary, 'It would make me more satisfied, if I could visit the poor & sick, & teach classes'; of even more interest is her desire to open up their home to the destitute; she writes of 'the harder & more self denying work of going about among a few poor, or gathering them to the house'.[46] There is an account she gives in the life of her husband of a Newgate prisoner who had been seduced and then abandoned by her upper-class lover, and had then killed their baby. Josephine had read about the case and wanted to visit the woman in prison, to comfort her and to tell her 'of the God who saw the injustice done, and who cared for her', but it was George who suggested that they might take her into their Oxford home as a servant.[47] In her evidence to the Royal Commission on the Administration and Operation of the Contagious Diseases Acts in 1871, Josephine stated that she began her rescue work first of all in Oxford, and it may have been this woman's case that she was referring to.[48] It was a remarkably courageous act of the Butlers, but it was also an act that could appear ostentatious to unsympathetic onlookers. A comment made years later by Benjamin Jowett suggests the kind of response Josephine must have aroused in Oxford. Writing to Florence Nightingale in 1869, he gave his view of Josephine's later rescue work in Liverpool: 'she is very excitable & emotional – of an over-sympathetic temperament, which leads her to take an interest about a class of sinners whom she had better have left to themselves'.[49]

By the summer of 1856 Josephine was pregnant with her third child, and was possessed by a guilty feeling that she was 'not *doing* enough for God', and depressed at the recognition that her state of health was a great hindrance. Indeed, Josephine's health was so precarious that she began to doubt whether she was to be called to active work at all, or whether she had been chosen to lead a life of prayer: 'I am in a great measure unable to walk, combating daily with infirmities & languor; with child; & peculiarly disabled from physical effort'.[50]

Earlier that year, George and Josephine had decided to venture all their capital in investing in a project that would provide them with a permanent home in Oxford as well as a permanent income. George was involved in a number of reforming schemes in the city and was on the side of those who wanted to liberalize the university by releasing it from the conservative influence of the heads of individual colleges. He now showed his reforming spirit by applying to the university authorities to grant him a licence to set up a private hall which would provide less expensive accommodation for undergraduates.[51] Butler Hall, situated at 15 St Giles's Street, was a fine-looking two-storey Georgian house built in sandstone. George was able to combine his work as Principal of Butler Hall with the curacy of nearby St Giles's Church, and Josephine seems to have been very happy in her new home. In time, the scheme promised to provide for the future of their growing family.

According to the biography she wrote of her husband, Josephine suffered more than usual from the Oxford damp in the autumn of 1856, damp caused by a great flooding of the surrounding countryside. George took her down to London to see a specialist, Sir James Clark, who had once been the royal physician. At the end of the consultation, Sir James turned to George and said, 'Poor thing, poor thing! you must take her away from Oxford'.[52] '*Rest* & quiet' was the only treatment recommended by Clark, after he had examined Josephine's heart, as well as 'slight palliatives & soothing things'. Like the many other consultants to whom Josephine turned, Clark told her 'that God is my only Physician (which I knew), and that all my ailments were so complicated with the spiritual and intellectual being that it would be an impertinence in them to think they could manage me'.[53]

It was the first time that a doctor recognized that Josephine's physical ailments, painful and enervating as they were, and even dangerous, were triggered by anxiety and depression. George bought her the palliatives that she had been prescribed, but privately Josephine prayed for forgiveness for her spiritual weakness, as she saw it, in resorting to opiates: 'dear Lord', she wrote in her diary, 'grant me a little oblivion – put me out of pain – If I take opiates, Thou knowest it is terror wh drives me to seek oblivion in them'.[54] In one painful passage in her diary, her distress is so great that it seems she was even tempted to think about taking her own life: 'Lord, Thou alone canst hold me, & keep me from open sin, from this desperate unrecallable act . . . Take my loved ones, & be my Covenant God, & keep them for me & then slay me – take me & take me *soon*, unless Thou make another "way to escape" – Lord, shall I do it? – *hold back my hand*'.[55]

As an immediate yet temporary measure, George took a house at Clifton, near Bristol, where the warmer climate would help restore her health as her confinement approached. 'This was no light trial,' as Josephine acknowledged. 'Our pleasant home must be broken up; all the hopes and plans my husband had cherished abandoned'.[56] For him to carry on his work alone, and for them to be separated for an indefinite time, was something they could not envisage. George asked his sister Catherine to come to Clifton to nurse Josephine. This was an inspired choice, since Catherine had herself worked amongst the poor in London for some years, and she was able to give her brother's wife much comfort and much advice about the sort of work she wanted to do in the future. Catherine herself was to accept Bishop Bowen's invitation to join him as his wife and fellow missionary in Sierra Leone in the autumn of 1857, 'her one idea of happiness being complete devotion to the cause of God and suffering humanity'.[57]

George, meanwhile, prepared to close up Butler Hall and began again the rounds of applications for academic posts. In 1856 and 1857 he applied for and failed to get two Classics professorships. Hatty recorded this solemn fact in a wickedly funny cartoon of a ragged and barefoot George and Josephine leaving Oxford to seek employment elsewhere. George steps out resolutely, with all his worldly goods tied up in a handkerchief on a stick over his shoulder, and a bedraggled Josephine creeps meekly behind him, weighed down with baby Stanley and a romping-looking Georgie. In fact, they had become seriously worried about their future, when George was offered the post of Vice-Principal by the Board of Governors of Cheltenham College, a private boys' school with an already strong reputation in the teaching of the classics.

4

Eva

'The brightest of our little circle'

JOSEPHINE NOTED THAT her husband's appointment at Cheltenham College marked 'the cessation of material difficulties and anxieties',[1] yet George's new responsibilities were considerable. As well as taking on the duties of Deputy Principal, he was responsible for a number of boarders (these would grow to as many as thirty) who lodged at the house provided for the Butlers, on the junction of Priory Street and London Road. Named the Priory, the house, or mansion, rather, dated from around 1820. An advertisement from 1828 provides a detailed description of the interior:

> It contains, on the basement, a roomy kitchen, scullery, larder, laundry, butler's pantry, wine and beer cellars, and every domestic office; – on the ground floor a handsome vestibule (from which springs an elegant staircase with fancy iron balustrade and mahogany continued rail and oak stairs), a breakfast parlour . . . fitted with statuary marble chimney pieces, enriched by cornices and flowers; a dining room 30 feet by 17 ft. 6 in. connected by folding doors, with a drawing room of 22 ft. by 17 ft. 6 in. opening through French windows to a neat lawn.[2]

There was a second drawing room on the first floor, together with 'two spacious lofty, and airy bedrooms, adjoining on each side, and a dressing room, each leading from a spacious landing place', and on the second floor there were six more 'excellent bed rooms' with a magnificent circular skylight above the landing. An idea of the size of the Priory can be gathered from the fact that a previous owner held a ball there which was attended by 800 guests.

George entered fully into the intellectual life of Cheltenham. He was invited by the headmaster to join a gentleman's debating society whose members met once a month at each other's houses to consider mostly literary subjects. Their family doctor, Dr Claude Kerr, was a member, as was the retired actor William Macready, who became a good friend of the Butlers. Josephine recorded very little of her life at Cheltenham, however, so we know little of the family's involvement with their schoolboy boarders. The new babies presumably occupied her a good deal during their first years there. Their son Charles Augustine Vaughan (known variously as Charlie, Carlo or Carlino), named after Charles Vaughan who succeeded George's father as headmaster of Harrow, was born at Clifton, shortly before their arrival in Cheltenham, and their fourth and last child, a daughter, Evangeline Mary, was born on 26 May 1859. Then a woman of thirty years of age, Josephine had no more children. Her doctors may have advised her against further pregnancies. Josephine later reminded her niece Edith, 'Think how many years I was laid up, scarcely able to walk about my house. For 5 years after Stanley's birth I was so weak & useless', and there is evidence to suggest that Charlie's birth especially left her in delicate health.[3] That she had no more children is an interesting matter, but it may have been that 'a serious injury' which she later referred to, sustained in one of her confinements, meant that she was simply unable to have another child after Eva was born.[4]

Two of Josephine's sisters were then lodging in Cheltenham: Eliza, who married a second time in the summer of 1861 at the age of forty-two, and Fanny. From Fanny's diary we know that Josephine continued to suffer from bouts of illness. In 1862, for example, Fanny was put in charge of the Butler children while Josephine underwent a water cure at the Malvern Springs, and an undated letter survives from Georgie Butler to his father, who was then away from home, informing him, 'Dr Kerr says Mama has got a sharp attack of Rheumatics and must stay in bed a day but she will be better soon. We are praying to be good boys and not to do mischief. Mama does love you so very much dear Paps, and we all love you'.[5] Although never strong physically, there is no indication from Josephine's diary that her years at Cheltenham witnessed a return of the terrible mental and spiritual anguish she suffered at Oxford. She now had four young children to supervise, as well as the pleasant society of her sisters to enjoy, and she became especially close to Eliza's already grown-up daughters, Edith and Constance. There is nothing to suggest that she was not utterly content and fulfilled in her domestic role.

Josephine's home life was merry, due largely to her husband's boyish sense of fun, but Fanny also observed 'a good deal of amusing chafing and fun going on between her and the boys'.[6] To his young sons, Papa was 'Paps', while Josephine was given more idiosyncratic titles, among them 'Mauddy', 'Mudsie', 'Melchis', and, what seems to be Charlie's invention, 'Fruiterartereeteroo', or 'Dear Fruit' for short. At Easter 1861, they all went over to Boulogne for a brief holiday, and at hotels in Dover, Folkestone and Boulogne, George and Josephine kept up a comical mock diary for the private entertainment of their boys, written in both hands. One of George's more surprising contributions was the riddle: 'What part of the Scriptures do two young ladies fulfil when kissing each other? They do unto one another what they would have men do to them.' He also made their mother the subject of delightful nonsense rhymes such as the following, which makes gentle play of Josephine's poor appetite and her inclination to thinness:

Poor Mama – she was a case
That once had something in her
Of stomach now she'd not a trace
A sinner without a dinner.

And when at last the dinner came
She marched in quite defiant
She ran full tilt at every course
Refreshed like a giant.[7]

Their years at Cheltenham witnessed great changes to the Grey family circle. Josephine's mother died on Friday, 17 May 1860. Fanny and her sister Emily, recently widowed, were at Dilston to nurse their mother in her final months. Emmy had married at twenty a Gateshead man, William de Pledge, in 1856, but she was left a young widow with three babies by the time she was twenty-four. Hannah Grey had been an invalid for some years, and John had arranged an upstairs room to be specially furnished for her, 'apart from family care and fatigue'. It was a gesture thought much of by his daughter, Fanny, and she would observe her father come up to his wife after the day's work was done, sitting by Hannah's reclining chair, his hand resting on hers, 'patting and fondling it'. She died suddenly, yet quietly. As her maid remarked, 'It was just like mistress: she made not a bit of fuss about dying'.[8]

Fanny happened to be in Cheltenham with the Butlers when the telegram arrived from their father. Josephine left straight away for

Dilston, and George joined her later for the funeral at which he was to officiate, 'his form bent, his face saddened'.[9] George returned to Cheltenham soon after, leaving Josephine behind to comfort her father. It was while she was away that Eva, exactly a year old, managed to stand on her feet for the first time, as Georgie, now six and a half, informed his mother:

> My Dear Mauddy,
> I hope you will come soon. I learn my lessons every night. Mr Tibbs pulled out one of my teeth to-day. I have got a new flannel-shirt so as it will not get dirty. I hope you are quite well. Eva can stand on her own legs for a little time. We went to the fields to get some flowers. We got such cow-slips. A huge bouquet that [Aunt] Eliza could hardly hold them.
> I send a kiss to you and Grandpapa.
> I am your own dear Georgie Butler.[10]

Fanny noted in her diary that her husband, George Smyttan, also went up to Dilston for her mother's funeral, and that it was he who chose the quiet corner in Corbridge churchyard for their mother's grave.[11] That same year, George Smyttan's name was removed from *Crockford's Clerical Directory*, and it appears that by the autumn of 1860 he and Fanny were no longer living together as man and wife.[12] By then, Fanny was back, alone, at 'my little home' in Cheltenham, 'an invalid and in anxiety'; here she received letters from her father, 'full of kindness, softening sympathy and judicious advice', letters which, belonging to a painful period, she did not keep.[13]

It seems evident that all Fanny's troubles arose from her marriage. From her diary one is impressed by her remarkable meekness. It seems unimaginable that such a wife would desert even the most disreputable of spouses. Fanny, one feels, would have borne all. One can only suppose that the Reverend Smyttan abandoned her. After 1860 he simply disappears from view. We know only that he died ten years later, at the age of forty-eight, at Frankfurt-on-Main.[14] A year after her mother's death, Fanny was installed as mistress of Dilston, as her widowed father's companion, but she continued to be troubled by news of her husband. In the summer of 1862 ('a time of great trial and perplexity to me external to my home life with my dear father', was how Fanny described it), her brother George and his wife were down in London, and 'were obliged to write to me on what they knew would be a trouble to me'. John Grey would gently hint to visitors not to disturb Fanny because she had suffered a good deal.

The year 1862 was also an eventful one for other members of Josephine's family. In March, her niece Edith was married to a young Swiss banker, Ludwig Leupold, whose business was in Genoa, where they were to live. Eliza, too, left Cheltenham after her daughter's wedding, to set sail for China with her second husband, Norman Masson. None of the Greys remained unmarried. Josephine, Hatty and Tully were blessed with long and happy marriages. It is remarkable, though, that so many of their brothers and sisters married again. Both surviving brothers, George and Charles, took second wives, and Emily, born the year Queen Victoria came to the throne, and living long enough to see women get the vote, married a surprising three times. She married her second husband in March 1862. Jasper Bolton, the younger brother of Charles's wife, Emily, succeeded Charles as Lord Derby's land agent in Tipperary. They had five children of their own on top of Emmy's three children from her first marriage. Their first child, Edith Rhoda, born in December 1862, would marry Josephine's son, Stanley.

That year, John Grey, now seventy-six, began to make preparations for his retirement from the Greenwich estates. In the summer, Hatty chose to visit England with her husband and a large party of his relatives from Naples who had come to see the Crystal Palace. She brought with her her baby Josephine, whom they nicknamed 'Doe'. The baby, 'a white child with quiet eyes', was beginning to crawl: 'I do not profess to care for babies much', was Fanny's comment.[15] At Dilston, they received a number of visits from old servants who both wanted to see Hatty and to say their farewells to their old master. John Grey saw to it that the existing servants 'had their sprees also' before the household was broken up, and Fanny sent a detailed account of their various treats and holidays to her sister, Eliza:

> There were cheap trips on the newly opened line, the Border Counties, branching up the North Tyne from Hexham. There was a trip to Edinboro' one day for 4 *s.* there and back, leaving at 5 in the morning, returning at 10 at night . . . Hatty's maid (who had never been to Scotland) asked to go too, so we were left with Neale and young Hannah . . . and Papa sat up for the wanderers and brewed them whisky toddy on their return.[16]

Josephine's father retired in 1863 on a pension of £600 a year, to be succeeded by his son Charles. He moved to Lipwood House in the village of Lipwood, not far from Dilston, noted for its restorative waters. Fanny came as his housekeeper. The hardest task she faced was to urge upon her father to take anything he needed from the old house; the only item he insisted upon taking to Lipwood was the portrait of their mother that hung above the fireplace in the morning room.

John Grey's final duty as master of Dilston was to host the annual summer entertainments for the workhouse children from Hexham, in June 1863. The Butlers were all there, too, and joined in the children's games in the Castle Field. Tea and spice cake were provided as refreshment, and Fanny noted that Eva 'looked happy in her small benevolent way, going from one little girl to another on the sloping bank, peeping into their cans to see if they required replenishing, and urging them to take more'.[17]

Josephine herself had been so poorly that winter that her father came down to Cheltenham to be with her. Fanny was the guest of the Butlers at Easter 1864, and she found Josey stronger than she had expected: 'tho' still looking delicate, her arm in a sling as she had strained her hand', she was 'able to turn more rapidly and cheerfully from one thing to another'.[18] Fanny was taken to the school gymnasium to see eleven-year-old Georgie at his exercises, and she was trailed around the house by little Charlie and Eva: 'I would glance up to see two little round happy faces and bright eyes very wide open, and noses flattened against a window pane, in grave childlike observance of my doings'.[19] They would sometimes hold up a fat guinea pig for their aunt's inspection. Fanny was also there to record the entertainments got up at Easter for the boarders. On Easter Eve, Josephine, together with Fanny and Eva's governess, Miss Blumke, organized a mass egg painting and decorating for the younger boys, 'with the usual accompaniments of rags and lemons, butter and soot, dirty paws and greasy plates, filthy towels, cracked eggshells, and burning hands, dirt, laughter and disorder'.[20] Georgie was entrusted with a magic lantern show, and then his father joined them for the older boys' entertainments: charades, and the card game 'snip-snap-snorum-high-cockleorum-jig'.

It was little Eva who really touched Fanny's heart on this visit to Cheltenham. She had made her aunt a pincushion as a leaving present, and Fanny bought her a trinket in return: 'her little face flushed all over with a pleased surprised glow, & she flew to my arms to hide the warm face against my heart. Then, looking up, exclaiming in her loving impulsiveness, "I will make you *two* pincushions, Aunt Fanny, I will make you *two* pincushions".'[21]

*

The summer of 1864 had been spent in the Lake District, where the Butlers had been lent the house of their good friend James Marshall, the brother of Eva's godmother, Mrs Myers. The house overlooked Coniston Water. 'It was a beautiful summer,' wrote Josephine. Yet, a few days after their return to Cheltenham, 'a heavy sorrow fell upon our home; – the brightest of our little circle being suddenly snatched away from us'.[22] On the evening of Saturday, 20 August, Eva fell from the banister at the top of the hall stairs. She remained unconscious for three hours and then died. She was five years old. A. S. G. Butler said of his grandmother that 'the shock to her system remained like a scar; and it was perpetuated through her children to us. Even at St Andrews, thirty years later, it was mentioned in a hushed voice. My sister and I grew up with the shadow of the disaster still there'.[23]

For nearly three decades Josephine was unable to write about the death of her daughter. Then, after her husband's death in 1890, she began to search through family correspondence, and came upon a bundle of letters of condolence dating from the autumn of 1864. Josephine now made a startling confession to her son, Stanley: she told him how, until George's illness began in the late 1880s, 'for twenty-five years I never woke from sleep without the vision of her falling figure, and the sound of the crash on the stone floor. It had taken possession of my *brain* as well as my heart . . . I have since then had a dread of sudden and *violent* death'.[24] Quoting largely from the letters she wrote and received at the time of Eva's death, Josephine was able to write a full and deeply moving account of the event in her biography of her husband. It was with anguish that she recalled a brief conversation she had with Eva on the afternoon before she died. Eva had found a pretty caterpillar in the garden, and had run up to her mother's room to ask for a little box to keep it in. Josephine handed her a box and then said, 'Now trot away, for I am late for tea.' She did not see her daughter again until George picked up her body at the bottom of the stairs.

> Never can I lose that memory, – the fall, the sudden cry, and then the silence! It was pitiful to see her, helpless in her father's arms, the little drooping head resting on his shoulder, and her beautiful golden hair, all stained with blood, falling over his arm! Would to God that I had died that death for her! If we had been permitted, I thought, to have one look, one word of farewell, one moment of recognition! . . . We called her by her name, but there was no answer. She was our only daughter, the light and joy of our lives.[25]

Arthur Butler recalled that he and his sister Emily arrived a few hours after the accident, and 'never did I see more crushing, touching sorrow'.[26] It was not until she was near death herself that Josephine could communicate the true horrors of the night she lost her daughter. In a private account, written especially for Georgie, she promised to share with him some memories of his sister 'of which I have not yet felt able to speak, for I have been paralysed with grief'.[27] It was only now that she felt equal to describing the hours when Eva lay dying, how the little girl who loved her mother so dearly 'that I have seen her even start out of sleep at the sound of my voice', never gave a sign that she knew her mother and father at her bedside. 'Her eyes wandered with an expression of terror, and her convulsions were terrible to witness'. Then, at the end, a change came over her. The convulsions ceased and an expression of serenity passed over her face. Some of those present believed this to be a sign that she was coming round, 'but I knew it was death and I bade the servants who were sobbing and weeping to be still'.

> She opened her eyes and seemed to see some glory approaching, and her face bore the reflection of that which she saw. Her look was one which rebuked all wild sorrow, and made earthly things sink into insignificance. It was as if she said, '*Now I see God*'. She gave one or two gentle sighs, not of pain, but of sweet relief and contentment, and her soul passed away . . . I thought when I saw her beautiful form in her coffin all crushed and bruised, what a sad death it was for one so sweet and gentle, but I tried to take comfort in the thought that Christ died a more cruel death . . . and she was made like her Lord in her cruel death.[28]

To Josephine, Eva was a saint upon earth: 'She was so perfectly truthful, candid and pure. It was a wonderful repose for me, a good gift from God – when troubled by the evils in the world or in my own thoughts – to turn to the perfect innocence and purity of that little maiden'.[29] The very afternoon before her death, she had been asking Miss Blumke, her governess, how far off heaven was, and would they touch the floor of it if they climbed to the top of Battledown Hill, and Josephine recalled her once saying, 'Mammy, if I go to heaven before you, when the door of heaven opens to let you in, I will run so fast to meet you; and when you put your arms round me, and we kiss each other, *all the angels will stand still to see us*'.[30]

Because of the nature of Eva's death, an inquest was called two days later at the Priory, on the evening of Monday, 22 August, in order to ascertain 'whether her death resulted from any carelessness on the part of those who had charge of her'.[31] Only Maria Blumke and the butler, Robert Hardman, were called upon to testify. The report of the inquest in the *Cheltenham Mercury* gave no indication that Josephine was present. Eva's body was still in the house, and was viewed by the coroner and jury. The statements of the two servants provide far more prosaic, yet altogether more harrowing accounts than that given by Josephine. It was revealed, for example, that all four children were in the habit of straddling the banisters, despite their looseness, and of sliding down them on their chests. It was thought that Eva's attempt to do this by herself, having left her governess in the schoolroom to say goodnight to her parents who were downstairs in the drawing room, led her to her fall of some forty feet. Eva fell at 7.15 p.m., Miss Blumke testified, 'I screamed out, and Mr Butler rushed out of the drawing-room. When I got down the butler had just picked her up. I don't think she was sensible. I did not see her sliding down. I saw her feet disappear'. There seems at first to be some confusion in the *Mercury*'s version of what happened, between Mr Butler rushing to his daughter and the butler's reported action, but Mr Hardman himself offered yet another account of the sequence of events. He testified that he was coming out of the dining room into the hall when he saw something fall: 'I believe she fell upon her shoulder. A boy coming out of the pantry picked her up, and I ran for the doctor. I saw she was not dead, but was quite insensible, and never moved'. The pantry boy is not mentioned by Josephine. In all her private and published accounts of the tragedy, of which there are several, the only person to take little Eva in his arms is George.

Robert Hardman was unable to contact the family physician, Dr Claude Kerr, but he managed to raise a Dr Abercrombie, who got to the house before 8 p.m. There was really very little he could do for the child, however. Eva remained insensible until her death at 10.15 p.m. The cause of death was recorded as 'a severe concussion of the brain and injury to the upper part of the spinal cord'. George was spared the stand at the inquest, and the coroner moved that the jury find for Accidental Death: 'it appeared that there was not the slightest blame attributable to anyone'. He did say, though, that the banister at the top of the stairs appeared to be faulty, and hoped that Mr Butler would be informed of this so that it might be repaired.

Eva's cruelly accidental death was seen by George and Josephine as part of the divine order of things. They received several letters of condolence which said much the same. A friend of George's, the Reverend Francis Atkinson Faber, wrote of how he, too, had lost a child through an accident, and charged them not to dwell on the manner of death, but to think only of their daughter's state of grace. The Edinburgh physician and writer, John Brown, had special words of comfort for Josephine, speaking of his wife's strength of faith when they lost a baby girl of three months, 'dying in a moment': 'when the stroke came she had the divine secret of submission'.[32] The Butlers needed no such advice, but they must have questioned why God had chosen them to be bereft of a daughter, and why Josephine was to be denied a daughter's companionship. In *Recollections of George Butler*, Josephine described how their faith was, if anything, strengthened by their loss.

> Do the words 'accident' or 'chance' properly find a place in the vocabulary of those who have placed themselves and those dear to them in a special manner under the daily providential care of a loving God? Here entered into the heart of our grief the intellectual difficulty, the moral perplexity and dismay which are not the least terrifying of the phantoms which haunt the 'Valley of the Shadow of Death' – that dark passage through which some toil only to emerge into a hopeless and final denial of the Divine goodness, the complete bankruptcy of faith; and others, by the mercy of God, through a still deeper experience, into a yet firmer trust in His unfailing love.[33]

Twenty-five years after Eva's death, Josephine gave such spiritual counsel to Stanley and Rhoda whose first child, named Josephine after her grandmother, suffered from spinal disease as a little girl. Prompted by a statement she had read by Annie Besant, describing how her religious faith had been wrecked by the death of her baby, Josephine had written a letter to W. T. Stead for publication in his paper, the *Review of Reviews*, in which she told how she herself had 'suffered frightfully and was in darkness'. It was not God whom she blamed for the death of Eva, however, but the Devil: 'I never threw it in God's face that he had killed my child . . . The heart of God was pained for my heart's pain; He hated the author of my pain'. This, too, was how Josephine comforted her son and daughter-in-law until they 'got over their rebellion'.[34]

Before Eva was buried, their friend from Oxford days, the sculptor Alex Munro, was called to the house to make a death mask. He left with the Butlers the very first plaster cast he took. Josephine later described to Hatty its distressing appearance: 'with the thick eyelashes still clotted with the gummy tears wh were squeezed out when she was dying from the poor broken head. Every little mark was reproduced in the first caste'.[35] From this cast, Munro made a plaster medallion and a marble bust, a copy of which was given to Uncle Monty. It is a highly sentimentalized study of angelic innocence. Eva clutches a dove of peace to her breast, and her famous golden curls are swept back to reveal a broad and pure brow. She resembles an angelic version of Alice in Wonderland. Yet George praised Munro for executing 'the most perfect *likeness* of our dear child that marble is capable of conveying'.[36] A rather more unconventional representation of Eva was designed by a Cheltenham friend, William Riviere, who had just taken up a post teaching Art in Oxford. He had heard what Eva had said about meeting Josephine in heaven, and presented the Butlers with a sketch of just that, 'with our dear child coming forth to meet her mother'. To George, this was not a morbid or mawkish fancy, but a 'beautiful idea, most tenderly and gracefully expressed in your drawing'. Munro's commission was completed by a 'broken lily' medallion for Eva's gravestone in Leckhampton churchyard. The grave itself remained in their minds. When the Butlers moved to Liverpool in 1866, they continued to pay the keeper of the graves an annual sum of twenty shillings to tend the grave, and in the rootless years after her husband's death, Josephine chose to return for a time to Cheltenham. Despite her evident loneliness there, she confided in Stanley, 'I have a curious & comforting feeling of companionship in being so near Eva's grave'.[37] At Josephine's death, the busts and bas-relief made by Munro were distributed amongst the boys. The cast itself, kept in a tin box, Josephine directed to be left to Georgie: 'Tho' sad to look at, it has a peaceful expression, and the closed eyes and beautiful long eyelashes and high smooth forehead are very sweet'.[38]

Another memorial by a Cheltenham friend, 'a little device by Miss Elliott, which she gave to me, with a printed letter in the centre, done by Eva – "My Papa, I love you"', was also left to her eldest son. Eva had been a sweetly loving daughter to her middle-aged papa. She would pet him with extravagant hugs and kisses, and then 'would fly off and tax her little fingers by making him something – a pin cushion or a kettle-holder. She made him blue, pink, white and striped pincushions and mats for which he had not much use!' recalled Josephine.[39] Her husband's love for Eva 'was wonderful', Josephine wrote in George's biography. He was, indeed, distracted in his grief, but it was a deeply personal and private grief, and incommunicable. Monty praised his brother's 'beautiful self-control', but Josephine was deeply shocked to come upon him one day in his study, 'alone and looking ill. His hands were cold, he had an unusual paleness in his face, and he seemed faint'. She knelt at her husband's feet, 'and shaking myself out of my own stupor of grief, I spoke "comfortably" to him, and forced myself to speak cheerfully, even joyfully, of the happiness of our child . . . After this, I often went to him in the evening after school hours, when, sitting side by side, we spoke of our child in heaven'.[40] Josephine believed that talking to George of Eva's happiness 'helped my own soul', but it must have been a shock to her to be without George's consoling strength at such a time.[41] She wrote out a prayer for her husband, dated 25 September 1864: 'My God, I pray not for myself alone, but for him who is as dear to me as my own soul'. The prayer closed with an anxious plea for the unity of their marriage:

> Suffer us, till life ceases, to bear each other's burdens. Knit our hearts together in steadfast love. May we walk together in the narrow way, upheld by mutual prayer, and our children with us. Perfect in Heaven the love begun on Earth. Smite us in an eternal bond, and let nothing put asunder those whom Thou has joined together.[42]

It was the young Georgie, not quite twelve years old, who seems to have been his mother's greatest strength, and she would never forget his 'gentleness and quiet behaviour' that autumn.[43] Her own grieving had to be put by as her greatest fears were reserved for seven-year-old Charlie, who had been Eva's closest companion: 'a little *pair*', was how she described them.[44] She could not recall their ever having quarrelled. Despite Miss Blumke's statement at the inquest to the effect that all three boys were playing in the yard when Eva fell, Charlie had been in the hallway, and was the only witness of his sister's death, apart from the butler: 'It was a terrible shock to his poor little nerves and brain'. Charlie's sad expression in early photographs was 'not natural to a child', felt Josephine. A surviving photograph from the period attests to this, suggesting a traumatized little boy. As a child, Charlie was subject to headaches and delirious visions, and would suffer from melancholia and a variety of physical disorders into manhood. His mother described him as 'highly sensitive and easily put out of tune'. Dr Kerr advised that Charlie should not be subjected to lessons as yet, and further, that he should be kept out of the house as far as possible. In the record of Eva's death written for her three sons before her death, Josephine recalled how

> Father hired a little open phaeton drawn by a pony, which I could drive myself. It was a fine autumn and winter, and I devoted myself to this little stricken brother. We drove about the lanes continually, and he gathered flowers and made little bouquets to place in vases around her picture. But he never smiled or laughed. It was strange to see that settled mournfulness in so young a child. Once we went to call on Mrs Myers (who was Eva's godmother). I was sitting in the garden with her and speaking of my Eva, and tears were on my face. Charlie ran up to me with a bunch of flowers 'for Eva', as he used to say. When he and I got into our little carriage again, he gave a sharp little cry, and threw his arms round me. I stopped our pony, and said 'What is it, dear?' and he said 'O Mudsie, what you said to Mrs Myers'.[45]

Josephine gave away Eva's clothes to a poor family, but all the remaining relics, locks of hair, thimbles, a needle-case, pencils and suchlike were left to Charlie. Nearly forty years after Eva's death, when Josephine was again living at Cheltenham, Charlie cycled over to see her. She later described to Georgie how she had called Charles to see an old plaster cast of Eva which she had had cleaned up by a sculptor, 'and was very sorry I did so – he burst into tears, and turned away, sitting down at my table, *weeping* for a long time, and saying "O my sister". For days afterwards he would stand gazing at it silently'.[46]

Josephine's belief that Charlie's mental and physical health was lastingly affected by this event is borne out by his unsettled career. Charlie first worked as a foreign press correspondent, a post that took him to Germany and Greece; he endured a brief and harrowing spell as 'Gunner Butler' in the Sudan; and was a gold miner in South Africa and Western Australia in the 1890s. He did not marry until he was in his early forties. Significantly, the picking of posies in remembrance of his dead sister becomes a poignant motif throughout their lives. On the Butler family holidays to Switzerland every summer, Charlie was noted for his gathering of different varieties of gentian. This was a pastime which he never gave up. When he was ordered to Switzerland for his health in 1894, Josephine wrote to her Butler sisters-in-law that Charlie was sending her 'twice a week, boxes of lovely Alpine gentians gathered on his walks'.[47]

Josephine nursed her youngest son through his grief, and then ten-year-old Stanley came down with diphtheria. In her diary for 30 October, Josephine wrote,

> Last night I slept uneasily. I dreamed I had my darling in my arms, dying; that she struggled to live for my sake, lived again a moment, and then died. Just then I heard a sound, a low voice at my door, and I sprang to my feet. It was poor Stanley, scarcely awake, and in a fever. I took him in my arms, and carried him back to his bed . . . My heart sank. I wondered whether God meant to ask us to give up another child so soon.[48]

Stanley recovered, but Josephine's health finally gave way, and Dr Kerr ordered mother and son to spend the winter in Italy. They were invited to Edith's villa at Sestri, outside Genoa. Hatty travelled from Naples to meet her there, and described how her niece showed her into the drawing-room, where she found Josey, 'sitting in the twilight by the fire, her fragile figure in its deep crape, looking very still outwardly, but the soul, no doubt, working within'.[49] Between them, Hatty and Edith provided just the comfort Josephine needed. Stanley had the company of two of Hatty's boys, and Edith transformed the drawing room into a cosy dressing-room for her aunt, complete with teapot. Edie also hunted up an old packet of letters from thirty years earlier. They were from the late Mrs Grey to Edith's mother, Eliza, who would then have been at school, and they proved of special sustenance to Josephine. The letters referred to the illness and death of their infant sister, Ellen, of whom Hatty had no recollection. Even though their mother's faith remained firm, Hannah had written to her husband, 'Dearest, I am not unthankful, nor do I repine; but in walking the street, if my eye rests on a little fair-haired babe in its mother's arms, or sees a little one with tottering feet and chubby hands, my heart sinks within me. Oh! how many darts pierce a bereaved mother's bosom which no one knows of!'[50] Josephine found these letters deeply touching, revealing as they did how her mother 'had been treading the same path, mourning for her child': 'They are both gone,' she said, 'and mother has found her child again.'[51]

She drew comfort from the letters, but she was not cured. Josephine's first attempt to return to England brought about a breakdown in her health from which she nearly died. It has been suggested that she had fears about a return to Cheltenham which were dangerously suppressed and resulted in hysterical paralysis.[52] Hatty, who determined to accompany her sister on the sea voyage back to England, first became alarmed when Josephine complained of claustrophobia, as if the walls of her cabin were pressing in on her. She had to get out of her bunk to lie down in the passage, where Hatty made her more comfortable with a pillow, and bathed her forehead with vinegar. Hatty then called up their attendant, 'Old Grumpy', to provide a bottle of champagne and a tumbler, and he 'routed up' a maid who brought a pot of hot tea. Josephine was able to return to her bed later that night, and in the morning she felt able to walk about on deck, but after breakfast she retired, again complaining of sickness. While Hatty coaxed the captain to secure Josephine the best place in the boat (and coax she did: he ended up offering his very own cabin!), 'Johnny came up with a face of terror, and shouted, "Mama, come to Aunt Josey". I went, and found her in convulsion'.[53]

> Her face was grey, and her hands rigid like those of a corpse. Her eyes were quite closed. I bent over her, and asked, 'Do you know me? Try to know me. Say Yes'. She seemed to make a great effort and said 'Yes', but as if her tongue and jaw were stiff and could not move. By-and-bye a little more naturally she said, 'I think I am going. Dear George; Dear George!' Then she became rigid and unnatural. And her eyes, which were wide open, saw nothing . . . They gazed right through me, and through the ceiling far beyond, as if following something which was going upward, and she said, but not in her own voice, 'My little darling, she went so quick, so quick'.

Hatty made a wild offer of £1,000 to the captain of the mail steamer if he would bring the vessel ashore, but this was quite impracticable, as well as against regulations. There was little to do but keep Josephine as warm as possible, and pray for her recovery. Hatty's overriding thought was of course for her brother-in-law: 'He sent me his wife to cherish and heal, and I had taken her away and killed her'. But the captain *had* acted. His distress signal was answered by the north-bound mail vessel now on its way to Leghorn, and a small boat was lowered to transfer the sick English lady and her party. While Hatty gathered together the frightened boys, she found that 'a gentle, burly, brown sailor had taken [Josey] up, mattress and all, in his arms, like a German baby on a pillow, and was about to carry her down the ladder into the boat'.

On board the return vessel, Hatty found herself among sympathetic and resourceful passengers. A Venetian schoolmaster diagnosed 'congestion' of the heart and brain, and set about applying mustard poultices and stone hot-water bottles. Josephine was smothered in blankets, and ether was forced into her mouth, while the captain and his wife joined Hatty in massaging the frozen hands and feet. They kept this up for a good hour until she came round, and Hatty saw her face 'unlock as if something melted'. As the steamer came in to dock, the good captain 'stroked her hand and cooed over her and said "Bisogna avere coraggio, *my dear*", bringing out the only two English words he knew triumphantly, as if they were a spell'. The ship's second-in-command was sent on ahead to secure a room at the Washington Hotel in Leghorn, and brought back with him a friend of Edith's husband, a Dr Pietro Capanna. The doctor wrapped up Josephine in his own coat which was lined with yellow fox skins, while the enterprising sailors fitted up the captain's little boat with a mattress on the floor and iron hoops from which they suspended a tarpaulin. 'Then there was a general stuffing into her little handbag of the pocket handkerchiefs of the crew filled with flour and mustard' to make mustard poultices. When leaving the first ship, Hatty was asked what should be done with their luggage, and had only had time to shout, 'Meuricoffre, Naples'. 'I am rich in cotton handkerchiefs of all colours,' she reflected, 'but in *nothing else*.' When they reached the hotel, Dr Capanna reappeared,

> panting and puffing and too blown to speak, but producing with triumph out of a red silk bundle two gorgeously embroidered night gowns, stockings and night caps, with treble rows of stiff goffered frills, etc. He had been to his home and rifled the wardrobe of Mme Pietro. Oh, proper English sisters, don't blush! The very simple-minded way in which these Italian men do such things saves one's feelings.

Throughout the spring of 1865, Josephine continued to suffer from a 'long drought in my soul', and on Easter Sunday she was unable to attend church, or to visit Eva's grave.[54] 'When so weak,' she explained, 'I often feel as if my heart were breaking – not with misery, but with its heavy burden of desire, love & sorrow. Then I just have to put my hand in Christ's, and ask Him to put His hand on my heart, & keep it quiet.' Josephine's spiritual diary for that year reveals that her distress went far beyond the natural grieving of a bereaved mother to an encompassing sympathy for the sufferings of the world. This '*spirit of vicarious suffering, the grace of perpetual intercession*,' was, she considered, 'perhaps the noblest of all graces.'[55] What is most interesting about this admission is the specific class of society to whom she was now dedicating her prayers. It is, I believe, the very first reference made by Josephine to the wretched sufferings of prostitutes.

> I long to have a hundred voices, that with all of them I might pray without ceasing that Christ will come quickly, & deliver for ever the poor groaning world: the slaves from all their woes, the victims also & slaves of lust in our own land, the poor women who are driven as sheep to the slaughter into the slave market of London . . . We are all involved in the guilt of society, in the destruction of the innocents, in the denial of happiness to the young, of purity to children.[56]

5

The House of Rest

'Some pain keener than my own'

IN JANUARY 1866 the Butlers began a new life in Liverpool, when George was invited to become the new headmaster of Liverpool College, which all three boys were to attend. They rented a large house at 280 South Hill, Park Road, in an area of Liverpool now known as the Dingle, in walking distance of the college which was at Mossley Hill. Liverpool College was a day school and took between 800 and 900 pupils. It was a relatively new school, founded in 1840, and its unusually high proportion of boys from a commercial background, of a variety of nationalities, races and religious persuasions, afforded George the opportunities he sought to institute a number of educational reforms, such as emphasizing the teaching of modern languages rather than Latin and Greek, and his pioneering interest in the teaching of Geography. Under his principalship, Liverpool College soon became one of the top schools in the country.

When she first settled into their new home, Josephine described how her husband and sons 'began their regular life at the College' while she, wife and now redundant mother, was left alone for many hours every day, thinking continually, 'How sweet the presence of my little daughter would have been now.' Deep depression followed in which books were discarded half-read, the piano abandoned, and her watercolours remained in their box.

> I became possessed with an irresistible desire to go forth and find some pain keener than my own – to meet with people more unhappy than myself (for I knew there were thousands of such). I did not exaggerate my own trial; I only knew that my heart ached night and day, and that the

> only solace possible would seem to be to find other hearts which ached night and day, and with more reason than mine. I had no clear idea beyond that, no plan for helping others; my sole wish was to plunge into the heart of some human misery, and to say (as I now knew I could) to afflicted people, 'I understand. I, too, have suffered'.[1]

Taking instruction from Charles Birrell, minister of the Baptist Wavertree Chapel in Liverpool, who was married to her cousin Harriet, Aunt Margaretta's daughter, Josephine put this wish into action. As she said, 'It was not difficult to find misery in Liverpool'. Josephine's starting point was the Brownlow Hill Workhouse where Charles Birrell made regular visits. It was an intimidating place: the largest of its kind in the country, it could take up to 5,000 inmates. The modern Catholic Cathedral now occupies its site, and only a row of the original redbrick outbuildings, laundry-rooms, survive, standing opposite the University College building. Its size (Josephine called it 'a little town in itself'), and its prominence at the top of Brownlow Hill, meant that it dominated the skyline of Liverpool, a grim warning for its people.

It was to the 'oakum sheds', the cellars where women picked oakum that Josephine first made her way. This was regarded as productive labour. The unpicked fibres of old rope were used for caulking boats, but it was hard and degrading work, thought fit only for paupers or convicts. It was the punishment for unmarried mothers or prostitutes, such as Esther in Elizabeth Gaskell's 1848 novel *Mary Barton*, who is committed to prison for a month for 'disorderly vagrancy'. Others, the sick and homeless, for whom the workhouse was the last recourse, especially in the biting winter months, were voluntary admissions, desperate cases, prepared to pick oakum in return for shelter and for a meal of bread and water. By whatever means they arrived there, oakum pickers were commonly regarded as women for whom there was no hope of reclamation. Nobody wanted them as servants; not even the charitable refuges for fallen women would touch them.

Stepping down into the dark and fetid oakum sheds Josephine was faced by some three hundred strangers. At that time a dozen of the most wicked, 'violent, strong amazons', were in custody at Liverpool County Jail, awaiting trial for the brutal murder of one of the matrons, whom they had beaten to death. The replacement matron was so nervous, Josephine said, that 'she pushes me in among them and then flies to her own room'.[2] Josephine herself took a step back and leaned for a minute in silent prayer against a wooden cask. 'Dear Fanny,' she wrote to her sister, 'I never addressed a word before such a mob!' The effect she would never forget. The women began at once to circle around her, curious to know her business. She then described how she 'sat on the floor among them and picked oakum. They laughed at me, and told me my fingers were of no use for that work; which was true. But while we laughed we became friends'.[3] Josephine then bid them pray, 'God be merciful to me a sinner!' and, as if in response to a charm, all fell to their knees upon the damp bricks. She knelt too, and heard a great moaning and weeping rise up from the cellar floor: 'It was a strange sound, that united wail – continuous, pitiful, strong – like a great sigh or murmur of vague despair, piercing the gloom and murky atmosphere of that vaulted room, and reaching to the heart of God'. Josephine instinctively knew how to talk to such women with quiet authority and without patronizing them. Women rejected by society as 'ultimately bad', she always found 'courteous and gentle' towards herself, and 'bowed down with weeping' when she talked to them. She was sure that no one had spoken lovingly to them before. When she visited the sheds a second time, the matron took care to exclude those women regarded as most vicious and depraved. In a rare attempt to replicate working-class speech (Josephine's prostitutes generally speak like ladies), she reported what a certain Catherine Lynch had told her: 'The matron, she locked ten of us out when you was here last, and yet you had put down all our names. And one poor creature who was going for to hear you speak, the matron told her as how you didn't want anything to do with the likes of she, and the poor creature was broken-hearted and wept all the day. We knows you are a good Christian to God and that you wants to make us love God as you do yourself – May the Lord reward you'.[4]

In the late summer of 1866, Hatty and Tell visited England, again bringing with them their youngest daughter, Josephine, to see her grandfather in Northumberland, and then the Garstons and Butlers in Liverpool. They had already lost one daughter, Beatrice, in 1865, to a cholera epidemic in Naples. While at Dilston little Josephine fell ill, and she died before they reached Liverpool. Hatty later spoke of her sense of gratitude to George and Josephine for receiving them with their little burden: 'I recall all [George's] kindness and goodness to me, since old Oxford days, until that crowning goodness of receiving us at Liverpool with our dead treasure, as his guests, the pretty guest-chamber made ready for her, in spite of all the unhealed wounds the sight must have re-opened in your hearts'.[5]

Little Josephine's death was not seen as a curse upon the Butlers' new home, but as a divine sign of the way forward for Josephine's work with the destitute women of the city. They buried the child in the Smithdown cemetery (now Toxteth Park cemetery). Within a few months, Josephine buried the first prostitute she took into her care in the plot next to little Josephine's grave. The association in Josephine's heart between these dead children and the female penitents begging to be ministered to is understandable, but, in the way it was articulated, not always easy for us to accept. Josephine recorded that before Hatty returned to Naples they visited the wretched Liverpool streets and some of the hospitals, and 'our impression was the same – namely that there were children & mothers far more to be pitied than ourselves & ours. Our darlings were safe with God'.[6] They took with them photographs of their dead daughters to show to the destitute women. From Naples, Hatty wrote to her sister, 'I cannot help thinking that our darlings will, in some way hereafter, surround these victims with love and consolation, and that they will still have a sweet childhood which they never had on earth'.[7] Josephine took the association between the deaths of their children and her rescue mission among the prostitutes of Liverpool even further: 'I have a certain feeling that the love & the sacred souls of these poor girls are given to us in return for the loss of little Eva & Josephine & Bee. *Nothing* can repair *that* loss. Still, it seems as if God wd give us souls while he gives us sorrows'.[8]

Of course, many of the prostitutes she met *were* mere children, and it was with obvious delight that she told Fanny that 'pretty little Martha', whom she and Hatty had first seen in the workhouse infirmary, 'calls me "Mother dear"'. She was equally disposed to adopt an intimate tone with the older women. One elderly woman asked if she was too old for Josephine to take care of her: 'Poor woman! She looked a little like my mother used to look, and I could not help saying to her, "My mother, I will do what I can for you – meanwhile, trust in God and pray to Him", and she trotted off quite happy to *wait*'.[9]

The connection between the death of Eva and the work in which she had begun to involve herself may be seen in Josephine's somewhat impulsively seeking out a three-year-old orphan girl, Polly, in the workhouse, 'because she so strongly resembled our Eva in the face'.[10] She placed Polly with a good woman she knew in Clifton, a Mrs

Braybrooke, but she rarely visited the child herself, perhaps because she had soon 'grown out of that likeness'. As with so many of the young women and girls she helped, Josephine inspired considerable personal devotion in poor neglected Polly. Travelling to Bristol on business in January 1873, Josephine wrote to her friend Mary Priestman of her intention to visit the girl: 'Tho' I seldom see her, she lives upon the thought of being my lady's maid some day!'[11]

Josephine's immediate response to the suffering she saw in Liverpool was to open her own home to the disease-ridden or to those women desperate to reform but who could not get a place in a refuge. The very first prostitute Josephine removed from the hell of the oakum sheds was a twenty-four-year-old consumptive by the name of Mary Lomax, known only as 'Marion' in Josephine's published accounts of the case. Mary's was a familiar enough story, perhaps. She was born near Matlock in Derbyshire to a farming family, and had been working as an under-maid in a well-to-do house. She was 'not fifteen when the gentleman sent her up to his room to fetch a cigar case, and followed her, and shut the door . . . Then followed childbearing, shame, concealment, in which the parents, strong in north country virtue, treated their child with a harshness of which they afterwards bitterly repented'.[12] Mary then came to Liverpool seeking another situation. Josephine confided to her niece Edith that Mary's future career was not unblemished. She became attached to a sailor who went off to sea and deserted her. 'She became reckless, staid out one evening too late, & lost her place',[13] and then, looking about the town for another place, Mary was, according to Josephine, 'literally kidnapped' by a Mrs Mandeville, the brothel keeper of one of the more 'select' brothels in Liverpool 'who goes about covered in diamonds, & has 50 or 60 fine girls in her house'. Mary was a great beauty and the gentlemen would ask for her specially, so that when Mary's uncle came to Liverpool in search of her, she told how 'the women in the house put her into an empty boiler and covered her with carpets and drugged her, and swore to her uncle that she was not in the house'.[14]

When Mary became consumptive, Mrs Mandeville's clients complained about the state she was in and she was thrown on to the streets one November night in 1866, coughing and spitting up blood. She made her way to Brownlow Hill, where a pauper nurse had to stop her from poisoning herself. It was there that Josephine saw her some time later. 'I had just caught one peculiar look of her wild beautiful eyes,' wrote Josephine, and without even introducing herself, she stepped over to Mary's bed and began to stroke her long black hair away from her hot forehead. Mary later told her that 'the turning-point in her life was my stroking her hair with my hand. She says my hand felt so nice, & a choking came in her throat, & she felt she could die happy if she might have her hair stroked so again!'[15] Significantly, it was as a mother that Josephine first addressed Mary: in a sudden impulse she said to her, 'You shall come home with me dear, & I will nurse you in my own home, & you shall be my own daughter.' Mary 'replied with a gasp of astonishment, grasping my hand as if she would never let it go again. I brought her home'.[16] The next day she hired a cab and collected Mary from the workhouse. When they pulled up in the driveway outside the Butlers' house, George was there to meet them, '& giving her his arm, he led her gently upstairs as he would have led any lady visitor, speaking courteously to her'.[17]

Josephine leaves no record of the feelings of her husband, her sons, or even her servants, whose home was so dramatically upturned. Only their housekeeper, Jane, is mentioned as 'a helper in all our work, a silent woman with rare good sense & much graciousness'.[18] Yet, in admitting prostitutes into her home, among them girls she named as Martha and Elizabeth Jane, some of them absolutely destitute, others diseased and close to death, Josephine was endangering not only the career of her husband, but also the moral well-being of her three schoolboy sons. When the Butlers moved to Liverpool, Charlie, their youngest, was just ten years old, Stanley twelve, and Georgie fourteen. Yet there was never any attempt to segregate the boys from their new house guests. That would have been difficult anyway: it was not long before George was exclaiming that his wife had 'very nearly fill[ed] the house as full as it will hold of the dears'.[19] And fill it they did, with girlish chatter as well as consumptive coughing. The women themselves could hardly believe that this beautiful home was to be theirs. Josephine described how, once Jane had settled in two of their first admissions in the cellar, she went down to see that they were comfortable: 'both the poor ragged girls insisted on kissing me and cried so, "*Oh!* Mrs Butler", which expressed a great deal'.[20] Very soon every available room was put to use, and five girls were staying in the Butler house.[21] Nor were the girls confined to their rooms. When Martha was well enough she would 'crawl' downstairs for family prayers.

George and Josephine said nothing to the girls about their past lives, nothing about *sin*. 'It was not our habit to do so', said Josephine.

'My husband and I always felt that *human* kindness & loving action should come first & last'. They knew that there was only one power which could bring about repentance, 'namely *Love*'.[22] When Mary had been with them for some ten days, George asked Josephine whether she thought he might go up to Mary's room and offer to read from the Bible to her. 'I said, "Do dear", & then I left them alone'. George returned some time later with an amazing story. He had begun in his gentle way to talk to Mary about Jesus Christ her Saviour when she stopped him and said, 'O Sir, you need not tell me about Jesus Christ. I know Him, for I have seen Him.' An anxious George asked her, 'How so?' Mary replied, 'Sir, you have brought me to your own beautiful home. You have treated me as if I were your own daughter, as if I had *never done anything wrong*. That is what I mean. I have *seen* Jesus'.[23]

Mary Lomax was the particular favourite of the boys, and, astonishing as it sounds, the bedroom she shared with Martha was situated right next to the schoolroom. Josephine wrote to Fanny, telling her how, three days before her death, Mary produced a poem she had written for Josephine which Catty (Stanley) had copied out in his neatest hand: 'I saw some grand secret going on between them and then she pulled it from under her pillow and gave it me. I would not like people generally to see it because of its praise of me. But anyone would forgive her exaggerated ardour about the first person who had ever shown her *real* kindness'.[24] Mary herself was half ashamed of the twenty-line composition, feeling that it was 'not half so nicely put as it ought to be'. It is the only first-hand account we have of Josephine's tender ministering.

> What worthy offering can I make to one I love so well:
> My heart seems nigh to break when on her gentle love I dwell.
> When I think of how she found me so wretched and so low,
> So torn with pain and sickness, so plagued in guilt and woe;
> How sweet she said she loved me, even me the wicked one,
> And answered my despairing words with joyous hopeful tone;
> While smoothing back with gentle hand the strayed locks of my
> hair,
> She whispered low within my ear the sacred words of prayer.[25]

Mary lived with the Butlers for three months before she died, and in that time her room became, in Josephine's words, 'a kind of centre of religious life'. The sick prostitutes she took into her own home were all devout, or, if without a religious education, embraced religion with nothing short of fervour under George's tutelage. Indeed, they were what Josephine described in an unfortunate phrase: 'just of the kind I want, dying Magdalenes who seem to be yearning for some hope of mercy and pardon'.[26] News of Mary's conversion spread quickly and all sorts of people came up to the house wanting to see her and 'ask her prayers'. Josephine wrote to her niece, Edith, of 'a chorus of thanksgiving going on all round me you know!'[27] People were understandably quite astonished at what the frail Mrs Butler had achieved in such a short time, yet for Josephine it was simply the harvest time of her long years of prayer and meditation: 'it does not in *the least* surprise me. I should be surprised if it were not so,' she said. Other, more cautious visitors would tell her that she should not expect to see such miracles often, to which she would say to herself, 'But I *do expect* more miracles; & if I had never *expected* this one of Mary you would not have been sitting moralizing over it, for no one would have seen it'. She was delighted 'to see stuffy *Christians* startled by seeing the poor lost dregs of humanity dancing into heaven before them!'[28]

Liverpool was short of refuges and there simply were not enough beds to offer shelter to those female penitents discharged from the workhouse who were willing enough to reform. There was a Catholic institution out of town, and a Protestant penitentiary which Josephine criticized as 'prison-like in character'. She was 'stabbed to the heart' to hear that on a single day sixteen oakum pickers had been released from Brownlow Hill and, with nowhere to sleep that night, had been tempted back into a brothel. 'The devil is very busy and outwitted me,' was Josephine's comment.[29] She resolved not to be outwitted again, but the situation was desperate, and there was still nowhere suitable for middle-aged and elderly prostitutes deemed too old to reform, or for women guilty not of an immoral career but simply of homelessness, who were impoverished and unlikely to gain any employment save the very lowest. These 'honest poor', many of them Irish, often shoeless and bonnetless, fought off starvation by selling in the streets sand (used then to clean floors), or battered vegetables.

As Josephine put it, God simply would not leave her alone, but sent 'hint after hint' to begin establishing her own refuge for these female outcasts.[30] One such hint came from a Dutch doctor at the workhouse hospital. On a visit to the oakum sheds, Josephine was told that Dr de Zouche of the infirmary wanted to speak to her in his office. She went 'and he *sprang out* to meet me so eagerly. He is a shabby little Dutchman with very little command of language, but most kind eyes, and a trembling about the mouth as if he were going to cry'. He wanted her help for his two hundred patients, many of whom came in from the streets to die. She was shocked by the wretched conditions in the hospital:

> It breaks my heart to walk along hundreds of beds and see death, death, death, and often such pitiful yearning faces, as if they *longed* for a word of hope. The carriers from the Dead house look in every morning and say, 'anyone for us?' That means, 'is there a corpse here?' And sometimes the answer is, 'Yes, *two*'. I go down about every other day when able, and God seems to have given me some miraculous strength. The place is so large that it measures about half a mile perhaps each time through the house.[31]

It was the Butlers' own doctor, Dr Moore, who after one of his visits to the girls at their house, startled Josephine by saying, '"Mrs Butler, if you should ever start a little hospital of your own, I am at your service. I or my son will attend it *regularly* & you shall have our services & all medicines free of all expense!" Was it not generous?'[32]

Josephine did begin to think about a hospital or 'Home' for the destitute, and it was, fittingly, Eva's godmother in Cheltenham, Mrs Myers, to whom she turned for advice. She also learned much from her close involvement with Jane Cragg, matron of the Benediction House just down the road from the Butler house, at 56 South Hill Road, which took a great number of young girls.[33] Josephine was further encouraged by like-minded women who had invited her to meet them in Manchester in early 1867. They were, she declared, 'some of the nicest and most real people I ever met'. They had heard of her mission, but her name was already known to them, for Josephine had been one of the 1,500 female signatories to the first petition submitted to Parliament in favour of women's suffrage, presented by John Stuart Mill on 6 June 1866. Manchester became the centre of the suffrage movement, and the very first suffrage committee, of which Miss Lydia Becker was the Secretary, was formed there in 1867. Josephine found Lydia Becker a most impressive woman. She also met an inspirational schoolmistress, Mrs Glayn, a woman so very shy that she flushed up when talking to Josephine of her work among the poor, yet 'is president of a society about "*women's work*"'.[34] Josephine would later lament the fact that she was unable to campaign for the repeal of the Contagious Diseases Acts in Manchester due to what she perceived to be the strength of *anti*-suffrage feeling in the city, aroused by Lydia Becker's work there. In time, she would also come to question Lydia Becker's methods, but for now she was rightly humbled to meet women of such experience, and was full of praise for the women of Manchester, saying that she had learned much more from them than she could herself offer by way of information and shared experience. It was a significant meeting, a turning point, because it demonstrated to Josephine, for the first time, what social reforms could be achieved if women would combine to work together and form local committees, committees which might develop into national movements. It was a step from the personal to the political, from an amateur, localized, amelioration of a social problem to a professional, politicized, articulation of social wrongs. It was a step she took, seemingly, without a moment's faltering: within a year Josephine would become the first President of the North of England Council for Promoting Higher Education of Women, and a year after that, Honorary Secretary of the Ladies' National Association for Repeal of the Contagious Diseases Acts.

For the present, uppermost in her mind was establishing her own refuge in Liverpool. At that time any private individual could set up such an establishment. There were no regulations, no boards or committees to satisfy, but Josephine's original ambitious plan did grow out of consultation with the Brownlow Hill Committee, who sanctioned her idea of a refuge to take in destitute women once they were discharged from the workhouse. On approval of her scheme she was promised a house with fifty beds and an income of £200 a year. She would need to hire a matron and an assistant matron, and her own idea was for the women to stay on for a year's probation, and to be taught skills that would enable them to secure honest labour when they left, when they would be provided with a character reference 'equivalent to a certificate by which situations may be obtained'.[35] Josephine wrote to Mrs Myers of her elation, saying that she could hardly sleep at night for thinking of the joy it would be if her refuge should 'be the saving of a great number of women'. She was convinced that as many as two hundred women would follow her to a lodge if she could set it up. The Committee procrastinated, however, and refused to finance the scheme unless she could prove to them that she could run such an institution satisfactorily. 'But how can I?' she asked.[36] Her heart failed her as she thought about how she was going to face her oakum pickers with the news: 'it almost seems cruel to preach industry, purity, prayer, and then to leave them in *hell* – a place more corrupting than even ordinary prison'.[37]

Finally, in the new year of 1867, the Butlers themselves secured a property near their home, for which they paid a yearly rent of £250. Although Josephine intended to meet much of this expense through subscriptions and small donations, it was a serious financial commitment for the Butlers, whose own house rent was only £150 a year. The building could house up to thirteen women, and was to be called a 'House of Rest', a name that had taken Josephine's fancy from a refuge she had visited in Brighton. Dr Moore, as he had promised, attended without making any charge: 'He talks so lovingly to them, and often has to take off his spectacles to wipe the tears from his old eyes'.[38] Josephine's only financial plan, if it can be called that, was to pay ready money for everything, so that she would know 'when I actually fall short, but *I do want money*'.[39] She welcomed '*any* gifts however small, or contributions down to a shilling'. She found three annual subscribers who would give her £35 a year, but she needed a great deal more. She made some interesting allies for a headmaster's wife, such as a 'roaring Radical' upholsterer called Jeffreys: 'When I told him that the principle of equality was so dear to me as to make me enjoy picking oakum in the oakum sheds, he offered me beds with bedding for my hospital at sum of 5/0 cash. He is very vulgar, but a very generous man'.[40]

Women whose illnesses were not mortal and whom she helped to restore to good health, Josephine confessed, 'I hardly know what to do with'.[41] Despite the fact that the Brownlow Hill Committee finally withdrew their offer of financial support before the end of February, Josephine wrote to the Mayor of Liverpool twice in March to urge upon him the social benefits of an industrial scheme for women that was both self-supporting and encouraged independence among inmates. She tried to persuade the Mayor that the class of women she intended to help were those over the age of sixteen, who had so far not become prostitutes but who were '*in danger*', either through exposure to overcrowding in wretched lodgings, or from the fact that there were so few industrial openings for working women in Liverpool, which, as a busy seaport, required predominantly heavy labour at the docks.

> Women here exceed men in number, and of these women an unusually large percentage have to support themselves. Sudden failures of dockyard employment, deaths at sea, and the virtual widowhood and orphanage of the families of many sailors who are *not* dead – causes like these leave

> unsupported many women who have married too young to have had any opportunity of learning a trade or practising for domestic service. It is mainly to such widows and orphans that I would offer an Industrial Home.[42]

She could not wait for the help of outside agencies, though, and on Good Friday her first Industrial Home, a 'very small temporary lodge – part a workhouse for poor destitute girls to work in', was officially opened with a service of thanks led by George.[43] George's notes for the order of service survive, and they are testimony to his wonderfully delicate manner with women of the poorer class. Instead of delivering a sermon, George offered a commentary in plain and simple language on the two chosen lessons from the Old and New Testaments: 'We do not wish to pry into the secrets of your past lives', he assured them, as he read from Matthew 11: 28, 'Come to me, all ye that labour and are heavy laden, and I will give you rest', and he asked them to join him in singing Psalm 25, of which the seventh verse reads, 'Remember not the sins of my youth, nor my transgressions'.[44] Most touching was George's selection of a reading from Matthew 5: 1–20, and of his impressing upon his congregation, 'Hereafter you may fulfil the command, "Let your light shine before men"'.

At first, the women at the lodge could earn a nominal sixpence a day (with which they 'are delighted'), making women's and men's clothes, both recycling material from donated garments and making up outfits from new cloth: 'I have expended a good deal in *materials* to make clothes for the poor and have got several women fitted out to return to their homes in Ireland or America which they were prevented doing by *nakedness*'.[45] However, the former oakum pickers sewed so fast that Josephine could scarcely keep them supplied with material. Eventually, they were able to take in laundry and then one room was given over to a small envelope factory which was patronized by local businesses.

One thing Josephine never had to contend with was opposition from her family. She did declare herself too radical for the Greys, but all her sisters, to varying degrees, and her many nieces, gave Josephine unquestioning support from the very first, although in the early days of her work in Liverpool, only Eliza's married daughters, Edith and Constance, were old enough to confide in.[46] Josephine called upon her sister Fanny to come and assist in the nursing at the House of Rest, so as to free her for her workhouse visits, 'the heaviest part of my work now'.[47] She had kept the whole mission secret from Fanny until the little hospital had been set up, but was now 'bursting' for her sympathy.[48] She was, though, determined that none of her family should be asked for funds, and forbade her sisters to send any money. She would accept only old clothes, linen, blankets, slippers, brushes and combs and suchlike. Money itself was not an issue, or so Josephine claimed. Even though she had to raise funds personally, Liverpool was a very wealthy city, and one that already supported 'grand big charities'. She did find, however, 'that there is a little clumsiness in the administration, and not as much personal effort as there might be'.[49] Josephine had only two methods of raising subscriptions: by praying, which she believed 'the best way', and by personal application to wealthy individuals. The citizens she pursued most vigorously were 'young unmarried men of *means*, and I have, thro' our connections with universities, more opportunities of meeting young men than many have, and I must say some have given most kindly',[50] although, she remarked to Edie, 'it is oftener the good and pure ones and not the fast ones who give'.[51] On occasion, a written word from Josephine was enough to turn a young man away from vice. One night, a girl to whom Josephine had written urging her to repent showed the letter to a young man who had been pestering her. He apparently 'staggered and turned back, and *bolted*!'[52]

Even with the hints offered by Mrs Myers and Mrs Glayn, and with other models before her, such as Mrs Gladstone's Magdalene 'retreat' for incurable cases in London, Josephine was still very new to the work. Yet not once did she show any sign of a lack of confidence, or any anxiety about the responsibility for so many women's souls. She remained clear-headed, and was modest about the precise nature of her role. She spoke to Mrs Glayn of soon being in a position to devolve all responsibility to the 'abler hands' of a professional matron. Her new friend urged her to think again: 'Well! But still you must go often and see them, for it may be that no one could do exactly your part of the work. Whenever we see that we are *loved* by wretched and guilty people, we must consider that we have a gift from God which must be used for Him'.[53] This was thoroughly understood by Josephine, and by George, who, despite his demanding duties at the school, would stop by the House of Rest every evening to hold prayers. If ever her husband was unable to make his evening visit, Josephine would take his place.

Josephine was clear in her vision of the style of management she wanted for her House of Rest. Her 'private and small affair' was to be quite distinct from those large religious institutions and penitentiaries where fallen women were reclaimed at the cost of rigid and punitive discipline, places such as Angela Burdett-Coutts's Urania Cottage at Shepherd's Bush, with which Dickens was associated, and which had opened in 1847: 'I think for the present I shall *do* as regards hints about work and discipline. I am *quite* sure about love and gentleness being the chief power'. In this she had Jane Cragg's approval. The Butlers' House of Rest was, she told Josephine, 'just what she had dreamed of for years', and she was moved by her sense that the women Josephine took in 'all seemed to her to be so assured of the love of God and to feel that the Good Shepherd had really found them'.[54] Josephine was equally determined that the religious instruction offered to the women should be 'very wide and simple and unsectarian'. She had a short catechism for them to repeat, which would 'give them a simple cheery hope in Christ our Saviour'.[55] Josephine found she could not accept the Catholic worship of the Virgin Mary practised by many of the women who came to her, and she did her surreptitious best to convert them. In her estimate, about half of the three hundred oakum pickers were Roman Catholics, many of them Irish. These women would often ask Josephine why, when she led them in prayer, she only prayed to Jesus, never to Mary. Sometimes, she said, she would 'teach them a prayer which the priests could not object to'. On occasion, though, she went further than that, recording with satisfaction the deathbed scene of one girl at the workhouse infirmary who had always before prayed to 'Mary, Mother of God', but who 'never ceased during the last hour of her life to cry, "Jesus, pardon me, Jesus receive me, Jesus help me", and died very peacefully'.[56]

Even though Josephine envisaged a uniquely liberal regime for her own House of Rest, she had to deal with larger institutions around the country, as far afield as the Roman Catholic 'Good Shepherd' in Hammersmith, London, which could take up to eighty women, to which she sent on female penitents who were in good health, but who needed a period of rest and training before setting out into the world. One penitentiary that Josephine was particularly keen should admit cases from Liverpool was Mrs Tennant's Home of Mercy at Clewer, near Windsor. Gladstone had first sent a young Oxford prostitute to Mrs Tennant in 1849. Within three months she had eighteen new inmates, many of them camp followers of the Windsor barracks, whom she trained for domestic service or prepared for emigration.

Mrs Tennant's story was no doubt an inspirational model for Josephine.

One of the reasons she was in need of her sister Fanny was so that one or other of them could accompany these women on the train to a new refuge if such a move was thought necessary. As it was, it took a considerable amount of planning to find places in the right kind of refuge. Josephine was, for example, cautious of putting too many women who knew each other into a single institution lest they talk themselves out of their new lives and drift back into sin. She also had to hold her tongue when faced with the prejudices of some refuges. One of the women she had taken in was at first viewed doubtfully by the chaplain at a refuge in Birmingham because she was nearly thirty. He wrote to Josephine 'such a *hard* letter, saying, "I fear she is too old to reform, but I'll give her a trial however unsteady she may be, poor creature"'. Josephine objected to the idea of her being too old to reform, and felt that if God could grant repentance to 'the grey-haired fathers of families and the churchgoing religious merchants who have kept her for their private prostitute', he would do so to 'poor Ellen, who has had so few advantages and who left her sins at the *first call*'.[57]

The name of Mrs Butler soon became known amongst the destitute women of Liverpool, who were quick to recognize that it was a very remarkable woman who would sit and pick oakum with prostitutes and thieves, and open up her home to the homeless, offering hope of salvation and respite from material want. Some weeks she was quite 'overwhelmed with poor penitent women swarming up from the town. At all times of day they come asking for me'.[58]

One day in the centre of town, she was spotted by a little girl with trembling lips, her 'toes coming out of her ragged shoes', who chased Josephine in the busy streets, 'halooing after me'.[59] Josephine stopped, but 'could hardly hear her story for the rattle of buses'. The girl told Josephine that she was an orphan, and that she had been a prostitute for a very short time, 'and was longing to go to a Refuge'. Josephine handed her her card, and invited her up to the house. She then drove home, but had 'scarcely got to my room and was taking off my hat at the window, when I saw the poor lost thing, running up and down the road looking first at my card, then at all the houses, and not knowing which gate to go in at. How she must have *run*, poor child, to get up so soon all that way'. Josephine managed to settle her with Miss Cragg at the Benediction House. One Sunday a friend of Mary Lomax's arrived, having heard of Mary's conversion. Her name was Ellen

Weald, she was thirty years old and strikingly tall and handsome, a higher class of prostitute who worked from her own rooms under the name of Mrs Blackstock. She stunned Josephine by turning up unannounced, 'her eyes red with weeping and a rather black gown on', stating that she had sold up her apartment and all her belongings, and was willing to go into any penitentiary the lady thought fit. Josephine 'could scarcely get breath to speak'.[60]

Josephine would go into brothels without fear or squeamishness in order to talk to prostitutes, or Charles Birrell, the Baptist minister, would supply her with the addresses of destitute women living in the city. 'Courage, my darlings', she would say to them. 'You are women, and a woman is always a beautiful thing. You have been dragged deep in the mud, but still you are women'.[61] One of the first inmates of the House of Rest was an unmarried mother, Margaret Winstanley. Hollow-eyed and emaciated, plainly dying of consumption, Margaret was too weak even to hold her own baby. She had been living with a very poor married sister in a cellar underground, and it was in this cellar that Josephine sought her out. Margaret's story was 'a sad one', and, according to Josephine, her collapse dated from the birth of her child, oppressed as she was 'by the sense of her sin and the wreck of her life'. The sister was willing to take in the child if Josephine offered a home to Margaret, and she promised to bring the baby on visits. Josephine gives a moving and sympathetic account of her visit to that wretched cellar, but particularly engaging is her response to Margaret's illegitimate child: 'She has a most beautiful baby of 6 months who gurgled and crowed at me and seemed to think life full of joy and fun. It kept putting my boa to its little nose and smiling when it tickled it and then grinning at me'.[62]

Josephine encountered one 'fine 1st Class prostitute' whose select clients, married men and wealthy merchants, made appointments by letter. She failed to convert her, but the woman still returned her call, eager to tell of her previous night's adventure. She had, she told Josephine, 'entertained a gentleman, a clergyman, who asked me *which* Mrs Butler it was who had been to see me. He said he knew Mr Butler of the College'. The woman herself commented on the immorality of married men in Liverpool. Prostitutes did not give her names of their clients; nor did Josephine seek them, but it rankled that she might share the company of these very men, who 'go about smiling at dinner parties' while the women they consort with in secret 'are *branded* openly'.[63] As she saw it, her fellow townsmen were in league with the

Devil, undoing all her patient work, which she regarded as God's work, among these women.

One reason for Josephine's self-confidence in establishing her House of Rest is of course that it was a divine calling. Like the large institutions, she sought to reclaim these women for society, training them for domestic service in England or preparing them for emigration, but primarily Josephine sought to reclaim their souls for God. Many of these women, whom she referred to as her flock, were dying. Within two or three years, Josephine would be fighting for women's civil and legal rights, but at this time it was 'for their *souls*'. Indeed, 'An extraordinary kind of revival of dead souls' was how she described her work in Liverpool.[64] Amongst the dying she certainly found plenty of penitents. The city prostitutes Josephine encountered, or rather, the prostitutes whose stories she chose to record, either privately in letters or publicly in published accounts, bear little resemblance to the rowdy drunken women recorded in recent studies of Victorian prostitution.[65] Dr de Zouche assured Josephine that she need not fear coarse speech from his patients. He told her: 'I know they may have fallen very low, but I assure you I never heard a word from one of them which a *lady* might not speak. I can scarcely believe that they have been such sinners'.[66] And indeed, Josephine was much struck with their delicate appearance: 'so young and fair often – muttering such passionate prayers through their white lips'. De Zouche's patients responded to their new lady visitor, and would confess to her, pulling her down towards the pillow to whisper in her ear, 'I have been a *great* sinner'. Josephine responded in equal measure, although she sometimes overreached her lay role: 'One day I felt moved to say to a woman who was *just* dying, "Woman, thy sins are forgiven thee", and I just spoke the name of Jesus again and again. She looked at me, poor skeleton, with deep sunk eyes *burning* with a kind of thirst of soul, and gasped, "*I believe it*"'. Josephine could be forgiven this attempt to make up for the fact that only one (Anglican) chaplain was engaged to minister to the four thousand or so workhouse inmates, as many as a thousand of whom were in the infirmary. It was not unknown for the chaplain to be driven away with curses by some of the women. One woman who died 'in agonies from a kick in the side given her by a man who *kept her*', had rudely rejected the chaplain's attentions, and had become so violent that the doctors called Josephine over to try to soothe her. At first she spat out at Josephine, 'Don't speak to me. I am lost.' Josephine made no attempt to interfere, but knelt by the bedside in silent prayer. Her quiet presence was tolerated, and when Josephine rose to go, the woman seized her arm and said, 'You won't go – you won't. I will not die. I dare not die'. They told Josephine that she raved all day and night, '*shrieking* for me to come and help her . . . "When will Mrs Butler come . . . *come, come*, will you"', and fell back on the bed cursing God.[67]

Another distressing death was that of Mary Lomax, who died of consumption at the Butler house on a bitterly cold and snowy day in March. Since her arrival, Mary had become almost another sister to Josephine. She told Edie, 'She is just like one of *us*. She talks as Hatty & you & I might talk to each other'.[68] Mary's death throes began in the early hours of the morning. Josephine was wakened by the anxious servants and at once took her place by the bedside. George looked in before leaving for the college with the boys, his eyes filled with tears, and although she could barely speak, Mary reassured George, 'Yes, God is with me, sir; I have perfect peace.' The death struggle lasted twelve hours. Gasping for breath, she begged for the windows to be opened.

> Her long black hair thrust wildly back was like the hair of a swimmer, dripping with water, so heavy were the death dews. She became blind; and her intelligent eyes wandered ever, with an appealing look, to whatever part of the room she thought I was in. Towards sunset she murmured: 'Oh come quickly, Lord Jesus'. During that long day she continually moved her arms like a swimmer, as if she felt herself sinking in deep waters. Then her poor little head fell forward, a long sigh escaped her parted lips, and at last I laid her down flat on her little bed. My husband and sons returned from College, and we all stood round her for a few minutes. She had become a household friend. She looked sweet and solemn then, her head drooping to one side, and with a worn-out look on the young frail face, but a look, too, of perfect peace.[69]

Josephine herself dressed the coffin, buying expensive blooms of white camelias which she banked up around the corpse: 'With her hands crossed on her breast, and dressed as a bride for her Lord, she looked quite lovely'. George conducted the funeral service. It was not until the funeral that Josephine met Mary's mother. She later described how she came upon her, 'kneeling by the coffin, in an agony of grief and anger', raging about her daughter's original seducer. 'She said (her body rocking backward and forward with emotion): "If *that man* could but see her now! Can we not send for him?" and she added: "Oh, what a difference there is in English gentlemen's households! To think that this child should have been ruined in one and saved in another!" '[70]

The decision to bury Mary in a grave adjoining that of her little niece, Josephine Meuricoffre, deserves to be seen not as a sentimental gesture, but as a symbolic act, or even a political act, signifying as it did the allegiance of Josephine Grey, like her father before her, to the cause of the poor. And though her friendship with Mary was cut short by her early death, Josephine would be supported by Mary's words to her for many years to come. She had warned Josephine of the bitter trials ahead of her in fighting the evils of prostitution, and told her, 'When your soul quails at the sight of evil, which will increase yet awhile, dear Mrs Butler, *think of me* and take courage. God has given me to you, that you may never despair of any'.[71]

6

Wasted Lives

'The aches and pangs of ignorance'

IN THE SPRING of 1867 another female visitor walked up the drive of the Butler house. Not a prostitute, this time, but the future principal of Newnham College, Cambridge, Miss Anne Jemima Clough, surviving sister of the poet, Arthur Hugh Clough. A. H. Clough was a contemporary of George Butler's at Oxford, and the two young men had become good friends when George took a reading party over to Grasmere, where the Clough family lived. Born in Liverpool, the daughter of a cotton merchant, Anne Jemima had set up her own girls' school in Ambleside and had been involved in the campaign to open the Cambridge Local Examination to girls under the age of eighteen; this was granted officially in February 1865. Following this success, campaign leaders Emily Davies and Barbara Bodichon formed a committee to press for university entrance for female students, their objective being the founding of a university college for women. Anne Clough was likewise preoccupied with the idea of higher education for women, but her plans lay along quite different lines from those of Davies.

It was chiefly to sound out George Butler, rather than his wife, that Anne Clough called at their house in 1867. The higher education of women was, wrote Josephine, but one of the subjects 'concerning which my husband advanced with a quicker and firmer step than that of the society around him', and she reflected that Anne Clough must have been 'heartily glad to find herself in a house where not a shadow of prejudice or doubt existed, to be argued down or patiently borne with'.[1] George Butler believed strongly that the social position and salaries of headmistresses and schoolmistresses should be equal to those of their male counterparts. Such equality could be merited only if female teachers had access to comparable education, training and qualifications.

Promising moves had been made in this direction. Whitelands College, the first teacher training college for women only, founded in 1841, was followed in the next thirty years by several more, but these colleges trained women to teach in elementary schools and drew their trainees from the working and lower middle class. Middle-class families were reluctant to allow their daughters to teach in elementary schools, and an 1858 pamphlet by Angela Burdett Coutts argued that they were not, anyway, well enough educated to qualify for entry.[2] The Governesses' Benevolent Association founded Queen's College in Harley Street, an Anglican college which attracted the support of visiting male lecturers from London University, as did the Unitarian Ladies' College in Bedford Square. However, neither of these colleges really offered aspiring young teachers and governesses much beyond the standard of secondary education. In 1864 the Schools Inquiry Commission accepted a petition from Emily Davies's Schoolmistresses' Association asking them to look into the current provision of state education for girls; evidence to the Commission exposed the continuing poor teaching standards of female teachers and established that better teacher training was required.[3]

From the meeting between Anne Clough and the Butlers grew the North of England Council for Promoting the Higher Education of Women, through which they sought to raise the position of governesses and schoolmistresses to the status of a profession; at present they did little more than receive employers' charity. George Butler was committed to the cause but was firm in his conclusion that women themselves should fight this battle, and that he himself was merely a 'supplement'.[4] It was with such encouragement from her husband that Josephine stood as the first elected President of the North of England Council, with Anne Clough, its originator, as Secretary. Committees were formed in four principal northern cities: Anne Clough and the Butlers were the leaders of the movement in Liverpool, Elizabeth Wolstoneholme in Manchester, Theodosia Marshall and Lucy Wilson in Leeds, and a Miss Keeling and her clergyman father in Sheffield.

To confront the poor training and lack of recognized status of women teachers and governesses, the Council devised what they called a University Extension Scheme. This was to be a series of local lectures for young women, given by a university lecturer who would make regular visits to the four northern cities. In the future it was hoped that a regular course of such lectures might lead to a special, certificated, examination which would serve as a teaching qualification.

Their first roving lecturer was James Stuart, a bright twenty-five-year-old Cambridge scholar and fellow of Trinity College. The young man became an instant friend of George and Josephine. He said himself that George Butler 'was one of my most intimate friends . . . a very perfect English gentleman', and to Josephine, Stuart was 'like a son or a brother'.[5] He would later befriend Georgie and Charlie Butler who were both at Trinity College, Cambridge. Stuart had, quite independently, thought up an inter-collegiate lecture system at Cambridge which in many ways anticipated the spirit of the University Extension Scheme. His great educational project was to break down class barriers and he aimed to develop what he called a 'peripatetic university', whereby Cambridge lecturers would make lecture tours of all the big towns.

In the summer of 1867 Josephine and Anne Clough invited him to provide a course of instruction in Educational Theory, for which he was to be paid £200 for eight-week courses in each of the four cities. Stuart held out for giving the women access to particular subjects. He got his way. That autumn of 1867 Stuart made his first lecture tour, speaking on Physical Astronomy, no less, in Liverpool, Manchester, Leeds and Sheffield. This northern circuit expanded rapidly, and by the following autumn three lecturers covered a total of nine towns. The Butlers' friend, Frederick Myers, the son of Eva's godmother, and an ex-pupil of George's at Cheltenham, although never a council member, was a great promoter of council schemes, and he too would later become one of their roving lecturers.[6]

George Butler delivered an inaugural speech in each of the four original towns. To deprive women of access to higher education was, he pointed out, to deprive *half* of society. It was 'suicidal to the welfare of society' to force women 'if wealthy, into a round of fashionable frivolity, or if poor, to a humdrum existence – needlework and household duties', and also destructive to the institution of marriage, driving husbands to the pub or the club.[7] Women were predisposed to make excellent teachers, he said: how, then, could society continue to provide no national training schemes, no national certified examinations, in order to raise standards? George promised extra-mural courses in Natural History, Maths, English History and Literature. Subjects as yet under discussion included French, Italian, European History and Literature, and, more surprisingly, the Growth of the Indian Empire, and the Rise of the US Colonies.

As Frederick Myers observed, 'These lectures, then, are a small thing accomplished, but they are a great thing begun'.[8] They certainly attracted a great many young students, 550 in all, who amazed Stuart with their diligence and serious application. He had expected twenty or thirty students to respond to his question papers, but three hundred did so in the first week. The town circulating libraries 'had to change the character of their books', to meet the demands of these young women. Scientific works were what they now requested; sensational novels remained on the shelves![9] At its height, the Council had representatives in twelve towns and cities as far afield as Glasgow and Cheltenham. Eventually, local committees took responsibility for hiring lecturers and determining the subjects to be offered, a development which freed Clough and Butler to work on other projects.

What is surprising about Josephine's energetic involvement in the work of the Council is that at the same time she was involved in the running of her House of Rest and the Industrial Home, as well as keeping up her visits to the Brownlow Hill workhouse, and was equally active in the agitation demanding protection for married women's property and earnings which followed the 1857 Matrimonial Causes Act. A Married Women's Property Committee, centred in Manchester, was established in April 1868, with Josephine and Elizabeth Wolstoneholme acting as joint secretaries, and Lydia Becker as Treasurer. When Anne Clough invited Josephine to involve herself in the North of England Council she opened up a new world of possibilities to her, introducing her to wholly new circles of principled men and women who understood how to organize committees and how to put pressure upon the government, people such as radical Quakers Jacob and Ursula Bright, radical MPs like Charles Dilke, Anthony Mundella and Richard Marsden Pankhurst, the latter prominent as a radical, and a Nonconformist, and unsurprisingly, in view of the career of his future wife, a feminist. It was he who drafted the 1868 Married Women's Property Bill.

One of the last times Josephine saw her father was to ask for his signature to the petition in support of this Bill. He gave it gladly, and just as she was leaving the room he called her back, saying, 'Stay, my dear, let me put *JP* after my name. Maybe if they knew what an old magistrate I am they would think my signature had more weight'.[10] John Grey died suddenly on 22 January 1868 at the age of eighty-three. Fanny was the only daughter with him when he died, and it was she who telegraphed the news to her brothers and sisters. Josephine and George set off at once, and Josephine later wrote an account of the funeral for Hatty, describing how she herself had dressed the coffin. After a terrible stormy night, during which Lipwood House shook, 'the river roared and the windows rattled', and Josephine and her brothers and sisters 'all cowered over the fire, and talked of him and of old days', she awoke to a beautifully bright Sunday morning, 'such a breath of coming Spring', and stepped out into the grounds to pick stems of evergreen since 'there was not a flower to be found': 'I . . . made stars and crowns of evergreens, and covered the coffin with them, and built them up at the sides, so that he lay in a bed of cheerful shining green. The evergreen suited him best, with its hardy perennial look, and his memory will be like it, ever green'. She fancied she could hear her father say, 'O lassie, you are making me far too smart!'[11] Josephine's *Memoir of John Grey of Dilston*, which she saw published the following year, was a moving account of her father, as well as being a commercial success. Second and third editions were issued in 1874 and 1875. It was translated into Italian with a preface by the Italian Prime Minister, and an admirer even wrote to Josephine from Naples telling her that her biography of her father 'will raise the character of the nation abroad'.[12]

It was through her work on the Married Women's Property Committee that Josephine met Albert Rutson, Private Secretary to the Home Secretary, Henry Austin Bruce. Bruce had sent him to confer with the ladies of the Committee, and while there he heard of the North of England Council's lecture scheme. Rutson was an old acquaintance of George's from Oxford days, and he and Josephine seem to have achieved an instant rapport: she began writing to him weekly letters as if he were an old and valued confidant. Rutson had evidently expressed his concern that she was doing too much in taking up an executive position in two quite separate movements, but Josephine reassured him that she was not so taken up with public work that she had no heart for anything else. She wanted him to know that 'I sometimes feel heartily weary of all that we are doing, and very tired in myself. I don't think I could go on at things if it were not for the possibility of retiring into a fair sweet world of my own, my real home and life. To be one hour in the presence of God, with every voice silenced except His, refreshes me more than sleep, or change of scene or anything else'.[13]

Albert Rutson also took a very personal interest in Josephine's House of Rest, visiting her patients when he was in Liverpool, and now and then sending her half a sovereign from his own pocket. Josephine invited the girls themselves to decide how they would like to spend Albert's treats and, as she said, 'put it to the vote'. On one occasion, those who were well enough chose an afternoon's drive. Josephine wrote to Albert that she had 'hired an old shabby large open carriage twice on some warm spring like days we had, and packed five or six of them in, and covered them all over with rugs and cushions'.[14]

A year on since its founding, the House of Rest now accommodated as many as forty women. At midnight on 4 March, Josephine woke suddenly with 'the feeling that one of the forty souls under our care was passing away'. She slipped out of bed and knelt down to pray. The next morning she wrote to Rutson to tell him that a girl named Fanny had died that night, a Catholic girl he had seen when she was already very ill. Josephine had found her already laid out, 'as white as the white sheet over her, pennies laid upon her eyes, and crocuses about the bed'.[15] The matron told Josephine that Fanny, too, had woken in the night, and had been praying at just the same time. Indeed, she had prayed for two and a half hours, and when the matron tried to quieten her, Fanny whispered, ' "I am weaving Mrs Butler's crown". Poor soul, it was very touching. She said, "tell them when I get to Heaven I will be very busy. I will ask for a place to be got ready for Mr & Mrs Butler and their children. I will see to it"!!!'[16]

Josephine herself was not at all well at this time. The shock of her father's death, added to her winter rheumatism, saw her in a very bad way in February 1868. She was convinced that daily exercise would be 'quite a blessing to me',[17] and Albert Rutson was so concerned for her health that he generously arranged for Josephine to have the temporary use of a horse and then picked out a horse for her to buy. The idea of having her own horse again was thrilling to Josephine, but she had very precise and sober requirements:

> Often I find it the reverse of a recommendation to be told that a horse has been used as a lady's horse, for many ladies fidget their horses and make

> them restless. I can do with any amount of spirit, but I like a business like horse, who does not make a flourish and a splash, and curvette and coquette, as park horses do, but who will leave the stable at a walk and walk steadily 5 miles if one wants it . . . is it thorough bred or nearly? I like the colour of black or dark brown very much.[18]

Albert's choice was approved. Fittingly, the horse was named Black Prince, the name by which John Grey had been popularly known at election hustings in the past.[19] It was the tonic she needed, and by the spring she was writing to Rutson, 'Black Prince is growing handsomer every day, and *so* conceited. He snorts and praises himself in an intolerable manner! . . . On May Day I rode him with long wreaths of daisies and spring flowers hung about him, which Charlie made'.[20] To eleven-year-old Charlie his mother must have looked like a fairy-tale queen.

It was at this time that Josephine was putting the finishing touches to her first published article. It was also her first independent contribution to the work of the Council, a twenty-eight page pamphlet entitled *The Education and Employment of Women*. Rutson had offered to act as her go-between with a potential publisher, Alexander Macmillan, whose *Macmillan's Magazine* was a journal strongly supportive of efforts both to improve state education and to widen access to education for all disadvantaged classes.[21] Josephine was divided over whether she would reach a wider audience through publication in the magazine, or whether it would be better to ask Macmillan to publish her article separately as a pamphlet. She posted Rutson a 'rough specimen of my tract' in early May, and although much excited at the prospect of publication, she cautioned him not to be too deferential when dealing with the great publisher. She stressed that the article 'was written at the request of the Vice Chancellor and Dons of Cambridge . . . The figures etc. they wish to have *soon* before them'.[22]

The prevailing opinion was that *any* woman was qualified to teach because of her innate womanly qualities. Furthermore, as Josephine argued,

> the phrase 'to become a governess' is sometimes used as if it were a satisfactory outlet for any unsupported woman above the rank of housemaid. When we see advertisements in the newspapers, offering 'a comfortable home', with no salary, as sufficient reward for accomplishments of the most varied character, we sometimes wonder at the audacity of employers [and] our surprise has in it something of despair.[23]

At the heart of this question lay the problem of class: neither lady nor servant, the typical governess was a 'gentlewoman of reduced means'.

Josephine made impressive use of statistics compiled from the census returns of 1851 and 1861, and information gathered from societies such as the Governesses' Institution and the Schoolmistresses' Association in order to break the 'conspiracy of silence' which kept society in ignorance of the economic position of women. The facts were sad and shocking: five hundred applicants answered an advertisement for a situation as a governess at just £20 a year, a sum regarded as so paltry that women willing to accept such wages, 'and their name is legion', were refused registration by the governesses' institutions; another advertisement for an *unpaid* nursery governess was answered by three hundred; and the competition for female telegraph clerks at the Post Office was so great that demand had brought down the weekly wage from eight shillings to just five, 'a sum on which a woman can scarcely live unassisted'.[24] As well as shocking her readers with such figures, Josephine brought these anonymous women to life by quoting from anecdotal evidence. Teachers told of bodily privation, of how 'night after night when they went to bed, they have tied a band around their waist to keep down the gnawings of hunger', and also of, to quote one woman, 'the *pangs of ignorance*, this unquenched thirst for knowledge, these unassisted and disappointed efforts to obtain it, this sight of bread enough and to spare, but locked away from *us*'.[25] To raise the standard of the education provided for female pupils by half-educated schoolmistresses and governesses, poorly paid and low in social regard, Josephine advocated colleges for women offering 'a higher education than schools can offer', and the introduction of a university certificate which would act as a teaching qualification.

Josephine's concerns were wider than the single issue of the higher education of relatively well-to-do middle-class women. This is borne out by the terms of her disagreement with Frederick Harrison, a fellow of Wadham College, Oxford and perhaps the leading British Positivist of the time (he had served on the Royal Commission on Trades Unions, which sat from 1867 to 1869, and was increasingly influential in reformist circles). On 7 May 1868, Josephine wrote to Albert Rutson to tell him that she had just received a 'most *horrible* letter' from Harrison, attacking her views on female education and employment. That Harrison wrote to Josephine suggests how well known she was becoming, but she had been surprised to hear from him, especially since he had clearly not yet read her pamphlet. His position on female employment, as set out in his letter, she called 'Satanic theories': 'He says *no* occupations ought to be open to women, not even light trades, they ought *never* to work, nor have the *means* of working . . . that working men do right to drive women out, etc., etc., etc.'.[26] George, too, was outraged by the expression of such opinions, in particular because implicit in Harrison's position was acceptance of a situation that could be solved only by polygamy or well organized prostitution: 'he is so sensitive about the dignity of women that he could not bear such arguments being written to *me*'.[27] Interestingly, Josephine's letters to Rutson combine frankness about such matters with a covering reference to George's responses and rather nervous reminders about confidentiality. As she continued in her work, such cautiousness would disappear.

Josephine's immediate response to Harrison was to write back to him, setting him straight about the facts of the situation, and enclosing a copy of her pamphlet. Josephine had read a good deal of Comte, the founder of Positivism, who had died in 1857,[28] and she knew many Comtists personally. Positivism strangely combined the most progressive attitudes to society, seeing itself as positive because it sought social and moral improvement through analysis and criticism, with hierarchical and regressive beliefs. Among these were its attitudes to women, whom it saw as the repositories of feeling, a moral force to be honoured and venerated. Women were to renounce property and remain in the home as domestic goddesses, inculcating in the young the home affections which were to be the basis of social good. Honouring Comtists for some things, Josephine wrote to Harrison that their views on women were 'the rotten part of their system': 'They pretend to hold women up as superior beings, for *worship* (a thing which every sensible and honourable woman rejects with scorn), because she knows that God alone is to be worshipped; while at the same time they are in *practice* the most shallow and cruel in their theories of and treatment of women'.[29] She had specific challenges to make, too, astonished at Harrison's apparent acceptance of the fact that (quoting his letter to her), 'The wages of women are invariably lower than those of men', saying, 'You assert this as if it were a law of nature such as that trees are green, one which cannot alter'. 'Why', she asked, 'are women paid less than men?' Then, on the question of Harrison's view that marriage was the only career open to women, she posed the question of the two and a half million surplus spinsters and widows,

> for whom there is the alternative of starvation or prostitution. Thousands are actually now starving: I do not mean of the *lower* classes, but of the middle class. Thousands are driven to prostitution, a profession which theories such as yours do more to encourage than any amount of actual profligacy. I have worked much among that unhappy class. I know hundreds of them intimately. I know their histories and the causes of their present state.

This was a point she had dared express in her pamphlet, phrased, of course, most carefully: 'Many a woman rejected from the shop-till or housekeeper's room for ignorance and inefficiency, is compelled to . . . embrace the career, the avenues to which stand ever wide open, yawning like the gates of hell, when all other doors are closed'.[30] Josephine reported to Albert Rutson that some people were shocked by what her pamphlet revealed about middle-class women: 'these are *men*, who had no idea that there was *any pressure for employment* among us'.[31] Harrison seems to have regarded Josephine as an ill-informed society lady. Abruptly she terminated her letter to him, 'I have lived among the middle and lower classes. I know nothing of fashionable society or aristocratic or grand London people. The few times I have been among them I found they did not understand my language, nor I theirs.'[32] She apologized to Rutson for any rudeness of hers towards Harrison, but she made no such apologies to the man himself, saying that she could not help but write indignantly: 'I have spoken the truth. *I am ashamed of my countrymen*. It is a subject which justifies a little anger if any subject ever did'.[33]

Yet although she could write an articulate and forthright reply to Frederick Harrison, Josephine was greatly disturbed by the episode. Both heart and brain were, as she said, overtaxed, and a deepening depression manifested itself in actual bodily illness, until she confessed herself 'nearly blind with the pain behind my eyes'.[34] On 22 May she wrote to Rutson of her four days and nights of physical and spiritual malaise. George had asked William Carter, a recently qualified young doctor, to attend her. Carter, whose practice was at 78 Rodney Street, a short walk from the workhouse, recognized at once that 'sadness of heart which had brought it on', and visited the house every few hours. By now delirious, and confined in a darkened room, Josephine claimed that she was possessed by a nightmarish vision of

Frederick Harrison and his kind: 'I used to cry out for some way of escape for starving women, and saw thousands of them being swept up with a broom and hidden like ashes under a huge grate, by political economists, and I kept saying, "O take care. They are tenderer than you"'.[35] The very next morning, allowed to get up for the first time in days, she wrote again to Rutson, warning him not to let Harrison near her since she might not be able to forget how she saw him in her delirium.[36]

At the end of May 1868, once *The Education and Employment of Women* was published, Josephine travelled to Cambridge to seek support for the University Extension Scheme and to deliver the Memorial to the Senate of the University. She made it a personal mission, and although she had been ill and was still suffering from severe headaches and neuralgia, she determined upon a one-woman tour of the colleges to solicit support for the Higher Examination.

Josephine saw little of Cambridge itself, dividing her time between a marathon of interviews and hours spent alone in a darkened room. She recognized, though, that her appeals to the Cambridge dons were strengthened by her pallid looks, noting, 'I do think that seeing me suffering does not lessen the weight of anything I say', and that she was 'touched with the open-hearted sympathy of the *older* men'.[37] Her physical sufferings were a serious matter, though, and she confessed that the 'unceasing and sharp pain in the head and face . . . gets so bad it quite terrifies me'.[38] At home, three days after she left for Cambridge, all the servants went down with diphtheria. It was left to George to get in a professional nurse and pack the flushed boys off to Aunt Tully. Josephine began to think that 'some evil influence has had to do with my own painful sufferings, and the feverish attacks the children had'.[39] The doctors could only offer opiates to help her sleep. She was fully alert during the daytime, however, and counted no fewer than forty-eight university men to whom she had appealed individually, giving away so many copies of her pamphlet that she begged Macmillan to print more. She was certainly pleased with the number of converts, and found at the very least a sincere interest in all she was doing, but was 'not impressed by any great intellect'.[40]

Josephine stayed on in Cambridge until Saturday, 6 June in order to present the Memorial to the Senate. Fresh petition forms, signed by many governesses and schoolmistresses, were coming through the post right up to the deadline, and at 11 a.m. that morning she had to paste on new sheets containing 182 new signatures. Members of the

Senate complimented her on the impressive list, which included the names of Florence Nightingale and Harriet Martineau, as well as a good number of titled ladies and some famous wives, among them Mrs Tennyson, Mrs Gladstone and Mrs Froude, wife of the historian, James Anthony Froude. Josephine herself addressed the Senate, asserting that the Higher Examination would 'test and attest' the educational achievements of women. It was a neat phrase, and James Stuart believed that it told with Senate members, who at once accepted the planned examination, which became known as the Cambridge Higher. Josephine felt on the brink of success. There was much work to be done, however. Fifty-nine letters relating to the cause awaited her when she got back home.

The Cambridge Higher Examination for women over the age of eighteen was officially sanctioned by the university in 1869 and thirty-six young women were entered for it in its first year. Much of the credit for this should go to Anne Clough, but Josephine played a very influential part in the organization and leadership of the campaign. Referring to her Cambridge mission Miss Clough said, 'the charm Mrs Butler put into all the details she gave, showing the desire of women for help in educating themselves, made the subject, which might have been considered tedious, both interesting and attractive, and thus drew to the cause many friends'.[41]

A board was set up to examine the Cambridge Higher: it was made up of prominent Cambridge men, a total of twelve fellows and seven professors, among them Professor John Couch Adams, the discoverer of the planet Neptune, and the author Charles Kingsley, Professor of Modern History, who had been one of Queen's College's first visiting lecturers. The ambitions of the North of England Council did not stop there. Josephine addressed James Bryce on the subject of Oxford University granting a similar examination. Further, she suggested that the proposed new university in Manchester, a project that Bryce was deeply involved in, might serve as a suitable examination centre for women living in the north of England or in Scotland.[42]

The schemes put in place by the North of England Council were not the only reforms then being sought in relation to the higher education of women: indeed, Josephine Butler and Anne Clough were, in some respects, working in a quite contrary spirit to the ambitions of another educational reformer, Emily Davies. Anne Clough had some experience of working with Davies, who in 1866 had founded the London Society of Schoolmistresses, a branch of which Clough formed in Liverpool. When the North of England Council was established in 1867, Davies appears to have welcomed the presence of Anne Clough and Josephine Butler at meetings called to promote her idea of a separate university college for women at Cambridge, and Josephine appears at first to have given her every support.[43] However, Davies was concerned that Cambridge's approval of the Higher Examination would make it more difficult for her to achieve her own more radical demand that women be admitted to study for degrees.[44] On her side, Josephine was concerned that Emily Davies's demands for university entrance, and for a separate women's college, were arousing so much opposition (from the university itself and from the public), that their own council schemes would suffer. She was also impatient with Davies's fostering of a rivalry between them, writing to Albert Rutson: 'she is so clearly in the wrong that I do not care to prove her to be so . . . these masculine aiming women *will* fail'.[45]

While enlarging their northern circuit of the University Extension Scheme, Butler and Clough were, like Davies, beginning to think about securing lectures for women in Cambridge itself, both to make their presence felt in Cambridge and for the practical reason of making life easier for lecturers. As Josephine explained further to Rutson, 'I would prefer beginning it humbly – taking a Boarding House merely, within reach of Cambridge and working up for examinations given by the Cambridge Syndicate'. The boarding house scheme, 'Merton Hall', in fact laid the foundation for the second women's college at Cambridge.[46] Clough started out in 1869 with just four students, although ladies resident in Cambridge were also invited to attend the lectures.

James Stuart was once again involved, this time giving lectures on Mathematics, and he had also engaged himself to lecture to students at the house Emily Davies had taken in Hitchin in Hertfordshire, thirty miles or so from Cambridge. When he had begun lecturing for the North of England Council, to appease those who feared the consequences of young unmarried women coming into direct contact with itinerant professors, a fastidious scheme was devised by which the lecturer would distribute sets of questions or essay titles at the end of a meeting, enabling his anonymous students to correspond with him by post. 'Thus the dangers attaching to personal intercourse would be avoided,' recalled an amused James Stuart. It was also thought proper that a man should take the chair at lectures, 'it being thought at that time unsuitable for any lady to address any assembly, even though it consisted, as in this case, entirely of women'.[47] One can imagine the laughter when Stuart reported back to Josephine and Anne Clough that the 'masculine aiming' Miss Davies was even more anxious about propriety than they were, and, during classes at Hitchin 'sat in the room and knitted all the time'![48] In some ways, Butler and Clough were thinking along far more radical lines than Davies, who envisaged women taking the male degree within the safe bounds of a female college, while Anne Clough suggested that her female students attend the same classes as Cambridge undergraduates, an idea that Josephine strongly supported: 'The idea of a mixed class is *good* and I will consult Mr Stuart and George – I think we should encourage mixed classes wherever we can'.[49]

A year later, relations between the two camps broke down utterly when Davies snubbed Josephine's invitation to work together. Josephine informed Anne Clough, 'I have had an answer from Miss Davies, to whom I wrote very courteously. She shortly and *not* courteously declines to have any connection with us. So let her be!'[50] Both Emily Davies and Anne Clough succeeded in their aims: Davies's house at Hitchin laid the foundations for Girton College, Cambridge, which was established in 1872, and Merton Hall became Newnham College, Cambridge in 1875, with Clough the first Principal. Josephine, we may assume, will have been pleased at the success of both colleges, and, interestingly, one of the early Girton students became her sister-in-law. Miss Agnata Ramsay, who in 1887 secured a first-class degree in the Classical Tripos, became Monty Butler's second wife, and one of their sons, James Ramsay Butler, became a future professor of history at Cambridge.

The wider concerns expressed in *The Education and Employment of Women* and in the letter to Frederick Harrison became more and more Josephine's preoccupation, and she undertook a new project, editing a collection of essays entitled *Woman's Work and Woman's Culture*. In January 1869 she was in London to negotiate a contract for this book, again with Macmillan. The whole family travelled with her to stay with George's sister Louisa and her husband, Frank Galton, at their home overlooking Hyde Park. While George took charge of the boys, filling the holiday with some serious museum-visiting, Josephine was coached by her brother-in-law in preparation for her interview with Macmillan, who called in person to meet Josephine on a Saturday evening. To her mother-in-law, Sarah Butler, Josephine described how, 'In the morning Frank put me through a rehearsal of my interview with Macmillan and taught me how to drive a hard bargain, and then when Macmillan came, Frank looked so eager and mischievous that I laughed, and could not make any bargain at all'.[51] Once the business of a contract for the book had been settled, Josephine was able to relax, but she could not be persuaded to join in the family sightseeing. She said she always felt like 'a moulting bird mewed up, in London, and pine for some sign of the country, and some glimpse of the fair sky'.[52]

Back in Liverpool, Josephine and George now slept in separate bedrooms because she was coughing up so much blood. Josephine assured her mother-in-law that George's 'dressing-room is a long way off, so that he cannot hear me cough at night'.[53] She suffered worst, she said, when the family were at school, and she was either naturally calmer in the evenings, or made a greater effort to appear so. The doctors told her that only one lung was now working, and the pain in her chest was often 'very bad'. She was losing a great deal of blood, and in a scene reminiscent of Mary Lomax's dying hours in which she begged for the bedroom windows to be opened despite the icy wind outside, Josephine described how she too preferred sitting by an open window: 'It might look like madness to a looker on, when I am coughing so, and choked with phlegm and blood, but if I remained in a close room during those fits I should faint away. I *have* done so twice, and that is *worse*'.[54]

The issuing of *Woman's Work and Woman's Culture*, was pre-empted to a degree by the publication of John Stuart Mill's *The Subjection of Women*. Josephine was fully aware of Mill's thesis, and declared that it had 'electrified the public with its boldness', but she clearly regarded her own volume as on a par with Mill's.[55] That the two titles came out within a matter of weeks indicates how topical a subject the 'Woman Question' was in the late 1860s, but it should not blind us to the very different aims of the two authors. John Stuart Mill pleaded for the enfranchisement of women, and the necessary opening up of higher education and the professions that would follow, on two fronts. It was firstly, he argued, for the greater good of society, 'doubling the mass of mental faculties available for the higher service of humanity'. Women would exert a moral influence upon the government and human relations would be ordered by justice instead of oppression. Secondly, he held that enfranchisement would also increase individual happiness and produce true marriages of like-minded people, who would share interests and ideas. He also wanted the professions to be opened to women to remedy 'the dull and hopeless life to which [society] so often condemns them . . . the feeling of a wasted life'.[56] He gave no specific examples of female employment, however, beyond alluding briefly and vaguely to women professionals, MPs, doctors, lawyers and civil servants. For Mill it was never a question of *trades* being opened to women, never a question of women being in a position simply to earn enough money to support themselves or a family, as it was for Josephine. *The Subjection of Women* addresses itself chiefly to the position of the middle-class, leisured wife, the sole remaining slave under English law, as Mill described her. His position was utterly opposite to that of Frederick Harrison: 'Marriage is the only actual bondage known to our law. There remain no legal slaves, except the mistress of every house'.[57] Although many of Mill's views were shared by the Butlers, his championing of the cause of exclusively middle-class married women suffers by comparison with Josephine's wider social vision.

Woman's Work and Woman's Culture reflects the diversity of women's interests then occupying Josephine, who was careful to include essays equally from male and female contributors. James Stuart and Elizabeth Wolstoneholme wrote on women's education, while the questions of married women's property and female suffrage were also addressed. Female employment was the central subject, with an essay by Jessie Boucherett on 'superfluous women', one on medicine and another, by George Butler, on teaching as a profession for women. Woman's work was also the subject of Josephine's lengthy introduction which begins rather defensively, in particular stressing repeatedly that the essays in the collection, including the editor's introduction, had been written before *The Subjection of Women* came out, but does go on to assert that the issues addressed were not 'women's questions', but '*social* questions', and to remind men of the educated classes, 'born to an inheritance of monopolized privileges', that 'wherever there is monopoly on the one hand, there is loss and waste on the other'.[58] She argued that women of *all* social classes could very well descend into prostitution if all other means of earning bread honestly were withheld. Again Josephine alluded to prostitution itself with the greatest care, referring to the familiar 'paths of hell', and to italicized '*destruction*', but having gained the trust of her genteel readers, she proceeded to keep the subject before them for much of the sixty or so pages of the introduction. She was not to be silenced because this 'subject was thought too painful a one to be specially treated in a volume for general reading'.[59] Indeed, this made it all the more needful, in her eyes, that it should be confronted.

It was, she said, a 'most ungentle irony' to preach that woman's sphere was the home and woman's natural career wifehood and motherhood. She asked, as she had of Harrison, where that left the two and a half million single women for whom there simply were not husbands enough to go round. She insisted though, in common with Mill, that this was not solely a matter of economics, and concluded her essay by making a strong case for the beneficial social and moral consequences of admitting more women into employment, and qualifying them for that employment. She urged her readers not to fear industrial freedom or higher education for women, but to welcome them, promising that such changes would not revolutionize the home but strengthen family life by restoring the dignity of women: 'At the present day women are cheap; their value in the great world's market has sunk to a very low ebb. Their attitude, speaking generally, is that of cringing for a piece of bread'.[60]

Once her book was out, Josephine began to gather information from women all over Europe. She began at the top, first petitioning Queen Victoria's eldest daughter, Victoria, now Crown Princess of Prussia and the head of a Society for the Employment of Women in Berlin, for statistics regarding female employment in Germany. Victoria herself referred Josephine to her sister Louise, Duchess of Argyll, in March 1869. Josephine was no doubt on the lookout for likely patrons for the cause, and being able to refer to the English princesses would have been useful in this regard. Both princesses were naturally conservative: Victoria counselled Josephine to look to 'wise and experienced *men*' for answers. She was '*not* enthusiastic for women's suffrage . . . nor for lady lawyers or lady clergymen (as have been heard of in America)', and, sensitive to the unpopularity of the expression, 'Women's Rights', which she said, 'has become a species of watchword from which the general public turns with ridicule and disgust (and not unjustly)', she urged extreme caution before taking any decided steps.[61]

Yet the Princess's catalogue of suitable occupations for women of all social ranks encompasses an extraordinary list of possibilities. For a woman who regarded *knitting* as an occupation not without its hazards ('in Germany it has been found by Physicians to develop forms of nervous disease if too much practised at an early age'), she had some unusual suggestions, which included up-to-date occupations such as telegraphy and stenography as well as, more surprisingly, photography, lithography and marquetry. She saw ladies' colleges 'as a necessity', and felt that a college education ought to include 'a general knowledge of *Law*, added to a particular knowledge of the laws relating to their own position'.[62] The Princess drew her long letter to a close by saying 'I cannot conclude without saying how much I admired your letter, and with how much sympathy it has inspired me'.

In a rather touching gesture of womanly solidarity, Princess Louise wrote, enclosing a letter she thought would interest Josephine, from Elizabeth Garrett Anderson, the first British woman doctor. Louise had gone to see Garrett Anderson before the latter left for Paris to sit for her MD, and declared: 'She is one of those who *can* prove how much women can learn, if they put their whole heart, and soul, in what they are about'.[63] The correspondence was dropped abruptly when the Princess was embarrassed to receive a package of suffrage material from Josephine. Yet Josephine continued to write to the princesses, even on the unsavoury topic of prostitution, sending repeal pamphlets to Alice, Grand Duchess of Hesse, in October 1872.

Perhaps prompted by Princess Victoria's advice that she should seek out 'wise and experienced *men*', Josephine wrote to John Stuart Mill to confide in him her aspirations for an international society for promoting women's interests. Mill replied on 22 March rather stiffly, asserting that the improvement of social, industrial and economic conditions for women was inseparable from 'their claim to political rights', although he added that any genuine effort to improve the position of women in society should be applauded. He did, however, warn her away from any notions of international solidarity, telling her that the states of Europe were too disparate and multifarious to think of imposing a universal set of legislative demands.[64] On the question of female suffrage Mill was, of course, preaching to the converted. It must be stressed that Josephine had never ceased to pronounce that this injustice lay at the root of all manner of inequalities meted out to women. She had, after all, signed the 1866 suffrage petition which Mill had presented to Parliament. His second point about interfering in European affairs she would not accept, and continued to dream of forming an international women's association.

In April 1869 Josephine opened a correspondence with a Russian society led by a Mme Troubnikoff. She made much of Princess

Victoria's royal backing, and managed to create the impression that it was Mill who had sought her out, rather than vice versa. At present, Josephine was simply making enquiries and gathering information about the opportunities for higher education for women, but she wanted to know '*especially* what is the industrial position of women in Russia', and what access, if any, they had to 'a technical education'.[65]

In the years immediately after the death of the repressive Tsar Nicholas I in 1855, there were increased opportunities for Russian women to participate in philanthropic efforts. Like Josephine, Maria Troubnikoff and her colleague Nadezhda Stassoff were respectable ladies with aristocratic connections.[66] Their efforts, too, were similar to Josephine's own. They provided cheap housing for poor women and aimed also to provide employment. They organized nurseries for the young children, communal kitchens and sewing workshops. Stassoff set up a Sunday School for illiterate working women, and the two women tried to establish a Society of Women's Labour in 1865. Then in 1867 they led a campaign for the advanced education of women.

Josephine sent them notice of her forthcoming periodical *Now-a-Days*, which would offer information about developments in women's higher education, not just in Britain but across Europe. It was Josephine's hope that the Russian ladies would contribute to the magazine, from which she warned Maria Troubnikoff not to expect '*literary* merit at first'.[67] Elizabeth Wolstoneholme and Jessie Boucherett backed Josephine with articles for the first edition, but unfortunately the paper has not survived. It is possible that it never went beyond the first issue, yet it showed quite remarkable self-confidence to take on such a project. Josephine's approach to the Russian women was repaid with sincere warmth and spirited enthusiasm. Mlle Stassoff commended her idea of an international association, and enthused, 'We joyfully avail ourselves of this opportunity of entering into relations with the women of England, pursuing the same ends'.[68]

These were an extraordinary few months for Josephine. Just days before the launching of her magazine she made her maiden public speech at a North of England Council meeting held at George's school. For Josephine to have made anything short of an impressive speech would have reflected awkwardly upon her husband, and she and George had also invited a great number of friends, members and non-members, to the house for a party afterwards. 'I was not at all nervous,' she wrote a week later to her mother-in-law, 'George stood beside me, and was *very pleased.* His face beamed at me so, and the audience was very sympathetic. My speech lasted 20 minutes!'[69]

Josephine kept up her association with the North of England Council until 1871, when she resigned as President.[70] She had by this time become more and more involved with the campaign to repeal the Contagious Diseases Acts, which was to be her 'Great Crusade'. She was also aware of the obloquy that was increasingly associated with her name because of this involvement, which was something that she resigned herself to. She took care never to go anywhere without an invitation, and she wrote candidly that 'some of my best friends have told me that they must get rid of my name in their schemes or committees for good objects'.[71]

Josephine herself gave a further reason for dropping her educational activities:

> The regulation of vice – the enslavement of the women of the people in its most horrible form, was in full operation, while we were trying to elevate women in the higher or happier ranks (and rightly so) by seeking for them equal educational advantages with men. I felt then as if we were building a beautiful house on the top of a bad drain, or upon a malarial swamp. The inmates could never be sure of health and vigorous life with such a fatal poison lurking in any part of the foundation of their dwelling. There were many, I believed, who would continue the educational work; but comparatively few who would care to go down to the deeper and more hidden work, and to encounter the special difficulties, the disgust and the sorrow which met us *there.*[72]

This is an important statement in that Josephine makes the crucial distinction between the work of the Council, which, as was specifically noted in its rules, was formed 'to deliberate on questions affecting the improvement and extension of the education of women of the upper and middle classes',[73] and her future work towards the repeal of the Contagious Diseases Acts, on behalf of 'the women of the people'. Hitherto, Josephine had made personal, private efforts to alleviate the suffering of poor women in Liverpool. Her decision to accept the leadership of this public, political campaign confirmed once and for all her class allegiances. And in doing so she proved herself her father's daughter. Many years later Josephine wrote to her son Stanley, 'without any radical affectation, I do love the people with all my heart'.[74] Modern readers should not be suspicious of such a declaration. Certainly the poor themselves, men and women, took Josephine Butler to their hearts, and never detected in her any affectation or condescension.

7

The Contagious Diseases Acts

'This work of darkness'

IN THE SUMMER of 1869 the Butlers made a tour of Switzerland, visiting Lucerne, Grindelwald, and finally La Gordanne, the Swiss home of Hatty and Tell. The trip was financed by George's mother, and was intended to improve Josephine's health. Yet, as well as benefiting from the rest and a change of air, Josephine arranged a little international conference, in reality two or three women's meetings, through which she strengthened the network of support for women's higher education on the Continent. Josephine eventually met Maria Troubnikoff in Geneva, where she and Hatty were asked by a Madame Goegg to address a drawing-room meeting of Swiss, French, German, Italian and Russian ladies to consider how best to voice their opposition to the system of regulated prostitution on the Continent. Madame Goegg had said to Josephine that the English were fortunate to have no such system of state regulation and the legislative distinction it made between men and women: 'We are talking about the advance of women, but we can make no advance, we, who are afflicted with such Regulation, until we have got rid of it'.[1] At the Geneva meeting, inspired by what Josephine and Hatty had to say, the ladies at once formed an International Women's Association to call for the abolition of the system of regulation.

From Hatty and from her niece, Edith, Josephine had for some years known about the Police des Moeurs, the bureau in continental countries responsible for arresting, registering and examining prostitutes: 'in fact I knew of its existence as early as 1864'.[2] This was the year of Eva's death, after which Josephine had spent the autumn recuperating at Edith's house in Genoa. It was also the year that the first Contagious Diseases (Women) Act was passed in Britain, which was to a degree modelled on the European system of regulated prostitution, and which, within a radius of eleven army camps and naval ports, sought to control the spread of sexually transmitted diseases in the army and navy by the forcible registration and regular internal examination of women who were believed to be prostitutes. Those found to be diseased were detained for periods of up to three months. It was a temporary piece of legislation with a limited life of three years, and was replaced by a new Act in 1866 which added Chatham and Windsor to the number of subjected towns, and introduced the enforcement of fortnightly examinations of prostitutes. When Josephine heard of this second Act, 'It seemed to me as if a dark cloud were hanging on the horizon, threatening our land. The depression which took possession of my mind was overwhelming'.[3]

When the Butlers returned to England in the autumn of 1869 they learned that a third Act had been passed. At Dover, there was a letter waiting for Josephine from Daniel Cooper of the Rescue Society, who had led early opposition to the Contagious Diseases (CD) Acts, telling her that the system of which Madame Goegg had spoken was in existence in England, 'and had been extended by an Act of Parliament whilst we have been abroad'.[4] Josephine was at first incredulous, and dashed off a pencilled note to James Stuart asking him to make enquiries; Stuart confirmed to her that a third Contagious Diseases Act had just been passed through Parliament, extending the province of the second 1866 Act to cover a total of eighteen towns in the British Isles. The maximum period of detention for a diseased prostitute had been extended to nine months. In Josephine's words, 'A small clique in Parliament had been too successfully busy over this work of darkness during the hot August days, or rather nights, in a thin House, in which most of those present were but vaguely cognisant of the meaning and purpose of the proposed constitutional change'.[5] The Act received Royal Assent on 11 August.

The CD Acts were administered by units of plainclothes policemen seconded from the Metropolitan Police. In the subjected areas they were known as 'the spy police', and were hated for their surveillance and harassment of prostitutes and working-class women, illiterate women many of them, whom they treated with little regard for their legal rights. The lock hospitals in which diseased women were detained were loathed, too, for their harsh regimes. It was a system regarded by the Rescue Society as one which *hardened* women, confirmed them in their prostitution and condemned them to it.

The fact that the number of subjected districts had risen within a few years was alarming enough, but it was the desire of the Harveian Medical Society of London to extend the legislation to cover the *entire* civil population, or at the very least, London, and to adopt fully the European system of licensed prostitution. Their 1867 report led to the formation of the Association for the Promotion of the Contagious Diseases Act of 1866 to the Civil Population, a cause that had the backing of the medical journal, the *Lancet*.

There were also doctors prepared to speak publicly *against* the Acts, and their objections were not solely on the grounds of the doubtful effectiveness of periodical examinations to curb the transmission of sexual disease, but on the grounds that the Acts were immoral, both in condoning prostitution and in forcing the degradation of regular examinations upon women, and women alone. Also awaiting Josephine at Dover was an emphatic telegram from a Nottingham doctor, Charles Worth, asking her to lead a campaign to fight for the repeal of the Act: 'haste to the rescue'.[6] Dr Worth and other medical men opposed to the Act had tried to prevent its passing, but had become convinced that since the legislation related to women alone, 'these women must find representatives of their own sex to protest against and to claim a practical repentance from the Parliament and Government which had flung this insult in their face'.[7]

As well as receiving appeals from medical men, Josephine was urged by Elizabeth Wolstoneholme to lead the opposition to the Acts. Wolstoneholme organized a crucial meeting in Bristol on 30 September 1869. The National Association for the Repeal of the Contagious Diseases Acts was founded within days of this meeting, and Wolstoneholme wrote to Josephine telling her all about it. Remarkably, Josephine kept these communications from George for three months. She was uncertain whether this was truly a divine call to action, and fearful of the public role she was being asked to adopt on such a shocking social question, which was far from her acceptably feminine, personal rescue work with individual prostitutes. She was also unsure how her husband would react to such a proposal. Josephine later confessed to Millicent Fawcett, 'God did not choose for that work a perfect woman who recognised at once a divine call. Few know how imperfect, how hesitating that woman was'.[8] An entry in her spiritual diary for September 1869 gives some indication of her state of mind:

> It is now many weeks since I knew that Parliament had sanctioned this great wickedness, and I have not yet put on my armour, nor am I yet ready. Nothing so wears me out, body and soul, as anger, fruitless anger; and this thing fills me with such an anger, and even hatred, that I fear to face it . . . If doubt were gone, and I felt sure He means me to rise in revolt and rebellion (for that it must be) against men, even against our rulers, then I would do it with zeal, however repulsive to others may seem the task.[9]

Ultimately, Josephine recognized how this anger, similar to that which had brought on her crisis of faith at the age of eighteen, should now be channelled: a 'well-governed' hatred against injustice, tyranny and cruelty is what she prayed for at this time. 'This is perhaps, after all, the very work, the very mission, I longed for years ago, and saw coming, afar off, like a bright star. But seen near, as it approaches, it is so dreadful, so difficult, so disgusting, that I tremble to look at it'. After many sleepless nights, in which her pillow was 'literally wet with tears',[10] Josephine determined to tell her husband of her conviction that God was calling her to take up this new work.

> It seemed to me cruel to have to tell him of the call, and to say to him that I must try and stand in the breach. My heart was shaken by the foreshadowing of what I knew he would suffer. I went to him one evening when he was alone, all the household having retired to rest. I recollect the painful thoughts that seemed to throng that passage from my room to his study. I hesitated, and leaned my cheek against his closed door; and as I leaned, I prayed. Then I went in, and gave him something I had written, and left him. I did not see him till the next day. He looked pale and troubled, and for some days was silent.[11]

Eventually, George was able to discuss the matter with his wife. He foresaw what it would mean for Josephine and for himself, but 'spoke not one word to suggest difficulty or danger or impropriety in any action which I might be called to take', and gave her his blessing, 'Go! and God be with you'. She never ceased to regard George's attitude 'with wonder and admiration. I think there are not many men who would have acted thus,' she said. She would constantly remind others of the debt she owed him, saying that she 'could not have responded to such a call, if I had not had such a man as my fellow worker & supporter'.[12]

George was to make a public statement of that support later that year at a women's meeting at Gravesend, which he attended in order 'to show how completely Mrs Butler and he were united in spirit, as regards the work to which she had recently devoted herself.'[13] It may have been that George felt called upon to make such a public statement in order to counter scandalous allusions in the press suggesting that marital unhappiness had driven Mrs Butler to take up this work on behalf of her fallen sisters. She was assailed with 'violent and cruel criticism' from many quarters. During the early years of the campaign, it was said that 'there was probably no other woman whose personality was so frequently discussed'.[14] In particular, the *Saturday Review's* 'nicknames for Mrs Butler were of the most offensive kind', while on the floor of the House of Commons, Cavendish-Bentinck referred to Josephine as 'a woman who calls herself a lady', and Sir James Elphinstone declared, '*I look upon these women who have taken up this matter as worse than the prostitutes*'.[15] Josephine herself referred to 'social ostracism', but recorded only one incident where she was shunned in public. Years later she admitted to her niece (and daughter-in-law) Rhoda, 'I felt it most once at the Harrow speeches, when all Uncle George's old friends (except one) turned their backs on me – *literally*, & avoided having to speak to me. It made him unhappy for weeks'.[16]

The newly formed National Association, at its inception, excluded women from membership, and so a separate movement for women, the Ladies' National Association for the Repeal of the Contagious Diseases Acts (the LNA), was formed by the end of 1869 with Josephine at its head, and her sisters, Tully and Fanny, among the initial subscribers. The Association was conceived during a visit Josephine made to Quaker friends of hers, Mary Priestman and her sister, Margaret Tanner, who lived at Durdham Park in Clifton: 'You can picture these two ladies and myself, sitting face to face, in gentle consultation. '"What shall we do?" One of them replied, "Well, we must rouse the country". Brave woman! So gentle, so Quakerly, yet convinced that we three poor women must rouse the country. Indeed God does use the weak things of the world to confront the strong'.[17]

There were four Priestman sisters: Elizabeth married the MP John Bright, and their daughter Helen Bright Clark would also become a prominent member of the LNA – 'like pure gold', is how Josephine described her; Margaret, whose husband Arthur Tanner had died in 1869, became the LNA Treasurer; while the two remaining unmarried Priestmans, Miss Anna Maria and Miss Mary, would become Josephine's most trusted colleagues and most intimate friends ('you know how at home I feel with Bristol friends').[18] The sisters were, she said, 'my strong phalanx', 'you dear, true, unselfish women, whose labours are unremitting for love and justice'.[19] When they were unable to attend an important meeting, Josephine felt the loss of their sisterly support keenly: 'It makes quite a blank for *me*. Your loving faces, your quiet presence at meetings have been more of a *power* to me than I knew till I begin to look for them & not find them'.[20]

By her own account, Josephine plunged into her new role as public speaker: 'I scarcely knew what I should say, and knew not at all what I should meet with'.[21] James Stuart arranged a meeting at the Mechanics' Institute in Crewe, where he had given lectures in the past. A group of the principal workmen were assembled: railway workers, engine-makers, and boiler-fitters.[22] It was later noted by Benjamin Scott, Chamberlain of the City of London, and a prominent member of the NA, to be 'a new thing, and, withal, a startling one at that time for men to hear a political address delivered by a woman . . . It was surprising and refreshing to men to find themselves spellbound by the passionate eloquence of a gentle sweet-voiced woman, who lifted their minds . . . Their imaginations were aroused'.[23] Some of the men at Crewe had served their apprenticeship in Paris and had seen for themselves the social effects of the continental system of regulated prostitution. They could affirm the truth of Josephine's statements, and they pledged their support for her campaign. From Crewe she travelled on to Leeds, York, Sunderland, and finally Newcastle, addressing foundry workers and steam-engine makers, which is where she spent the New Year, before returning home to Liverpool. It was her first absence from home in the service of the cause, and she and George exchanged letters on New Year's Eve and on New Year's Day. Josephine thanked George for sparing her at this time, 'I feel deeply how good it is of you, dearest, to lend me to this work', but he couldn't forbear alluding to the fact that 'our being apart is exceptional', and he urged, 'Be sure to let me know if you are not well, and I will fly to you at once'.[24]

At the end of the year the *Daily News* reprinted four letters by the sixty-seven-year-old Harriet Martineau, under the pseudonym 'An Englishwoman'.[25] The letters protested against the Acts and also put forward proposals for alternative activities in which soldiers might be occupied. Martineau spoke of the new Ladies' National Association, defending its members as 'some of the most honoured of the matronage of England, and the names of some of the most distinguished of intelligence and culture'.[26] The letters now appeared on 28, 29 and 30 December 1869, and on 1 January 1870. On New Year's Eve,

Josephine wrote in high excitement to a Quaker friend in Leeds, Mrs Ford, urging her to get hold of the *Daily News*: 'They are far the best things written. I do *bless the writer*, to whom it may cost her life. Make everybody read them. Send stamps to the *Daily News* office, and ask for all *four* numbers with the letters'.[27]

On Friday, 31 December, the *Daily News* also published 'The Ladies' Appeal and Protest', signed by 124 women, under the auspices of the newly formed Ladies' National Association, among them Harriet Martineau, Florence Nightingale, and Josephine's old colleagues, Elizabeth Wolstoneholme and Lucy Wilson. It was drawn up 'as a result of the working of the best brains among us', and in later years Josephine would look back on 'The Ladies' Appeal', saying, 'Nothing better than that protest has ever been written since'.[28] The legislation, the ladies argued, had been passed through Parliament without the knowledge or consent of the people it represented, while the law failed to define clearly the offence which it punished. Unjustly, it punished only one sex, and the punishment itself was cruel and violated the feelings of women: their reputations, their freedom, and their very bodies, were, so to speak, in the hands of the police. Such legislation had not stamped out disease or raised the morals of society in Paris and other continental cities; but the reverse – it encouraged depravity, since the moral restraint upon young men was removed by a piece of legislation that regarded prostitution as a necessity. Finally, the question of sanitary control could never be separated from the moral aspect, and society would be better served by legislation that looked into the social and economic *causes* of prostitution.

'The Ladies' Appeal and Protest' was published again in the first issue of the repeal movement's newspaper, the *Shield*, which began as a weekly paper in March 1870. The protest became a petition and by the time it was delivered to Parliament, 2,000 women had signed the protest, including Josephine's sisters Tully and Emily. An MP wrote to Josephine telling her of its effect: 'Your manifesto has shaken us very badly in the House of Commons. We know how to manage any other opposition in the House or in the country, but this is very awkward for us – this revolt of the women. It is quite a new thing; what are we to do with such an opposition as this?'[29]

Before she reached home, Josephine wrote to her mother-in-law, telling her something of her latest work, but she was unable even to name it in her letter: 'I have been about on a sort of preaching tour on behalf of a question of social importance of a rather sad & painful kind'.[30] George's mother was assured that she spoke mostly in Quaker meeting houses or church schoolrooms, '& *only* to women'. This was simply not true. This letter was quite unlike the one Josephine wrote to Sarah Butler six months earlier, in which she triumphantly described her maiden public speech in Liverpool on the subject of women's higher education, but any anxieties Josephine may have had regarding her mother-in-law were unfounded: Sarah Butler was, she said, 'the first in the family to write us words of sympathy concerning that part of our work which is misunderstood by so many', and when she died in 1872 she bequeathed a sum of money to Josephine, 'to help "our good work"'.[31]

Such nervousness about the public role she was taking on was characteristic of the early stages of the campaign. At a large meeting of working men ('no women or boys admitted') at the Richmond Hall in Liverpool on the evening of 18 March 1870, where Josephine was to be the principal speaker and the only woman present, the chairman, while praising Mrs Butler for her moral courage in taking up this cause, felt it necessary to offer, in the words of the *Shield*, 'a gracefully apologetic explanation of the motives which actuated members of the Ladies' National Association to take the part they had assumed in connection with this vital moral question'.[32] George Butler then rose to defend the 'unusual' presence of the 'lady' upon the platform, arguing that although women were rightly regarded as guardians of the moral purity of their homes, there were occasions in history when the moral purity of the nation was so threatened that women were compelled to leave the privacy and sanctity of the domestic sphere 'and take a lead in directing the energies of their countrymen'. He asked them to think of his wife as a latter-day Joan of Arc. After Josephine's speech, her cousin's husband, Charles Birrell took the platform and, professing not to see the necessity of apologizing for women's public involvement in this matter, nevertheless alluded to his personal knowledge of how painful it had been for Josephine to take her 'unusual step'; in the *Shield*'s account of the meeting, the editor took pains to emphasize Josephine's womanly style of speaking, her 'admirable calmness, dignity and simplicity of manner'.[33]

Although her speech was thus protectively hedged in by the comments of her chivalrous menfolk, what Josephine had to say to the working men of Liverpool must have taken their breath away. She began by explaining the moral iniquities and legal injustices of the Contagious Diseases Acts, and their bearings upon the women of the working classes, drawing frequent outbursts of applause 'of the most heartfelt description' from her audience, who otherwise listened to her 'with the deepest attention'. In the second half of her speech, Josephine reminded her audience of the story of Wat Tyler, one of the martyred leaders of the Peasants' Revolt of 1381. This had also been the subject of her speech to seven hundred working men in Birmingham earlier that month, which was misrepresented in the press as a piece of irresponsible rabble-rousing. Josephine was not to be deterred: 'I will say that whatever was righteous and noble in Wat Tyler's anger I desire to see aroused in the men of England now'. She urged the men of Liverpool, many of them newly enfranchised under the 1867 Reform Act, to rebel, not with physical force, but with moral indignation: 'This power is yours.'

The Liverpool speech demonstrates that Josephine was in no need of male apologists: she felt nothing 'unusual' in addressing a hall filled with working men. 'My brothers' is how she addressed them, and this was not empty rhetoric, but a bond she felt.

Josephine would often allude to the pain involved in her decision to accept the leadership of the women's protest. She did this not to appease male audiences, however, but to encourage more timid women, of all classes, to follow her lead. On one occasion, at a meeting of ladies held in the Mayor's Parlour, Manchester, in March 1870, Josephine spoke for many women who, like her, had suffered 'restless days and nights, for their hearts had been well nigh broken' before they felt able to take up such work.[34] The Manchester branch of the Ladies' National Association was formed that night. Mrs Garrett, the wife of the rector of Christ's Church, Moss Side, was deeply impressed with Josephine's speech, and went home to tell her husband of 'the calm and gentle words' with which Mrs Butler 'opened out [her] grief'. He wrote to the editor of the *Shield* at once, 'My wife fears, very justly, the injurious effects which so great an anxiety may produce upon Mrs Butler's frame, if strong help is not soon given to her' – and promptly offered his services![35]

Josephine's gift for public speaking, according to James Stuart, 'familiarized people with the appearance of women upon the platform', and 'conduced so greatly to forwarding women's suffrage'.[36] As Benjamin Scott wrote, 'It required great courage for anyone to speak in public on this subject, and it required unparalleled courage for a woman to do so, at a time when women were expected to be silent in public affairs'.[37] Yet the first time Josephine spoke in public 'it was perceived at once that she was particularly fitted to do so, by a gift of great eloquence, a voice of singular sweetness and clearness, a manner always graceful, and a spirit always brave': 'it was the spirit that breathed through her words which had made the movement what it was, and which subsequently raised it to the height of its great success'.[38] According to the American suffragist Elizabeth Cady Stanton, who heard Josephine address many Quaker meetings, her ardent style of address was 'not unlike that one hears in Methodist camp meetings from the best cultivated of that sect; her power lies in her deeply felt religious enthusiasm'.[39]

Josephine told the working men of Birmingham that she saw her involvement in the repeal cause as a natural extension of the liberal reforms championed by her father, those 'great questions like negro emancipation, Roman Catholic emancipation, repeal of the corn-laws, extension of the franchise, and national education'.[40] She asked the people of Wigan: 'shall the same country which paid its millions for the abolition of negro slavery now pay its millions for the establishment of white slavery within its own bosom?'[41] and invited her audience at Carlisle to see their opposition to the government's institution of white slavery as analogous to that of the campaign for Negro emancipation:

> Let us think on that great anti-slavery movement . . . Let us remember, too, how from such small beginnings the movement gathered strength and flowed on like a mighty river; and how at last that great woe of slavery, like poor, blind, chained Samson in Hebrew times, laid hold upon the mighty pillars of the commonwealth of America, and shook them with a giant's grasp till the great fabric lay a mass of ruins and rubbish, from the midst of which the slave rose up free.[42]

The connection between Negro slavery and white, sexual slavery was made frequently, and the repealers became used to speaking of themselves as 'Abolitionists'. Josephine received letters of support from Victor Hugo and Giuseppe Mazzini making the same connection, and Josephine and George would often find strength in 'the labours and fortitude of the heroes of the great American conflict'.[43] After the death of Eva, Josephine had found comfort in reading a life of the early Abolitionist, John Woolman (1720–77), a Quaker preacher and 'an apostle of practical love',[44] and in her speeches and writings she would often quote Woolman's saying, 'Only love enough, and all things are possible to you.' She would also often use the defiant declaration of Abolitionist, William Lloyd Garrison (1805–79), so often that it might be taken as her watchword: 'I will be harsh as truth, and as uncompromising as justice. I am in earnest – I will not equivocate – and *I will be heard*'.[45]

Remarkably, Josephine, on her tours of northern cities, appears to have made a different speech in each one. She was famed for these heart-stirring addresses. Later she affirmed, 'Mine is not an official voice, wh seems to say, "Allow me! Excuse me, I beg your pardon gentlemen", all thro'.[46] To a conference of Manchester men, in May 1870, she spoke of women who turned to prostitution from 'starvation hunger', and declared, 'Two pence, gentlemen, is the price in England of a poor girl's honour', yet, under the CD Acts, girls such as these 'are to be no longer women, but only bits of numbered, inspected, and ticketed human flesh, flung by Government into the public market'.[47] In answer to those who would have it that women such as these were 'lost, irreclaimable, unsexed, mere animals, harpies, and the like', she insisted on their humanity, inviting members of her audience to 'spend a week with me among these poor women, and then say whether they are not altogether human beings like ourselves, with hearts and consciences'. She went on:

> When you make a law which includes all unchaste women as 'common prostitutes' you err and you oppress; and when you say that fallen women in the mass are irreclaimable, have lost all truthfulness, all nobleness, all delicacy of feeling, all clearness of intellect, and all tenderness of heart because they are unchaste, you are guilty of a blasphemy against human nature and against God.

In April 1870 Josephine conducted a ten-day tour of the garrison towns of Kent, together with Daniel Cooper and other members of the Rescue Society and of the London 'Midnight Mission'. Her seeking out unfortunate women in the subjected districts was, in a sense, a return to the rescue work for which she was so well fitted, but now, as well as offering a woman's sympathy she had to record evidence from prostitutes and the fallen themselves regarding the abuses of the system instituted by the Acts. It was in a spirit of defiance that she informed advocates of regulation, 'that ladies are not afraid to face the devil himself in the search for truth'.[48]

On 11 April Josephine was in Dover, where she found five women imprisoned under the Acts for refusing to attend the examination. She was conducted to 'cells with grated windows and heavy doors where delicate girls were immured – for what? For refusing the ghastly indecency, the shame and the pain which the Act commands them to endure, without any proof that they are what it pleases to call them'.[49] They were kept in solitary confinement for much of the day, but she found two of the women together, 'washing in a dark corner, fenced off by a chain or rail'. Josephine leaned over the barrier to speak to them, and the girls came near to her, 'looked earnestly through the gloom in my face, and asked, "O Madam, what does the *Queen* say?"' She could not answer them, but she could assure them of the sympathy of women throughout the country. 'In expressing this sympathy I never fail to tell them how we *hate* the sin of their lives while we are indignant at the law which degrades them still further. But many of the women I saw were *not* prostitutes'.

The name of Josephine Butler gained an immediate and long-lasting regard amongst the prostitutes of Dover, where the inmates of Mrs Hyde's rescue home for young women whom she had not had time to see on this visit earnestly petitioned her to come and talk to them if ever she returned to their town.[50] Eighteen months later, an Association worker reported how one girl responded when she offered her Josephine's letter for distribution amongst the fallen: 'she seemed quite to bless Mrs Butler's name, and accepted eagerly to read that lady's Appeal and some other papers'.[51]

On 13 April, Josephine's forty-second birthday, George posted her birthday wishes, telling her that it was 'hard to be long parted from her', and closing with the hope that God would grant them 'some years of rest and happiness before we quit this earthly scene'! In a previous letter, sent on 11 April, he urged her to bring back some of the girls she found to their Industrial Home in Liverpool, but also suggested a visit to Cheltenham: 'It would be nice to put a fresh wreath of immortelles on darling Eva's grave'.[52]

Josephine also spoke to the young soldiers in these towns. Some new recruits looked to her 'no more than 13 years of age; some might have been 17, 18, or 20, but they were extremely youthful in appearance'.[53] At a brothel in Chatham, a vast room in which two hundred or so girls were sitting with the soldiers, she was struck by the 'business-like exhibition', and 'the want of anything like gaiety or mirth'. The girls openly displayed their tickets signed by the examining surgeon which confirmed that they were free of disease. Some even pinned them to their dresses, and Josephine noted that 'many of the boys and soldiers had those tickets fastened to their hats, passing them from one to another with remarks as to the date of the last examination'. Some young men gathered round Josephine when she entered, and told her that there simply were no other forms of amusement, and that all the soldiers came there: 'They expect us to be bad, and so, of course, we *are* bad'. As the boys began to tell her something about themselves, 'one burst into tears and said, "Oh, madam, you will not go away; you will stay amongst us, and try to do us good".' Josephine stressed that throughout this tour, which involved several visits to brothels, she 'met no personal annoyance, no rudeness whatever – although the places were crowded with men in a horrible state of intoxication'.[54]

It was on this initial tour of the subjected districts of Kent that the hypocrisy of the whole system was revealed to Josephine. A prostitute in Canterbury who chose to go to prison rather than submit to the examination told her that it did seem hard that the magistrate who committed her to prison had paid her 'several shillings a day or two before in the street, to go with him'. This was not an isolated case,[55] and Josephine was so roused that she issued a threat to the magistrates of Kent, saying, 'I should be glad to speak respecting their relationship with certain poor and persecuted girls of those towns'. She assured them that the repealers would not cease until they had obtained 'an equal code of morality, *one standard* for men and for women alike, equal laws based upon an equal standard'.[56]

Josephine also learned of the full horrors of the examination procedure from the women themselves, some of whom she persuaded to testify at women-only repeal meetings held in these towns. She sent one woman's account to a Dr J. J. Garth Wilkinson, who quoted from the letter in a pamphlet of his which argued against the Acts on medical grounds. Josephine had been told:

> It is awful work; the attitude they push us into first is so disgusting and so painful, and then these monstrous instruments – often they use several. They seem to tear the passage open first with their hands, and examine us, and then they thrust in instruments, and they pull them out and push them in, and they turn and twist them about; and if you cry out they stifle you.[57]

Another prostitute described her treatment at the hands of the examining surgeon as being pulled about 'as if you was cattle, and hadn't no feeling', and not, she concluded, 'to make you well (because you ain't ill) but just that men may come to you and use you.'[58]

The distressing case of one young woman from Canterbury, known as 'Sarah Waters' (Josephine protected the identities of all the women she interviewed), proved to be the experience of many women rather than the exception. Sarah was pregnant when she signed the voluntary submission form. She attended three examinations, and on each occasion was found to be free of disease, but, as Josephine reported it in the *Shield*, 'The instrumental violation of her person has caused her on each occasion great pain, and copious flooding. The [police] spy has gone to her home, into her bedroom, when she has been ill and retching'.[59] When Sarah refused to attend any more examinations while pregnant she was summoned to attend a hearing before a magistrate, who punished her with seven days' imprisonment. 'Now in six or seven months that girl will be confined,' wrote Josephine. 'That poor girl was threatened with miscarriage, and I much doubt whether she can ever be a mother after what she has been through'.

The final clause of the 1869 Act did make provision for the possibility of detainees giving birth while confined in the lock hospital, and the fact that under this latest Act the maximum detention period was extended from six to nine months (women were released only if found to be cured of disease) suggests that many women did enter lock hospitals when pregnant and were forced to see out their confinements there. Sarah Waters, though, was fortunate: the *Shield* reported that by the beginning of May she was being safely looked after by friends, far away from Canterbury, presumably sheltered by the Rescue Society.

In Chatham, Josephine sought out registered women in dancing rooms and 'low theatres'. Their overwhelming sense of degradation, together with the chronic pain suffered after their periodical examination, caused several women to blush and cover their faces with their hands as they told of their experiences to Josephine, and it took 'much gentle kindness' to get them to speak.[60] Others wept as they recalled the pain endured in the final weeks of pregnancy. One woman in Dover Gaol told Josephine that the visiting surgeon had refused to put off her very first appointment even though she had given birth three weeks before, and said, 'The man might have known that a woman in my state was not fit to go through all that horrible business'. There were cases in every subjected district of women who were prepared to spend months in prison rather than undergo an examination lasting a few minutes. Daniel Cooper was present when one Southampton woman received a prison sentence of fourteen days, and through her tears, defied the magistrate by saying that she would 'undergo fourteen *years'* imprisonment rather than go up to that beastly examination'.[61]

As well as making provision for pregnant women, the 1869 Act introduced a new clause concerning women whose appointment with the visiting surgeon fell at the time of their monthly period, something which was given no consideration at all in the drawing up of the earlier Acts. One woman working in a subjected district wrote to Josephine asking for professional advice on this matter, citing the case of 'a poor girl who suffers most violent pain' because she 'was compelled under many threats to submit to the examination during her monthly sickness. Please inform me if this is legal? From the Acts I believe *not*'.[62] Clause 3 of the 1869 Act gave the examining surgeon the authority to detain a woman at the local lock hospital 'for a period not exceeding five days', if, even though she 'is found by him to be in such a condition that he cannot properly examine her', he had, nonetheless, 'reasonable grounds for believing that she is affected with a contagious disease'. The same clause also provided for the occasion of a woman being drunk and disorderly, in which case she would be locked up 'for a period not exceeding twenty-four hours'.

Josephine had been away from home in the first week of May 1870, to address an important National Association conference, held in London on 5 and 6 May. She wrote to George, saying that it was her intention to 'lash the meeting with gentle & awful words'.[63] On the same day Josephine was one of a deputation to the Home Secretary to present to him the report she had written of outrages committed upon women in the Kentish garrison towns. Josephine added that John Bright had warmly approved of the two suggestions George had made about the future direction of the repeal campaign: 'a flying column of speakers for Elections, and resident solicitors in every garrison town'. All in all, George and the boys seem to have adjusted quietly to Josephine's new occupations when she was with them at home. She even let the youngest, Charlie, then thirteen, help her with her letter-writing, describing how, as a little boy, 'knowing nothing of the subject in question', he 'stood by my side busily stamping the many letters which I had to write'.[64] When she was absent, Charlie turned his attentions to his father. On her husband's birthday, 11 June 1870, Josephine was down in Plymouth. George assured her that they were 'all well. George and Stanley are in the town for the Oxford Local

Examinations. George has done well to-day in mechanics and hydrostatics'. He added that Charlie 'has so got into the habit of bringing your afternoon tea that he has just brought me some, and is very loving'.[65]

The question of legal representation for poor women put forward by George was first raised by a member of the Ladies' National Association, who, in a letter to the *Shield*, dated 11 April 1870, called for the setting up of an Aid and Defence Association, although Josephine requested that the new Association's funds also be used to provide for children whose mothers were detained in lock hospitals.[66] Prominent repealers immediately recognized the significance of the legal aspect of their work, which was to try to restore the civil rights of poor women. George gave £2 to the fund, John Stuart Mill and the Butlers' friend Frederick Myers gave £5 apiece, while one anonymous benefactor, 'A Friend to Women's Suffrage', started off the fund with a donation of £100, 'to help the poor outraged women in their brave resistance'.[67]

The arrests of individual women were challenged in the courts, and, locally, the organization of branch associations, the distribution of repeal literature and the holding of public meetings promoted awareness of the workings of the CD Acts. Nationally, the repeal movement came to prominence through its policy of bringing the question before every single parliamentary election: every candidate was to be asked to state his position on the Contagious Diseases Acts, and if the Liberal candidate was found to be less than firm in his opposition, it was determined to run a negative campaign against him. This was an extremely bold policy, since it enraged the government to lose good Liberals, or to see hitherto strong majorities drop sharply, and it risked making many enemies among the very MPs the repealers wished to win over.

In October 1870, the death of the Liberal MP for the Essex garrison town of Colchester, Mr Gurdon Rebow, was announced, and the party approved the candidature of Sir Henry Storks, whom the repealers knew well as an 'arch advocate' of the Acts. A veteran soldier, Sir Henry was an excellent choice from the government's point of view, a military man for a military town. As Governor of Malta (1864–65), he had been responsible for instituting the first CD Act in Malta, where, he claimed, the examination system had proved very successful in reducing the incidence of disease, so successful, apparently, that Storks only regretted that he was not authorized to subject soldiers' *wives* to periodical examinations.

The National Association decided to put up a rival Liberal candidate with the intention of splitting the Liberal vote. There was, of course, not the remotest likelihood of their own candidate being elected, and they required a martyr for the cause. Josephine's relative Sir George Grey was their first choice, a former colonial governor and a vice-president of the National Association, but Sir George was already on his way out to New Zealand.[68] The radical lawyer, Dr J. Baxter Langley, accepted the candidacy, and it may have been a personal appeal from Josephine that decided Langley to stand, despite the considerable Liberal party pressure on him not to.[69] In fact, a strange alliance of government supporters and local brothel keepers was determined that Langley would not be given a hearing in Colchester. He received many personal threats, and at a repeal meeting in the town's theatre his speech was drowned out by his audience, 'which howled and roared in a most hideous manner'. Members of Storks's committee were seen urging on the 'roughs': rotten vegetables, chairs, a sack of lime or plaster, and lumps of mortar from the ceiling were hurled at Langley.[70] Bruised and battered, Baxter Langley's friends on the platform led him through a back way to their hotel, the Castle Inn, at the bottom of the High Street. Among them was James Stuart, who had decided to participate actively in the cause.

They had left Josephine alone at their lodgings, keeping safe the gentlemen's watches and other valuables and listening to the yells of the gathering mob in the High Street. The crowd seem to have found out that she was there, and the landlord came to beg her to allow him to move her to an attic room nearby so that he could tell them that he was not harbouring any Association members. Before Josephine could get her things together, the window was smashed and stones were hurled into the room from the street outside. Langley, Stuart and the others arrived under a police guard not long afterwards, looking 'very pitiful objects, covered with mud, flour, and other more unpleasant things, their clothes torn, but their courage not in the least diminished'.[71] Josephine helped to patch them up with lint and bandages.

Josephine remained in Colchester for two weeks and her presence enraged their opponents, and, particularly, Liberal headquarters, far more than Dr Baxter Langley's candidature. She was even approached by one of Storks's agents who begged her to leave. Josephine first attempted to visit the women detained in the Colchester lock hospital, but was refused admission. She then took up her work in the town in a quiet and modest way, speaking to small groups of women in prayer meetings in schoolrooms or in Quaker meeting houses. The *Colchester Times* took pleasure in reporting that such a noisy crowd gathered outside the Osborne Street schoolroom that 'their demonstration had the effect of drowning the harangue of Mrs Butler'.[72] Josephine's name soon became known, and the LNA posters and handbills posted up about the town were torn down. In their place their antagonists posted exact descriptions of Mrs Butler's dress 'in order that she might be recognized and mobbed. Every day she had to alter her dress'.[73] While Stuart and the other men made do with rather cramped quarters at the Castle Inn, Josephine tried hotel after hotel without success. The landlord of the Castle advised her to adopt a pseudonym, and never to allow colleagues to call her by her name in the streets. Her colleagues were equally wary that any telegrams they sent from the town might be intercepted by the government, and Josephine instructed George, 'If I telegraph to you it will be in the name of Grey; you will understand',[74] but when she booked into the Tory hotel (perhaps the George) under a false name she was found out, and the landlord there had to get her out of bed under threats from the mob that they would set fire to the place unless Mrs Butler was delivered to them. A maid at the hotel took her through the back streets to the home of a working man and his wife, and they readily gave her a bed during her stay in the town.

On the evening after Dr Langley's public meeting was broken up, Josephine was due to hold a large meeting in the town for women only. The campaign team urged her to give up all thoughts of appearing in public. For one moment she thought of George and the boys at home, 'and a cowardly feeling came over me', but 'then it suddenly came to me that now was just the time to trust in God and claim His loving care'.[75] Dressing as a working woman, with no gloves or bonnet, a rough shawl held over her head and shoulders, Josephine passed unnoticed through the noisy, jostling crowds of men waiting outside the hall, and the meeting was allowed to proceed, even though 'every now and then a movement of horror went through the room when the threats and groans outside became very bad'.[76] While the mob waited for Josephine to emerge from the front of the hall, she was ushered through a back window by her fellow worker, Mrs Hampson, and together they slipped out into the dark streets. They did not know the way, however, and found themselves back in the High Street. By now Josephine was exhausted, and her friend left her to try to find them a cab: 'She pushed me into a dark, unused warehouse, filled with empty soda-water bottles and broken glass, and closed the gates of it. I stood there in the darkness and alone, hearing some of the violent men tramping past, never guessing that I was so near'. When all was quiet again she saw a movement of the gate, and she could make out the poorly dressed slight figure of 'a forlorn woman of the city', who pushed her way in and whispered to Josephine, '"Are you the lady the mob are after? Oh, what a shame to treat a lady so! I was not at the meeting, but I heard of you and have been watching you". The kindness of this poor miserable woman cheered me, and was a striking contrast to the conduct of the roughs'.[77]

Finally, Josephine found refuge in 'a cheerfully lighted grocer's shop', where the kindly grocer, a Methodist, seemed ready to give his life for her: 'He installed me amongst his bacon, soap and candles, having sent for a cab; and rubbing his hands, he said, "Well, this is a capital thing, here you are, safe and sound!"' While they waited, Josephine overheard women who had been at the meeting going past the shop and saying to each other, 'Ah, she's right; depend upon it she's right. Well, what a thing! Well, to be sure! I'm sure I'll vote for her whenever I have a vote!'

The episodes involving Josephine were not reported in the *Shield*, even though the earlier assault upon Dr Langley was recounted in detail. She agreed that it would do considerable damage to their opponents were they to publicize the unmanly nature of their assaults upon her, but Josephine preferred not to speak of it publicly: 'It is so *nasty*'.[78]

The election at Colchester was, as Josephine rightly considered it, 'a turning-point in the history of our crusade'.[79] Back home in Liverpool, sitting at the dining table with her family, Josephine received a telegram containing the coded message, 'Shot dead.' Storks was defeated. The Conservative candidate won by more than 500 votes. Storks managed to get 869 votes, but this was 500 or so less than the late member, and something like 600 electors had abstained. The London papers were clear that Storks had been 'shot down', not by the interference of Dr Langley's rival Liberal candidature, but by the presence of the ladies of the LNA. The *Spectator* ribbed Sir Henry with having been 'defeated by Mrs Josephine Butler', while the *Standard* offered mock sympathy, saying that the ladies had 'put their mark upon him': 'Sir Henry Storks is much to be pitied. He has offended Harriet Martineau and Ursula Bright, and we fear he is a doomed man'.[80] It was left to the *Shield* to point out the moral of the story of the Colchester election: 'No place could have been more favourable for the election of Sir Henry Storks than Colchester . . . The fortress seemed impregnable . . . We may take courage and feel sure that we can beat them anywhere . . . The future is full of hope.'[81]

In the latter months of 1870 Josephine worked on a book that would supply the staple principle of the movement to oppose the Acts. The medical and sanitary question would always be disputed by rival statisticians, and was, anyway, never of principal interest to the repealers. Yet the moral argument against treating women punitively while allowing men to sin with impunity was not strong enough to move a Parliament of men that regarded prostitutes as less than women, as 'unsexed', as 'sewers' to be kept clean. The repeal argument had to become political and constitutional in order to be taken seriously.

Distancing herself, here, from the debate over the *medical* violation of women, Josephine called her book, *The Constitution Violated.* She dedicated it 'to the Working men and women of Great Britain', and promised to show that in passing the Contagious Diseases Acts, Parliament had 'invaded and trampled on the liberties of the people'.[82] Advertisements for *The Constitution Violated* started to appear in January 1871, and in March it was reviewed in the *Shield* and justly praised: 'Mrs Butler has rendered great services to our cause, labours which can never be sufficiently estimated, but her book is the greatest of all'.[83]

Josephine described the Contagious Diseases Acts as waging 'an unequal war . . . against the weaker sex only'.[84] More particularly, the Acts persecuted working-class women: 'Ladies who ride their carriages through the streets at night are in little danger of being molested . . . To them this legislation involved no present and immediate diminution of freedom for themselves', but she warned that the political liberty of the whole country 'depends on the preservation of the rights of all'.[85] She began by challenging the fact that a suspected woman could be examined on the word of a police officer and a magistrate. The loss of a woman's virtue was regarded under the terms of the Acts as a 'minor case' not warranting trial by jury, yet, as Josephine pointed out, a poor woman's honour was often 'her only Capital . . . her only hope of getting a living in an honest situation'. She asked how an offence could be regarded as minor if it involved 'a repeated, and it may be lifelong, imprisonment?,[86] and quoted the Magna Carta, which promised: 'No freeman shall be taken, or imprisoned . . . unless by the lawful judgement of his peers'.[87]

She also questioned how martial law or the Admiralty Court could be given jurisdiction over the civil population, and pointed out that the Acts, while they were careful to make clear the roles and powers of policemen, visiting surgeons and magistrates, did not attempt to define 'a common Prostitute', which led to great confusion. In fact *any* woman seen in the company of men resident within one of the subjected districts was open to suspicion (Clause 4, 1869 Act). The law failed to acknowledge that there was no clear line to be drawn 'between the absolutely virtuous woman and the most degraded and evident harlot'.[88] Amongst the poor there were thousands of unchaste women who were not *criminal* women, but who were unjustly criminalized by the Acts.

The principal violation of a woman's rights, embodied in both the legislation, and the actual practice of the officers of the Metropolitan Police, was the issue of the so-called 'Voluntary Submission Form', which an arrested woman was required to sign, in order to give an examining surgeon the right to examine her body for venereal disease, or face imprisonment. As Josephine ably argued, whereas any other apprehended criminal was specifically advised *not* to say anything which might incriminate him, 'the woman, on the contrary, is . . . requested to criminate herself, and the War Office and Admiralty order that if she do not immediately criminate herself, she is to be threatened with penal consequence for her refusal'.[89] Clause 17 of the 1866 Act gave the impression that any woman might choose quite voluntarily to 'submit herself to a periodical Medical Examination under this Act for any Period not exceeding One year'. In reality, as so many, often illiterate, women testified to Josephine, the police did not explain to them what they were signing. Some were compelled to sign under threats, and some who defied the arresting officer testified that he had made her signatory mark for her on the form.

Josephine's final word was to demand the extension of the franchise for women: 'Legislation can never in these days . . . be just and pure until women are represented'. Using a phrase evocative of the English Revolution, she threatened a revolt of women in order to achieve the franchise: 'English women will be found ready again and again to agitate, to give men no repose, to turn the world upside down if need be, until impurity and injustice are expelled from our laws'.[90]

8

The Parliamentary Struggle

'Our cry is Repeal'

THE CAMPAIGN BECAME more and more concentrated on parliamentary procedures, which both exhausted Josephine and caused great strains in the movement over questions of styles of campaigning and how to respond to measures proposed by what might have been expected to be a sympathetic Liberal government.

At the end of May 1870, the Association's parliamentary representative, William Fowler, was granted a debate in the House of Commons to introduce a private member's bill to repeal the CD Acts. Before the debate could commence, all 'Strangers', meaning the press and those in the public galleries, were required to leave the chamber. Fowler regretted the secrecy of the debate, but proceeded to outline his objections to the Contagious Diseases Acts on medical, constitutional and moral grounds. At the end of his speech the Home Secretary, Henry Austin Bruce, announced that the government was prepared to set up a Royal Commission in the next parliamentary session to consider whether Fowler had a case to argue, and a large majority of MPs voted to adjourn the debate.

The announcement of a Royal Commission was received with suspicion. The *Shield* condemned it as 'simply a ruse to withdraw the matter from Parliament' and 'throw dust in the eyes of the country'.[1] Josephine thought it 'a scandal!' that a number of men should deliberate 'whether it *answers* to violate women by hundreds!!', and a protest against the Commission was issued by the National Association.[2] One of their chief objections was to the secrecy of its hearings. They felt that the matter should be discussed on the floor of Parliament itself where the debate could be public knowledge. Yet they had to modify their opposition and recognize the significance of the Commission's findings. They made adjustments to their administration accordingly. The office of the *Shield* was moved from South Shields to London, allowing for a wider and quicker circulation, and a guarantee fund with a target of £20,000 was launched in order to finance the gathering of evidence to put before the Commission.

The Royal Commission began sitting on 14 December 1870. Josephine was called to give evidence on 28 March 1871. George's duties at the school prevented him from taking her down to London, but, unknown to Josephine, he did write a private letter to the Commission chairman, William Massey, 'commending me to his kindly consideration'.[3] On the Saturday morning on which she was appointed to give evidence, Josephine received a number of letters and messages of support from friends and from working men's associations all over the country. When it was all over she wrote to George,

> It was an even severer ordeal than I expected . . . They had in their hands and on the table everything I have ever written on the subject, and reports of all my addresses, marked and turned down; and some of the Commissioners had carefully selected bits which they thought would damage me in examination. Frederick Maurice was not present, I am sorry to say; but Mr Rylands, Mr Mundella, and above all, Sir Walter James, I felt were my friends. The rest were certainly not so. To compare a very small person with a great one, I felt rather like Paul before Nero, very weak and lonely. But there was One who stood by me. I almost felt as if I heard Christ's voice bidding me not to fear.[4]

It was the harsh view which some members of the Commission took of poor women, and of the lives of the poor in general, that so distressed her, rather than any nervousness at being interrogated. She was particularly angered by Massey's attitude in accepting her presentation of a packet of letters and resolutions from working men: 'He said, "We may as well see them; for no doubt that class takes some interest in the question". I should think so! Let them wait till election times, and they will see!'[5]

Parliamentary records of her evidence demonstrate that Josephine was impressive in her appearance before the Royal Commission, as she condemned the double standard by which only women were punishable under the Acts, and the fact that the age of consent for 'women' was just twelve years old. She drew attention to the slave trade in the buying and selling of young girls, and stressed economic necessity as a major factor in the problem of prostitution, saying that there was an absolute lack of industrial training and industrial work for women. She was most compelling in her exposure of the contradiction implicit in the CD Acts which on the one hand had in mind 'the reclamation of women', and on the other 'the providing of clean women for the army and navy'.

But Josephine's refusal to be drawn into a fuller discussion of the working of the CD Acts was, if courageous, perhaps also misjudged. Astonishingly, it was recorded: 'She knows nothing of the garrison towns; . . . declines to give an opinion as to the operation of the Acts; has no interest in them'.[6] Her own feeling was that the answers she had given were inadequate and not articulated forcefully enough to move individual commissioners, but Frederick Pennington, MP immediately sent a telegram off to George, giving him a message from Peter Rylands, saying that Josephine's examination 'had passed triumphantly'. Rylands, the MP for Warrington and a Vice-President of the National Association, was particularly impressed by Josephine. She reported to George that he was overheard to say, 'I am not accustomed to religious phraseology, but I cannot give you any idea of the effect produced except by saying that the influence of the Spirit of God was there'.[7]

While the Commission was still hearing evidence, the repealers devised what they called a 'Monster Petition'. The idea was first publicized in the *Shield* for 17 December, where the petition was at first erroneously advertised as being for *men only*! The mistake was quickly rectified, and the text of the petition was published every week in the *Shield*. The aim was to collect 600,000 signatures, which was rather ambitious, but by the end of March 1871 the paper had amassed 250,283 women's signatures, which, according to the *Shield*, pasted together on sheets, stretched end to end for five miles. Josephine described to Margaret Tanner how she rode with their 'monster' in the train from Liverpool to London: 'Its Railway ticket cost me 17*s.* 6*d.* & it required 2 or 3 men to get it hoisted on the top of a cab at Euston'.[8]

On Thursday, 30 March, two days after she had testified before the Royal Commission, Josephine delivered the petition to Parliament. William Cowper-Temple and other members of the Commission gathered round, and Josephine was asked whether, as a woman, she had not felt nervous at having to appear before so many gentlemen. She said not, but rather disconcerted Cowper-Temple by saying that she had been, however, 'deeply troubled at the sight of so many men with so base & low a moral standard as you seem to have'.[9]

Josephine was among those permitted to stand by a door facing the Ladies' Gallery to watch the entrance of the petition, as the double doors were flung open to admit 'the hero (or heroine) of the day!' Reports, including those in *The Times* and the *Shield*, drew attention to the hilarity with which the petition was received by the House. 'An Eyewitness' wrote to the *Shield* to say, 'It is said that *the House laughed!* and yet it was one of the saddest scenes ever witnessed within those walls . . . – that such a prayer was needed to be sent up to a so-called Christian legislature!'[10]

By May there was still no sign of the commissioners' report. All that was left for Association members to do during this session was to continue to deluge MPs, in particular Mr Gladstone and the chairman of the Commission, Mr Massey, with further petitions and remonstrations. Josephine urged the Bristol ladies to continue to call meetings and to agitate, saying, 'Our courage must not fail us when we are so near to victory'.[11]

In a Ladies' National Association circular written the day after the Commission's report came out, Josephine said that, from the first, she had prayed that God would confound their deliberations, and that the outcome would be like the confusion of tongues at the Tower of Babel.[12] There was every bit as much confusion as she could have hoped for.

The Royal Commission concluded its sittings at the end of May and its findings were published on 7 July. There was not one report, however, but six in all. Anthony Mundella, the Radical MP for Sheffield, told Josephine that once the commissioners had finished signing the separate reports, they 'sat and *looked* at each other in a sort of astonishment!' The majority had signed what Josephine called a 'hateful compromise', but there were minority reports both for and against the principle of the Acts, and the very serious divisions within the Commission meant that any possibility of outright repeal was a long way off. It was small consolation that Mundella, Cowper-Temple and Applegarth, Secretary of the Carpenters' Union and the first working man to serve on a commission, had shown themselves converted to the Abolitionist cause. Josephine wrote a hasty note of apology to Cowper-Temple, whom she had told a few months back that 'he was on the road to ———!'[13]

Point after point of the majority report accepted that the periodical examinations had been successful in reducing the numbers of cases of syphilis. They sympathized with the repealers' argument that the Acts tolerated prostitution, indeed regarded it as a necessity. They also raised moral objections to the examination system and concerns about the nature of the examination itself, but concluded that the existing legislation would be pointless without it. The friends of repeal signed two minority dissenting reports, the first of which proposed that admission to state-funded lock hospitals be continued on a voluntary basis only. The second dissenting report disputed the sets of figures provided by witnesses. Their own studies suggested that the spread of syphilis in the armed forces had been better controlled in the period 1860–65 than during the latter half of the decade when the Acts were in full force, and they did not believe that the numbers of prostitutes had significantly decreased in Devonport and Portsmouth, pointing out that any fall in the numbers was due entirely to the successful work of independent rescue societies, and not at all to the operation of the Acts. Seven other commissioners stated in yet another minority report that the Acts 'should be gradually and cautiously extended', and Dr Timothy Holmes, house surgeon at St George's Hospital, submitted an individual report in which he called for the examination system to be extended for 'general use throughout the country'.[14]

One of the Commission's most significant points, and one which had direct bearing on Josephine's recent direction of the Abolitionist opposition, was their objection to the constitutional argument put forward by the repealers. The main report complained that the repealers' memorial to the Secretary of State, 'reads more like a vindication of the Rights of Prostitution than a grave argument against the Acts on moral and political grounds', and concluded that, in the opinion of the Commission, 'the temporary suspension of personal freedom in this instance . . . is not to be regarded as an infringement of a great constitutional principle'.[15]

Even before the commissioners' report was published, the *Morning Advertiser* had singled out Josephine for criticism, under the mistaken idea that it was she, not Emilie Venturi, who edited the *Shield*. The paper had tired of hearing how this one woman had the power to reform the moral atmosphere of Parliament, and it doubted her fairness and candour from the bigoted manner in which the *Shield* referred to the Royal Commission: 'We Englishmen are apt to think that it is best to commence legislation upon a doubtful subject by instituting a preliminary inquiry. Not so Mrs Josephine Butler, who being terribly afraid that the Royal Commission will not endorse her views to their fullest extent, denounces its verdict by anticipation'.[16]

The commissioners' main report also criticized the language of the repealers. The largest minority report, signed by the seven commissioners who wished to retain the Acts of 1866 and 1869, separately stated their indignation at the repealers' 'discreditable' style of campaigning: 'We see no adequate reason why we should yield to a clamour . . . which we believe to have been for the most part artificially excited'.[17] There was some foundation for these objections, and the Central Committee of the National Association was embarrassed at the personal nature of Emilie Venturi's attacks on members of the Commission in the *Shield*. Mundella agreed that this style of personal attack was detrimental to the cause: 'we must *convince* our enemies'.[18] Josephine's male colleagues repeatedly remonstrated with her for speaking with too much indignation, and James Stuart told her 'not to charge the Enemy in that bold way', but it grieved her to hear the repealers' male allies speaking in public with calm moderation.[19] She felt that 'anger is right in a woman on such a subject'.[20]

Josephine was often very outspoken, but it was one thing to remind audiences of working men of peasant revolt, and quite another to threaten the Home Secretary, as she did when she was one of a deputation who met him in May 1870: 'The men of Kent have not yet forgotten their countryman, Wat Tyler'.[21] She also, in an LNA circular sent out in March 1872, urged her fellow workers to petition Parliament in the strongest language, specifically attacking the '*surgical violation*' of women.[22] She not only represented the medical examination of women by the speculum as a form of rape, but also made the accusation against doctors, magistrates and MPs, that 'There is such a thing as the "medical lust of indecently handling women", as well as the legislative lust of ruling them with an iron hand for the purpose of gratifying vicious propensities in men'. In this she was supported by Daniel Cooper of the Rescue Society, who collected evidence to suggest that certain doctors did take an inordinate amount of time to conduct what was a very simple examination procedure.[23]

Josephine's strong language was sometimes extreme. In another LNA circular she referred to the examining surgeons as 'male beasts', each guilty of 'instrumentally violat[ing] hundreds of women every year'.[24] To label doctors as 'beasts' was not likely to do the cause much good, yet such was the language of the poor women themselves. Daniel Cooper could testify to the great hatred of the police and doctors among these women, who called them 'water rats', 'body snatchers' and 'beasts'.[25] On the other hand, however, we have Josephine's recorded objections to the methods of her colleague, Reverend Hooppell, headmaster of the Nautical School, South Shields, who roused meetings held exclusively for working-class *men* by demonstrating to them exactly how their womenfolk might be examined. Josephine protested that his 'habit of displaying at the meeting the instruments used at the examinations, & describing minutely their use' was 'needlessly & grossly indecent'.[26]

It was Josephine's belief that Gladstone 'abhors the Acts as much as we do'.[27] She believed, though, that more than half his Cabinet was against him, and that deputations would strengthen his hand. She had been given this information 'privately' by James Stansfeld, the radical MP for Halifax and at the time a junior member of the Cabinet. Stansfeld was strongly sympathetic to repeal and Josephine told her friends that 'Mr Stansfeld has been like a kind helpful brother to me. His sympathy is *complete*. I am confident he cares little for office in comparison with this question'.[28]

Josephine called upon ladies to send 'violent memorials' to the Home Secretary, Henry Austin Bruce, the Admiralty, and the Secretary of State for War, and on 21 July she led a deputation of ladies, together with fourteen MPs, to see Bruce. The procession of men and women who walked from the Westminster Palace Hotel to the Home Office was designed to cause a stir in much the same way as the monster petition had, and 'presented a striking appearance as it extended the whole length of Parliament Street to the Treasury'.[29] Bruce kept them waiting a full hour, and then behaved in a manner that Josephine described as 'sulkily defiant' and 'haughty'.[30] He objected most strongly to their bad taste in appealing to his personal instincts when he was there as a representative of the whole government, and his attitude was echoed by a report in *The Times* which chastised the female element of the deputation as 'unruly', 'disorderly' and 'insolent'. It was true that the deputation was reproved for shouts of 'Hear, hear!' and 'No, no!', regarded as quite out of place at a private audience of this kind.[31]

Worse was to follow. On 1 March 1872, Bruce published a bill that was widely represented as being a repeal bill to replace the existing Acts. The bill's incongruous title, 'for the Prevention of Contagious

Diseases and for the better Protection of Women', was a clear indication to Josephine of its 'contradictory provisions'.[32] Bruce's bill did propose to raise the age of consent to fourteen and included measures for the protection of girls under sixteen, but in the main the Home Secretary was proposing to repeal the Acts only to grant the police fresh powers over women they suspected to be prostitutes.

The most devastating aspect of the new legislation was the intention to extend its province from designated garrison towns to the whole of the British Isles. This was to reflect a change in army policy from the current concentration of troops in a few large garrison towns to a system which, by the creation of sixty-six new military depots, would provide for the localization of troops. Josephine's response was categorical: '*I and my ladies* will not *in any way* countenance Bruce's Bill'.[33] It was Bruce's claim that, 'If we have made the meshes larger, we have given the net a wider sweep', to which Josephine's response was, 'Why is there any net there at all? What is the net, and what is its purpose? The net is the Bill, which, with its meshes, is thus avowedly made so as to entangle women as much as possible all over the country.'[34] Her warmth in opposition to Bruce's bill is indicated by the number of circulars she wrote, and in particular by a weighty pamphlet, over fifty pages in length, which she issued in the summer of 1872. Entitled *The New Era*, extracts from it were reproduced in the *Shield* all through that summer. The pamphlet traced the history of regulation, which dated from an ordinance in Berlin at the beginning of the eighteenth century, and demonstrated Josephine's formidable powers as a researcher and her skills as a political polemicist. The crux of her argument against any legislation governing prostitution, of which Bruce's proposal was the most recent example, was very simple. For Josephine, no legislation dealing exclusively with an unrepresented class of society could possibly be fair: 'A parliament of men, if it deals penally . . . will deal penally with women only'.[35]

However, the immediate response of the National Association was to back the bill, believing that the government was committed to it and regarding it as their only chance to secure repeal. It was their plan to use the committee stage to strip the bill of its punitive measures against prostitutes and to preserve those clauses designed to protect young girls in Section 10 of the 'Bastardy Bill', for which the Conservative MP for Salford, William Thomas Charley, was responsible. The bill was due to have its second reading on 19 June. Thus Bruce's bill would become a simple repeal bill.

While Josephine fought to maintain a united opposition to the bill, the LNA's parliamentary leader, Fowler, saw his own repeal bill postponed again and again. 'What an apathetic leader he is!' Josephine wrote in despair,[36] and she got local committees to send him an ultimatum: either make a better effort, or stand down! He did eventually secure a hearing for his bill for 9 July, but days before this Fowler's young wife died in her first confinement, and he was ordered abroad by his doctors. More crucially, Josephine faced outright hostility from many members who failed to understand that the government bill was hardly a compromise at all. Personal opposition to Josephine was particularly crushing in Scotland where church leaders had never been comfortable dealing with a woman: 'They seem to look on me as a wild mad enthusiast who only does the cause harm.'[37] In London, also, MPs sympathetic to the cause were furious with Josephine. Peter Rylands, one of the Association's vice-presidents, was 'rudely contemptuous' and refused even to speak to her.[38]

In early June, Josephine sat down to write an analysis of their present situation for Hatty and Fanny, explaining to her sisters the significance of the new army reforms and describing the tactics of their opponents. Her despair at the contest over Bruce's bill was absolute: 'Thus after wearing out our lives, in a 3 years' struggle, wh has scarcely been matched in intensity by any struggle on record, except the anti-slavery movement perhaps in America, we find ourselves – *not* in prospect of victory . . . – but driven back to the position of trying to prevent their extension over the country'.[39] Most depressing were 'the defections in our own ranks', and the despondency: 'Our ranks are paralysed. Our coffers are empty'. 1872 became known as the year of the 'Great Defection'. Harriet Martineau comforted Josephine with the thought that every great and holy cause benefited from being 'sifted & sifted again & again, at whatever the cost', telling her that they would be the stronger with the departure of the 'unsound elements',[40] but Josephine was pained by the falling away of support just when they needed to stand firm and refuse to compromise. She wrote to her sisters that her past life seemed to her 'like playing at soldiers compared with the intense reality of the conflict into wh we have entered'. She was terribly upset that Hatty was unable to visit England that autumn as she had intended, 'tho' it seems as if no private grief could outweigh the weight of sorrow on account of my country wh I carry about continually'.

What she could not do was express such sentiments publicly. A male colleague had impressed upon Josephine that 'many a battle has been lost by an anxious face in a captain', and told her, 'For God's sake don't utter one word of discouragement: it is believed that you have faith to remove this mountain, & if the other people see you give way, the effect will be disastrous'.[41]

Earlier that year, the National Association had congratulated itself on putting together a medical petition addressed to the Home Secretary signed by fifty physicians and surgeons opposed to the Acts, but Bruce now received a petition from a thousand doctors who supported the system as it existed. MPs from the subjected districts also submitted petitions signed by the prostitutes themselves, who declared that they felt their rights in no way infringed, and that the Acts were a great advantage to their business! The *Shield* exposed these as highly spurious: prostitutes admitted that they had been forced to sign the petitions either by the arresting policeman or by the examining surgeon.[42]

With such a strong show of support for the existing Acts, and so little support among repealers for Bruce's compromise, Gladstone withdrew Bruce's bill on 15 July. 'From such a House of Commons there is nothing to hope,' responded the *Shield*. 'Our cry is Repeal, total, unconditional Repeal. Our strength is in the people'.[43]

Greater experience of parliamentary processes further convinced Josephine of the importance of the question of female suffrage. She and many other members of the LNA were also members of the National Society for Women's Suffrage, and in 1897 Josephine would claim that although for nearly thirty years she had laboured unceasingly on the exclusive question of the abolition of the Contagious Diseases Acts, she had sympathized deeply with every movement for moral, social and legislative reform, and believed that many of these movements had been energized by her own.[44]

One such matter of continuing interest to Josephine was that of the economic opportunities for working women, which was to result in her opposition to bills like the Nine Hours' Bill and the Shop Hours Regulation Bill, which sought to reduce the number of hours worked by women. Many working women were opposed to this legislation, and Josephine, echoing her earlier writings on female employment, saw such restrictions as inevitably pushing women out of work and into prostitution. She saw opposition to the Nine Hours' Bill as part of the same struggle as their LNA work.[45]

The intentions of the legislators were to 'protect' women, and to 'humanize' their toil. In a pamphlet entitled *Legislative Restrictions on the Industry of Women, Considered from the Women's Point of View*, Josephine declared that 'the practical result of those methods would be not to protect, but to oppress women', and asked why women of this class went out to work, if not through the need to support their families.[46] She also queried how such restrictions would benefit working mothers, or deserted wives and mothers, or spinsters supporting themselves. Referring to the Married Women's Property Act of 1870, which established the right of married women to their own earnings, she remarked, 'It would be a curious sequel to this instalment of justice if the House were to pass a law denying their right to earn'.[47]

In her arguments over the issue of women's employment, as with her campaign to repeal the Contagious Diseases Acts, it was Josephine's view that whenever law-makers enact measures which affect only women, *unrepresented* members of society, 'they, to whom these laws apply, have grave reason for alarm'.[48] Josephine's frustration over the lack of female suffrage is apparent in her response to a speech by her fellow Northumbrian Sir George Trevelyan in favour of the extension of the franchise to agricultural labourers, '& yet not a word about *us*'.

> I feel more keenly than I ever did the great importance of our having votes, *as a means of self-preservation*. We cannot *always* depend on the self-sacrificing efforts of noble men . . . to right our wrongs . . . if we become (tho' more than half the nation) the one unrepresented section under a Government wh will become more & more extended, more popular, more democratic, & yet *wholly masculine*, woe is me! That people cannot see it![49]

Within a month of the withdrawal of Bruce's bill, another opportunity arose for the Association to publicize their cause in an electoral campaign. In August 1872, the Liberal Member for Pontefract, Hugh Childers, stood for re-election. He had served as the MP there since 1860, and was 'a popular & able member of the government'. As Ursula Bright, wife of Jacob Bright, MP, remarked, it would take 'a miracle' to defeat him.[50] There was, in truth, little chance of toppling Childers, but it was important for the repealers at least to dent Childers's majority and demonstrate the strength of their support.

The town was significant to the repeal movement as it was one of the new designated military depots created by the recent army reforms, and, as a former First Lord of the Admiralty (1868–71), Childers had been responsible for the application of the Contagious Diseases Acts at the naval ports of Plymouth and Portsmouth. However, whereas Sir Henry Storks had been a fervent supporter of the Acts, Josephine always maintained that Childers appeared to be rather confused about the issue.[51] During the election campaign, he produced some extraordinary statistics in defence of the Acts, and it was one of his claims that *all* soldiers and sailors suffered from sexually 'contagious diseases' at least once a year. Josephine regarded him as a tool of the government, who had been 'stuffed with falsehoods'.[52]

The Pontefract election, called on 15 August, seems to have taken the repeal Association a little by surprise and they did not put up a candidate. They did, though, send to Pontefract James Stuart and all their chief representatives in the North. Among these were Joseph Edmondson, and Henry and Charlotte Wilson, who were all to become important allies. Edmondson was a Halifax Quaker, who was there reporting the by-election for the *Shield*. Josephine came to know him as shrewd and principled, if rather too authoritarian in his attitude to prostitution. The same was true of Henry Wilson, a steel industrialist from Sheffield, whom Josephine came to work with very closely and whose wife Charlotte became more of a confidential friend. Wilson was an energetic organizer, active in many radical causes, a man impatient of delay, whose way was to bustle others into activism, particularly Liberal MPs. He would become a great admirer of Josephine, and was a support to her for many years.

Josephine received her notice to address the electors in a telegram from Ursula Bright just three days before the election, and was met by Stuart, Edmondson, the Wilsons and National Association agent Fothergill. As at Colchester, the repealers had a rough time of it. The full wrath of the opposition was reserved for the women-only meeting held by Josephine. The only place that the women could find for this meeting was a large hayloft on the outskirts of the town. James Stuart had gone on ahead to check that all was ready for them: he found the floor strewn with cayenne pepper in order to make it impossible for them to speak. A woman helped him to douse the floor with a bucket of water, and then to sweep it as best they could, but it was still 'very unpleasant for the eyes and throat'.[53] Stuart stayed long enough to see Josephine and Charlotte Wilson safely there and then left them to attend another meeting held by Childers. The large room quickly filled with women, and Josephine began by leading them in prayer. While she was speaking, someone set fire to the bales of straw in the storeroom below, presumably with the intention of smoking the women out, and curls of smoke began to rise through the floorboards. To their horror, they saw head after head of angry-looking men appearing from the trapdoor, until they crowded the room: 'There was no possible exit for us, the windows being too high above the ground, and we women were gathered into one end of the room like a flock of sheep surrounded by wolves'.[54]

The men swore at them with much 'profanity and obscenity', shaking their fists in the women's faces. 'Their language was hideous', according to Josephine, to whom it was clear that some of them had a vested interest in the evil the women were opposing. Just as the men were about to seize Josephine and Charlotte Wilson, a brave young working woman, 'strong and stalwart, with bare muscular arms, and a shawl over her head', broke through the crowd of men, escaped through the trapdoor, and ran with all her might to get help from the repealers attending the other meeting. When she found Mr Stuart she could only cry out, 'Come! Run! They are killing the ladies.'[55]

Stuart's breathless arrival only seemed to enrage the men further, and they tried to pitch him out of the window head first. He managed to get away but other men outside the barn now began to throw stones up to the windows and broken glass flew across the room. In the midst of these extraordinary scenes, two helmeted Metropolitan policemen were seen to peer up into the room through the trapdoor, but withdrew without making any attempt to restore order. 'At that moment,' recalled Josephine, 'Mrs Wilson and I whispered to each other in the midst of the din, "Let us ask God to help us, and then make a rush for the entrance".' Protected again by working women, they made a bold dash for the trapdoor, and not stopping to make her way down the ladder in her long skirts, Josephine took one leap to the floor: 'Being light, I came down safely'.[56] The others were allowed to follow, and she and Charlotte led the distressed women, many of them weeping, back to their hotel, the Red Lion. There, they held an impromptu meeting, which, once he had heard of their rude treatment, the landlord permitted, although the ladies were begged to keep all the windows closed and the lights down low.

The whole town was shocked that the ladies had met such a reception, and a number of respectable witnesses, men and women, came forward to name the 'roughs'. Sixteen or more men were identified, among them an accountant, two grocers, a tallow chandler, a joiner and a bricklayer, who were 'led on by two persons whose *dress* was that of gentlemen'.[57] These were apparently members of Childers's committee.

Josephine was sent donations for election work because of the way the ladies were treated at Pontefract, but elsewhere the behaviour of the roughs met with approbation, and the insults of the mob were taken up by the London press. In a front-page article, the *Saturday Review* strongly criticized the clamour of 'females', 'presided over by a person of the name of Butler', who, by the circulation of their literature, attempted to foul the minds of the children of Pontefract, so that 'factory girls as they went to their work speculated aloud upon the examination of women'. The paper condoned the violence with which 'those dreadful women who appear on the eve of every election' were seen off.[58] As the *Shield* was quick to point out, factory girls were precisely the class of young women upon whom the police were hired to spy, and who were compelled to undergo such examinations. In Josephine's report of the campaign at Pontefract, written for the *Shield*, she described her feelings on listening to Hugh Childers assuring the electorate that 'honourable women would not be interfered with', and, further, that he would vow to say no more about the legislation lest he should cause distress to the ladies in his audience.

> My heart filled with pity as I looked down on the *ladies* he thus addressed; poor, humble, toil-worn women, many of them holding infants to their breasts. It seemed indeed a cruel mockery for Mr Childers to make this parade of delicacy in speaking of this matter to women, most of whom were of the same class as those now subjected, in our garrison towns . . . and all of whom might have been exposed to personal outrage.[59]

To his surprise, Childers found that these women did not blush at the subject, but 'fairly yelled at him' with 'a sharp fierce cry of derision'.

The repeal movement had some success at Pontefract. One third of the 2,000 registered voters abstained and Childers was estimated to have lost up to 150 votes. Yet the Pontefract election had taught them that towns needed to be thoroughly prepared on the question prior to local elections. For this, more effective organization was required. Two electoral associations were founded soon afterwards: the Northern Counties League, with Henry Wilson as Secretary and Joseph Edmondson as Treasurer, in the autumn of 1872, and the Midland

Counties Electoral Union, with its centre in Birmingham, formed in December 1872, with Robert Martineau, nephew of Harriet Martineau, as its leading figure. These new branches of the National Association demanded their own independent salaried electoral agents who could be dispatched about the country with relative ease.

This was a contentious issue. There was a great deal of mistrust of salaried working-class agents among those who gave their time to the movement voluntarily, but Josephine wasn't one of them. She had lost patience with local committees who were not pulling their weight, and who, she felt, relied upon her effort to make good their defects. She wanted someone who could give his whole time to the work, and she went ahead and hired an agent of her own without seeking the authority of any committee. Henry Bligh, who had been a soldier in the artillery in India and at home for some twenty years, had written to the *Shield* offering his services. Josephine arranged to meet him in Newcastle and engaged him on the spot. She liked particularly 'his good moral character and humility', and pointed out to Wilson that 'he has had twenty years of training in implicit obedience'.[60]

At the close of 1872 Josephine made use of an opportunity to speak to Gladstone personally when he accepted George's invitation to preside over the school prize-giving ceremony at Liverpool College, a few days before Christmas. She wrote to Fanny in a tone of mock awe at the thought of receiving the Gladstone ladies in all their finery, for Gladstone had promised to bring his wife and daughters with him: 'It burdens me more than any public meeting of repealers, but I must be brave! . . . I have bought a new bonnet for Mrs Gladstone's edification!!!'[61] Josephine and George had personally to supply the funds to entertain the Gladstone party, which the Tory directors of the school had bluntly refused to do. The reception was a great success, and Josephine managed to get Gladstone to herself as far as was seemly, and as far as was possible in a room full of people eager to be introduced to the Prime Minister.

The chance to converse with Gladstone in an informal setting could not be turned down, but it would have been in bad taste for his hostess to assault him with the political issue of the CD Acts. She reported to Wilson that she led him as *close* as she possibly could to the subject she had at heart, but that she got no encouragement from Gladstone to go further. She then seized upon related subjects, such as marriage, domestic life, purity, Christ's law of purity as binding on all, and even contraception, or rather 'the deadly evidences we have in certain modern designs for allowing physical evils'.[62]

Gladstone was taken aback by the weightiness of her conversation, and Josephine realized that he was not used to conversing with 'sensible women'. It is a pity that she failed to appreciate any solid qualities in his wife, Catherine, who for many years had been committed to rescue work amongst prostitutes, and who had also lost a little daughter, five-year-old Jessie, who died of meningitis in 1850. Josephine complained to Wilson that she had been trapped with her for an age, and she felt that her true feelings about Catherine Gladstone were too rude to record. By her own account, Josephine had Gladstone mesmerized, and not just by the intellectual force of her comments, it would seem, but also by the surprise of being challenged on intimate matters of sexual morality. 'He seemed struck, and took fire, as it were, when I spoke. Indeed, he would have become so absorbed, that the guests, I saw, were wondering, and for decency's sake I twice turned the other way and talked to the Tory mayor on my other side'. She appears to have found Gladstone equally attractive, considering him 'certainly loveable – I felt, if I had the opportunity, I could *with ease* carry him to the deepest questions and plead with him as a woman can with a sensitive refined man of intense feelings and keen intellect'.[63]

The encounter was a coup for Josephine, and this was due in part to George's cleverness at the toast-making, in which he gave what was an audacious speech in view of his still delicate position at the school. That autumn he had refrained from appearing at repeal meetings, and Josephine explained to Wilson that George took care over absences from the college.[64] Yet now George made bold use of the school prize-giving to publicize Josephine's campaign, reminding the assembled guests that as well as being the headmaster of Liverpool College, he was also the husband of the President of the Ladies' National Association. Gladstone proposed a toast to Mr and Mrs Butler to thank them for their hospitality, upon which George rose to thank him:

> He said that he felt it a *great honour* to have his name coupled with mine & to be identified with me – that we were closely associated in a great social and public movement, it was well known, & that we worked with one heart in them; & that the way in wh they had drunk our health wd cheer us in our work, & that it was not merely as his wife, but as his companion in efforts for social reform that he felt thankful & proud to be thus publicly mentioned together with me by the Premier!![65]

After a few moments of stunned silence from the school governors, 'Mr Gladstone shouted, "hear, hear!"' It was far more than they could have wished for, and if Josephine had not observed that Gladstone drank very moderately she would have sworn that he was drunk!

Their financial situation was a continuing anxiety for the Butlers, and Josephine was also aware of the movement's need for funds. Josephine wished that every lady who had any 'would sell her jewels . . . I have already sold the few I had worth anything',[66] but what little annual income she got from her marriage settlement went on her House of Rest in Liverpool. On reading the list of subscriptions to the National Association in the *Shield*, headed by sums of £100 and £50, George was distressed at being unable to match them. He gave £1, Josephine 10 shillings, and he already gave away an eighth of his salary every year, about £100 'in £1 & £5 subscriptions to charities & educational matters'.[67] Josephine asked Henry Wilson if he would write to George, 'saying to him that smaller subscriptions are expected & welcome'.

Their three boys were able to go up to university only with the aid of scholarships, and much 'screwing & contriving which none of our friends are probably aware of', on the part of George and Josephine. Georgie was an Exhibitioner at Trinity College, Cambridge, where his father had begun his studies. George never hid from his son how dependent they were upon the beneficence of friends and relatives. Enclosing a gift of £30 from Uncle Monty, he wrote to his son, thanking God for the many people who were assisting him in his university career:

> Even if I were suddenly cut off, you have, with your grandfather's legacy (about £400), the means of carrying on your studies at the University. Indeed, you have now, with your Exhibitions and this £120 a year, exclusive of your dear grandmother's legacy of £20, Uncle Spen's present – I forget whether it was £5 or £10 – and half of £100 which James Stuart placed in my hand to start some of you at college, & which I propose to divide between you & Catty, as a help towards your college outfit.[68]

In March 1873 Georgie won the Bell scholarship, which was open to students across the whole university. Josephine was thrilled to read the announcement of this in *The Times*, and wrote proudly to the Wilsons: 'He is working so hard, & his chief motive is – dear lad – to get some money to make it easier for us to go to Switzerland to take a rest some time . . . He is *quite* a freshman at Cambridge, you know, & it is not usual for a freshman to get a *University* scholarship'. 'He is very industrious,' she added. 'He would not belong to our family if he was not'.[69]

The Butlers were to receive financial aid to help with recuperative travel from another source. In the autumn of 1872, Josephine had caught a severe cold after addressing an open-air meeting in Plymouth. Back in Liverpool she had two doctors in attendance, and was kept in a darkened room. She could not move for bodily pain. The doctors told her that she had escaped the threat of jaundice, but Josephine felt very much as if she *had* it, saying, 'George was very frightened on Saturday'.[70] She was ordered to rest for three to four weeks, and in fact did not leave the house for three months, but she was not resting. Despite suffering what she described as 'a terrible heart attack' in October, she continued to work, sending out pamphlets and circulars, and complained that she was 'getting almost deformed with stooping over my desk such long hours'.[71] Josephine had rallied for Gladstone's visit, and she managed to hold some meetings in Bath the following Easter, but she was quickly set back by any activity like this and seems glad to have had an excuse not to go on a tour of Belfast. She was suffering from congestion of the lungs and fever, and was haemorrhaging: 'I must own that the future of *my* work looks a little uncertain,' she confided to Robert Martineau.[72]

By May 1873, the doctors offered her an ultimatum: travel to southern Italy or even Algeria, or become very seriously ill. Martineau had already contacted Wilson and Joseph Edmondson, and between them they secretly organized what was to be the first of several subscription funds in forthcoming years, collected by fellow workers to finance a continental holiday for Josephine. The very grave concern of her colleagues for Josephine's well-being, and their delicacy in organizing collections of money, demonstrates their recognition of her worth to the movement as their leader, and also the personal veneration and love that Josephine inspired in the men she worked with. Martineau wrote to Wilson that he had heard from Josephine that she must get away to Switzerland if she were to be able 'to stand another year's fight'. He had also understood that money was short and was pleased that 'all will be made easy for them'.[73]

Two hundred pounds in donations no bigger than £10 was the sum they fixed upon. It was estimated that the Butlers would probably not spend more than half that on the holiday itself, and they were concerned to phrase their letter to Josephine in such a way as to arrest any temptation she might have to give away any unspent funds to the Ladies' National Association on her return. Martineau was also keen to make over the gift to *both* Josephine and George: 'I mentioned *Mr* Butler because I know how desirous she always is that he should be noticed. And after all it is *his* money that is being spent'.[74] Josephine was overwhelmed with gratitude. She knew well that she was in need of spiritual refreshment as well as bodily rest. She also needed, for a time, to turn her back on England. She told Wilson, 'I want to get *south of the Alps. I never feel warm* . . . I have not felt warm since July 1869'.[75]

9

Europe

'Running one's breast upon knife points'

AFTER THE DIVISIONS in the repeal movement prompted by the introduction of Bruce's bill in 1872 and the subsequent 'Great Defection', 1874 witnessed yet another falling away of support. The general election that year was a double blow to the Abolitionists: not only did Fowler, their parliamentary representative, lose his seat, but the fall of Gladstone's government meant that their parliamentary canvassing had to begin all over again. 1874 became 'the year of discouragement', 'a time of . . . deep depression in the work'.[1]

Among the core of the movement, however, a new spirit was moving. On 25 June a select band of workers representing the various repeal societies met in York to consider the direction of the work before them. The centrepiece of the conference was a speech by the Reverend C. S. Collingwood, which gave a devastating summary of their position within the context of European regulation, pointing out how limited had been their vision that they could remain an exclusively *national* concern and act in isolation. It was not just the like of William Acton or the *Lancet* with whom they had to do battle, but international medical congresses backed by every government on the Continent. 'What (they ask) are a few women, a few noisy agitators, a few hundred thousand petitioners . . . what are we against so-called science, and all the allies it invokes, against Kings and Prime Ministers?'[2] He put the question whether they should have accepted the legislation offered by Bruce and withdrawn from the field, and answered it himself, '*No! a thousand times no!*' The York conference took up the challenge, and a resolution was passed by which the LNA were asked to open correspondence with anti-regulationists in every European nation.

The movement was also energized by the declaration by James Stansfeld, now free of office, of his commitment to the repeal of the Acts. In a speech in Bristol on 15 October he condemned the Acts as 'immoral and unconstitutional and calculated to degrade the manhood and womanhood of the country'. He announced his sympathy with the women of the movement who had been 'hounded down and hooted at' and vowed that neither he nor they would desist until the Acts had been repealed.[3]

Stansfeld had moved in radical circles all his adult life, and in fact was married to a sister of Emilie Venturi who edited the *Shield.* As Liberal MP for Halifax, he had been put under considerable pressure by his constituents, including Joseph Edmondson, to state his opposition to the Acts, even if it meant resignation from the Cabinet. Now he said, 'I have cast my lot with these men and women'. It was clear to him and to all others that in doing this he had sacrificed his political career. To Josephine it was a fresh call to battle.

Josephine did her share of making contacts with anti-regulationists abroad, but it was slow and dispiriting work. How much more speedy and more effective it would be if one could speak directly to the peoples of Europe. This she quickly determined to do, and she arranged with Stansfeld that she would keep a journal for him detailing her progress. She was also given considerable financial support: the Society of Friends provided the largest grant, and the LNA and Northern Counties League guaranteed Josephine £50 apiece. The Priestman sisters also sent a modest little sum they had collected privately. Her son Stanley was to be her chaperon at the start of the tour, and George and the rest of the boys were to join them once term had finished.

Josephine set off for Paris on 11 December with letters of introduction (the Quakers were especially useful in this, and she also had one from the new Foreign Minister, Lord Derby), and prayers. The Priestmans sent her a 'sweet little illuminated verse', and when she opened her bible for words of comfort on the crossing, out slipped an envelope directed in her husband's hand, 'To my dear wife; to be used when we are separated from each other'. Enclosed was a prayer in which George commended his wife's safety to God. Josephine kept it about her, in her pocket-book, and took it with her as a talisman wherever she went. She read it every night.

Josephine's way was prepared by a Swiss gentleman, M. Aimé Humbert of Neuchâtel. That he had ever heard the name of

Josephine Butler seemed to her an act of Providence. When sending out announcements of her tour to likely people on the Continent, Josephine picked out some names and addresses from a directory she had found on her travels that summer which provided details of the heads of various charities abroad. She addressed one letter to a M. Humbert of Neuchâtel, but the postman delivered it to a different man, M. Aimé Humbert, who had long opposed the system of regulation. Aimé and his wife, Marie, would become firm friends of the Butlers, and their daughter, Amélie, Josephine's devoted amanuensis. Humbert had been Minister of Public Instruction for ten years, and President of the Chambres des Etats Suisses for one year, and was able to provide Josephine with many valuable introductions to influential contacts in Paris, Lyons, Marseilles, Genoa and Turin. He even drew her up a street map of Paris so that she could plan her day-to-day movements.

Money was tight, but Josephine was by now an expert economizer. She and Stanley took humble lodgings on the Boulevard Magenta, just three 'very tiny rooms' between them, but they were on a floor by themselves, so they at least enjoyed some quiet and could receive visitors with a degree of privacy. They sampled the dinner there on their first evening but did not much like it or the company. Soon they discovered a cosy café in Montmartre which 'only cost us two francs each and was so good!', and decided to dine there every day.[4] Josephine's only major expense in Paris was the hiring of a cab and driver for the week. Stanley found her a charming young coachman 'with a sweet face, and so quick and obliging', but who, unsurprisingly, couldn't 'make out the character and business of Miladi at all'.[5]

It was evidently a comfort to George that Stanley, now a twenty-year-old undergraduate, accompanied his mother, and Josephine certainly felt the need of a companion when crossing the Channel, at the very least. She confided her dread of such crossings to George: 'If I have *anyone* with me to give me stuff when at the last gasp, it gives me confidence'.[6] Curiously, any difficulties that might arise from Stanley's presence in Paris seem not to have been anticipated either by Josephine or by George, who presumed that his son would occupy himself with artistic study, and he wrote him out a list of the best works to be seen at the Louvre. George jokingly reminded Josephine to 'tell him not to do as the Parisians do while in Paris',[7] but Parisian vice was unavoidable: within a few days of their arrival, her 'dear innocent steady Stanley' was invited to a ball in a brothel which was in actuality an orgy, 'where people dance *nudé*, and where, Josephine was informed, one sees 'the brilliant *demi-monde* lending itself to every kind of degradation'.[8] She was thankful that her son was so alive to the traps laid for unsuspecting young men! In the evenings he would tell his mother of all he had seen and heard, and spoke of his disgust.

In fact, Stanley's innocence was as much at risk in his mother's company as in his solitary wanderings. Josephine does not seem to have realized at first how awkward it was for Catty when people came to their rooms to talk about her work, and it took several days before she acknowledged to her husband that he was too young to work with her. Indeed, she felt that Cat's presence, although he was loving and companionable, added to the burden of her anxieties. Companionable he was, nonetheless, and he did much to lift his mother's spirits. Josephine described a splendid dinner at the Montmartre café with Stanley and a friend ('*7 courses*, all for a few francs!!!'): 'The two boys were so merry over it, and made me laugh quite indecorously, it was a great relief. Catty's French to the waiters was so funny'.[9] Her only care was for their coachman, waiting outside the restaurant in the falling snow. The very least she could do, she felt, was to send out a glass of wine.

When M. Aimé Humbert first heard of Josephine's continental crusade he wrote to her blessing her for her courage but warned, 'You are about to confront not only the snows of winter, but the ice which binds so many hearts'.[10] It was, in actuality, the hardest winter for many decades. Josephine complained to Hatty that she was suffering greatly from the fog and the cold, which made 'the conflict with gigantic evil seem harder'.[11] She complained too of half-cold tea, uncarpeted rooms and ineffectual fires. At their first lodgings in Paris, she and Stanley resorted to bribery to get the maid to pile up the coal. When she heard this, Hatty wrote back by return of post of her fears for Josey's weak chest: 'I longed to be with you, that I might at least run about after you with spirit lamp and tea caddy, or muscat wine, cloves, and sugar, to cheer you'.[12]

It was a difficult task that Josephine had set herself. Her French was excellent, as was her Italian,[13] but to speak in public in a foreign language, and to conduct arguments, often specific not just to a country but to a region, demanded a good deal of careful preparation. She later confessed to the Wilsons that it was 'a daily struggle with difficulty', and any free hours were spent sitting in the cold, desperately looking up forgotten words in the dictionary and learning by heart the arguments she was to use, for fear that 'some blunder of my foreign tongue might provoke ridicule and laughter'.[14] At one meeting in Paris she had to conduct an argument so rapidly with an angry man in the audience that George Appia, an Italian pastor recently come to Paris, stood behind her chair and translated her replies sentence by sentence. It was only in writing to Hatty that Josephine could truly unburden herself: 'Going from city to city, tired and weary, always to meet with sharp opposition and cynicism, and ever new proofs of the vast and hideous oppression, is like running one's breast upon knife points, always beginning afresh before the last wound is healed'.[15]

The French system of regulation dated from the Napoleonic Code of Law and the title given to the special police, the Police des Moeurs, or Morals Police, was a misnomer: their business was to enforce the sanitary regulations by which prostitutes were obliged to abide. 'Morality', in the inverted values of this society, was a matter of physically clean prostitutes, disease free, 'safe' women. To Josephine's mind it was a system that falsified consciences.[16] 'Immoral' prostitutes were women who flouted the rules governing their appearance and manners in public, and even their hours, or more seriously, those who resisted regular examination by state-approved doctors. These women were, if caught, imprisoned. Brothels were only permitted to send one woman at a time on to the streets. In effect, prostitution had to be kept hidden.

The French position was to tolerate prostitution as an unfortunate necessity. It was accepted that men had a biological need that only prostitutes could service, and so a system of surveillance was thought necessary to examine the health of the women providing the service. Officially recognized prostitutes, known as *filles soumises*, were either attached to brothels, *maisons de tolérance*, and underwent a vaginal inspection weekly, or operated independently from their own apartments. The latter, known as *isolées*, were submitted to fortnightly examinations. All of these women were licensed by the government and 'inscribed' in the police records, which Josephine called the 'Book of Hell', and 'at once [were] made public property – a thing not a woman![17] They were provided with a ticket or *carte* listing the dates of their regular examinations with the doctor's stamp proving that they were clean. On the reverse of this *carte* prostitutes were reminded of the rules governing their appearance in public: they were, for example, required to be 'simply and decently clad'; they were forbidden to be on the streets or to work as prostitutes at all during daylight hours, or after 11 p.m.; they were not allowed to take up a station on the pavement, nor to show themselves in windows; and there were rules governing whom they could approach and how.[18]

The most significant threat to the whole system of regulation, and to the control of syphilis, was the number of unlicensed *insoumises*, that is, unsubjugated, unsubmissive prostitutes, or *clandestines*, those women who operated independently and who resisted inscription and, thereby, the hated examination. These were often women, many of them married, who took to prostitution seasonally when unable to find any other work. For them, the life of the *clandestine* was greatly preferred, even though they risked imprisonment and forcible registration if they were caught. Once they had been entered in the police register it was exceedingly difficult to persuade the authorities that they wished to reform, and have their names removed. Josephine was concerned that many women who were driven to temporary prostitution by economic circumstances were unable ever to escape their classification as prostitutes. Her foremost argument against regulation, though, was the sexual injustice that lay at its heart. Although the sexual contract required two willing partners, the state and its institutions did not recognize any criminality in the male client.

The regulations were enforced without much sympathy, and working people described to Josephine many abuses of the system of enrolment. Individual policemen told Josephine that rather than protect a girl from inscription, they regarded it as their duty to register any unmarried woman who was known, or suspected, to be sexually active, lest she 'become diseased and communicate the disease to *honest men* (I am quoting the very words spoken to me), to *honest men*'.[19]

Many of Josephine's objections to the French system, including the hypocritical intent merely to conceal the fact of prostitution, were shared by the English doctor, William Acton, who visited Paris in the late 1850s to gather material for his influential study, *Prostitution* (1858). Acton was a supporter of the Contagious Diseases Acts in England, yet he, too, observed at first hand that, 'Such a system appears better suited to heathen times, and to grate harshly on Christian civilisation'. He concluded, though, that 'it has, however, at least, the merit of being logical, and is, apart from its cruelty, in accordance with common sense. It sees . . . a vice incurable, irrepressible, and, therefore, seeks to regulate it'.[20] The result was that 'In London a man has prostitution thrust upon him; in Paris he has to go out of his way to look for it'.[21]

The episode which dominates Josephine's account of the Paris campaign in *Personal Reminiscences of a Great Crusade* is her interview with Charles Jerôme Lecour, Chief of the Police des Moeurs, a scene which will be repeated with Signor Vigliani, Minister of Justice and Police in Rome, and with the Procureur Général in Geneva. We read how Josephine, a solitary, unprotected, anonymous woman, entered M. Lecour's palatial headquarters on the banks of the Seine and walked past the marching guards, through the massive gateways and up the vast stone staircase, passing liveried servants and preoccupied officials, until she came to a door over which, in large gold letters, were the words: '"Arrestations, Services des Moeurs". I was faint and out of breath, and an old guard stared at me with curiosity as I gazed at those mendacious words . . . it so clearly and palpably means the "*Service de Debauche*".'[22]

Lecour kept her waiting in an ante-room for half an hour, and when he did finally admit her she had to sit quietly with a newspaper while he concluded two other interviews, one with an elderly man who was protesting in vain at his daughter's name being placed on the register. From behind her newspaper Josephine watched and listened. She found Lecour shallow, vain, verbose, his countenance 'repulsive', and likened him to 'a shallow actor, an acrobat, a clever stage-manager'. Yet this man, 'chattering and gesticulating like an ape', held in his hand 'the keys of heaven and hell, the power of life and death, for the women of Paris!'[23]

At last the great man was ready to receive her. By this time she was angry and stood before him, declining to sit. She told him who she was, and why she had come to Paris: 'He said he knew very well who I was. His manner became rather excited and uneasy. I continued all the time to look very steadily, but not rudely, at him'. Lecour talked more and more, as if to drown her with words, and she found it difficult to say a word in reply. So excited was Lecour that he admitted to Josephine that the number of cases of syphilis in Paris had actually increased under regulation, and was continuing to increase. Asked to explain why this was so, Lecour extraordinarily attributed it to the 'increasing "coquetry" of women'.[24] Refusing to listen to Josephine's talk of economic conditions, this 'barber's block' proceeded 'in a most disagreeable manner' to act out a seduction before her very eyes, in order to demonstrate how prostitutes preyed upon innocent and '*honest* men', as he insisted upon calling them. He gave Josephine a copy of his latest book on the subject in which, she observed, he 'appeared to regard every woman who is not under the immediate rule of some man as he would a volcano ready to burst forth under his feet'.[25] Incredibly, Lecour misinterpreted his lady visitor's unshakeable demeanour for one of pure unworldliness, and sexual ignorance. 'He seemed to think that I was an ignoramus.'

Yet Josephine was given every assistance in her investigations by Lecour. He provided her with a letter of introduction giving her *carte blanche* to see whatever she wanted in the St Lazare prison, which housed recalcitrant prostitutes, and added a postscript to the letter, asking 'that every facility should be given to the very honourable lady from England'. Josephine commented on the strange ways of Providence: 'Here was the very head of the much-hated Morals' Police himself sanctioning all I might wish to do with a great flourish, and full of vanity in the performance'.[26]

Josephine made her way, unaccompanied, to the gates of St Lazare prison. As she approached, a great black prison van overtook her, splashing through the melting snow, followed by an escort of armed gendarmes on horseback. It was a grim sight, and the crowds in the street instinctively fell back. The prison van was strongly secured and had no windows. To Josephine's mind, it looked like a hearse. The great prison gates swung open as if by magic and swallowed up the chilling vision. She wondered 'What powerful ruffians, what dangerous, strong-sinewed criminals' they were escorting to prison with this show of force. Only a few bewildered and helpless *girls* 'guilty of the crime of not ministering to impurity in accordance with official rules'. She exclaimed to herself: 'O manly, courageous Frenchmen! You cannot govern your own passions, but you can at least govern by physical force the poor women of your streets, and swagger to your hearts' content in your hour of triumph, as you proudly enter the prison gates with your trembling caged linnets'.[27]

Once the prison gates had again closed before her, Josephine was unsure how to gain admittance. The guards on duty pretended not to understand her, but she was persistent, and to get rid of her one nodded towards a small iron-barred door within the gate: 'Vous pouvez battre,' was all he said. 'Yes! I could "beat" no doubt,' she wrote, 'but my hand made no sound or impression at all against that heavy iron door.' It seemed typical of their work on the Continent, 'beating at the outside of a strong Bastille of misery and horror'.[28] Emboldened, she picked up a stone from the gutter and proceeded to beat on the door with that. It had the desired effect. She produced Lecour's letter and passed through the gates of St Lazare.

The deputy matron, a nun, took Josephine over the whole of the prison. The visit took hours, and yet Josephine found it impossible to write about what she had seen. The conditions at St Lazare had already converted one English doctor to the repeal movement at home. Dr Drysdale, formerly an apologist for the Contagious Diseases Acts, had gone to Paris in 1867 to study the French methods of containing disease. Speaking at a repeal meeting in March 1870, he described how he was 'horror-struck at the gloomy prison into which poor helpless women could be thrust without trial, to linger for months at the mandate of a low police functionary or medical inspector'.[29] Josephine left behind only one recorded scene, and, significantly, chose to write about only one type of Parisian prostitute – more of her 'caged linnets'. These were the women she saw in the recreation yard situated in the centre of the prison, where just a few square yards of blue sky were visible to the inmates who, in twos and threes, tramped though muddied slush in the freezing air. 'It was a sight to wring the heart of a woman, a mother! Most of them were very young, and some of them so comely, so frank, so erect and graceful, in spite of the ugly prison dress'. She was forbidden to speak or signal to them, impotent to console, although she longed to speak, and thought the inmates wanted it, too, 'for their steps slackened as they came round, and they paused when they got near me, with looks of kindness, or gentle curiosity. One knows enough of the heartless, artificial, or hardened women of Paris, but my memory recalls *these* who were the raw material, fresh from nature's hand'.[30]

In Paris, without any shame, gentlemen would describe to her the efficiency of licensed brothels. Josephine wrote to James Stansfeld, 'There is *no decency here*, but I try to conceal it and bear on for the sake of the work I have in hand. To think that I am a woman and that women are thus spoken of to my face.'[31] Some brothels she saw for herself. Minors were not permitted, and any child prostitutes were discreetly hidden when Josephine made her inspections. Yet she did visit, by the invitation of Lecour, a certain institution which housed hundreds of former child prostitutes, 'four hundred I think', little girls from the ages of five to eleven, some as young as Eva. Child prostitution had been excused to Josephine as a fact of life, because 'Our society is very corrupt, and men require *variety* in vice', and her female guide at the reformatory expected her to praise a system that kept such children off the streets. Instead, Josephine expressed her horror, asking, 'By what process of corruption have your men come to that they victimize these infants?'[32]

Despite the prominence given to such encounters in her published accounts, Josephine wrote proudly to Stansfeld of the extraordinary success of her mission which was far beyond anything she had hoped for: 'This is a fact, and I know you won't think me boasting if I say it is. It is God's work and not mine'.[33] It took her just half an hour to persuade Pastor Théodore Monod, who 'was not right on our question and had been bamboozled by doctors', and who promptly dropped to his knees in prayer! She was frankly bewildered by the sheer number of conversions. Many people sought her out at her lodgings, often following her late at night after meetings to offer their congratulations, attentions which she found burdensome, as she was sometimes 'choking' for a cup of tea. One memorable visitor was the chief commissionaire of 'Cook's' Hotel, a 'mahogany coloured' African from Tunis. Josephine explained the nature of her work to the man, who 'looked distressed and modest, and his eyes filled with tears'. Humbly he offered his services. In faltering English, he urged Josephine to work in particular amongst the young men of the city, giving her some addresses of friends in need of guidance. He told her that he had travelled the world, but had never encountered such flagrant and confirmed vice as in Paris. When they parted, he offered Josephine a blessing in the name of Jesus Christ. 'I looked at him rather hard, and he replied to my look, "Yes, that is the Master I serve"'.[34]

In Paris, Josephine found herself under constant surveillance by the police, and although her work was never interfered with, it was restricted to private interviews with individuals or drawing-room meetings in private homes. Public meetings were then outlawed by the government, as were all pamphlets of a political nature. This restriction meant that Josephine was unable to reach large numbers of the common people, whose daughters filled the police registers of licensed prostitutes. There was no way she could influence public opinion 'except privately from one to another'.[35] Josephine's ardent manner was, however, perfectly suited to such intimate gatherings, and, as she said, she won over many converts. At one such meeting the host whispered to her as she was leaving, '"we have lighted a fire tonight", and it seemed like it'.[36] She found not only audiences willing to listen to her arguments against regulation, but men and women eager to organize into societies that would be allied to the struggle for repeal in England.

She was able to make many useful and influential contacts through her drawing-room meetings, and some wholly unexpected conversions. Josephine had arranged to call at the home of Pastor Fisch of the National Reform Church, to whom she had written about her continental mission. The pastor was out, and his wife was holding an afternoon reception for ladies, 'rather a select little coterie'. Madame Fisch was in absolute ignorance of Josephine's name, and of the precise nature of her mission. Evidently the pastor had not thought Josephine's pamphlets fit reading for his wife. Despite receiving Josephine 'almost with the airs of a *grande dame*', she invited her to take a seat and introduce herself. Josephine explained, 'humbly but boldly (yes indeed!)' what her mission was in Paris, and 'Madame Fisch who had begun by listening with softly elevated eyebrows . . . evidently melted'.[37]

Any discomfort Josephine did experience was when speaking before aristocratic ladies, as at one drawing-room gathering, where 'the snow-white hands of these ladies and their exquisite complexions, made me feel like a working woman!'[38] But her refined audiences, and in particular the women, were drawn to Josephine and were moved to reassure her of their sympathy. One new ally was Madame André-Walther, who 'like a true woman' embraced the cause straight away. She also embraced Josephine, greeting her at their first meeting with 'a loving kiss with her arms round my neck'. This fascinating lady was 'quite a queen', Josephine observed, noting that 'all the best public men go to her to consult her about Public matters'. She supported Josephine in her work, and on one occasion insisted upon seating herself next to Josephine while she addressed a crowded mixed drawing-room meeting for three-quarters of an hour, after which she said, ' "donnez moi ta main, mon enfant", and she took my hand and kissed and patted it so lovingly. That was better than any applause'.[39]

The Butlers arranged to meet up in Paris in the third week of December. They were to spend Christmas and the New Year as guests of their friends the Closes, the Dean of Carlisle and his family, who had a holiday home at Cap d'Antibes. Georgie crossed the Channel with one of the Closes, and Charlie was to make his way over with cousin Fred Meuricoffre. This left George to travel alone. It is amusing to read Josephine's letters of advice to her husband, she, the experienced traveller! George was warned not to risk a cold by travelling at night, and to be on the alert for thieves: '*Don't get your pocket picked*, darling, in crossing the Channel. I wear all my money almost next to my skin!'[40] Josephine was more than ready to postpone her work, telling George, 'rest with you will be so sweet'. She had felt isolated, and she made it no secret that she would have been glad of James Stuart's intelligence and comradeship, 'for this work in Paris is certainly the most difficult I ever did'.[41]

At Antibes, with her happy family about her once more, she could for a time put the horrors of Paris behind her. The weather was warm enough to risk a Christmas Eve picnic by the sea, although Josephine confided in Hatty, 'The Closes don't seem to feel cold at all, and fires are not much approved of!'[42] Josephine would certainly have been encouraged to speak of her experiences by the Closes, who sympathized with her work. Later, when George returned to Liverpool for a conference there on 25 January, over which he presided, he read aloud a letter of support from the seventy-eight-year-old Dean. Dean Close had written, 'I believe these Acts to be based on error; I believe them to be cruel, immoral in every item, and unconstitutional'.[43]

From Antibes, Josephine travelled by the coastal train to Genoa to stay with her niece, Edie, for a few days, before she took up her work once more in Rome. This was to be the longest leg of her journey, but she now had George with her, and also James Stuart. In their concern for Josephine, they interspersed campaigning with sightseeing. Josephine was clearly delighted with the plan: 'My husband is so good a guide in Rome, that we need no other; he seems to know every stone of it, at first sight, and all about that stone, even to the disputes historians have had over it!'[44]

As in England, a system of regulation had been established in Italy very recently, and popular resistance to it, both by the people and by radical and liberal politicians, was more readily mobilized than in France. Several Italian states had already begun to experiment with the French model of regulation in the 1850s, and it was instituted in Piedmont by Prime Minister Cavour in February 1860, during the struggle for liberation from Austrian rule and for Italian unification. Gradually it became the law throughout the whole of Italy, Rome being the last to take it up, in 1870. The heavy-handed ways of the Italian Morals Police, the Polizia dei Costumi were greatly resented, as police harassment of innocent women became notorious: over a twenty-four-year period in Bologna, over 50 per cent of the women forcibly examined were neither prostitutes nor infected.[45] There was also the shame to be borne of having a female relative confined in the Italian equivalent of the lock hospital, the *sifilicomio*. Even worse, some communes lacking a special *sifilicomio* sent diseased prostitutes to be treated in the prison infirmary. In Florence, Josephine learned of the lengths to which peasants would go to protect their daughters from such humiliations: 'A peasant girl escaped from one of the Government houses of infamy and fled to her parents' cottage. She was followed by the police who endeavour to "reclaim", that is, *bring back to bondage*, every girl who escapes. The parents barricaded their house; a struggle followed, and blood was shed'.[46]

In Rome, Josephine had the support of a new apostle, a well-connected young politician named Giuseppe Nathan, the youngest of fourteen children born to a prominent Jewish banker and his Italian wife. Together with many of his brothers, Nathan had involved himself in local agitation against the system of regulation, and Josephine reported to Henry Wilson that they were 'a first rate family to have got on our side, for they are so esteemed in Italy'.[47] Like Josephine herself, Nathan had first turned to rescue work when made desolate by personal tragedy. His young English wife had died giving birth prematurely to a stillborn baby after they had been married for just one year. Josephine found him 'hardly able to speak, trembling and crushed'. She spoke to him gently yet firmly, telling him that there was still 'work for his broken heart . . . He looked upon it as a call from Heaven'.[48] Nathan's contact with individual prostitutes who were desperate to reform and to remove their names from the register drove his political condemnation of regulation, and convinced him to give up his life to the cause, a campaign that he took to the working people all over Italy. He was a mesmerizing speaker, 'full of Italian fire', as Josephine described him. For another six years he led the movement to repeal the Cavour Law but without success, only to die at the age of thirty-three in 1881.

With Nathan Josephine addressed meetings at which plans were made to form an association in Italy to continue the campaign for repeal, and Nathan was also able to arrange for Josephine audiences with sympathetic politicians, although she was equally determined to put her argument to unsympathetic officials. Just as she had faced Lecour in Paris, so Josephine sought out the Minister of Justice and Police in Rome, Signor Vigliani. His reception of Josephine was 'cold and scarcely courteous', and he proved just as intransigent as Lecour, speaking of prostitutes as '*not human* at all'; the fact that men made use of them was 'something to be regretted', but their needs had to be provided for. He said, 'A woman who has once lost chastity has lost every good quality. She has from that moment "*all the vices*". And so pleased did he seem with this theory that he smiled and repeated it,

"Once unchaste, she has *every vice*".'[49] Vigliani was clearly a man not to be touched by the arguments of an Englishwoman, however expertly they were put.

From Rome, Josephine went to stay for a week with Hatty in Naples, while George made his way home. It was terribly important to her that she was able to spend this little time with her sister who was just then not well enough to accompany Josephine in her work. While on her foreign travels Josephine would keep Hatty up to date with developments, and was often more candid in this correspondence than she was in her letters to her husband. Hatty was her strength. She had written to Josephine at midnight on 31 December, between the old year and the new, addressing her as 'Beloved of my soul', writing of Josephine as a crusader carrying 'the standard of the fiery cross over the sea and into another land', and thanking God who 'surrounds you with His shield'.[50] From Naples, Josephine wrote to George about how she longed to have Hatty, the companion of her childhood, associated with her in her work: 'You can imagine how sweet it is to me; and how full, and tender, and penetrating are her sympathy in, and her understanding of, the whole matter'.[51] Hatty was herself engaged in similar work: she assisted at her sister-in-law Sophie Meuricoffre's industrial home for widows and young women, she donated money to Catholic refuges (although they did not permit her, as a Protestant, to work with 'friendless girls'), and she founded a Sailors' Rest in Naples, which provided visiting British seamen with comfortable, orderly and free lodging. Three successive British consuls in Naples praised the Sailors' Rest for stamping out all disorderliness 'on the part of our sailors'.[52]

Josephine's visit to her sister seemed 'to stand out in a sort of glory', and on her return to Rome she wrote to her, 'I can hardly believe I am separated from you yet – the memory of your presence is so strong'. On the train, she had kept Vesuvius in sight from the carriage window for as long as she could, and then, 'about 4 I ate the cakes and drank the tea, and tried to make believe that I was once more having tea with you after one of our drives, but I felt chokey. My heart was too full'.[53]

Stuart had assisted Nathan in arranging some good meetings for Josephine. They had a busy time in Florence, where she met politicians, clergy, doctors and the press, working to stimulate the campaign against regulation. They then travelled on to Milan where they held a large conference that was well attended by politicians, and medical men. Astonishingly, one doctor, who made a long speech in favour of regulation, was so moved by the earnest discussion that followed that he publicly recanted.

Stopping briefly in Turin, Josephine crossed over into Switzerland. This was to be 'A hard ten days' work'. The diversity of civic authorities and of legislation in the individual cantons, as well as the prevailing respect for the police, created unlooked-for difficulties. She was at her most nervous in Geneva, where she seems to have been deeply affected by hearing horrible stories of the degradations suffered by the prostitutes here: 'Of all the places in the world it is the one (so far as I know) where the poor women (children many of them) are most *cruelly* treated'.[54] The streets were clear of vice. Prostitutes were 'Never seen – how beautiful! They are carefully *locked up*'. Brothels flourished and brothel-keepers, *tenaciers*, were powerful and influential. The moral atmosphere was cold, punitive and repressive. It seemed more than Josephine could bear: 'the anxiety, the strife, & above all the *horrors* revealed to me of Geneva vice'. An elderly baker named Wolff came to her hotel to tell her of 'his angel visits to these poor women': some he managed to rescue and hide from the police, but there were others whom he was unable to get to who had committed suicide, 'and *he*, elderly hard sinewed man, with not much sentiment about him, burst into tears'.[55]

Josephine felt that she spoke better in Switzerland than in France or in Italy. As she herself was well aware, her fragile appearance was always a powerful aid in converting the faithless, and her pallor was much commented on in the Swiss press. The Berne *Pilgrim* gave an account of the profound impression 'produced on those present when this pale and timid lady reproached strong men for the crime of trampling upon the weak'.[56] The fact that she was a woman braving this iniquitous subject caused a sensation in itself, yet Josephine proved to the Swiss that women could and should take a leading role in this crusade: 'These English women are remarkable; they unite with their great freedom a dignity seldom seen elsewhere'. A friend of Hatty's from Lausanne, M. Buscaret, echoed these sentiments, saying that everyone in Geneva and Lausanne was impressed by the nobility and compassionate spirit of her sister, and he could not help thinking of the phrase, 'When men cease to be men, it is needful that women should become men'.[57]

Not all were so impressed. Josephine described how the Procureur Général of Geneva at first refused to shake her hand after a bitter argument: 'At last he rose up . . . and said that it was after all too delicate a subject to discuss with a lady'. Josephine continued to hold out her hand, and was at last rewarded with the tips of his cold fingers. It was an effort for her, as she always felt as if she were 'untrue to my poor, fallen, enslaved sisters, shut up in the prison house of this system', when she shook hands with a supporter of regulation, but she tried to remember 'that the heart may be changed, and that the man may yet repent'.[58] The effort cost her more than she was prepared to admit in her published accounts. In a letter to Hatty, written at Neuchâtel on 5 February, she writes: 'Well, I was full of anger and rage . . . and I grew suddenly quite faint and without any pulse at all in the evening. I lay down flat on the sofa and presently Stuart came with a bottle of champagne (fancy for a teetotaller!) and *made* me drink a large glass full, and do you know it really revived me'.[59] Josephine needed more than champagne to revive her, though, and she began to feel '*dangerously* worn out'. She needed rest, but since the Swiss would not allow meetings of men and women together she had double the work: 'Stupids! . . . that makes *9 meetings* within one week. It is too hard work'.

Five days later, as she travelled from Berne to Lausanne on the last stage of her Swiss tour, Josephine began a letter to George: 'We have come to *vingt-cinq minutes d'arrête* (*sic*) somewhere, so I shall write to you. I am in one of those large, roomy railway carriages, with chairs and tables and a fireplace piled up with logs'.[60] She described her sleigh ride with Marie Humbert, down the Jura to the industrial centre, La Chaux de Fonds, where she had been invited to address a group of workers. To George, with his artistic eye, she wrote of the glories of the winter scene. To Hatty, she gave a rather more prosaic account of having to set off in the sleigh at six in the morning in order to meet 'the "Chemin de fer de Jura Industriel" which zigzags down the mountain, and I got here at 8½, half dead'.[61]

Josephine was nervous about her return to Paris. It gave her 'a kind of sickness and sinking of heart the moment I enter it'. She was also suffering physically, and she described to Hatty her terrible journey over the Jura, especially from Pontarlier down to Dijon, when it was so cold that it was painful to breathe the air, 'and even in the carriage, with foot warmers, and my large rug wrapped round me from head to foot, I could scarcely keep my senses. The cold made me fall asleep for very faintness'. It was almost midnight when she arrived at Dijon: 'My lips were so stiff I could hardly ask for what I wanted'.[62] Hatty was cautioned not to mention this adventure to George.

It is remarkable how Josephine seemed always to recover with renewed energy from the kind of physical and mental exhaustion she had experienced in Switzerland. During her return visit to Paris, in mid-February, Josephine began to feel that the city could in fact be moved. Meetings were perhaps better organized this time, and she was now joined by the capable Aimé Humbert who had a meeting with Lecour's predecessor, Mettetal, and argued the question with him for a gruelling two hours, after which Josephine found him with his head in his hands, 'groaning, "Ah! C'est une dure croisade".'[60] She sent him off to the Louvre to see a painting of 'St Marguerite, the patron saint of purity, trampling down the hideous dragon, and looking so calm and peaceful'.[63]

This time Josephine was heartened by the defiant spirit of the French women. Accounts of one memorable meeting were often reprinted. This was a mixed meeting, at which there was a large number of women, 'a queer sort of democratic mob (*not* working people, but people of our own class, rather)'.[64] Josephine was warmly received and listened to sympathetically, but when she had finished, an advocate took the floor and began to say 'all the untrue and cowardly things which men generally say when defending the enslavement of women'. He was not allowed to speak for long. The women began to hiss and then to shout him down, or, as Josephine put it, to 'yell': ' "Mais les hommes, les hommes?" Their indignation and right judgement, and the sharp questions they flung at him, delighted me'.[65] Josephine sat back in a corner, and thanked God silently.

The closing episode of Josephine's continental tour was organized by Pastor George Appia's sister, Louise, who took her to a church refuge for young girls who had been rescued from prostitution. It does not appear in any of Josephine's official accounts, but she described the visit to Hatty: 'She quite reminded me of you, darling, in her way of feeling and speaking, and in the *sweet* way in which she petted me, and made a ridiculous fuss'. Louise introduced Josephine to the girls, explained to them about her work, and then told them that she wanted them all to 'look at her – look at her well, that you may never forget, for perhaps you will never see her again. She is your *friend.* She is *our* friend. She has come to Paris to say that our bonds shall be broken – look at her and love her, my children'. The children then performed for Josephine a hymn about their bonds being broken, 'and at the end Miss Appia played a few wild *minor* notes on her harmonium, which seemed to express the sadness'.[66]

Josephine described this final visit to Paris to George on the eve of St Valentine's Day. She had received a 'sweet Valentine' from her eldest son ('Stupid lad'), but as for her husband, a perfunctory news-letter would have to suffice: 'This is my valentine to you, darling. Will you forward it to Edie. It will tell her that I got the Geneva statistics today which she sent. They are very useful – always the same story over again'.[67] It was now time for Josephine to leave Paris. The police, she said, were watchful, yet they had been unable to charge her with any illegal activity. She chuckled to herself as the express hurried her on to Calais: '"not caught this time" – I thought'.[68] George was to meet her at Calais, and see her over the Channel. They would stay overnight in London before catching the train back home to Liverpool. George had reported that he and the boys were missing her sorely, and 'were all in rather "doleful dumps" . . . but we agreed to "keep our pecker up"'.[69] When she got to London she went straight to bed with tea and hot water bottles at the Victoria Hotel. Yet she was determined to see both her university boys, and after only a few days' rest in Liverpool she set off to visit Stanley in Oxford, then on to Georgie in Cambridge, and then straight on to London for a repeal conference in early March.

Josephine wrote out detailed records of all her meetings abroad, and these she requested to be circulated amongst her family and close colleagues. Letters to George went back and forth between Tully and Edie or Hatty. These were often franker accounts than the versions which appear in her books *The New Abolitionists* (1876) and *Personal Reminiscences of a Great Crusade* (1896). The original account in a letter to Hatty of the Paris meeting in which the women shouted down the male advocate was thought too incendiary for colleagues at home, and she certainly didn't want it broadcast in the *Shield*. Josephine cautioned her sister, 'Don't let anyone see this note, darling, except *women* perhaps'.[70]

Given the involvement in these matters of women like Josephine Butler, it is easy to forget that the membership of women in the repeal movement continued to be a problematic issue. Josephine's one-woman mission to Europe inspired women whose lives were significantly more restricted than those of their British sisters, yet at home some still doubted whether it should be a woman's question at all. Such misgivings were referred to in a speech at the London meeting on 3 March at which Josephine made her first public appearance since her return home. Stevenson A. Blackwood remarked that

that very day he had heard concern expressed about the involvement of ladies in this question. He answered: 'It has been forced on them by a Parliament of men. (Hear, hear.)', but he also had some personal news for the doubters: 'I am thankful to say that my own wife has allowed her name to be enrolled amongst the Vice-Presidents of the NA – (Cheers) – and I trust that many more will follow her example and the example of the other ladies'.[71]

Josephine had to provide an account of her activities for the Quakers, who had helped finance her campaign, and she also kept a journal for Stansfeld which she posted in instalments, as letters, and which he was often asked to pass on to Fanny. These contained material which she could not make public, and which she could barely express in private. In the account written for Stansfeld which covered 20–22 December, Josephine referred to the child prostitution of Paris: she had heard of certain houses where 'these poor young slaves are . . . "farmed by the night", others *by the hour, night and day*', but she was unable in the letter to tell him all that she had seen and heard. It was 'too painful to dwell upon'.[72] This would become a familiar apology. The horrors she had heard of, or had actually witnessed, were too far removed from the experiences of her colleagues at home to be spoken of, certainly by a woman. The problem of utterance went deeper than this, however, and amounted to a fear of living through those experiences in the telling. Alluding briefly to the child prostitutes of Geneva, Josephine could only tell Hatty: 'I dare not recall what I have seen at Geneva, dear, not tonight, for I have no one to cry and moan to – and my heart would break'.[73]

Four days after her arrival in England, Josephine was already writing to Henry Wilson to propose an early '*friendly* conference' to discuss official plans for the founding of a European federation made up of local societies in all the countries she had visited, which would act as a sister movement to the repeal campaign at home. The various continental committees were anxious for suggestions and advice, and she wanted to send them 'a more *authoritative* note of encouragement . . . than a mere private letter from myself would be'.[74] She was firm that England would not always have to advise and direct that work, but that the organizations abroad wanted to be connected with the English movement at first, and needed all the 'moral support' they could give.[75] It was her intention that each country would, in time, be self-funding, although it was clear that Britain would have to bear the costs of publishing useful literature during the early stages.

At a conference of Friends at the Westminster Palace Hotel on 4 March, chaired by Stansfeld, Josephine, echoing Collingwood's York speech of 1874, warned the assembly to avoid insularity: 'I take blame to myself for having, to some extent, shared the idea that England was the only country in which any stern resistance has ever been made to this modern tyranny and immorality'.[76] In her private letters, too, she was having to make the same plea. To Joseph Edmondson, she wrote, 'I am convinced that we should be simply fools if we were to be contented with achieving our own repeal victory',[77] and she urged Wilson, never an enthusiast of the Federation, that 'in defeating "White Slavery" in England alone, we should be merely lopping off a branch of the poisonous tree, so to speak. We should still have the old parent tree, with its deep roots and strong trunk standing in neighbouring countries'.[78]

The inaugural meeting of the British, Continental and General Federation was held in Liverpool on 19 March 1875, with Stansfeld its appointed President, Josephine and Wilson as joint secretaries, and Stuart as Treasurer. It was agreed that the scope of the Federation was 'the abolition of female slavery and the elevation of public morality among men'. Foremost among its resolutions was the principle that 'all legal guarantees of personal liberty must be equal for the two sexes', and that 'the law must not provide or tolerate any official registration of prostitutes, or any official recognition of prostitution as the status of a social class'. It declared that 'no regulation of prostitution may exist'.[79]

It has been suggested that Josephine was unwilling or unable to devolve power, that, having conducted her mission to Europe virtually single-handed, she was slow to recognize that her new allies, men such as Aimé Humbert and Giuseppe Nathan, were better fitted to carry out the work of the Federation.[80] Yet Josephine's most pressing concerns on her return to Liverpool were precisely to acknowledge the independence of the Federation, and to create an official salaried appointment for Aimé Humbert, who devoted much of his free time to Federation business but could not afford to give up his £400 salary and work full time. Josephine believed that Humbert was uniquely qualified for such a position, and was increasingly irritated because men like Edmondson and Wilson were waiting for testimonials from abroad rather than simply trusting her judgement. She had been away for three months, travelling widely in France, Italy and Switzerland, investigating systems of state regulation, confronting its proponents, addressing countless public meetings, canvassing support, organizing repeal associations, and doing all this with the help of just a few chosen associates. At home she felt burdened by the slow work of committees. She was beginning to feel that it was a more exhausting business trying to defend her European mission to English colleagues than it had been to conduct the crusade itself.

10

Martyrs to the Cause

'Crying in the Wilderness'

BRITISH INTEREST WAS quickly diverted from Josephine's European Federation when, on the afternoon of Easter Sunday, 30 March 1875, the body of a thirty-six-year-old widow, Mrs Jane Percy, was discovered floating in the Basingstoke Canal. Mrs Percy was an actress who had complained publicly of harassment by the special police at Aldershot (one of the subjected districts). She had been accused by the special police of being a common prostitute, and had apparently drowned herself in the early hours of 30 March rather than sign the voluntary submission form. As soon as Josephine heard the news, she dispatched her most trusted agent, Mr Henry Bligh, to Aldershot. As an ex-soldier, Bligh was an excellent choice for investigating the case, and he had already had experience of working as a 'spy' for the repeal movement amongst soldiers in the subjected districts. Much of what we know about Mrs Percy comes from Bligh's accounts.

On the morning of Tuesday 1 April, the day of the inquest into Mrs Percy's death, Josephine took the train to Sheffield to confer with Henry Wilson and to urge him to join Bligh. Wilson travelled down to Aldershot the next day. There was no question of Josephine going in person. She had been unwell since her return from Paris, and on her arrival in Liverpool after her visit to Sheffield, Dr Carter kept her under observation for the next ten days. Josephine wrote to her niece Edith that she had not dared tell George how bad she was: 'I have such a painful cough, deep down, & spitting of blood, & am so tired, I can hardly hold up my head . . . I have been kept up with quinine & stimulants, & iodine rubbings & plasters, & everything one can think of. I hate wine, but have had to drink it to keep off actual blindness and fainting'.[1]

Josephine's personal involvement in the Percy case was limited to her care of Mrs Percy's daughter, Jenny. One of the reasons Josephine was not more obviously active in the case was, of course, her deep interest in developments abroad, as she followed the progress of the new European Federation. It was with exhilaration that she received news from Edith that Genoa was in ferment over the Percy case, and that the Italian press had gone wild about it: 'If we could only get *The Times* to report the Italian agitation! . . . It is like a sudden revolution!'[2]

On Josephine's return to England at the end of February, she had believed that the tide of support she had mustered throughout Europe would serve as an example and an inspiration to the various branches of the Abolition movement at home. Yet, when the first news of the Aldershot scandal broke, Josephine recognized that Mrs Percy's sensational death would do far more to publicize the cause and win them new members. Sir James Stansfeld declared publicly that in his opinion the Aldershot case 'marked the turning-point in this great agitation, and in this sacred cause',[3] and in the letter to Edith quoted above, Josephine wrote that Mrs Percy's 'dying appeal has sounded throughout England, and roused the country as no appeals of ours could do, & every newspaper records it'. In fact, three national newspapers carried leaders on the case (not, though, *The Times*), and Josephine rejoiced that the 'conspiracy of silence' in the press was broken at last. In Parliament, Lord Charles Beresford, who had drawn up a bill calling for the extension of the CD Acts to cover every seaport in the kingdom, saw that it would be unwise to attempt to introduce such a measure at this time and hastily withdrew it.

Mrs Percy, a professional singer and actress, had lived and worked in Aldershot for the past twenty years. Her husband, a writer of pantomimes and burlesques, had died a year earlier after a long illness, leaving Mrs Percy to bring up her daughter, sixteen-year-old Jenny, an actress and dancer, and two little boys of seven and four. In early March 1875, Mrs Percy was visited by a Metropolitan Police officer who seems to have had the Percy house under surveillance since Mr Percy's death. Both mother and daughter had apparently come to the notice of the special police, because they had been seen late at night in the company of different soldiers. This was probably true: they were often escorted home by soldiers, since they had no other male protector. Mrs Percy refused to attend an examination for syphilis and was subjected to an intimidating interrogation by Inspector Godfrey of the Metropolitan Police, who was alleged to have shaken his fist in her face and threatened that he would make her sign the voluntary submission paper, 'or drive her out of Aldershot': he 'seemed to take a hatred of her,' Jenny Percy told Josephine.[4]

The Percy case came to public notice when Mrs Percy wrote a remarkably articulate letter which appeared in the *Daily Telegraph* on 12 March 1875, giving an account of her persecution by the police, 'as the means of bringing to the notice of those persons who have thought it their duty to agitate for the repeal of the [Contagious Diseases] Acts, a proceeding which I cannot but stigmatize as a shameful and high-handed use of the power given to the police under its provisions', and saying that the possibility of submitting to an examination at the lock hospital 'would have completely disgraced me in the eyes of all my acquaintances'.[5]

The police continued to harass Mrs Percy, making it impossible for her to find employment as a performer, so that she was in great distress about how to provide for her children. On the afternoon of Sunday, 30 March her corpse was discovered. An undoubtedly flawed inquest reached the verdict of 'death by drowning', a verdict which seems to have been governed by police anxieties that a verdict of suicide would lead to criticism of their methods.

Mrs Percy's was not, perhaps, a wholly uncontroversial case for the National Association to become involved with, and Josephine was not entirely free of ambivalent feelings about her. However, there was never any suggestion that Mrs Percy *was* a 'common prostitute', and there were several testimonies to her respectability and good character. It has been said that 'the case was worked for all it was worth' by the NA,[6] and Josephine's privately stated opinion to her niece, Edith, that 'Every good cause deserves martyrs' reads badly when taken out of context. She regarded it as 'a noble act of [the] mother to drown herself rather than be forced into infamy, and this poor woman's death will, I believe, be a means . . . of shaking the system more than anything we can do'.[7] All parties, including the Association, realized that it was most necessary to get Jenny Percy far away from Aldershot, and far away from police interference. Josephine invited Jenny to come to her house in Liverpool until a situation could be found for her, and George offered to stand *in loco parentis*. However, Josephine made it very clear to Wilson that in offering a temporary home to Jenny, 'I do it simply as a private person, not for the Association'.[8] Josephine arranged for some regular schooling for Jenny,[9] but Jenny liked to carry out errands for her mistress, running about and 'chattering immensely', going to the post and waiting on Josephine: 'she *prefers* this, & waits rather nicely'.[10] Eventually, Josephine found her a good situation as a domestic servant in Liverpool.

The transcription Josephine provided of Jenny Percy's account of the persecution of her mother and herself by the police is perhaps her most significant contribution to the Percy case. Jenny's statement gave a full account of the irregular conduct of Inspector Godfrey, as well as a convincing and highly moving description of her mother's despair.

> At the different places where she acted, or stayed, she found a warning had been sent beforehand, that she was a bad character . . . She always had Inspector Godfrey's face before her, and his threat on her mind, but she *spoke very little* to me about it. She seemed as if she could not bear to speak of it; but she did tell me that she could never be the same person again . . . She told me that she would choose death rather than do as Inspector Godfrey wished her to do. I would indeed, rather die than go through THAT.[11]

Even though this transcription does seem to reproduce the authentic voice of the sixteen-year-old girl, certain of Jenny's statements make her sound like a dyed-in-the-wool Abolitionist. Towards the end of the interview, Jenny not only criticized the Acts but gave a rallying cry on behalf of the repeal movement: 'But what a *law* this is. I could never have believed there was such a law; surely everybody ought to fight against it'.[12] Jenny also took the Abolitionist line on regulated prostitution: that registration *makes* prostitutes. In her final statement, she told Josephine,

> No girl can live in Aldershot; they *won't leave you alone*. Mamma told me she knew several girls who were as good as the best in the land, and who were forced to go to the Lock Hospital, and who are now amongst the most wicked of the bad characters at Aldershot, and they tell you themselves they were forced into it, and now they care for nothing.

The Percy case was invaluable to the repeal movement for increasing awareness of the way the Contagious Diseases Acts were enforced. The National Association held two 'Indignation' meetings in May 1875, at the second of which George Butler read out Jenny

Percy's statement. A 'Percy Fund' was raised, ostensibly for the relief of the orphan children, but a greater proportion of the money was used for Association business – for pamphlets, advertisements and circulars; money was rather grudgingly eked out to the young Percys.

'Mrs Percy's case certainly has roused the people,' Josephine remarked to Henry Wilson.[13] In Liverpool on 8 April a meeting of working men was announced as 'An Inquest upon an Inquest'. With dramatic flourish, Henry Bligh invited the five hundred assembled working men and women in the Queen's Hall, Birkenhead, to throw their offerings to the Percy fund upon the stage. £1 6*s.* 8*d.* was collected that night.[14]

Josephine became almost jealous of the furore over the Percy case, since the scandal at home distracted Association members from the mounting calls for assistance in France and Italy. When asked by Stansfeld to organize the collection of subscriptions to the Percy fund from all the 'baby' foreign committees, as she styled them, committees which had not yet begun to raise any money for *themselves*, she felt he was forgetting that the Italians had suicides of their own. In the end, she sent a total of £8 to the Percy fund, in the name of committees in Paris and Switzerland, '*all out of my own pocket* to satisfy Mr Stansfeld'.[15]

Earlier in 1875, Sir Harcourt Johnstone had introduced a bill to the House of Commons for the unconditional repeal of the CD Acts. Its second reading took place on 23 June in an atmosphere greatly influenced by the aftermath of Mrs Percy's suicide. To a House dominated by the Conservatives, Johnstone argued that 'it was no business of the state to provide clean sin for the people',[16] but by far the most influential contribution to the debate came from Colonel Claude Alexander, MP, who had been asked by the NA to investigate the circumstances of Mrs Percy's death. His findings, influenced by spurious information about Mrs Percy's character and contrary to the findings of the inquest on her death, were not at all what the National Association wanted to hear. The repeal motion was heavily defeated.

There was a danger that Josephine would, after Mrs Percy, be the second English martyr of the Contagious Diseases Acts. By the middle of May 1875, even though she had undertaken to receive Jenny Percy at Liverpool, Josephine confessed to the Wilsons that things were going badly wrong:

> I am losing my head. I never had sudden faintness & giddiness. I am trying to work less, but all these different languages bother me. Would you kindly return me a *copy* of my last accounts sent to you – some items in my book here have got blurred – like my own head. Forgive me if I make horrible mistakes. I am really frightened. I address all my letters wrong now![17]

She was experiencing palpitations and at times lost her sight and her hearing. Dr Carter ordered absolute retirement. She was not even to *open* letters. It was a horrifying prospect. She had been fully involved in the work of the Federation, and, impatient with the *Shield*, she had declared that she would launch her own Federation journal.

Henry Wilson, the Sheffield industrialist, and his wife Charlotte were the only people with the authority to carry on her work, and yet they were hardly the most enthusiastic over developments abroad: 'I am filled night & day with terror – among the worst terrors one is that all my friends will blame me for dragging them into this foreign work'.[18] It was arranged that Nathan would send Wilson weekly bulletins from Italy, and she asked only that Wilson enter summaries in her 'news book'. He need not actually write to any foreigners! Josephine was not to be left unattended and James Stuart came to stay to give what comfort he could. He reported from the sick-room on her progress, saying that he was making her do nothing. He made sure all her requests were met, the very first being for 'a fat book' the Wilsons had about the struggle against slavery, which Stuart promised to read to her. She wanted to know how the Abolitionists could bear having to see the slaves suffering for so long 'while they were not strong enough yet to relieve them'.[19]

Although Josephine was supposed to dictate any communications she wanted to send, an occasional memo in pencil did find its way to Charlotte Wilson. One asked for her colleague's prayers:

> for there are promises in the Bible to Prayer & I do feel my case very precarious. I may go off some day to the surprise of all. To-day no restorative, quinine, brandy, ether. *None* have been able to raise me above fainting point & my head is stunned. I long to be restored for the sake of my beloved outcasts whom few love as I love them. Perhaps God will hear the united prayers of his people. I would serve him with a more simple heart, if I were restored by his Mercy.[20]

Upon receiving this fragment of a letter, Mrs Wilson left Sheffield on the first train 'to see if she might nurse dear Mrs B.', and Henry Wilson sent out a circular to Josephine's friends informing them of her critical condition and quoting freely from her letter.[21]

It is important to seek to understand what lay behind this breakdown. At different times in her life, Josephine was prostrated by illnesses which seem to have had a nervous or psychological cause, the illness which led to their leaving Oxford, for example, or the suffering which followed her correspondence with Frederick Harrison, which was an earlier instance of how 'my spirit can be darkened' until 'my bodily sight is darkened too'.[22]

Her breakdown of 1875 seems to have been of a similar kind, but more serious. It may have been caused by her failure to persuade the English repeal movement of the importance of her continental work. Her politics of *inclusion*, her embracing of sexes, classes, cultures and nationalities, was thwarted from within the movement: hence her complaint that hundreds of foreign letters were reaching her eyes only, and her impatient desire to set up her own journal from her own home. Her illness appears to have been the outcome of her anguish about the sufferings of European women. This becomes clear in a letter to Joseph Edmondson, written a year after the onset of her breakdown, in reaction to his scepticism about her reports of medical outrages on women in France and Italy:

> Nothing of this kind surprises me in the least. What *does* surprise me is that persons like yourself should, at this period of our agitation, think such outrages 'almost incredible' . . . *It is well to be sceptical.* But bye & bye, let me assure you, you will have to hear & have *proved* to you, *worse than these outrages.* Look back & see whether any horrors I have told you of the system have not been more than realized by experience. I have *never* exaggerated, but if I were to tell you now what I saw in Paris, & what was the nature of things which were the real cause of my breaking down, you would *not believe me* . . . I have determined long ago to hide down in my own heart *what I know* because if I spoke of it, you would all say '*prove it*' . . . It *will* all come to light, but be prepared for worse & worse.[23]

Significantly, at the time of her breakdown, Josephine was proofreading the first major pamphlet she produced for Europe. It was written in French, drawing on a number of speeches she made on her continental tour in the winter of 1874–5, and was later appropriately entitled, *The Voice of One Crying in the Wilderness.* With George's support, Josephine decided to publish it 'simply as the utterance of a woman'.[24] It was quickly translated into other

European languages, the Italian edition by Giuseppe Nathan, but was not translated into English or published in England until 1913, seven years after Josephine's death.[25] The *Voice* is certainly a powerful voice, unorthodox, radical, and decidedly a woman's. She begins with 'two words from the mouth of a woman, speaking in the name of all women'.

> And these two words are – We rebel! I grant that this is not the language of science; it is not the formula of statistics or of hygienic deduction; no – it is simply the outburst of that condemnation which has been kept voiceless through centuries . . .; it is the protest of all womanhood, a cry of horror, an appeal to justice.[26]

Josephine comes as the saviour of 'Oppressed women', who 'have needed to find this voice in one of their own sex. She is here, and she comes to proclaim uprising and deliverance'. She comes as a female Christ: 'The degradation of these poor unhappy women is not degradation for them alone; it is a blow to the dignity of every virtuous woman too, it is a dishonour done *to me* . . . "Inasmuch as ye have done it unto one of the least of these my brethren, ye have done it unto me".'[27] Josephine faced her critics stoically: 'I care little that men accuse me . . . of mere sentiment, and of carrying away my hearers by feeling rather than by facts and logic. Even while they are saying this, they read my words, and they are made uncomfortable!'

The repeal movement could not afford to lose Josephine. Margaret Tanner, the LNA Treasurer, told Wilson that 'the bare thought of her being ill paralyses some of our workers who almost exist by her inspiration'.[28] Josephine's value was also recognized by Jane Ord, who wrote to Mrs Wilson that her life was precious to them all, especially 'to those poor outcasts for whose sake she wishes to live'.[29] Eliza McLaren, writing from Stirling, expressed her faith that God would 'graciously restore our leader to us',[30] while Edmondson felt that 'if she were given to us in answer to our prayers we must cherish the precious gift', and heartily concurred with the Wilsons' idea of repeating the present of money given to the Butlers two summers ago. He and his wife had had the same idea, and offered £10, 'as before'.[31]

With the gift of money from their friends, George again hired a carriage so that Josephine could take the daily drives Dr Carter recommended. She was gradually recovering, and Dr Carter was able to comfort Charlotte Wilson with news of Josephine's steady progress: she was still sleeping,with the help of opiates, but was no longer nauseous, and could take nourishment. He told her that 'so much depends on the feelings in her condition', and warned, 'I do not entertain much fear of *complete recovery*. But she must never again be subject to the fearful mental and physical strain which she has had to endure now for 6 years'.[32] George sent a rare bulletin to Wilson at the end of May, assuring him of his wife's improvement: 'Just now she is out gardening, it being still rather cold for driving'.[33] Josephine was herself able to write to the Wilsons a week later to say that she was 'much stronger & more hopeful so long as I sit in the garden, eat, sleep, & am a cumberer of the ground'. She was prompted to write to express her thanks for the gift of money, saying that she was so touched that she could hardly help crying, and doubting whether she was worth saving: 'If I come out of this with a weak intellect for instance.'[34]

Even though James Stuart stressed to the Wilsons that Josephine must feel free from all sense of responsibility for the movement, her foreign mission continued to preoccupy her. As well as proof-reading *The Voice of One Crying in the Wilderness*, a postscript to a letter Stuart wrote to Wilson pointing out his ignorance of regulation in Europe, was clearly dictated by Josephine; and Stuart would press the Wilsons, daily, for cheering news of the cause, because 'Mrs B. likes getting bits of news'.[35] She seems also to have been checking up on Wilson's activity in Federation matters, asking for translations of letters to foreign ladies' committees, herself sending a pencilled memo, quite a scribble, to Charlotte Wilson a few days later, asking, 'O *have* you got my Federation circulars done? *Please* let me have some . . .'[36]

At the same time that Josephine was labouring to persuade her closest colleagues of the importance of the European Federation, she was called upon to defend the setting up of a separate branch of the repeal movement for working men. While she was abroad in the winter of 1874–75, Dr Carter, together with her Liverpool agent, William Burgess, had organized a number of meetings for the working men of Liverpool, and on 23 February, after a crowded meeting at the St James's Temperance Hall, it was decided that the Working Men's National League (WMNL) should be formed. Its leader was to be a local basket-weaver named Edmund Jones, who had been converted to the cause after hearing Josephine address a meeting in St George's Hall two years earlier.

Henry Wilson reacted to the news with consternation, rather

inconsistently both resentful that the new League would need subsidies from the established repeal organizations and alarmed at the independent character of the League. He had never liked Burgess, but to Wilson Burgess was merely an agent in this affair. He seems to have written to Josephine, accusing her of having encouraged the working men, and demanding that she do all in her powers to dismantle the League. As Jones's paper, the *National League Journal*, remarked in its first issue, 1 August 1875, 'The wonder is that the town which has the honour of claiming Mrs Butler as a resident should have been so long without such an organization'.[37] In what is clearly a reply to the letter from Wilson, Josephine told him that the Working Men's National League had already been formed when she returned from abroad, and that she was 'only too thankful to see the working men moving without being *pushed* by people above them'.[38]

Since Josephine's first public speech on the question of repeal to an audience of working men at Crewe, she had encouraged meetings amongst the working people throughout the country, and in Liverpool had gathered around her a number of intelligent working-class agents. She often expressed a preference for her working-class allies. At an open-air meeting in Plymouth in September 1872, she was shivering on a hay-cart, lit by four torches held over her head so that she could be seen by the crowd, when a working man 'took off his rough coat, & climbed up on the cart side & put it tenderly over my shoulders'.[39] She was treated with similar delicacy by her fellow speakers, one of whom was a George Mitchell 'who could not read till he was 20'. She wrote to Anna Priestman: 'I felt much more at home in the cart with Mitchell than on the platform with Lord Napier & Sir J. D. Coleridge'.[40]

Georgie and Stanley were away at university when Josephine became ill, each at one of their father's old colleges: Georgie went up to Trinity College, Cambridge in 1872, and Stanley to Exeter College, Oxford a year later. The strain of their mother's public life had also begun to tell on them. Georgie appears to have become jealous of his mother's public career. In a letter which perhaps dates from Josephine's seeing him off when he first went up to Cambridge, Georgie begged his mother to have a private set of photographs taken for the family's use, as opposed to the official set that was for circulation among abolition workers. What he wanted was a photograph 'where you had your

1. Hannah Grey. 'We owed much to our dear mother, who was very firm in requiring from us that whatever we did should be thoroughly done'

2. John Grey. 'In daily intercourse, his truth, purity, and nobility of mind shone out in all he said, and still more in what he did'

3. Watercolour sketch of Josephine Grey, painted by her mother in 1844

4. The ruins of Radcliffe Castle in the grounds of Dilston Hall. 'Our home at Dilston was a very beautiful one . . . It was a place where one could glide out of a lower window, and be hidden in a moment, plunging straight among wild wood paths'

5. (*left*) Fanny Grey: Fanny assisted Josephine with her rescue work in Liverpool and was one of the original members of the Ladies' National Association; 6. (*right*) Hatty Grey and her husband, Tell Meuricoffre. Hatty was her best loved sister: 'She is just the same size and everything as myself. People will think there are two Mrs B.s!'

7. (*left*) Emily Grey and her second husband, Jasper Bolton. Emily was one of the first signatories of 'The Ladies' Appeal and Protest' and was consistent in her support for Josephine's work; 8. (*right*) Edith Leupold, the daughter of Josephine's eldest sister, Eliza. Edith lived in Genoa and was actively involved in anti-regulation agitation in Italy

9. George Butler. George's vision of marriage was 'namely, a perfectly equal union, with absolute freedom on both sides for personal initiative in thought and action'

10. Portrait of Josephine Grey, by George Richmond, June 1851, six months before her marriage to George Butler. Richmond's portrait fits exactly Hatty's description of her sister at this time: 'Josey looks so pretty just now. She gets a kind of rich glowing colour, and her eyes look lustrous, with light dancing in them'

11. View of 'The High', Oxford. 'I had come from a large family circle and from free country life to a University town – a society of celibates, with little or no leaven of family life'

12. Marble bust of Josephine, by Alexander Munro, 1855. 'Every instinct of womanhood within me was already in revolt against certain accepted theories in Society'

13. Letter from Josephine to her Butler brothers-in-law, December 1853 (on the anniversary of Georgie's christening): 'Hatty is so kind to my little chap, & gives him long lectures, wh he listens to, looking up in her face all the time'

14. Cartoon of George and Josephine leaving Oxford, by Hatty Meuricoffre, 1856

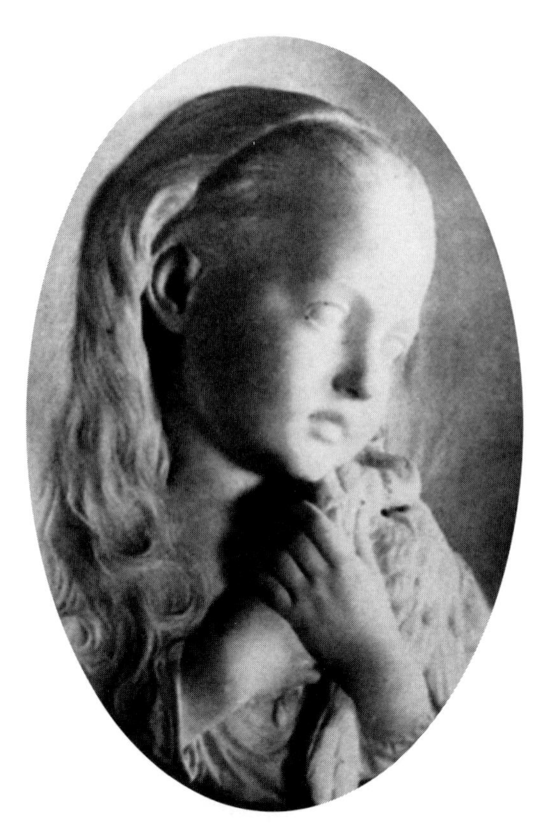

15. Marble bas relief of Eva Butler, by Alexander Munro, 1864. 'Never can I lose that memory – the fall, the sudden cry, and then the silence! . . . Would to God that I had died that death for her!'

16. Charles Butler, *c.* 1864. Charlie was the sole witness to his sister's death. Josephine wrote that it was 'a terrible shock to his poor little nerves and brain . . . in very early photographs done of him, one sees what a sad expression he had – not natural to a child'

17. Josephine Butler, 1869. Queen Victoria's son-in-law, Prince Leopold, wrote that Josephine was 'by many people considered the most beautiful woman in the world, she is very clever & a great speaker; but she has done herself a great deal of harm by violently taking up a subject which had better be left alone, by ladies at any rate'

18. (*left*) James Stuart. Nicknamed 'Thick' by the Butler boys, Stuart became a firm friend of the family. Josephine, who regarded him as 'a son or a brother', was 'most thankful for Thick's brains' in her campaigns; 19. (*right*) James Stansfield. Stansfield sacrificed his political career to lead the parliamentary campaign for the repeal of the Contagious Diseases Acts. 'It would be difficult to exaggerate the value of such services to our cause,' wrote Josephine

20. (*left*) Henry J. Wilson. A Sheffield industrialist, Wilson proved himself a fearless agitator for the Cause, and, together with Josephine (whom he regarded as 'my chief'), he directed the campaign in the North of England; 21. (*right*) Charlotte Wilson. As well as being a trusted colleague, Charlotte quickly became a close friend and confidante of Josephine's. They first worked together at the Pontefract Election, in 1872, when they braved cayenne pepper, smoking straw and the insults of a hired mob

22. Josephine Butler addressing a public meeting: 'It was a new thing, and, withal, a startling one at that time for men to hear a political address delivered by a woman . . . It was surprising and refreshing to men to find themselves spell-bound by the passionate eloquence of a gentle sweet-voiced woman' (Benjamin Scott)

23. Handbill from the Pontefract Election, August 1872

It appears from the Handbills issued by MR. CHILDERS this morning, that

HE IS AFRAID TO MEET US,

And answer our questions on the Contagious Diseases Acts.

THEREFORE

MRS. BUTLER

REQUESTS THE

WOMEN OF PONTEFRACT

TO MEET HER AT THE

LARGE ROOM, IN SOUTHGATE,

(USED BY MR. JOHNSON AS A SPINNING ROOM),

THIS EVENING AT SEVEN O'CLOCK.

MRS. BUTLER will shew that the Bill of which MR. CHILDERS says he is now a supporter, while pretending to Repeal the "Contagious Diseases Acts" is an extension of their principle to the whole country.

MRS. BUTLER will shew that MR. CHILDERS belongs to a Government which has extended these Acts not only to this Country but to the Colonies and Dependencies of the British Empire.

JOSEPHINE E. BUTLER, Hon. Sec. of the Ladies' National Association.

24. The Police des Moeurs making an arrest in Paris. 'O manly, courageous Frenchmen!' wrote Josephine. 'You cannot govern your own passions, but you can at least govern by physical force the poor women of your streets'

25. Delegates attending the 1877 Federation Congress in Geneva. *Standing*: Aimé Humbert (*second from left*), James Stuart (*fourth from left*), Georgie Butler (*first from right*); *sitting*: Margaret Tanner (*first from left*), Josephine Butler (*third from left*), with George standing behind her

26. 'The Startling Adventures of a Young Lady who was Drugged and Abducted', from *The Day's Doings*, 1871

27. W.T. Stead's Christmas card from Holloway Prison

28. The Ladies' Gallery, House of Commons. Josephine campaigned for women to be allowed to listen to debates on the Contagious Diseases Acts from the Ladies' Gallery, arguing that 'if men were so bad as to enact such an outrage on women, they must endure to answer for their act face to face with us'. It was from the Ladies' Gallery that Josephine witnessed the success of Sir James Stansfield's motion, on 20 April 1883, that 'This House disapproves of the compulsory examination of women under the CD Acts'

29. Josephine in widow's weeds, Elliott & Fry, *c.* 1890. One friend commented, 'The Warrior Spirit has been greatly revived in her'

30. Butler family photograph, Ewart Park, Northumberland, Christmas 1897. *From left to right:* Stanley Butler, Mia holding baby Hetha, Charles Butler, Rhoda (*standing*), Margaret, Bobby (*sitting on floor*), his sister Josephine, Georgie Butler (*standing*) and Josephine Butler

31. Josephine writing *Personal Reminiscences of a Great Crusade*. Josephine addressed this photograph to her granddaughter, Josephine: 'Granny thinking what she is going to write in her Book'

natural expression; not one where you look as if you knew you were in a photographer's shop':

> You may think this is sentimental, but indeed it is the only way in which I can express it. When I look on your dear face, it calms me and makes me more contented . . . [Will you] wear exactly the same clothes and hat as when I was with you at Euston Station (with your black thing on over your dress) and get photographed like that . . . Because you looked so dear and nice, and I want to remember you like it. Can you get the photographer to give you a cup of tea before he takes you, to make you feel comfortable and at home, and will the Cat go with you? Don't let your hat come down over your forehead, but keep it back; I want to see your hair . . . I may not get so much out of spirits again, but if I ever should, I would look at your photograph and think of you, not as an agitator or anything great and grand, but as *my very own dear mother*.[41]

His brother Charles had been sent to a new school at Clifton in the autumn of 1874. It had been difficult for Josephine to send 'our last son' away, but it was felt that his health would benefit from the south-western climate.[42] It was at Clifton that his mother recuperated after her earlier breakdown in health in 1856, and Charlie had been born there. He had succeeded Stanley as editor of the Liverpool College school magazine, but he had had to give this up earlier that year because he was 'so very delicate just now'; Josephine described him as looking like 'a languid hop-pole, with a creole's complexion, & a melancholy, unchildlike smile. Poor lad, my heart aches to look at him'.[43] He had to sit an entrance exam for Clifton in late September 1874, and Josephine begged the Priestmans to take him in on his first night, and to invite him over for tea now and then: 'My husband and I will now be left *quite* alone, & we feel rather desolate . . . Don't think me too weak if I ask you to send me the enclosed telegram as soon as Charlie arrives. You need not tell *him*'.[44] She also enclosed a '*sweet* photograph of our 2 eldest sons, at Oxford and Cambridge'.

Charlie seems to have confirmed Josephine's belief that her son was too delicate for public school, although it is probable that his ill health was related to anxieties about his mother. He began to suffer from fainting fits, just like Josephine, and was ordered home. Josephine wrote to Miss Priestman to ask if she knew anyone suitable to accompany Charlie on the train. She could not of course go herself, and George was overwhelmed with exams and preparations for the school prize-giving: 'he *must* travel *lying down*, for he has a bad abscess and is very weak: he has suffered great pain . . . *I dare not* let Charles travel alone'.[45] Miss Priestman went herself to the school to enquire about travelling arrangements, but had an unfortunate interview with the headmaster, who 'blew up' poor Charlie because the school doctor had not informed him that the boy needed to be sent home, *and* evidently had a sharp word or two for Miss Priestman, as Mrs Butler's representative. 'Percival *hates* me,' explained Josephine, 'and it seems he let it out in his anger – what can you expect of a man who loves the *Acts*?'[46]

Once home, Charlie made an immediate recovery. On 19 June, George was able to take Josephine and the boys down to Derwent Water for a week's holiday, and the family then stayed in Keswick while George left for London on business. Josephine wrote to the Wilsons of her feelings of isolation: 'I suffer so deeply in mind – no one to consult with – the debate [of Harcourt Johnstone's Repeal Bill] tried me more than any illness – the *blasphemy* . . . to see those men pleading for wickedness in such an exalted tone & in the name of Jesus! Please friends, pray for me. I am ill, and darkness sometimes comes'.[47] Back home in Liverpool, she made plans for a summer holiday abroad using the money they had been given: 'I think George & I will *dawdle* up the Rhine & go somewhere in Switzerland where we can live in a pension – not a hotel'.[48] That very afternoon, however, these plans were abandoned after a visit to the bank manager: they found so little in their account that they decided to go instead to Northumberland. Her illness and Charlie's had been heavy expenses, what with bills for the chemist and the doctor and for the drives she had been ordered to take. The morning after their appointment at the bank, 'George, I observed, did not eat a bite of breakfast'.[49]

Writing from the Rothbury Hotel, roughly half-way between Dilston and Milfield, on 25 July 1875, Josephine assured the Wilsons that she was just as happy to be in her native country as to go abroad. George had to begin work again on 5 August, but Josephine could not yet face returning to Liverpool because home was 'crowded with associations of work, & as soon as people know I have got home, they call all day, & claims thicken and gather as you know'.[50] The Butlers left for home on 4 August, but, after just a fortnight, Josephine was off on her third holiday, to stay at the Chatsworth Hotel, in Edensor, Derbyshire, where she was attended both by James Stuart who continued to act as her amanuensis, and by her brother-in-law, Arthur Butler, who, she said, was 'struck with pity for my delicate looks'. He put his pony carriage at her disposal, and proved a very pleasant companion.[51] George joined them at weekends.

Judging from her depleted correspondence, Josephine had a quiet autumn. However, the exertion of delivering the annual report to an LNA meeting at Chatham, on 18 October, led to a high fever and the loss of her voice. George made the uncharacteristic move of forbidding his wife to attend any more ladies' meetings and confining her to the house. Josephine, in a rather flurried letter, apologized for any hasty words of George's to Miss Priestman: 'He naturally felt that if I was to pay with such suffering for every effort I now make, he must use his influence to keep me at home'.[52] She was permitted to attend the NCL annual meeting at Sheffield in mid-November, and stayed overnight with the Wilsons, but she warned them not to expect a single speech from her: she could say no more than '(literally) a *few* words, for I cough even after a brief conversation'. The Wilsons were forewarned about her invalid's trappings, her 'medicines & cordials & mustard poultices', and she hoped it would not trouble them to see her 'medicine claret on the table'.[53]

In fact, Josephine did manage to address two separate women's meetings, one immediately after the other. The Albert Hall in Sheffield could not contain the extraordinary numbers of women who had come to see her, and so, having delivered an inspiring speech on womanly unity, she slipped out to the nearby Nether Chapel to address the remaining women. She also spoke at the Northern Counties League evening meeting in the Albert Hall, presided over by George, at which Mrs Butler 'was received with loud and prolonged cheering'. A full report of this speech in the *Shield* gives us a flavour of her skills as a public speaker. Making the audience laugh with jokes about the weakness of her voice, she went on to speak of the cowardice of the Acts, imposed by the rich upon the poor. She was frequently answered by calls of affirmation from the assembly, and indeed, would often invite such responses: '"Working men", cried Mrs Butler, "can you bear the thought of it?" ("Never".) "If prostitution is a necessity, I call upon Mr Cave, Colonel Alexander, and Mr Gathorne Hardy each to contribute a daughter". (Tremendous cheering.)'.[54]

When Charlie went up to Trinity College, Cambridge he seems to have been concerned that his mother would again work herself too hard and make herself ill without her son at hand to check her. He wrote her a mock-serious letter from Cambridge begging her to put her family before her public duties, if she felt unwell:

> *Please* Meelchis,
>
> Don't write too much. If you are ever rather tired & doubting whether to finish a letter to some Birmingham worthy or not, think of *us* . . . & let the Birmingham worthy be hanged . . . because we would compel you to stop if we were present: so bear us in mind, as if we hear of any further offence we shall on our own responsibility send round threatening and abusive letters to all your correspondents.[55]

Stanley, too, wrote lovingly from Oxford, 'All the good there is in me I owe to you, & I shall cherish your words & teaching as long as I live. Dear Meelchis – you have been everything to me, & I look upon you as the only means by which I may arrive at anything good'.[56] All three boys kept in close touch with their mother while they were at university. Charlie sent her diagrams for bulb planting and detailed instructions to help her with the upkeep of the garden, even giving her advice on how to take cuttings and on soil content, and she was requested to send him parcels of tea from Liverpool: 'we do not get nice tea here, at all'.[57] In 1876, Josephine wrote to twenty-two-year-old Stanley giving him advice on his handwriting: 'If you cd attain to a fixed good writing, it wd be an advantage. I am thinking of it chiefly in relation to yr examinations. It counts for something, does it not?'[58] Two years later, when Stanley was mountaineering in Switzerland, he left his mother in charge of his finances, relying upon her to forward him cheques and pay Oxford bills for repairs to his spectacles, his boots and his bicycle. George and Josephine had been alarmed at not hearing sooner from Stanley when he was on this particular trip. A number of mountaineering accidents had been reported in the newspapers, and Uncle Monty had telegraphed them to say that one of the masters at Harrow had been lost on the mountains and the body not yet found. Josephine wrote to Stanley of their anxiety while they waited for word of him:

> I could not sleep at all, & had often to sit up all night, the palpitation was so violent . . . Poor Paps was so anxious about you. You would have thought his whole happiness was wrapped up in you – & indeed I think it is. He used to get up at 6 every morning, & keep the front door open, or walk up & down the front, waiting for the postman, & when the cards came at last, his eyes were quite juicy with thankfulness and relief.[59]

*

The late 1870s were lean years for the repeal movement. Successive repeal bills were defeated, and although the majority against lessened, so too did the number of MPs who could be brought to vote upon the question. Stansfeld confessed, 'Every time that I address myself to speak upon this question I lift a heavier weight'.[60] In 1877, a year when he was advised by Gladstone to postpone the introduction of a new bill, English Federation members devoted their energies to preparing for the International Congress of the Federation which was held in Geneva in September. It was a huge undertaking, with five hundred delegates from fifteen countries attending. The conference was divided into five sections: Hygiene, Morality, Legislation, Preventive and Rescue Work, and Economics. Before it began there was great alarm at the prospect of a prohibitionist proposal from a Swiss delegate that all prostitution should be made illegal and heavily punished. This would make rescue work very difficult since any prostitutes coming forward would incriminate themselves, and, even worse, it would result in an *increase* of police powers. Josephine sent a circular to all her friends urging them to vote against it. She was equally opposed to another proposal, this time from Swiss women, that for reasons of delicacy some of the sessions of the Hygiene section should be for men only. She told them that no English male delegates would agree to attend a meeting from which women were excluded, and she appears to have packed the Legislation and Hygiene sections with English women so that such proposals would be defeated. Josephine herself delivered a stirring address to the Hygiene section in which she denounced the forcible examination of women:

> You have no right, gentlemen, to outrage any woman whatsoever were she the most guilty, the most fallen, the most lost in the world. You have no right to extinguish the last spark of womanly feeling in the prostitute's heart, and all hope of rehabilitation which is possible for the most fallen . . . Nothing can give you the right to force her to unveil the most sacred part of her physical nature.[61]

There was a great deal of drama over the voting on such issues, with lengthy arguments about voting procedures. At one session this had gone on so long that the German delegation rose to leave, wanting to dine. Josephine with her back to the door refused to let them, shouting that no one could dine until the voting was over! The British women dominated the voting in the Legislative section and then attended the Hygiene session where similar arguments over voting procedures meant that the meeting lasted until midnight. At 11 p.m., Georgie, who was there as Josephine's personal press officer, ran to her hotel to tell her that a long row of British women were 'all sound asleep'. She found, though, that one of them, Mrs Bright Lucas, had been deputed to wake them whenever a vote was taken!

The Congress ended satisfactorily and produced a two-volume study of the European system of regulation, 'scientific, statistical and closely reasoned'. It confirmed the Federation's demand for the abolition of all systems of regulation, and reaffirmed its commitment to equality for women in law and in economic opportunity. It also urged that rescue homes should operate, not penitentially, but through Christian love and sympathy, and that an international system should be set up to prevent the trade in young girls for prostitution. Most valuable of all, perhaps, was that the Congress brought together delegates from so many nations to hear about 'the appalling position in which women were placed by current economic conditions – the desperately low wages, the exclusion from nearly all trades and professions and the resultant steady increase in prostitution'.[62] 'This Congress has had a wonderful effect,' wrote Josephine.[63]

Josephine was also able to devote these years to her writing. In 1876, she had published *The Hour before the Dawn*, which was a remarkable attack on the sexual double standard and a plea for understanding for the prostitute, in which she challenged the reader, 'What was her life, and what was yours? . . . What is there in such a one that makes her a greater sinner than yourself? Be honest!'[64] She gave an insight into her religious faith, saying that it was when she felt the stirring of love and pity in her heart for the wretched and destitute that she recognized the love and compassion of Jesus Christ. Most interesting of all is the passage in which she reveals something of the spiritual crises that seem to have been behind breakdowns in her health:

> When my soul was in darkness on account of sin – the sin, the misery and the waste which are in the world – the cruelties, the wrongs inflicted and never redressed, and the multitudes who seem to be created only to be lost . . . I could not love God – the God who appeared to my darkened and foolish heart to consent to so much which seemed to me cruel and unjust.[65]

Her crises of faith are also alluded to in *Catherine of Siena*, her most well known work of this period, a book so characteristically well researched that it is difficult to imagine how she found time to write it. Her aim was to portray 'the real woman', not the superhuman saint, and she found much to identify with in Catherine, whose 'zeal and fire would naturally carry on to impatience', who found it difficult to tolerate being impeded in her work by 'the stumblings and errors of others', and who had a 'tendency to rule in too despotic a manner'.[66]

Josephine saw all three of her sons in London in early 1879. She had an appointment on Thursday, 6 March to meet Benjamin Scott, George Gillet and a number of Quaker bankers described by Josephine as 'grey beards', who wished to discuss the candidature of Benjamin Lucraft, a working man, cabinet-maker and a leading member of the WMNL, for the Tower Hamlets constituency at the next general election. An opening prayer was proposed and they all dropped to their knees. George Gillet was just offering a special prayer for Josephine, 'when the door silently opened & in crept Stanley, looking half afraid'. Gillet explained to the gentlemen that this was Mrs Butler's son, 'and the grey beards assented by a subdued tapping of feet & umbrellas on the floor'.[67]

Before returning home to George, Josephine intended to hear the women's suffrage debate in the House of Commons scheduled for Friday afternoon at 5.30 p.m, which was to follow Leonard Courtney's introduction of a resolution in favour of the suffrage. Charlie produced tickets for a matinée performance of *She Stoops to Conquer*, but Georgie and Stanley, who were now working in the Civil Service, had to go back to work, and Josephine, Charlie and James Stuart went. They were out of the theatre by 5 p.m.: 'I was so thirsty with laughing (!) that kind Charlie took me to a little tea & coffee shop he knows of, just opposite the House of Commons, & gave me a cup of tea which revived me . . . I then climbed up the long winding staircase to the Speaker's Gallery'.[68]

Henry James, the Liberal MP for Taunton, made a powerful speech *against* female suffrage and infuriated Josephine by quoting the Queen's own words, to the effect that 'we women are not fit to govern or to manage public affairs, & every good woman must abhor all such masculine avocations', words Josephine considered 'neither Queenly nor womanly'. She fancied she saw Gladstone rebuking James, '& James looking very sulky'. Then the Irish MP Alexander Sullivan 'spoke so beautifully about women' and said that the 'false & miserable things' said by James had made him into a determined suffragist. Isabella Tod of the Belfast LNA put it down to the influence of Sullivan's strong-minded female relatives and whispered in Josephine's ear, 'I am proud of my Irishmen'.[69]

The division took place at half past one in the morning, and, as expected, a heavy majority of 114 voted against the bill. Josephine wrote to Fanny that she 'ran down stairs before the numbers came out, & ran thro' the empty deserted streets to the Hotel'. She had only had some soup for her lunch and was very hungry, but all restaurants were now shut, as well as the kitchen at the hotel. 'I crawled up to my room & was preparing to tie a belt round my waist to stay the pangs of hunger,' she wrote, when she saw that Stanley, fast asleep, had left her out a large bun and some soda water, 'knowing my way of forgetting "the flesh"'.[70]

The Federation Congress that year, 1879, was held from 20 to 27 August at Liège in Belgium. Josephine and George made a tour of Germany in July and at Bonn met up with Charlie, who was clearly delighted to have their company. The weather, though, was appalling. At Koblenz they were 'half-drowned' with the constant rain and flooded roads: 'we look at all the pretty views from under dripping umbrellas,' she wrote to Stanley.[71] Mercifully, they were dressed for it. Josephine had thick boots and a short rough petticoat: 'We are not doing the fashionable at all'. They had intended to take the train to Switzerland where Georgie and Stanley were mountain-climbing, but their father was not up to the journey, and they decided to stay put.

Josephine wrote to Stanley of the success of the conference, which was due in part to the choice of Liège rather than Brussels. By not holding their conference in the capital city, the Abolitionists were avoiding possible confrontation with local brothel keepers and, perhaps, obstruction by the Police des Moeurs. In Liège, a heavily industrialized area, the working men were strongly supportive of the aims of the Federation. The famous Lancashire textile manufacturer William Cockerill had set up factories at Verviers and Liège, and his son John had established a foundry and machine factory at Seraing in 1817. The delegates were invited to speak in Seraing, on the River Meuse; Josephine was awed by 'the picturesque wild beauty of the scene, the vomiting flames from the works, the palpitating of the steam hammers', and reported that the workmen understood them perfectly.[72]

Emilie de Morsier, a delegate from Paris, thought the particular success of this conference due to fundamental agreement among the delegates upon the question of personal liberty and the rights of the individual. She cited Benjamin Scott's stirring speech: 'You are not free,' he said to the citizens of Liège, 'Liège is not free; Brussels is not free; and Paris is not free . . . so long as any woman may be deprived of her civil rights at the caprice or tyranny of a police agent, or through the denunciation of a scoundrel.'[73]

On the first afternoon, Madame Nicolet of the Liège branch of the Federation convened a women's meeting at her Maison Hospitalière. This was a form of industrial home modelled on Josephine's in Liverpool and had been inspired by Josephine's last visit to Liège in 1876. She was proud to call it a true 'child of the Federation'. The select meeting at the Maison Hospitalière was held 'for ladies who were more timid & fastidious', and Madame Nicolet warned delegates to 'use no expressions which would shock'.[74] Madame de Morsier captured the audience with stories of individual girls whom she had successfully rehabilitated on their release from the St Lazare prison, and then went on to the more radical work of the Federation. It was left to Josephine 'to finish their afternoon's education by planting a few painful thoughts in their hearts about the terrible wrongs of poor women & their own guilt if they did not help them'. By the time she had finished, 'We were very glad at last to see some pocket handkerchiefs called into service'.[75]

One new delegate was the elegant and beautiful Baroness de Stampe, daughter of the ex-Prime Minister of Denmark, who became an intimate of Josephine's almost immediately. A large women's meeting was advertised for the Thursday evening, and the four women speakers representing four nations, Josephine, Countess Schack from Germany, the Baroness de Stampe and Madame de Morsier, retired to rehearse their addresses: 'We ran a good deal into each others' bedrooms all the afternoon to consult together, and Madame de Morsier corrected the grammar of the other three'.[76] Madame de Morsier was indefatigable in the role of translator: Benjamin Scott simply handed his speech to her on the platform at one meeting and then sat down again; and she translated the speech of Benjamin Lucraft, one of several English working men delegates, sentence by sentence as he went along. The ladies had all determined to speak in French, however.

They had been warned not to expect much of a reception since the hall they had chosen was attached to a Protestant church, and it was thought that Catholics might object. In fact, 'women came pouring in till the little hall was crammed'. Windows and doors had to be kept open for the sake of those seated inside as well as those listening outside. The Baroness was the first to speak, but, said Josephine, she put 'so much of the tone of revolt in her speech that I thought it prudent to tone it down a little afterwards'. The delegates could hardly get away at the end of the meeting as women crowded round them, asking questions and holding their hands. Josephine slipped out first and settled herself in the waiting carriage. She found herself watched by a silent group of a dozen or so ragged little girls who had been prohibited from entering the hall, 'just of the class who will be the victims of the future to the evil we are fighting against'. She saw one of them clasp her hands together and heard her sigh, 'O-o-o-o-h – qu'elle est belle, cette dame Butler.'[77]

Liège may have been a more than usually high-spirited conference. Yves Guyot found fun in everything, '& goes off like a soda bottle'. He was 'such a nice chap,' she told Stanley, and when they all dined together they 'laughed so much that the people of the hotel think moral reformers are the merriest people in the world, & it is well they should think so!'[78] On the last night, Aimé Humbert chaired a vast public meeting with an audience of between seven and nine hundred, so Josephine estimated, to whom he introduced the speakers one by one, giving a brief description 'while he pointed to each like a showman with a wild beast show. It was very difficult for *us* to keep our countenances'. Humbert was inclined to get carried away when speaking, and Josephine would tap him on the back with her fan when she felt his time was up. At dinner that evening, he proposed a private resolution for the delegates, that in future ladies' fans were to be prohibited on the platform: 'he accuses me of having given him such thrusts in the back with my fan that he was quite sore'.[79]

In sharp contrast to her leading role at the Liège Congress, Josephine accompanied George to the Headmasters' Conference at Eton in December 1879 simply as headmaster's wife, or 'Mrs Liverpool', as she jokingly described herself. George and his brother Monty were there to promote the teaching of Modern Languages. There were only nine ladies present at the dinner set for two hundred, and they were seated alternately with the gentlemen at the top table, 'Mrs Liverpool with Mr Rugby, Mr Liverpool with Mrs Winchester, and so on'.[80] Pretty Mrs Eton, decked in velvet and jewels, was not to Josephine's taste, but she made a new friend in young Mrs Winchester, Laura Ridding, who 'came and sat nearly two hours in my room over the fire'. Laura was the eldest daughter of Lord Selborne, the future Lord Chancellor, and she was a Poor Law guardian. Her husband, George Ridding, was an old friend of George's from Oxford days, a tutor at Exeter College when the Butlers were there in the early 1850s, and a strong opponent of the Contagious Diseases Acts.

Monty and his wife Georgina asked them back to Harrow on the Sunday, and Josephine then spent a couple of days in London making final preparations for the annual LNA meeting in January. From there, George and Josephine stopped off to see her sister Eliza at her school.[81] The pair of them were so exhausted that they readily accepted Eliza's invitation to spend Christmas Day with her, since the Butler boys were all away from home. Eliza had quite a family party with her: her sister Fanny, who 'trembles all over at the least exertion, poor thing', and nieces Constance and Adela Grey. Eliza's boarders had all gone home for the holidays, but the three governesses remained. George Butler, the only gentleman in the house, threw himself into the charades on Christmas Eve, playing a variety of characters from Solomon to his old dancing master, improvising a violin from a poker and tongs: 'He nearly killed them with laughter'. Constance and the English governess acted Jael plunging the nail into Sisera's forehead, a curious choice for a Christmas party, and then, at Eliza's instigation presumably, they played out an instance of the excessive prudery of the elder German governess 'who is very firm'. She was in the habit of instructing Eliza's pupils to turn away their heads whenever they passed a gentleman in the streets! Contie impersonated the poor governess, who was rather shocked by the levity of the proceedings, while the younger German governess dressed up in George's hat and ulster as one of the fearsome gentlemen.

For all his high spirits, George was not a well man and on the journey home to Liverpool had one of his, now frequent, attacks of sickness and diarrhoea. Josephine managed to get him into a saloon carriage so that he could lie down, and she nursed him carefully when they reached home, but she acknowledged that he was looking 'rather old and grey'.

11

The White Slave Trade

'The Slaughter of the Innocents'

IN JANUARY 1879, Josephine had written a circular to all English members of the Federation, calling on them for great individual effort. She warned them that it was 'not by official machinery that we shall conquer, but by self-sacrifice & by unwearying missionary zeal', and, not shy of presenting herself as an example, she looked back to the extraordinary success of her own continental mission in the winter of 1874–75.[1]

On Josephine's return to England in the spring of 1875, the one subject that she had shrunk from publicizing was her knowledge of the extent of child prostitution on the Continent and of the trade in English minors, innocent and respectable girls, who were abducted and imprisoned in foreign brothels against their will and subjected to degradations and cruelties unimaginable to incredulous friends at home; this was only hinted at in her April 1875 letter to Joseph Edmondson. She was aware that a reputation for exaggerating facts such as these would reflect very badly upon her leading role in the repeal movement. It was not until five years after her own foreign mission that Josephine felt able to speak out boldly. She was supported by the collaborative efforts of an association of Quaker bankers in the City, the leading force among them Benjamin Scott, Chamberlain of the City of London. Scott, aided principally by Mary Steward, a member of the Ladies' National Association, Alfred Dyer, a publisher who issued much of the repeal movement's literature, and George Gillet, a banker, formed the London Committee for the

Exposure and Suppression of the Traffic in English, Scotch and Irish Girls, for the Purposes of Foreign Prostitution.[2]

It was Josephine's belief that the current 'fashion', as she put it, in sadistic crimes against children was directly linked to state regulation of prostitution, and the words of an adversary, Charles Lecour, she felt supported her. She quoted from his 1870 book, *Prostitution in Paris and in London from 1789–1870* in which he stated that men 'cease to be satisfied with the human merchandise prepared and guaranteed for them by the State, and go out of their way to seek excitement and novelty; hence the violence practised on children'.[3] She further argued that once prostitution was perceived to be tolerated, even facilitated, by the state, so would men seek 'to be stimulated by the brutality of rape and violence in addition to other acts of impurity. The younger, the more tender and innocent, the more helpless and terrified the victims, the greater their value in the eyes of these accursed beings'.[4]

Young English girls were recruited to brothels on the Continent because England had such a low age of consent; in Belgium a woman had to be twenty-one to register as a prostitute. Under English law, the seduction of a child under twelve years of age was a felony; between the ages of twelve and thirteen it was a misdemeanour; yet above the age of thirteen it was not a legal offence, although it was a misdemeanour to abduct a girl under the age of sixteen with intent to seduce. The only girls given the full protection of the law up to the age of twenty-one were heiresses. As Josephine observed, 'The law appears to proceed upon the principle that those who require every possible protection shall have none at all'.[5]

In the autumn of 1879, an Englishman who was in Brussels on business had visited a brothel and had been offered a young English prostitute, Ellen Newland. She was in great distress and appeared close to suicide. Ellen confided her story to this man, saying that she had been abducted to Belgium and was kept a prisoner. He shied away from becoming personally involved, but he did inform Alfred Dyer of the girl's situation and begged him to do something to rescue her. In late February 1880, Dyer and Gillet went over to Brussels to investigate. Working closely with a new ally, an advocate named Alexis Splingard, they posed as wealthy clients, and asked specifically to see English girls. They also visited the hospital wards reserved for diseased prostitutes, accompanied by a Brussels minister, Pastor Leonard Anet, as the regulations required. It was their plan to take statements from the prostitutes, and even rescue the girls if possible. In this latter work they would be assisted by Mary Steward, a married woman and a Methodist, who had a large experience of rescue work.

Within a matter of months, Alfred Dyer and George Gillet provided the proof Josephine needed to support the assertions she had made. Theirs had been a highly dangerous mission, and also highly frustrating, since they faced obstruction both from the Belgian police and from British consular officials. Nevertheless, Dyer and Gillet returned home in the spring of 1880 with indisputable evidence of a widespread and organized traffic in British minors. A pattern emerged whereby a girl would be induced by an apparently respectable foreign gentleman to go with him to Brussels under the promise of a highly paid situation abroad, or even, in some cases, marriage. On arrival, he would hand her over to a 'friend', in most cases a brothel keeper, who would escort her directly to the office of the Police des Moeurs, where falsified documents would be handed over. She would then undergo a physical examination before being registered as a prostitute under a false name and a false date of birth. The girl would be placed in a brothel from which it was hazardous, if not impossible, to escape. She would be told that she could not leave until she had earned enough money to pay back her fare for the crossing, and she would be warned that if she did try to escape she would be put in prison for registering under a false name. The girls were barely treated as human beings; rather they were merchandise, stripped of their names, forbidden their own clothes, imprisoned, starved or beaten if they refused to go with clients, or sold on to other brothels if they proved troublesome. Even in death they were subjected to shocking degradations. M. Lenaers himself, the Chief Commissary of the Police des Moeurs, admitted that 'their teeth, if good, were extracted for dentists' uses, and their hair cut off to be made into artificial coiffures for ladies of fashion, and their disfigured bodies, scarcely cold, flung into the common ditch used for such debris, and concealed under quicklime'.[6]

Under Dr Carter's orders, Josephine had for some time been dictating all her business correspondence to an amanuensis, but on 1 April 1880 she wrote a private letter to Carter, explaining the peculiar details of a case discovered by Dyer, the horrors of which it was scarcely possible to exaggerate, or even to communicate at all, publicly or privately. The case involved an English girl, Adeline Tanner, a very pretty girl of just nineteen, yet who appeared much younger. She had been recently orphaned and had come up to London to look for a situation. She met a foreign gentleman calling himself M. Sullie who convinced her that he was in love with her and wanted to marry her. 'Sullie' was in fact the pseudonym of Edouard Roger, the owner of a brothel in Brussels, who would periodically come over to London to recruit young girls. On this particular trip, in September 1879, he had also abducted two other girls, one a very young girl known only as 'Baby Nelly'. Roger took the three girls to Brussels where they were examined by the police surgeon and then registered as prostitutes using false birth certificates produced by Roger (Adeline under the name of 'Ellen Cordon'), certificates which stated that they were all over the age of twenty-one. Roger's accomplice, Anne Parent, acted as interpreter. According to M. Schroeder, the Deputy Chief of the Police des Moeurs, 'The girl Tanner appeared to be pleased to be registered', and even danced for joy.[7]

Adeline was imprisoned in Roger's brothel at number 3 rue des Commerçants, 'A splendid house, devoted to first class visitors'. She was there for just seventeen days, however, during which time she suffered brutal treatment: 'She was *torn*, & ill with their violence, but it was of no use. "No gentleman could go with her"'.[8] 'The case is peculiar,' Josephine explained to Carter, '(& most useful for us), because this child was at once pronounced *unable* to be a prostitute, owing to the exceeding smallness of her person & to some defect.' Instead of keeping Adeline on at the brothel for other sexual practices, or simply throwing her out on to the streets, Roger seems to have regarded the girl's deformity as a personal slight, and he determined to *make* her penetrable at all costs.

What followed is scarcely believable, and is as difficult to describe now as it was for Josephine, a hundred and twenty years ago. For something like five months, Adeline, not knowing a word of French, was detained at the Hôpital St Pierre in Brussels, where she was at first treated for a painful vaginal abscess. Then, she was forced to undergo an operation with an instrument to enlarge her vagina. According to Josephine, '*They nearly killed her*'. The English girl was a medical curiosity: visitors would arrive at all hours of the day, for whom she had to lift her nightdress and reveal her 'deformity', and student doctors would crowd around her bed to witness her operations. Adeline told Dyer, 'They did not even give me chloroform, but the students held my hands and feet, whilst the operator seemed to cut and tear away at my living flesh'. She had, she thought, seven operations, and said, 'The principal doctor seemed to hate me, and take a pleasure in prolonging my torments'.[9]

When it became evident that no amount of interference would

render her fit for normal sexual relations, let alone a career as a prostitute, Adeline was put in prison for fifteen days for the crime of registering herself with the Police des Moeurs using false documentation. Mary Steward was there to rescue her once she had served her prison sentence, but told Josephine that she 'found her like a crushed worm, hopeless, sullen, & at times quite wandering in her mind'.[10]

Josephine herself nursed a number of other English girls rescued from Brussels, 'refugees' she called them, at home in Liverpool. One was Emily Ellen, aged twenty-two, who had also been decoyed by Edouard Roger, and for five weeks was confined at the same brothel as Adeline Tanner, registered under the false name 'Eliza Land'. Emily was intractable, weeping constantly, telling her story to every English or American client, and finally locking herself in her room and refusing to entertain clients. She had been immured in a cellar so that her cries could not be heard, and starved, and beaten with a leather thong. When she came to Josephine, she was in great pain from unhealed sores on her back from the beatings given her by Roger and by the brothel mistress. Gently Josephine persuaded Emily to tell her story, and was present when Dr Carter examined her. The 'livid marks' on her back confirmed what she had said, and Josephine likened her to 'a victim of some cruel overseer of slaves' in the American South.[11]

Josephine's campaign to expose this white slave trade was supported by Adeline Tanner, by now restored to her married sister, who asked that her story be published for the sake of all the other English girls abducted to Belgium. She vowed that she would 'leave nothing undone to rescue the girls'.[12] Emily, too, agreed to testify. The Tanner case alone provided them with sufficient evidence to bring prosecutions against Roger and the hospital surgeon, and Alexis Splingard believed that they could go further and charge the Police des Moeurs with collusion. The next Federation meeting was due on 10 April 1880, and Josephine hoped to raise fresh subscriptions then to finance the publicity and the prosecutions. Josephine did not conceal that it was extremely painful for her to face again the subject of child prostitution, and said that she could do so only with the 'strength and comfort' given by her husband.[13] She had made the white slave trade the subject of her speech to the annual meeting of the Ladies' National Association in Woolwich on 29 January 1880,[14] and would continue to assert its existence in her speeches that year.

Now, prompt action was required. Josephine took up the challenge of the discoveries made by Dyer and Gillet, and in a long letter to the editor of the *Shield*, published on 1 May, gave a frank exposé of 'The Modern Slave Trade' between London and Brussels, acknowledging that it was difficult to speak of these things, and, indeed, to hear of them, but saying that she considered it 'a duty, even at the risk of scandalizing some of your readers'.[15] Josephine described how English girls from the ages of twelve to fifteen were kept prisoners in Brussels brothels, 'hidden away in padded cells, to prevent their cries being heard', and rarely living for 'more than *two years* after their capture'. It was, she said, impossible to exaggerate the horrors they suffered. At the Paris refuge run by Louise Appia, Josephine went on, 'one whole year is required to bring back a girl who has been in a maison tolerée from a state of mental alienation to one of moderate intelligence . . . For one year they are like "alienées" [lunatics], they do not know the right hand from the left'. Her final thoughts were for the male clients, often men old enough to be the children's fathers or grandfathers, who 'desire merely a *thing* to debauch – no longer a human being, but a *thing* in the shape of a woman'. Such men were beyond redemption.

The Conservatives were defeated at the general election in April 1880, and it was calculated that the repealers lost more than 150 MPs whom they had persuaded to be sympathetic to their cause. On 5 August, Benjamin Scott's London Committee sent a Memorial to Gladstone's new Foreign Secretary, Lord Granville, calling for a reform of British and Belgian law which would make it impossible for any British woman 'to be deprived of her liberty by fraud or force' or to be 'sold into slavery' in Belgium 'for the vilest purposes'.[16] Attached to the Memorial were individual depositions made by Alfred Dyer, Mary Steward, and by Adeline Tanner herself.

The triennial Federation Congress was staged in Genoa in 1880. Five hundred delegates assembled from all over Europe, George Butler representing the working men of Great Britain, and Giuseppe Nathan largely responsible for organizing delegations from working-class associations from all over Italy. As with the Liège Conference, it was a wonderfully uplifting time for Josephine. This time she had Hatty with her, and her sons, Georgie and Charlie (Stanley was now a lecturer at St Andrews University). Count Aurelio Saffi, who presided over the Congress, spoke in his introductory speech of his personal affection for the Butlers, recalling their hospitality in Oxford when he was in exile, and when 'the noble lady' sitting at his side, 'in the face of the world the stern and redoubtable champion of her sex', was 'an admirable wife and mother in the retirement of private life . . . only the guardian of the domestic hearth'.[17] Saffi also accompanied George and Josephine to a private audience with the aged Garibaldi, whose African servant, 'immensely tall & well-made', picturesque in a scarlet jersey, swept aside a curtain to reveal Garibaldi in his bed, surrounded by bouquets of flowers and looking 'sweet & benevolent'. He was able to say a few appropriate words to each of them, and told Josephine, 'Remember this, that though we pass away, and the leaders of the cause fall one by one, principles never die; they are eternal, world-wide, and unchangeable'.[18]

Although severely afflicted with rheumatism, Garibaldi liked to take a daily ride in an open carriage; Josephine described how the streets of Genoa would become 'a living mass of human beings, every window filled, and even the housetops covered with people, eager to see and greet the old hero'.[19] On one occasion his carriage pulled up in front of the Hotel Isotta, where the Butlers were staying. One of her sons, who was at the window, thought he was asking for Josephine. When she went to the window, Garibaldi, looking up and smiling, raised his crippled right hand to salute her.

Josephine received a deputation of working women at the hotel, who presented her with a written petition asking her to come and address them at their 'People's Hall'.[20] Some of the women carried babies in their arms, and one woman brought her five-year-old daughter, in order that she might see Mrs Butler and take her hand for, said the mother, 'when she is a woman she will be proud to think of this night, and no doubt she will be a better woman for the memory of it!'[21] When Josephine arrived at the People's Hall, she found the husbands, sons and brothers of these women waiting by the door to beg admittance. She was only too glad to welcome them.

The unanimity of feeling at the Congress took the English delegates by surprise. It was almost confusing to them to find their arguments already understood and judged by an enthusiastic and intelligent audience. The week ended triumphantly. The final resolutions of the Congress, which embodied the founding principles of the Federation, were announced publicly, almost operatically, from the balcony of the Carlo Felice Theatre, an enormous stone balcony which looked out upon the largest square in Genoa. The square was crowded as, in perfect order, each association arrived, 'with flags flying and trumpets sounding', and then 'each Resolution in turn was voted by acclamation by the multitude with deafening cheers'.[22]

George and the boys had to return home, but Josephine went on to Brussels to confer with Alexis Splingard, and was, as she said, 'filled with horror. Surely Sodom and Gomorrah will rise up in judgement against the Belgian capital'.[23] She was granted an audience with the *Bourgmestre* and aldermen of Brussels at the Hôtel de Ville, to whom she made specific allegations of collusion in the traffic in under-age girls against the heads of the Police des Moeurs, Schroeder and Lenaers. She then made her way home via Paris, but was delayed there for a few days because of a heavy cold. The delay turned out to be providential, for she was tracked down by a Belgian detective by the name of De Rudder, who had become so disgusted with the police collusion Josephine had alleged that he denounced his superiors in a written statement that he delivered to Josephine. De Rudder had an extraordinary story to tell. After Josephine had made her accusations, the *Procureur du Roi* in Brussels sent for Schroeder and asked him outright whether it was true that he permitted English minors to be entered in the police register of the city's prostitutes. Schroeder denied this, but then rushed off to see Lenaers to tell him what had taken place. Lenaers ordered two large carriages to call at certain brothels to carry off all the minors who were there, and sent them across the border into France. He then invited the *Procureur du Roi* to inspect the brothels to see if there were any minors among the prostitutes.[24]

Josephine gave the details of the particular charges made by De Rudder to Alexis Splingard, who found them 'corroborated on all hands'. This was the proof she needed, and she returned to England triumphant. When she reached Liverpool, George handed her an official notice from the Home Office stating that, under the Extradition Act, she was about to be summoned by a stipendiary magistrate to confirm on oath the allegations she had made about the Belgian police. M. Levy, a *juge d'instruction* in Brussels, was challenging her to provide details of a single case of outraged innocence in any brothel in the city. Thomas Stamford Raffles, the magistrate in question, called as soon as she was home, to ask when she would be able to make her deposition. Josephine was confined to bed and had completely lost her voice, but said that she would appear the next week, only too 'glad of the opportunity of telling what I know *openly*'. Alexis

Splingard came over to England at once to assist Josephine in any way he could, but he caught a chill crossing the Channel and was diagnosed with inflammation of the left lung: 'I won't let him get out of bed, poor man! He can hardly draw his breath. We are poulticing away'. Her niece Constance Grey also arrived to offer moral support, but she too was unwell, 'so we are a regular Hospital'![25]

The weekend before she was due to testify, George happened to travel to Oxford on the same train as Stamford Raffles, who appeared very nervous about having to take Josephine's statement. Josephine was still very poorly and retired to bed early, but before 5 a.m. she was awakened by a loud knocking at the front door. It was a 'confidential messenger' carrying a sealed package of letters for Josephine, sent by Benjamin Scott. Feeling a little confused in the cold, dark morning, she lit her candle in order to read 'a mysterious letter from the Guildhall, which contained also a telegram in cypher from Brussels, warning me that there was some trap being laid for us, and probably some collusion between the police of London and that of Belgium'.[26]

Both the City of London Committee and friends in Brussels urged Josephine to offer herself as a martyr to the cause and refuse to give evidence, even if it meant that she would be charged with libel for her writings in the *Shield*. She was told that it would 'arouse the public as nothing else could' for her to suffer the full legal penalty for refusing to answer. From Aimé Humbert, though, she received contrary advice. He was convinced that her allegations would be very difficult to prove, that the Brussels police would act at once to remove all documentary evidence relating to the child prostitutes in the city, and, of course, all girls from the brothels themselves, yet he wrote to urge her to be courageous and tell all she knew, even if it meant incriminating civic or legal authorities in Brussels. Josephine agreed. Alexis Splingard's life had already been threatened, and she, too, was ready to brave personal threats from foreign brothel keepers and police alike.

In the first week of November 1880, supported by the presence of George and some 'solid and honourable citizens of Liverpool', Josephine made a fearless deposition in which she gave particulars of several cases, naming individual officials, police officers and police surgeons, as well as the owners and managers of brothels and the men who abducted the girls from London to Brussels. She was able to produce two signed statements made by gentlemen living in Brussels, one of whom had been offered a child of twelve or thirteen at a brothel in the rue St Pierre known as the Sport Nautique; the other had been offered a twelve-year-old English girl at 42, rue St Jean ('The child flew to him in an agony of crying and weeping, and asked his help to get away. She said she was *never* allowed out of that room – never – never').[27] Official copies of Josephine's deposition were sent to the *Procureur du Roi* in Brussels and to Sir William Harcourt, Gladstone's Home Secretary, who immediately sent a lawyer, Thomas Snagge, to Brussels to gather evidence to test the authority of Josephine's allegations.

A few weeks after making her deposition in Liverpool, Josephine received a letter from Henri Boland, editor of the Belgian *National*, asking for help. He had been charged with libel by Lenaers and Schroeder and was summoned to appear before a commission now sitting in Brussels. He needed any documentary evidence of police collusion that she could provide. In particular, he thought that a copy of the deposition she had made in Liverpool would be of great use to him. Josephine responded to his request, upon which Boland, after reading Josephine's statement to the Commission, published the entire document in his newspaper, complete with the names of individual police officers who were charged with corruption, as well as the names of individuals who had risked much to supply Josephine and her friends with information. He also published a threat to the Police des Moeurs and to the child traffickers alike, 'that MRS BUTLER WILL NOT RUN AWAY'.[28] Josephine described what followed in her New Year's letter to Hatty: '60,000 copies of his paper were sold before the evening; a second edition was called for, and the next day 20,000 more were sold. Of course, at once his life was threatened, pistols were levelled at him . . . his office was besieged, and is still so, by people threatening him . . . For the moment this editor is a great man'.[29]

Josephine felt at first as though she had been betrayed by Boland and was concerned that through her naivety she had allowed many other friends to be betrayed. She then remembered that a year before, on 1 January 1880, she had prayed for just such an exposure of the cruelty done to women and girls on the Continent: 'I used to kneel and pray, "O God, I beseech Thee, send light upon these evil deeds! . . . flash light into these abodes of darkness. O send us light! for without it there can be no destruction of the evil. We cannot make war against an unseen foe" '. She had read that the Belgian newspapers all referred to that edition of the *National* 'as "a flash of lightning", and use almost the language of my own soul about it'. She was convinced that it was the hand of God.[30]

In Brussels, Lenaers and Schroeder were formally censured for their slackness in registering so many English girls without properly investigating their documentation, but no criminal proceedings were taken against them personally. However, the Belgian courts did now pursue the brothel keepers named by Boland, and as a result of that trial both Lenaers and Schroeder were dismissed from office. In all, twelve brothel keepers and procurers were charged on the various counts of abducting minors for the purposes of prostitution, of registering them under false documentation, and of imprisonment and assault. Isolated cases involving the debauchery of under-age girls had sometimes been heard in the Belgian courts, but this was a huge criminal trial, and the British authorities could no longer ignore the organized traffic from London.

Josephine was not able to attend the trial herself, but Mary Steward came up to Liverpool to collect Emily Ellen, who was to give evidence, along with two girls rescued from another brothel, Ellen Newland and Maria Higgleton. When Emily returned to Liverpool she told Josephine that she had accidentally met Edouard Roger in one of the corridors of the law court, and he had gone down on his knees in front of her, begging her not to testify against him. Adeline Tanner did not appear as a witness, but the other cases produced sufficient evidence to incriminate Roger. Dyer reported to the judge that Adeline was 'in a deplorable condition': she was still suffering from the abscess, and 'constantly spits blood'.[31]

At midnight on 15 December, a messenger knocked at the Butler house with a telegram for Josephine sent by Alexis Splingard: 'All condemned'. The next morning she sent an identical telegram to Hatty. All twelve accused, seven women and five men, were found guilty of the charges: ten received prison sentences and fines, and two brothel keepers who had assaulted Maria Higgleton in front of witnesses when she made her escape were each fined twenty-six francs. Roger's was the weightiest sentence, at two years and 300 francs. Thirty-four English girls who had been held against their will in various brothels in Brussels were released.

Following on this victory, the lawyer T. W. Snagge's report was published which confirmed that there was a systematic traffic in English girls to the Continent; that the girls were 'induced by misrepresentation and false pretences to leave England'; and that they were kept virtual prisoners, subjected to cruelty and forced against their will to become prostitutes. They were essentially treated like slaves, and 'were advertised to brothel keepers as *colis* (parcels) together with descriptions of physical features, real age, plus the age which could be credibly given to a client seeking a child, colouring and so on'.[32] Snagge himself discovered thirty-three individual cases. His findings were extremely useful to Josephine, although she was unhappy that, while he called for restrictions on the issuing of British birth certificates, and asked that the details of British girls registering as foreign prostitutes be forwarded to the Metropolitan Police, his position was not to criticize the trade of prostitution, but simply to ensure that it did not break the law.[33]

Josephine's response to the Snagge report was to prepare a Memorial to the Foreign Secretary, Lord Granville, petitioning him to make inquires into this traffic in young girls. Supporters for this campaign included ladies of high rank, a section of society hitherto unmoved by the campaign to repeal the Contagious Diseases Acts, and her Memorial contained the signatures of 1,000 ladies, among them those of Florence Nightingale, John Stuart Mill's stepdaughter Helen Taylor, the social reformer Jane Ellis Hopkins and Josephine's sister Hatty.

Before delivering the Memorial on 27 May, Josephine had written to Lord Granville to acquaint him with its subject. She closed her letter with a startling challenge: 'I added, "I shall be in London for three days, & will wait, if necessary, those three days *outside* your door, until your Lordship shall find it convenient to choose either to hear our petition or to order my removal!" '[34] The Foreign Secretary was quick to respond. He sent for Josephine at once, telling her that there was no need for her three-day siege, and that he had already acted upon her request. He professed himself to be absolutely in sympathy with his petitioners, and agreed that the law must be reformed, promising that on Monday, 30 May he would move for a committee of the House of Lords to take evidence upon this matter.

The Select Committee met for the first time on 28 June 1881: T. W. Snagge was one of the first witnesses to be examined; Alfred Dyer, George Gillet and Benjamin Scott were called to give evidence on 26 July. Dyer provided the details of a number of cases, and he read aloud to the Committee a statement made by Adeline Tanner, in which she declared that the white slavery that was allowed to operate between Britain and the Continent was 'the cruellest thing that ever existed'.[35]

In April 1881 Josephine had published a highly charged pamphlet entitled *A Letter to the Mothers of England.* In its simplicity, its brevity and its shocking narratives of seduction, Josephine's 'Letter' was very similar to Alfred Dyer's pamphlet published the year before, *The European Slave Trade in English Girls.* Josephine's pamphlet, addressed to 'mothers in the higher ranks of society',[36] was an uncharacteristically sensational one, listing case after case of abduction and enforced prostitution. One such described the trial, again in Brussels, of two women found guilty of kidnapping a young girl from her boarding school on behalf of the forty-three-year-old Baron de Mesnil. They each received a prison sentence of seven months, but the Baron '*was not even summoned as a witness at the Trial!*'[37] Other cases were even more shocking. The reader was then asked to imagine her *own* daughter being subjected to such outrages. Only very briefly does an argument surface about the inequalities in the law which left lower-class girls so vulnerable, or about Josephine's conviction that the sadistic treatment of children was directly linked to state regulation of prostitution.

At odds with the sensationalism of her pamphlet was her caution when speaking in public about the white slave trade. It was an extremely delicate matter, as can be seen from the way Josephine approached her address to the annual meeting of the Christian Women's Union, held in October 1881 in Liverpool. She was invited by Elizabeth Lundie to address a meeting on the third day of the conference. Her subject was preventive work, and 'ladies of a mature age only were invited to be present'.[38] She wrote twice to Elizabeth's sister, Charlotte Wilson, begging her to attend and speak in her support, anticipating that as soon as she approached the subject of immoral legislation 'a number of ladies will leave the room'.[39] Her hope was that she could persuade a few individual women in private conversation afterwards.

Josephine began with the story of her divine call in 1869. She then read out a letter from a group of Christian women in Switzerland who proposed measures to chaperon girls as they travelled between countries from one situation to another, lest they be decoyed by brothel keepers or arrested by police spies. Then she turned to the white slave trade between London and Brussels. There was 'a thrill of pain and horror' in her audience as she told them how young were some of the victims of this trade, and of the misery of their lives, yet Dyer's paper, the *Sentinel*, praised Josephine's speech, saying, 'so delicately and skilfully was the subject handled' that even the most refined ladies were stirred to swear their allegiance and to give in their names and addresses to the representatives present from the LNA.[40] In the event, Josephine appears to have spoken for too long, and there was simply no time for Charlotte Wilson or Maria Richardson of York, whom she had also persuaded to come, to contribute to the meeting at all, except to second the vote of thanks made to Josephine herself! She apologized to Charlotte, hoping 'she did not feel that it was a lost labour coming to Liverpool'.[41]

In July 1882 the Select Committee of the House of Lords submitted their report. The Committee's recommendations were weak in some respects: instead of making it harder to acquire a British birth certificate, the onus was placed on foreign authorities to check their validity.[42] Perversely, one measure worked *against* the protection of girls by giving the police unrestricted powers to clear the streets of suspected prostitutes without proof that they were there 'to the annoyance of inhabitants or passengers'.[43] However, the Committee did recommend two significant reforms: that the age of consent be raised from thirteen to sixteen, and, further, that the age at which a girl was protected from unlawful abduction be raised from sixteen to twenty-one.

Within a year, Lord Rosebery, Under-Secretary of State at the Home Office, drew up a Criminal Law Amendment Bill which acted upon the Committee's recommendations. The age of consent for girls was indeed to be raised to sixteen: any man having unlawful intercourse with a girl under thirteen could face penal servitude for life, and if the girl was under sixteen the maximum sentence was two years' imprisonment with or without hard labour. This was also the maximum sentence applied to the crimes of procuring and/or drugging women *of any age* for the purposes of prostitution, or for attempting to make them 'leave the country to become an inmate of a foreign brothel'.[44] Crucially, the evidence of very young children was to be admitted, and parents or guardians had the power to apply to a justice of the peace to enter a brothel under police protection if they believed that a girl was being held there against her will.

The bill passed through the Lords but was then shelved by the Commons. As W. T. Stead, editor of the *Pall Mall Gazette*, observed, 'No one in Parliament seemed to care about it'.[45]

12

Winchester

'A new sphere, a new stage'

GEORGE ANNOUNCED HIS retirement as headmaster of Liverpool College in a circular dated 2 March 1882. He was two months away from his sixty-third birthday. They had been thinking about retirement for some time: in April 1877 Josephine had expressed *their* wish to retire from the school work which had occupied her husband for twenty years, saying that they were 'feeling a little aged and tired, but late circumstances have determined us to hold on for some time longer'.[1] The Butlers were aware of the fact that the college would offer George a handsome testimonial on his retirement, 'and this we intend to *invest*',[2] but they had little money saved to rely upon in their old age. In 1875, and again in 1877, Josephine referred to unspecified financial losses. They were determined not 'to let it depress us, but it came at rather an inconvenient time'.[3] Josephine would freely confide in friends that for some time she and George had been unable to put any money aside from the college salary, all of which went on rent and household expenses, latterly on their sons' university education, and on extensive charitable subscriptions. To her niece, Rhoda Bolton, Josephine confessed, 'I don't know what we shall do to get our bread when we leave here'.[4]

In the late summer of 1878, Josephine wrote to Catty to say that his father had got a telegram from the elderly rector of Exeter College, asking him to preach the Latin Sermon at the University Church for the opening of term. This in itself was an honour for George, but for Josephine it was also a disappointment. She confided to her son, 'I wished it had been to tell him the old Don was going to retire and he hoped Papa would stand for the Rectorship'.[5] At that time, George had been headmaster of Liverpool College for twelve years, and Josephine felt disappointment for him that advancement, either in the academic world or in the Church, had not come his way. No doubt she also felt that her controversial public life, and his support for her campaign – his 'crotchet', as it was known – had been harmful to his career. Sir James Stansfeld expressed the belief that this was the case. Recent events in Paris had perhaps not helped in this regard.

Yves Guyot, a radical French journalist and a member of the Municipal Council of Paris, had been fined and imprisoned for writing articles critical of the Police des Moeurs and regulation. Josephine raised money for the fine from Federation friends in England, and she and George went to Paris to speak on his behalf before a commission of inquiry of the Municipal Council and also at a meeting where they, and others, spoke to a largely working-class audience of thousands. Josephine recalled the effect upon the audience of George's 'words of gentle force spoken in perfect idiomatic French'.[6] The outcome in Paris of Guyot's recent agitation and of Josephine's long-standing campaign there was that the Bureau des Moeurs with its regulatory police force was abolished in 1878. On his return to England, George found himself attacked in the London *Standard*, and the *Liverpool Mercury*, which asked if the governors of Liverpool College knew that their headmaster, a clergyman in the Church of England, had been addressing Republican mobs in Paris. George made a dignified response, but the newspaper attacks upon him must have unsettled some of the school governors.

George's failure to secure church preferment was a delicate subject. 'I scarcely like to express to yourself all I feel about you,' Josephine wrote, but she could not help praying for George daily that 'if it please God, all earth's rewards shall not pass you by'.[7] Hatty was perhaps freer to speak her mind, and told George that she was 'quite angry' that he had been kept waiting so long for recognition. George had recently been busier than ever with committee meetings about the proposed new university in Liverpool and with organizing a conference of clergy in support of repeal. Josephine would often find him in his study late at night 'with a pile of papers before him, leaning his hand on his head, asleep'.[8] She wrote to Stanley, 'Last night, he only got home at 10.15 & sat down & leaned back & said, "O *I am* tired". Dear old man, we will take him, please God, to some refreshing mountain place next summer'.[9]

There had also been a decline in the pupil intake at the college.

George's salary, as seems to have been current practice, was not fixed but dependent to a degree on college fees, 'which fall off in bad times'.[10] Ironically, it was the new university that George was working to promote that would 'absorb all the youth of the place who want teaching', or so he and Josephine believed. The college was 'dwindling down' markedly and it was feared that it might have to close.[11]

The day after George announced his retirement, Henry Wilson, unknown to the Butlers, sent out a private circular to all those friends who had subscribed to special funds for Josephine and George in the past, drawing attention to the Butlers' anxiety about their future. He referred to George's disfavour with some of the college governors because of falling recruitment, which Wilson felt had led to his resignation, and to his lack of preferment in the Church because of prejudice against the repeal movement. He and Robert Martineau were proposing that a fund of £3,000 or more should be raised for the purchase of an annuity for them.

Ostensibly, the annuity was to provide against George's retirement, but there was also the question of Josephine's likely widowhood in future years.[12] Robert Martineau at first believed that an annuity solely in Josephine's name would yield the highest interest, but he was taken aback rather on discovering her age: she was now only fifty-four, nine years younger than George, and so much younger than Martineau had thought that he feared he did not have enough to provide the Butlers with £200 a year: 'Have you got more to come in?' he asked Wilson, anxiously.[13] The generosity of the Butlers' friends was remarkable: Wilson and Martineau subscribed £100 apiece, as did MPs Peter Taylor, John Thomasson and Frederick Pennington, while an anonymous donor promised £300. Moreover, the annuity was to stand even if George did get preferment. It was Martineau's feeling that 'I suppose we say that in such a case we should only be too glad that they should have the extra comforts which this fund would give'.[14]

Josephine and George read of this gift beneath the trees in their garden one bright Sunday afternoon in May, their hearts 'filled to overflowing with wonder and gratitude'. Josephine felt that she had only done her duty, 'and barely that', while George, she explained to Martineau in her letter of acceptance, 'would rather I wrote to you for us both; for in his great modesty he persists in saying that any kind appreciation among our friends of a little work done on behalf of justice and purity, belongs to me of right, and not to him . . . he humbly puts aside any recognition for *himself*'.[15] She also referred to the sacrifice made by her husband, a sacrifice he had kept to himself. George had said to her, '"yes indeed, God knows what I suffered. But that is past". He allows you see some sacrifice in the past, though at the time he *never spoke* of it to me'.

Josephine clearly saw her husband's departure from the college not as retirement, but as entry into 'a new sphere, a new stage of our earthly home'. What she meant by this is explained in a letter she wrote to George that summer, from Hatty's Swiss home, La Gordanne: 'it is my longing that we both may be baptized with the Holy Ghost at this time, that the rest of our lives may be consecrated *fully* . . . and if there be any little sacrifice we can make in our daily life, of anything, let us do it, that we may make *room* more and more, for the spirit of God'.[16] Josephine had spoken of her husband's soon being in a position 'to help me more and more directly than he could do while superintending a great school'.[17] She even expressed a wish that they move nearer London, and nearer the Houses of Parliament, which was where her work was now increasingly concentrated. George's sacrifice, or the sacrifice of their 'united life', was only just beginning: their next few years were to be the most demanding yet, as Josephine's two campaigns, for the raising of the age of consent for girls, and for the repeal of the Contagious Diseases Acts, neared victory.

Then in June 1882 they received some very welcome news indeed. Mr Gladstone had written to George the previous Christmas, praising his achievements at the college, and he now received the following message: 'Dear Mr Butler, – I have much pleasure in proposing to you, with Her Majesty's sanction, that you should be appointed to the Canonry of Winchester, to be vacated by the Revd E. Wilberforce'.[18] When Hatty heard the news, she burst into tears: 'I did not realize till then how heavily had been lying on my heart the apparent non-recognition of your merits', she wrote to George, 'but perhaps I exaggerated what I took for a slight. I had however been fretting over it, and the reaction was delightful'.[19]

George's formal farewell to Liverpool College took place on 23 June. A speech from one of the school governors, George's friend Alfred Parker, praised the contribution the Butler family had made to education at Rugby, Haileybury, Harrow, Cheltenham and Liverpool, and fully acknowledged George's achievements at the latter. He asked his audience to consider how many generations of schoolboys had been sent into the world with the Butler stamp upon them, 'a stamp which does not tell alone of the highest scholarship, but which tells of purity, of honour, of manliness, of all those qualifications which English parents most desire their sons to possess'.[20]

On leaving Liverpool, Josephine was obliged to close the House of Rest. In a letter to Miss Priestman she said that she and George had assured 'all our poor hangers-on that we would find for them friends in their own town, but that we could not continue absolutely to support them, as we should have in our new home certainly a number of cases to help'.[21] Not all their rescue cases received this news graciously. A Mrs Gelling, whom Josephine had received at her little hospital when she was very ill and kept 'entirely at my own cost for several years', was placed with a good landlady in Liverpool, and Josephine wrote to a number of clergymen and friends enlisting their support. Mrs Gelling, however, 'had a very insolent and unpleasant temper, and quarrelled with everyone except myself'. Eventually, she began to quarrel with Josephine. Five years after the Butlers left Liverpool, she wrote violent letters, abusing Josephine 'for not sending regular supplies'! Mrs Gelling's story gives some idea of the scale of the charitable claims upon the Butlers, and explains only too well why they had not been able to put away any savings during their sixteen years at Liverpool. Josephine was often too busy with repeal business to raise money for her private rescue work in the city, and found herself 'hard put to it' and in debt to a number of lodging keepers. The calls on her purse were 'so far beyond what we can meet' that she was worried that she might have to turn away such cases in the future.[22]

The business of making preparations for the move to Winchester seems to have been left to Josephine. The boys' things had to be correctly identified and directed to their various addresses, and there were letters and papers to sort through, as well as furniture to sell. George had set about cataloguing his library, but he was not able to do much more, 'my poor old Love needing rather to be ministered to now than to minister'. None of her nieces were free to come to her, and Josephine felt keenly the want of a daughter's help. This was brought home to her when she came upon Eva's death mask. It was to Hatty that she confided her private grief:

> I am packing a little cabinet of Eva's, and in it is the *first* plaster caste of her dear face taken straight off as she lay dead, which no one sees . . . Every little mark was reproduced in the first caste; but it brings back the cruel nature of her death. The caste is so soft that to preserve it I must pack it in cotton wool and put it in my own box among my bonnets and best

> gowns; and it looks *so* pitiful. This is all I have by way of a daughter to help me move our home. Forgive this bit of a wail, dear . . . it is good it *should* come back to me in all its first pain now and then.[23]

There was the added distress of knowing that their dog, Bunty, now very nearly blind, deaf, and wretchedly insect-ridden, would not be able to adjust to a new home: 'He can only smell us, and he knows his garden still well enough to find his way to the trees on which he always scratches himself, and has scratched himself for 12 years'. It was left to Josephine to put 'dear old Bunty' to sleep. A chemist advised her how to do this using chloroform, but in the event she could not do it, and Bunty went with them to Winchester, where he died a natural death a few months later. They buried him in the garden, and George astonished his friends by carving a stone likeness of Bunty to mark the grave, bearing an inscription in Greek.

George seemed pleased with the move to Winchester, and, as Josephine later remarked, it was the 'only time I ever was mistress of a good house',[24] but it would never be a home to them in the way Liverpool had been: much of their eight-year residence at 9 The Close would be spent abroad, either attending Federation conferences or simply convalescing. The social climate of Winchester was markedly different from that of Liverpool, and it was a change in atmosphere that Josephine and George found 'rather abrupt'.[25] Winchester was both a cathedral town and a garrison town, and 'there seemed to be less breathing space, so to speak, socially and politically, if not intellectually'. When her niece Rhoda came to stay she found the atmosphere impossibly churchy: 'I hear all sorts of gossip about this old boy and that, some of them wrangle and are *so* jealous of each other'.[26] However, in the Cathedral Close itself, Josephine felt that society was 'less conventional and more liberal, in the best sense, than that of the city outside'.[27]

One good friend at 1 The Close was the Bishop's daughter-in-law, Mary Sumner, who would go on to found the Mothers' Union. For their first couple of years at Winchester, the Butlers enjoyed the society of the headmaster of Winchester College, George Ridding and his wife Laura, whom Josephine had met at Eton in 1879. Laura was involved in the work of the British Women's Emigration Society, which was based in Winchester. The Society was run by another clerical wife, the Honourable Mrs Joyce, daughter of Lord Dynover, whom Josephine described to Miss Priestman as 'a recent convert &

the best worker in Winchester', 'a Conservative, but good notwithstanding'.[28]

Hatty realized that Josephine's Liverpool wardrobe would not be quite up to Winchester standards for social calls and entertaining so she sent her sister a gift of 200 francs, with a direction on the envelope, 'To get a barège dress for Winchester' (a gauze-like, silky dress fabric).[29] Josephine had other ideas, though. She had had her eye on a large fur tippet. Complaining of the cold, she asked Hatty, somewhat ingenuously, 'Do you ever see any in Naples? They come down just to the end of the elbows, and to the waist back and front, and are *so* warm . . . and it looks so ladylike. I got besides with the money a muff to match'. As it was, social calls were a serious business. The Butlers moved to Winchester in the first week of November 1882, yet after one week in their new home, Josephine was faced with the prospect of having to return thirty calls made upon them by Winchester people despite the confusion she was living in at the Close, in the midst of plasterers, plumbers and mess. 'We shall be living in our *boxes* till November,' she told Charlie,[30] and to Miss Priestman she wrote, 'This house is a *ruin* . . . we are trying to build out rats and rain'.[31] Within days the builders took over completely, and the Butlers were living in lodgings: 'But do not spare me if I can do anything. I *wish* to work'.[32]

And work she did: by the New Year of 1883 Josephine had established a new House of Rest in a large elegant two-storey redbrick Georgian house in Canon Street, called Hamilton House. It was just a couple of minutes' walk away from the Cathedral Close. As with the Liverpool House of Rest, Josephine intended it to serve both as a hospital, and as a temporary home for those girls and mature women who were 'friendless, betrayed and ruined, judged for one reason or another not quite suitable for other homes or refuges'.[33] She hired a matron, a Mrs Hillier, to run it, and George held an informal service there every Sunday evening; 'the poor inmates looked forward all the week to his visits and delighted in them'. Some made their way to Canon Street independently, others were sent on to Josephine by the Salvation Army. One of these, a mere child who later died at the House of Rest, turned up on her doorstep with the plea, 'Please Missus, tell me who Jesus Christ is! I heard them telling about him'.[34]

Less than two years after their move to Winchester, Josephine also helped to form a branch of the Working Men's National League there. In early July 1884, a small group of earnest working men who were 'inspired with the right spirit' asked her assistance in holding a two-day conference. They had no money, 'So I paid *all* – for the hall (two days) and printing, . . . sandwich men, police etc., for there was a good deal of *previous* opposition, our Bills torn down etc.'[35] A local committee was set up immediately. The whole proceeding had cost £11, however, and Josephine reluctantly asked the LNA to meet £10 of the amount. She was ashamed that she was unable to pay for it all herself, but 'we have hard work here with our little hospital, and much expense'. She was willing to get them financial help, but never tempted to run their organization: 'I kept out of sight,' she told Miss Priestman, 'to make the meeting more of a Winchester movement.'[36]

On 19 July 1882, Sir James Stansfeld's repeal bill was given its second reading. It was received by the House with great respect, but MPs were advised to postpone voting until the recommendations of the Select Committee of the House of Commons on the Operation of the Contagious Diseases Acts were made known. The Select Committee sat for three years, which did delay the process of repeal, but its proceedings proved useful to the repealers, too. Its meetings were reported in detail in the *Shield*, and in particular the clever questioning by Stansfeld and Charles Hopwood of official witnesses.

Josephine herself was called before the Select Committee on the afternoon of Friday, 5 May 1882. She was dreading it: 'You can think what it would be to go before a lot of men, all of them asking the most cynical and horrid questions'. She was so oppressed by the responsibility resting on her that on the Wednesday evening she walked into the Salvation Army hall on Oxford Street to pray. A 'sort of holiness meeting' was in progress: 'People got up and stated their case. So I stated *my* case – partly. I was recognized, and some of them seemed to know what was before me, and they all prayed for me, and I went away *so* strengthened!'[37] But her nerves returned the next night as she sat up to prepare her statements, and she wrote to George, 'I find it *very* hard work learning by heart all the details I have to answer tomorrow; they say it looks bad to read from a paper'.[38]

In the event, it was one of their own MPs, Charles Hopwood, who put most of the questions to Josephine, and she gave an assured account of the history of the campaign, stating succinctly their moral and constitutional objections to the Acts, and listing the number of petitions they had presented to Parliament since 1870. She also gave her own observations of the effects of the Acts upon men and women living in the subjected districts. Judge Advocate-General George Osborne Morgan attempted to dispute the repealers' moral objections to the Acts by reminding Josephine that the legislation required every lock hospital to engage visiting clergy whose duty it was to try to reclaim the women confined there. He asked whether she was aware that witnesses before the Committee had testified to a certain number of women reclaimed in this way. 'I have read those statements,' was her reply, but she went on to inform Morgan that the women she had visited in the lock hospitals would say to her that 'the thing they cannot "swallow" (to use their own expression), is that the "parson" should be there, knowing for what purpose they are cleansed in the hospital'. Josephine was not afraid to tell the Committee that she would rather that *no* attempt was made to offer religious teaching to these women: 'I think it is a mockery of God'.[39] Morgan did his best to unsettle Josephine by getting her to admit that she had not visited a garrison town since 1873, but she declared that with regard to the *principle* of the CD Acts they were quite as good judges of the system 'away from the districts as we are in them'.[40] She reminded the Committee that the abolition of slavery throughout British possessions was carried by a parliament of men who had never seen a Negro slave, let alone a slave plantation.

The Committee, which was heavily weighted on the regulationist side, with nine of its members having army connections, published its report on 1 August, but did not recommend repeal. Responding to her colleagues' alarm, Josephine wrote to her northern friends urging 'rigorous action of a new kind': '*now*, I think, it is time to go straight forward . . . The languid or perfunctory workers will either receive new life, & run in step with us, or they *must* be left behind.'[41]

Josephine devised new methods of influencing Parliament. She recommended the immediate setting up of a 'powerful parliamentary committee', *not* to supersede the work of the National Association, whom they must be careful to conciliate, but 'to support, to fortify'. This was formed by the end of November, with Stuart in the chair, Wilson as Honorary Secretary, and Josephine on the Committee. There was also to be a national day of fasting and prayer early in 1883, even though 'to some it would seem fanatical'. This was to be the first of a series of prayer meetings in which it was Josephine's desire to include all denominations. The strong Quaker membership of the various repeal associations gave their unqualified support, and many meetings were convened at their headquarters at Devonshire House in Bishopsgate, but Unitarians and members of the established Church were hostile to the notion of inclusive religious gatherings of this nature. The lawyer William Shaen refused Josephine's invitation to sit side by side with Evangelicals like the Salvation Army, and even Stansfeld, who '*believes* in prayer', told Josephine that 'he would not wish to join *with others* in prayer'.[42] She wanted Lucy Wilson's support, but Lucy was a 'high ritualist, & for that reason will probably leave the room if prayer is offered'. Nonetheless, Josephine held to her principle of religious inclusiveness and boldly invited the retiring Governor of Hong Kong, Sir John Pope-Hennessy (whom she described as a Jesuit!) to speak at one of their public meetings on 25 January 1883: 'I love him for his *pity* for the Chinese women. His eyes flash & his thin hands tremble when he speaks of them'.[43]

She was giving offence not only to Church of England members, but also to the many prominent atheists among staunch repealers: Emilie Venturi, for example, who refused to have anything to do with Josephine's plan, telling her bluntly that she considered her faith in Christ 'an old & injurious superstition', and Ursula Bright, whom Josephine suspected to be an agnostic.[44] Despite his personal feeling about the prayer meetings, Stansfeld was insistent that they advertise them loudly in the national press, and many MPs wrote to Josephine individually, commending her recourse to prayer. Among their opponents there were equally strong objections. Cavendish-Bentinck, who had been present when Josephine appeared before the Royal Commission, she was told 'was rushing about the Lobby, cursing & swearing', shouting threats to Members who thought of looking in on the *Women's* Prayer Meeting. Writing to her son, Stanley, Josephine could not repeat his words, which were 'the most awful mixture of profanity & indecency'.[45]

Charles Hopwood had obtained time on Tuesday, 27 February to put before the House of Commons a resolution condemning the compulsory examination of women. Several prayer meetings were to be held, including meetings of men at the East London Tabernacle and at Devonshire House, as well as a vast mixed meeting at Exeter Hall. What became known as the women's prayer meeting was set for the date of Hopwood's resolution.

As well as united prayer, Josephine insisted upon the right of women to listen to the debate on 27 February from the Ladies' Gallery, a matter she discussed closely with the Wilsons. Many friends warned her against the waste of valuable debating time while MPs discussed whether ladies should be present or not, but for Josephine the question was 'one of principle'.[46] To her mind, the symbolic presence of women was of crucial importance, regardless of the unsatisfactory nature of their accommodation in the Ladies' Gallery, which visiting American suffragist, Elizabeth Cady Stanton, described as a 'dark perch' behind fine wire netting, from which it was possible to see very little, and 'a disgrace to a country ruled by a queen'.[47] Josephine felt that 'if men were so bad as to enact such an outrage on women, they must endure to *answer* for their act face to face with us'.[48]

She was very active in the weeks leading up to the day of the debate and the women's prayer meeting, and sent a circular to all Members asking them to give serious consideration to the question of whether women should be able to witness the debate or not. Josephine was quite prepared to be obliged to leave the House, she told them, 'But I wish that the onus of our absence should rest upon men . . . and I decline to take the responsibility of *staying* away which would be the act of a coward'.[49] Anticipating their cry that it would injure ladies to hear a debate on the question of the periodical examination, she had this to say: 'as long as any woman is obliged to *suffer* that outrage, I should be ashamed to speak of the pain to myself of *hearing* of it'. She also wrote privately to both Lord Harcourt and Lord Hartington, telling them that the repealers were appealing to God for justice and redress, and she enclosed a stern rebuke for Hartington: 'I said I hoped God would show him the horrible nature & unmanliness of *this* sin, in his *own personal life*, as well as the wickedness of the Laws'![50] Isabella Tod was equally bold in face to face encounters with MPs. During the week leading up to 27 February, she did valuable lobby work, '& no one can do it better than she', noted Josephine. Finding O'Shaughnessy, the chairman of the Select Committee, recalcitrant, Isabella and two other Irish ladies 'set upon him, in the House, & left him pale & with his two ears tingling! He won't forget it, *they say* . . . They talked the strongest brogue, & tears were shed! dear women'.[51]

Josephine booked an attic bedroom for herself at the Westminster Palace, a hotel popular with MPs, which also let out rooms to religious or charitable organizations, 'tho' I do not think they ever did so before, for a prayer meeting of women to pray for the degraded House of Commons!!'[52] She was warned that Charles Hopwood's motion might be deliberately crowded out by hostile MPs, but vowed that she would lead prayers until midnight if necessary.

The women's prayer meeting was due to begin at 5 p.m., and

Josephine decided to go to the Ladies' Gallery at 4 p.m., so that she would be able to relay news of the debate to the assembled women. By the time she got back to the hotel she found it full of ladies, and as many as two hundred would attend the meeting: 'Almost all the best known workers in benevolent things were there . . . several Lady Guardians of the Poor, some Members of Parliaments' wives etc.' And there, kneeling together with well-dressed ladies were poor women, among them prostitutes from the slums of Westminster. 'Many were weeping, but when I first went in they were singing, and I never heard a sweeter sound'.[53]

At 8 p.m. Josephine went back to the House once again, and recognized male friends from all over the country in the Strangers' Gallery, in the midst of them her son, Georgie, looking 'rather sleepy'. She tried to catch his eye, but he was not expecting his mother to be there and did not look up. Josephine had not eaten since breakfast and, knowing that she might have to sit up for several hours more, she ordered tea and toast in the ladies' room: 'I found a liveried urchin standing over a delicate little dinner of cutlets & vegetables served on a silver dish, & tea as well'. It was in fact Mrs Justin McCarthy's dinner, but she was so engrossed in listening to her husband speaking that she had forgotten it, 'So I ate it (& paid for it!)'.[54]

Josephine returned to the Ladies' Gallery in time to see Charles Hopwood, whose resolution had been crowded out by other business, ask the Speaker's permission to make a statement to the House concerning the manner in which he had been prevented from proposing it. He made a thrilling speech in which he said that 'Parliament & the Government must be prepared to have no peace on this question, for the country was roused, & nothing could lessen their determination'. He caught sight of Josephine a little later and took her out on to the terrace where, 'under a starlit sky, all the bustle of the city stilled, & only the dark water lapping under the buttresses of the broad stone terrace – the water into wh so many a despairing woman has flung herself',[55] he informed her of their current parliamentary position, and let her into the secret that ten Members, all sympathetic to repeal, had privately balloted for a place to move a resolution. In fact, it was Stansfeld who was successful, and 20 April was to be the date for the debate.

The day after Hopwood's resolution had been obstructed, Josephine, together with Stuart and Margaret Tanner, decided to go the House at 1 p.m. to see Members. Keeping to the protocol of sending in her card and calling out one name after another all afternoon was an arduous business. By 4 p.m. she could take no more of it. Next to the chamber was a grand circular hall in which Members could take refreshment, and when fairly full, as it was now, the hall resembled a vast public meeting. It was not unheard of for ladies to enter, but they were not expected to enter alone. Josephine decided to do so, and walked from the lobby through 'the heavy glass & brass doors' through which only MPs would usually pass. She found an elderly MP just inside the door and stood close by him, '*as if* he had taken me in under his protection'.[56]

Mr Whitwell knew Josephine, and he was only too pleased to bring MPs over to her. They came with pockets stuffed full of letters and petitions from their constituents begging them to vote for repeal, one MP being urged to do so by five hundred constituents' letters in one day. There were petitions from 'everywhere, every nook & corner & remote village or suburb', but the one that most moved Josephine was 'from 1553 inhabitants of West Ham': 'I knew that those were the poor working fathers and mothers whose children are stolen, & that they only had a week to collect those names'.[57] She was also proud of the petitions submitted by her family. Fanny sent in one, as did Stanley, and even a cousin, Albert Grey, the Liberal MP for South Northumberland.

The debate on 20 April 1883 was notable for Stansfeld's speech which demolished the arguments of the Select Committee's majority report. Particularly telling was his stress upon the fact that the Acts had failed to eliminate venereal disease. Josephine and many others kept their places in the Ladies' Gallery all evening until the division, which took place after midnight. The gallery steward then stepped over to her and whispered, 'I think you are going to win!' The House was so silent that she could hear herself breathe. From the Ladies' Gallery, directly above the Speaker's chair, Josephine could see the faces of the tellers as they filed into the chamber: 'I shall never forget when the vote was taken, and the two lines of men, the "ayes" & "noes" entered the door of the House'.[58] She knew the result of the division by their expressions of delight: Fowler was positively beaming, and the faces of Stansfeld and Hopwood were 'lighted up by such joy & surprise at the great and complete victory won after so many years of hard conflict, sorrow and disappointment'.[59] Once the figures were announced and the cheer was given, Josephine ran down from the Gallery to meet the members flocking out of Westminster

Hall. It was now one o'clock in the morning. She found Stansfeld waiting for her, the tears trickling down his face as he grasped both her hands.

A majority of seventy-two MPs voted to support Stansfeld's motion that 'This House disapproves of the compulsory examination of women under the Contagious Diseases Acts'. This had the immediate effect of suspending all clauses relating to the 'voluntary' submission and examination of women. Stansfeld explained the significance of his resolution in a long letter to M. Emilie de Laveleye, the new President of the Federation, who would be leading the forthcoming Federation Congress at Neuchâtel in September, saying that the government fully understood that the repealers' victory was conclusive and irreversible:

> I certainly could not have carried a Repeal Bill; but, though seeming to do less, I believe that I have in reality accomplished more, for I have succeeded in carrying, by a conclusive majority in the British Legislature, a resolution which is, in my opinion, fatal not only to the CD Acts, but to any possible system for the State Regulation of Vice.[60]

The vote won on 20 April 1883 was truly, as it was announced in the national press, the 'death-blow' to the Acts.[61]

Back in Winchester, Josephine began at once to discuss with local women how best to prepare the town for the total repeal of the Acts and the end, as she anticipated, of the system of state-run lock hospitals, but she also experienced at first hand the bitter hostility of brothel keepers towards the repeal movement. The air was 'filled with passion, and rage, and indecent fury, because we have deprived them of their prey'.[62] There was a good deal of support among the local clergy and aldermen for the Acts as measures to clear the streets of prostitutes, as George Butler and George Ridding were made uncomfortably aware at a meeting they held in Winchester on 28 June.

Rather than give in to the demand for absolute repeal, the government proposed to retain as much of the Acts as the House was prepared to accept, and the Marquis of Hartington, the Secretary for War, was asked to draft a bill. Hartington's Bill, as it became known, while maintaining the basic machinery of the 1866 and 1869 Acts, the special police and the police surgeons, proposed that submission to the examination, and to medical treatment, be purely voluntary. Josephine suspected that it was a trap and immediately prepared a statement for publication in the *Shield*, in which she denounced the new Act as simply the old Act 'with the addition of the horrible insult to women of *forcing them to ask as a favour that the abominable outrage should be inflicted on them*'.[63] Later that month, on 24 May, she addressed the annual meeting of the Society of Friends at Devonshire House, and made an extraordinarily dramatic plea for the rejection of Hartington's Bill. She had been very ill, confined to her bed for months, she said. 'With all the earnestness of a dying woman', she reminded her audience that any such legislation drafted by a parliament made up of men exclusively, and representing men exclusively, would prosecute women only, and '*will not touch the men*'.[64] It was often argued in the subjected districts that the Acts had at least cleaned the streets of openly soliciting women, 'But what of the *men* who torment us wherever we go?' she asked.

> Old as I am, and plainly dressed as I am, I cannot arrive at Victoria Station without being surrounded by a number of dissolute men. It is nothing to me; because, in the strength of God, I can defy any number of men. But, think what that is to a poor woman who feels tempted by the offer of money; or think what it is to a country girl just arriving in London.

Large numbers of repealers, including their own MPs, were unable to comprehend Josephine's outright rejection of Lord Hartington's proposals, however, and by August she had to face the fact that the party was 'hotly divided about the Bill'.[65] In a letter to the editor of the *Shield*, Josephine publicly declined to pronounce upon their position with regard to the bill and bowed to the judgement of their parliamentary leader, James Stansfeld.[66] Stansfeld was quite clear that they should not contest Hartington's Bill, but should fight to remove one particularly contentious clause in order to bring it more into line with their principles. This was Clause 5, which still insisted that a diseased woman be forcibly detained in a lock hospital until such time as she was considered cured. That autumn, at a meeting in Birmingham convened by the 'Political Committee' on 22 October, Stansfeld called upon repealers to embrace Hartington's Bill. Josephine was also on the platform, but said little. It was left to George to move the resolution expressing the hall's '*entire* confidence' in Stansfeld.[67] In the event, however, Hartington's Bill was dropped, and Hartington came round to the view that 'the effects of these Acts on the health of the Army were . . . very slight'.[68]

13

Child Prostitution

'O! What horrors we have seen!'

IN JANUARY 1885 Josephine was asked by Florence Booth, daughter-in-law of William and Catherine Booth, founders of the Salvation Army, whether she could receive a recent Army convert named Rebecca Jarrett at her House of Rest in Winchester. Josephine agreed to take her in, and there followed from this a remarkable friendship and a collaboration which led to Rebecca's involvement in the exposure of the trade in child prostitutes, one of the most scandalous episodes of the latter years of the nineteenth century.[1]

Florence Booth had been appointed to manage the first Salvation Army rescue home at Hanbury Street in Whitechapel in 1883, and it was in November 1884 that she had taken in Rebecca Jarrett. Rebecca was aged thirty-eight and terribly lame with a diseased hip. Weak with bronchitis, she was a confirmed alcoholic. She was too ill to be nursed at the Hanbury Street Refuge, and the Army got her into the London Hospital where she stayed for ten weeks to dry out: 'they never had such a bad drink case fancy from a girl of 13 or 14'.[2]

Rebecca was born on 3 March 1846, the youngest child of seven, to a rope merchant who kept a shop on the Old Kent Road.[3] According to Josephine's biographical sketch of Rebecca, her father deserted his family when Rebecca was very young and her mother drank heavily. Rebecca was in service at the age of fifteen and was seduced by a gentleman visitor to the house. She lost her situation when she became pregnant, and her seducer took her in. They lived for a time as man and wife, but her lover began pimping her and then seems to have abandoned her, making off with their child or children.

Rebecca supported herself by working as a prostitute, and eventually managed her own brothel.

There are several versions of Rebecca Jarrett's life. Josephine would have been familiar with the facts of Rebecca's upbringing from a private account Rebecca wrote out in an old copybook, 'just for yourself',[4] which no longer exists, but a later, fuller account, written when Rebecca was nearly eighty, tells a more sordid story.[5] It may have been that Josephine had wanted to make the narrative, in which she was writing a defence of Rebecca, less shocking to her readers, but there is evidence that Rebecca found it difficult to confront the facts of her early life. The fuller memoir reveals that her mother began pimping her at the age of twelve. Mrs Jarrett started taking her daughter to the notorious Cremorne Gardens, or to Ranelagh Gardens opposite the Chelsea Barracks, and 'in that gardens was as much wrong going on as there was in Cremorne'.[6] Following her mother's example, Rebecca began to drink: indeed, 'the drink was what I lived on for some years'. She left home at fifteen or sixteen, and over the years lived with a succession of lovers while managing a number of brothels. Her speciality was the procuring of young girls.

On Rebecca's release from the London Hospital in January 1885, she travelled down to Winchester. She missed the two women sent to meet her at the station and walked into Winchester. Not knowing the precise address, she asked several times 'for the faith healing cottage but no one seemed to know it . . . I was so disheartened for it was near 7 o'clock'.[7] Eventually, she was directed to the ladies at Hamilton House in Canon Street and 'got a nice reception'. The inmates were just about to have evening prayers, and the matron, Mrs Hillier, 'prayed for me directly then we had supper'.

Rebecca rested at Hamilton House for two months before Josephine and Amélie Humbert – Aimé Humbert's daughter, who was staying and working with Josephine – set about converting her. Her conversion, Rebecca put down to 'not their preaching but their care of me', and Josephine concurred, saying, 'If love and kindness will not bring them to God, no locking up in a Home will'.[8] Rebecca also recalled that Mrs Butler 'put the truth before me stern but kind'.[9] Rebecca was still battling not to drink and it was thought that active work would cure her despondency. Amélie Humbert asked her to help seek out fallen women and girls in Winchester and persuade them against the life. Thrilled to be given such responsibility, she wrote to Florence Booth, 'directly I get well I am to go with her for a week to go to all the gay houses and rescue the Girls down here so that I can get my hand into the work'.[10]

Josephine testified to Rebecca's extraordinary influence with girls of her own class: 'she would stand in the midst of a den full of men and women of the lowest type, get them down on their knees, pray with them and for them'.[11] One Winchester couple gave up their brothel after hearing Rebecca speak, and a local pimp vowed to reform. Throughout the spring of 1885, Josephine and Florence Booth communicated regularly about the wonderful success of Rebecca's mission. Josephine was full of praise for the Salvation Army's 'principle of sending class to class', the principle upon which she had set Rebecca to work, and she was perfectly candid in her admission that 'our old rescue methods are ineffectual'. She envisaged a whole army of women like Rebecca, who would draw in far more converts than she would ever be able to. They 'might go out into the streets & gather in such a full & blessed harvest of those poor girls. These are bold thoughts, dear Mrs Booth; & 99 Christian workers out of a hundred would probably cry out that . . . it would be a very unsafe experiment'.[12]

Rebecca recalled that she was 'well looked after by dear Good Friends each night Mrs Josephine Butler [and] the dear old Canon came to see me [or] I went to see them'.[13] More than once she overheard someone in the town caution Josephine against placing too much trust in her, but Josephine was always firm in her support. She also offered Rebecca hand-me-down garments and boots from her own wardrobe: Rebecca 'always wished to have a neat appearance'.[14] As Josephine stated, 'We were as sisters together, not "employer and employed"'.

Despite the extra expense, Josephine decided to set up a separate establishment in Winchester with Rebecca as matron, which would enable her to offer an immediate refuge to the girls she sought to rescue. They found a house at Bar End, High Cliff, overlooking the town, 'a good Home a nice large House', according to Rebecca.[15] Josephine named the house Hope Cottage: 'thank God', she said, 'one was rescued from a bad house after two years of a sinful life even before they got the furniture into the cottage . . . Another and another was got in'.[16]

Rebecca did not receive a salary for her work with Josephine. It seems that she spent her remaining 'last money from sin' on furnishing Hope Cottage,[17] while Josephine provided for its upkeep by collecting subscriptions, sure that God would 'supply *me* with the needful funds'.[18] Rebecca was given virtual autonomy over Hope Cottage. She had the rooms painted and made as attractive to the girls as the brothels they had left, and on Sundays she would invite other girls from such houses in Winchester 'to come and have tea'.[19] She was a diligent and professional manager of the Cottage, keeping accounts of all her expenses and a journal in which she recorded details of the girls she had spoken to on her nightly missions. One young woman who was successfully rescued by Rebecca testified to the sober atmosphere at Hope Cottage. The girls kept a quiet house, she said, sometimes attending Salvation Army meetings in the town, 'and after supper we had prayers and sang a hymn or two, but were generally . . . in bed about nine o'clock'. Rebecca was 'exceedingly kind, and studied our interest in every possible way . . . we had really got to love her'.[20]

Rebecca was also called upon to help a society of rescue workers in Portsmouth which was, like Winchester, a hitherto subjected district and still had large numbers of prostitutes. Her initial visit lasted a fortnight, and she was trusted to take the train down to Portsmouth with one other rescue case and an alcoholic 'of the superior class', whom she had been nursing at Hope Cottage. 'Dear Mrs Butler is going to see us off at the Station tomorrow and give us an allelujah parting,' she wrote to Florence.[21] Rebecca was so valued by the Portsmouth ladies that she was asked to stay with them overnight once a week. On one of these visits, Rebecca was looking for girls down White's Road when she came to a house that was unlocked and appeared to be empty. She walked up the stairs, thinking that she could hear voices above. There she confronted her past:

> I opened the door there in bed was an old man with two young children neither was 12 years of age as I knew the Mother was out working at the wash tub I made them both go home I sent up the vigilant man who was going round with me to deal with him.[22]

In the only surviving letter from Florence Booth to Josephine, written in late March 1885, she appears to have been in considerable distress about the number of young child prostitutes taken in at the Hanbury Street Refuge, and later recalled her shock upon realizing that there were '"walking our streets", hundreds of little girls of twelve, thirteen, and fourteen years of age'.[23] Josephine replied, 'Your letter falls in remarkably with the line of my own thoughts just now. Miss Humbert & I have been thinking much of the little girls who swarm our streets & whom the police & others tell us are tempters of men & "*incorrigible*".'[24] She understood that it was imperative for them to act in union to demand legislative protection for these children, both for the girls' own sake and because they were being used to justify a reintroduction of the CD Acts: 'The question of the little girls is urgent on all hands'. Josephine invited Florence down to Winchester and, in Florence Booth's own words, welcomed her 'with the tenderness of a mother and opened her heart to me'.[25]

The widespread prostitution of children was to become Josephine's main concern in 1885. In the second week of May a case was brought against the Chelsea brothel keeper and procuress, Mrs Jeffries, who was charged with 'keeping a bad house'. King Leopold II of the Belgians was her most prestigious client. In March 1879, Josephine had composed an address to King Leopold, a cousin of Queen Victoria, who was then visiting London, appealing to him personally to abolish the Police des Moeurs in his own country; she had some confidence that he would be touched by this direct appeal from a woman's heart: 'he is a good wise man, they say'.[26] She could not have made a greater misjudgement. Four years later, at the trial of Mrs Jeffries, the King of the Belgians was revealed to the world as a purchaser and trafficker of under-age girls for the purposes of prostitution. His taste was for virgins, and since England was the only country in Europe that had such a low age of consent, he would purchase under-age English virgins, as many as one hundred a year, it was alleged.

Mrs Jeffries had many other eminent and titled men among her Chelsea clientele: 'Princes and dukes, Ministers of the Crown and Members of Parliament were said to be among her customers. Witnesses were ready to swear to the presence of exalted personages and high officials'.[27] Before this evidence could be presented, however, the case was abruptly closed. The accused made a plea of guilty, and on 10 May was allowed to walk free after paying a fine of £200, 'just one quarter the sum which it was stated in court used to be paid to her annually by the King of the Belgians'.[28]

Less than a fortnight later an already compromised Criminal Law Amendment bill which now proposed to raise the age of consent to fifteen, instead of sixteen, as in Lord Rosebery's bill, was put forward by Sir William Harcourt, but was 'talked out' on the night before the Commons rose for the Whitsun recess. Only twenty MPs were present. It began to be rumoured that the House was 'honeycombed' with men of vicious propensities, and that 'both front benches' harboured guilty men. An investigation into the illegal practices of brothels 'could hardly be expected from legislators who were said to be familiar visitors at Berthe's in Milton Street, or Mrs Jeffries in Chelsea'.[29]

In part, Josephine blamed the press for reporting the Jeffries case too timidly. She argued that its failure to question the sudden termination of the case and its reluctance to publish the names of Mrs Jeffries's prestigious clients, led to 'the perpetuation of the most cruel and murderous tyranny' against defenceless young children.[30] The Jeffries case confirmed for Josephine her belief that 'the vicious example of the rich and great is a curse to a nation'. She wanted these men to be named.

In order to expose the extent of child prostitution, the continued traffic in girls and the 'systematic rape' of children, but also to shake the complacency of the Houses of Parliament, Josephine joined forces with the flamboyant editor of the *Pall Mall Gazette*, fellow Northumbrian William Thomas Stead, who was born at Embleton, less than twenty miles away from Josephine's birthplace. Stead had apparently pressed her to let him publish her evidence of child prostitution on the Continent after he had seen the published proceedings of the first Federation Congress. Josephine had felt strongly that she simply would not be believed: 'Mrs Butler wrote to me and said, "It is impossible; it is too horrible; no one would read it; no one would print it; you could not get it published"'.[31] Now, having seen what the methods of the editor of the Belgian *National* had brought about, Josephine, together with Benjamin Scott and Florence Booth's husband, Bramwell, asked Stead to use his paper to influence public opinion. Stead and Josephine made curious partners: in Josephine's letter to Stanley in February 1885 she had said, 'I don't know whether you ever read the *Pall Mall (I hate it)*'.[32]

Stead needed to prove a number of allegations: that children could be procured from their mothers; that so-called 'mid-wives' routinely examined girls to vouch for their virginity, and supplied drugs necessary to stupefy them while they were raped; and that a white slave trade still operated between Britain and the Continent. Following the example of Alfred Dyer's infiltration of Belgian brothels in 1880, Stead assembled a team of investigators whom he called, rather ostentatiously, the 'Secret Commission of the *Pall Mall Gazette*'. The team included Josephine and her son Georgie. They were to pose as wealthy clients, or, in Josephine's case, as a procuress, and were to enter brothels to see for themselves how many virgins were really for sale in London. It was a dangerous operation: their aim was not simply to compile reports of what they saw, as the basis of a series of sensational articles in the *Pall Mall Gazette*, but also to rescue any young girls who were offered to them.

A letter of 5 June 1885 to Miss Priestman suggests something of Josephine's involvement in the investigations of Stead's Secret Commission. It is the only surviving account left by Josephine.

> I have been for 10 days in London helping several friends in a most terrible investigation concerning the crimes (vice is too pale a word) of the aristocracy. It seems that all that goes on in Brussels & Paris goes on also in London . . .
>
> I have been about the streets all day & sometimes at night. O! What horrors we have seen . . .
>
> All this is not connected with the vices of the Poor but of the Rich, & there are guilty men on the Treasury Bench who begin to be most uneasy.[33]

She added that Georgie had volunteered to go 'in disguise into one of the high class dens where there are *padded* rooms. We have had to assume disguises'. They had spent nearly £100, buying children, and Josephine hoped that the LNA would pay 'two or three pounds of this'.

When Stead required proof that an organized trade in little girls existed, Josephine told him about Rebecca Jarrett and he asked to meet her. On 24 May, Josephine had a long talk to Rebecca about Stead and his investigations. She was extremely reluctant to see Rebecca return to London so recently after her conversion, yet the next day she let her do so. At Stead's Northumberland Street office, Rebecca rather falteringly recited her life story, and gave him a detailed account of her old methods of procuring virgins. Stead listened, astounded, as Rebecca told him that she had sold innocent children 'to dissolute customers, who for £10 or £20 could purchase liberty to rape with impunity'.[34] He needed proof of these practices and asked her to procure him a thirteen-year-old virgin from the child's mother, with the mother's full understanding that she was selling her daughter into prostitution, and then to take her across the Channel to Paris, as if for the purposes of prostitution.

Stead's proposition shook Rebecca. Josephine Butler had offered her a new life and career, and she was free from material want. She had been trusted with relative independence, and had experienced sisterly love for the first time. Instead of procuring girls for prostitution, Rebecca was now engaged in procuring girls for salvation: at this time she had '9 girls wich I had got off from their bad life I prayed with them each day told them How *God* had changed my Heart'.[35] Stead was asking her to put all this at risk and return to scenes of her wicked past. What caused Rebecca most concern was that he expected her to incriminate former friends and colleagues. He was insistent, and was even prepared to apply moral blackmail, saying that if she was truly penitent she must 'make amends' for her former crimes against children. He said himself, 'Jarrett pleaded to be spared this burden. I was inexorable'.[36]

Stead would not allow Rebecca to return to Winchester to take advice from Josephine, but said that he would write to Josephine himself, explaining the mission. This perhaps goes some way to exonerate Josephine, personally, from accusations that she was party to the exploitation of Rebecca Jarrett. She clearly had no idea that Rebecca was going to be asked to abduct an innocent child.

Rebecca returned to the city streets and looked up an old drinking acquaintance of hers, Nancy Broughton, who had once worked with 'Beck', as she knew Rebecca, in the laundry at Claridge's Hotel. Nancy introduced Rebecca to a likely mother, a Mrs Armstrong, who, together with her husband, was bringing up six children in a single room in a Marylebone slum. Rebecca offered Mrs Armstrong £1 for her pretty thirteen-year-old daughter, Eliza; Nancy Broughton (as procuress) was to receive £4. The child herself thought she was going into service.

The bargain was made on the evening of 3 June, Derby Day. Mrs Armstrong drank the proceeds, was arrested for being drunk and disorderly, and spent the night in a police cell. Rebecca took Eliza to a French midwife, Louise Mourez, and they were joined by Stead's assistant on the paper, Samuel Jacques. According to Stead, the examination to verify Eliza Armstrong's virginity was 'momentary, and no objection whatever was made by the girl. I was advised that the examination being made with consent was perfectly lawful'.[37] Stead chose deliberately not to inform Josephine of this proceeding until the deed was done, 'and then', she said, she went straight to Stead and 'protested against it'.[38] Eliza was pronounced a virgin by Madame Mourez: '"The poor little thing", she exclaimed. "She is so small, her pain will be extreme. I hope you will not be too cruel with her".' Mourez was given her fee of one guinea, and she then offered Jacques, who had attended the examination, behind a curtain, a shilling phial of chloroform for thirteen shillings.[39]

The party met up with Stead, who accompanied them to a Soho lodging house frequented by prostitutes, and Rebecca took Eliza aside to prepare her for bed. She attempted to give chloroform to the girl, but Eliza was frightened by the smell and they decided not to force it upon her. There was no need for Stead to prove that he had had the child drugged, but it would have meant that Eliza was spared the sight of Stead, somewhat unnecessarily, entering her room later that night. As it was, Eliza sat up in fright, crying out, 'There is a man in my room', at which Stead withdrew. Rebecca did all she could to soothe Eliza, and took her off to a respectable nursing home. There, once Eliza was asleep, chloroform was administered successfully, and the second examination of the night was performed by a gynaecologist, Dr Heywood Smith, in order to establish that the child had not been interfered with while in Stead's care. Rebecca was again present while the examination was carried out. The next morning she took Eliza to Paris, where she was put to service with a good Christian couple known to Bramwell Booth.

On Monday, 6 July, W. T. Stead began running his five-day exposé in the *Pall Mall Gazette*, entitled 'The Maiden Tribute of Modern Babylon'. In the first report, Stead spoke in plain terms of the social identity of the guilty and the innocent in this matter, accusing 'princes and dukes, and ministers, and judges, and the rich of all classes, [of] purchasing for damnation . . . the as yet uncorrupted daughters of the poor'.[40] Stead himself had negotiated for the purchase of seven girls between the ages of fourteen and eighteen, four of whom had a doctor's certification of their virginity. Most shocking of all was the chilling conversation he recorded with a prominent MP who offered to supply him with virgins at £25 each: 'it is nonsense to say it is rape; it is merely the delivery as per contract of her asset virginity in return for cash down'.[41] In an article entitled 'A Child of Thirteen Bought for £5' was the story of the purchase of Eliza Armstrong, her identity protected under the pseudonym 'Lily'. However, in the narrative as it appeared in the *Pall Mall Gazette*, 'Lily' was raped by the strange man who entered her bedroom while she was in a half-drugged state.

The next day, under headlines such as 'The Forcing of Unwilling

Maids', 'I Order Five Virgins', and 'Delivered for Seduction', Stead reported that young girls could be bought for as little as £5; that mothers were willing to sell their daughters' virginity; and that the children were made to suffer appalling brutalities. A procuress stated to Stead that she used to supply a virgin a week to one London physician for £10, who 'now takes 3 a fortnight from £5 to £7 each', and 'would take a 100 if we could get them'.[42] In rather lurid style, on 8 July Stead proclaimed:

> As in the labyrinth of Crete there was a monster known as the Minotaur who devoured maidens who were cast into the mazes of that evil place, so in London there is at least one monster who may be said to be an absolute incarnation of brutal lust . . . Here in London, moving about clad as respectably in broad cloth and fine linen as any bishop, with no foul shape or semblance of brute beast to mark him off from the rest of his fellows, is Dr———.[43]

On Thursday, 9 July, the paper threatened that it could expose the names of those men whose morality Stead had scrutinized, 'Princes of the Blood, and prominent public men'. On the same day Stead published a letter from Josephine which made the same threat. She had reacted angrily when appealed to personally by a member of the House of Lords on behalf of his class, and wrote, 'The great end which I personally desire to see, the end which I have long desired, is that the rich and aristocratic culprits in this matter should be judged by the people'.[44]

The campaign had revealed that child prostitution existed on an unimaginable scale. According to Stead, at Newport there was a refuge housing fifty girls under the age of ten who had been violated; at Farnham there were forty girls under the age of twelve, of whom only four had successfully prosecuted their assailants; and he later calculated that in June and July 1885 thirty cases involving forty-three girls between the ages of *three and thirteen* were brought before the courts.[45] These, of course, were instances which came to light, indications only of the extent of the problem.

Public reaction was extraordinary. A police guard was necessary to restrain the noisy crowds who jostled for copies of the paper outside its Northumberland Street offices. A writer in the *Methodist Times* said that a copy should be placed 'in the hands of every steady and respectable married working man',[46] but it had already reached a new audience. By the end of the month, mass meetings of working people all over the country were reported in the *Pall Mall Gazette*: in London, thousands turned out at the Mile-End Waste on 16 July, 1,500 at the Somerstown Railway Arches on 19 July, and 1,200 at Battersea Park on 26 July; the Liverpool Rotunda lecture hall was 'crowded with industrial classes' on 27 July; a demonstration at the Newcastle Circus on 29 July claimed an attendance of 4,000; and there were further large open-air meetings at Jarrow, Sunderland and Plymouth. Resolutions were passed at these meetings declaring that 'justice to children of the working classes demands that the age of legal protection should be raised to the age of 21 years'.[47]

On the same morning as the first issue of 'The Maiden Tribute' articles, a new Conservative Cabinet led by Lord Salisbury sat for the first time.[48] On the evening of 9 July, the day that Josephine issued her demand that the MPs and Lords tainted by this scandal should be named, the Commons quickly passed the second reading of the Criminal Law Amendment Bill, which had been adjourned in May. The next morning, Josephine wrote an ecstatic letter to the Priestmans: 'I never saw anything like the excitement in the streets & in the House of Commons. Such a judgement day for the vicious upper classes! . . . How wonderfully the protection of girls Bill passed last night on top of this wave of popular anger!'[49]

Having left Eliza Armstrong in France, Rebecca Jarrett returned to England and tried to resume her work in Winchester, but Nancy Broughton now revealed to fellow procurers and brothel keepers in London that Rebecca had turned traitor to expose their trade. She was followed to Winchester by 'certain companions of her former life', who, Josephine wrote, for nearly three weeks 'had haunted our neighbourhood & shaken Rebecca's nerves & feelings exceedingly by their threats'.[50] Josephine told Stanley that they had threatened to kill Rebecca, and that a police guard was posted outside both Hope Cottage and Hamilton House, where windows had been broken. At first, Josephine hid Rebecca at the Close, and it was from there that Rebecca wrote to Florence Booth on Federation notepaper, begging her to ask her husband, Bramwell, to hand Eliza back to her parents: 'now dear Mrs Booth do let me have her quick for the mother to see'. For her own safety, Rebecca was sent secretly to a Salvation Army barracks in Colchester, and was then taken to Jersey to a Salvation Army rescue home there, The Recluse. Back in Winchester, Josephine and Amélie Humbert closed up Hope Cottage.[51]

In London, the repeal movement used the scandals uncovered by

Stead to good effect, and the metropolitan committees of the various repeal associations worked together with the Salvation Army to organize a number of important public meetings. On 13 July, Josephine and Catherine Booth addressed a women-only meeting in the Prince's Hall, Piccadilly, and returned there the following day for a crowded mixed meeting presided over by Samuel Morley, MP. A great 'Indignation' meeting was scheduled for Thursday the 16th at Exeter Hall, but on the Wednesday Josephine took the train back to Winchester to begin packing for a family gathering in Switzerland. She felt guilty at deserting the 'dear Salvationists who have so nobly taken up our cause' and who so depended upon Josephine's judgement in matters of law and politics, but, as she admitted, 'I think I ought to leave, I am *so* tired'.[52]

Josephine was followed home to Winchester on the next train by an Inspector Borner who brought with him detectives from Scotland Yard. By the middle of July the Armstrongs, having recognized the story of 'Lily' as that of their Eliza, made a formal application to the police about their missing daughter, and now the police wanted to know Rebecca's whereabouts, in order to question her about the missing child. Inspector Borner's men went first to Hope Cottage, but finding it empty went to the Cathedral Close. Stanley Butler received an excited communication from Josephine, styling herself 'Your hunted old mother', in which she described how the Scotland Yard detectives had come to the Close and 'ransacked every corner'. Rebecca later told Florence Booth that they 'even watched to see I was not down the coal hole'![53] They then proceeded to Canon Street and questioned the women there. 'Winchester is quite turned upside down about it,' exclaimed Josephine. Inspector Borner threatened her with six months' imprisonment, but she laughed and told him, 'We are detectives like yourselves.'

On Thursday, 16 July, Josephine's niece, Rhoda, who was anxiously awaiting her arrival in Geneva that weekend, wrote to Stanley, 'I do so admire Aunt Josey having the courage to find out these awful things', but told him that she would 'not feel quite easy till I see her, they are kicking up such a row'.[54] Rhoda had not read the *Pall Mall Gazette* herself, she explained, because what Josephine had told her had 'quite sickened me', but with youthful indignation she declared she thought it 'down right wrong' that such evil men be allowed to live: 'A lot of women ought to go and slaughter them. I should love to help'. George finally got Josephine away from England on Friday the 17th. They met up with their party of assorted Butlers and Greys in Geneva, and then travelled on to Chamonix. It was from a hotel in Chamonix, on 26 July, that Josephine wrote to Arthur Naish of the Midland Counties Electoral Union, to explain why she had decided to leave England 'at the last moment' even though the *Pall Mall Gazette* was recording daily the surge in popular support throughout the country. Her six weeks' work with the 'Secret Commission', added to her other work, had taken so much out of her, she said, that George had been afraid she might break down.[55] Yet, far from resting, Josephine had begun energetically organizing the approaching annual Federation conference. Nor did she forget Rebecca. Friends in Winchester sent her a copy of the *Winchester Observer and County News* in which she herself and Rebecca were attacked for their unorthodox rescue methods. Josephine did not fear for her own reputation, having had years to become 'hardened' to misrepresentation in the press. She promised that as soon as they returned to England she and George would hold a meeting in the town, 'and at that meeting we shall give the whole story from beginning to end'. She wrote a letter of protest to the *Winchester Observer*, however, on behalf of Rebecca, as a woman who had 'acted an exceptionally brave and disinterested part' on behalf of the 'Secret Commission' of the *Pall Mall Gazette*.[56]

The Criminal Law Amendment Act was passed in her absence. On 30 July, the new Home Secretary, Sir Richard Cross, opened the debate on the third reading of the bill. It was passed by 179 votes to 71. The bill became law on 10 August 1885, and included a new clause raising the age of consent to sixteen.

Stead seemed to get rather carried away by this success. He began to talk of 'founding a Secular Salvation Army' as a counterpart to that founded by William Booth, 'with my paper as its war cry and myself as its General. It is a great idea'.[57] It was also his idea that the large public meeting planned for 21 August at St James's Hall be used to launch the foundation of a network of vigilance societies that would be responsible for identifying brothels and acting to suppress them. This worried Josephine sufficiently for her to send out a circular to LNA members, warning them against wasting their energy on such committees, and putting emphasis on 'individual enterprise and initiative'.[58]

Josephine expressed her approval of the staging of large public meetings to extend the work of the *Pall Mall Gazette* to a wider audience, but also warned obliquely of the dangers 'from the unrestrained chivalry of men' in dealing with 'the Criminal vices of men'.[59] She thought it anomalous that parliamentary discussions such as this were left 'exclusively in the hands of men', even though so many MPs 'came out so nobly'. She could see imperfections in the Act which she believed it would have been free of 'if some wise women had taken part in the discussion'.[60]

In her belief that the issue could not be separated from the question of suffrage, which was prominent in her speeches in July 1885, she was supported by Catherine Booth and the Priestman sisters. She wrote to Margaret Tanner, saying, 'Women must not rest until they possess the power wh Democracy is now extending so widely to men of directly influencing the laws by wh they themselves are to be governed'.[61] There was such a demand for the pro-suffrage article she had published in the *Methodist Times*, 'By Whom in Future are we to be Governed?', published on 8 October 1885, that it was reprinted separately as a pamphlet.[62]

On the front page of the *Pall Mall Gazette* for Tuesday, 25 August, Stead explained how the Eliza Armstrong case had been devised and carried out, and that week Eliza was handed over to her mother at the Steads' Wimbledon home. Josephine had not been informed of this, and on 1 September she sent a telegram to Georgie, asking him to consult with Bramwell Booth about the latest developments. In fact, on 2 September, prosecutions were brought against Bramwell Booth, W. T. Stead, Samuel Jacques, Rebecca Jarrett and Elizabeth Combe, the woman who had received Eliza in Paris, on charges of unlawful abduction. Louise Mourez faced the separate charge of indecent assault. Mrs Armstrong stated that she had believed she was placing her daughter in a good situation, and Mr Armstrong, a chimney sweep, pointed out that his permission, as would have been legally required, had not even been sought by Rebecca Jarrett. The Crown Prosecution case brought against the Secret Commission was restricted to the unlawful abduction of Eliza from her home. Ironically, the case was the first of its kind to be brought under the terms of the new Criminal Law Amendment Act.

Bramwell Booth advised Georgie that his mother's 'presence in London now would be a great help to them all', and Rebecca was no doubt in special need of Josephine's support at this time. Catherine Booth had been to see her, but Rebecca could only speak to her through bars. Georgie urged his mother to return to England, offering to meet her at Calais, or to send Stanley over, and he added an indignant postscript: 'What bullying it seems to pitch into the poorer agents in the case like Mrs Jarrett'.[63] Josephine, however, made the decision to continue with preparations for the Federation Conference which was to be held at Antwerp in less than a fortnight, and at which she and George were billed to speak, and then to return in time for the trial.

On the opening day of the conference, 16 September, Josephine talked at length about the recent events in England, describing how the moral force of provincial populations, and in particular the working classes, had compelled Parliament to push through the Criminal Law Amendment Act: 'it was not too much to say that a revolution had been accomplished in England in the last three months'.[64] She said that her aim was to stimulate the people to long-lasting action, and James Stuart similarly said that they based their hopes 'on the awakened conscience of the people', making the point that this had been achieved 'by fifteen years of education given by the crusade against the Contagious Diseases Acts', not simply by the *Pall Mall Gazette*'s revelations.

This was followed by an excited speech by Stead, in Antwerp while on bail. He 'was received with a long continued round of applause', and his furious condemnation of the whole system of regulation was met with delighted cheers. He spoke again at the large public meeting later that evening, introduced by Josephine, who justified the steps taken by Stead in the abduction of 'Lily' by the reluctance in Parliament to reform the laws to protect young girls.

As soon as the conference in Antwerp was over, Josephine left George with Hatty and returned to England to give support to Rebecca, but 'also in part to answer for her conduct'.[65] From Switzerland, George posted her special words of encouragement to give to Rebecca, telling her to take comfort from reading Psalms 30 and 31, which were remarkably pertinent to her situation: like David, Rebecca had 'heard the slander of many'.

The trial began at the Old Bailey on 23 October. The case against 'The Secret Commission' was founded upon the allegation that Eliza Armstrong had been abducted from her home. Stead had impressed upon Rebecca that she must 'purchase' Eliza Armstrong with her mother's full understanding that she was selling her daughter to a procuress, not to an agency for domestic servants. Rebecca assured Stead that she had acted just as he had wished. Stead had no reason to distrust her, particularly because of Josephine's faith in her. Mrs

Armstrong continued to deny Rebecca's version of their contract, however, and Stead could produce no evidence to support Rebecca's story. Her value as a witness was destroyed when she was shown to have perjured herself during cross-examination by lying to protect the names and addresses of former associates, brothel keepers and procurers. Josephine later described how she 'looked across the Court at me with an expression on her pale face which I shall never forget. That night, Rebecca spent several hours on her knees, weeping as if her heart would break'.[66]

Stead's condemnation of Rebecca's 'deception' was unequivocal, and from being the agent without whose collaboration he would have been unable to purchase a child like Eliza Armstrong, he treated her as if she were still a hardened procuress, as did the prosecution. It fell to Josephine to defend poor, confused Rebecca. She wrote to Stanley that Rebecca had 'had a good cry in the witness box', but that she herself was still 'in good spirits about the trial'.[67] She was called to take the stand on 2 November. 'Jarrett was strictly honest', she said, 'and could be trusted to the last farthing'.[68] Josephine denied strongly that she had attempted to conceal Rebecca's whereabouts from the police. On 7 November, the final day of the trial, Rebecca managed to pass a note to Josephine across the courtroom, thanking her for her love and kindness in supporting her throughout the trial, 'and more especially for your confidence in me after all the terrible things you have heard said of me by the Prosecution in this Court'.[69]

The two representatives of the Salvation Army, Bramwell Booth and Madame Combe, neither of whom had been involved in the actual abduction, were both acquitted. Stead was given three months' hard labour for the unlawful abduction of Eliza Armstrong, and Samuel Jacques, one month. Rebecca Jarrett and Louise Mourez were each sentenced to six months' imprisonment, Mourez with hard labour. The court made little distinction between the reformed procuress in Stead's employ, and the still practising 'mid-wife', the only one of the accused not to be aware that she was involved in a 'staged' abduction. In fact, Stead served only two months, and his original sentence was reduced. He sat out his term in a carpeted, book-lined room in Holloway Prison, from where he continued to write for the *Pall Mall Gazette*, while the lame Rebecca had to sleep on a plank bed two inches from the stone floor of her cell in Millbank Prison.

Stead had accepted his martyrdom with characteristic relish in his farewell leader, published on 9 November, and generously thanked the court for a fair trial. 'Perhaps Mr Stead may think that he himself was courteously treated,' was Josephine's retort, 'but what of the courtesy or even decent fairness shown in regard to Rebecca?'[70] Josephine sent a telegram to Winchester to give George news of the sentences. He had been thinking about her that morning in the Cathedral and had momentarily lost his place in the service, coming upon the words of Psalm 91, verse 11: 'For He shall give his angels charge over thee, to keep thee in all thy ways.' Josephine was coming back to him, but George's joy was mixed with disgust at Stead's vanity, and he wrote back, 'Tell Mr Stead, if you have an opportunity, to read Ecclesiasticus ii': 'Vanity of vanities, saith the Preacher, vanity of vanities; all *is* vanity'![71]

It was a costly autumn for Josephine. She calculated that she had had to travel up to London eighteen times 'about the Trial alone', sometimes there and back in the same day.[72] She was exhausted, but determined to counter the terrible slanders made against Rebecca during the trial. The day after Rebecca's sentence was delivered, William Booth reported to his wife that, 'Mrs Butler is fast at Winchester with bronchitis, working on a pamphlet on Rebecca Jarrett'.[73] This sixty-page pamphlet took the form of a biographical sketch of Rebecca in which Josephine hoped to 'present the exact truth about her in justice to herself'.[74]

As well as defending Rebecca in print, Josephine was busily campaigning for a reprieve. Together with Catherine and Florence Booth, she led a deputation of ninety women to the Home Secretary to protest against Rebecca's sentence, and presented him with one hundred petitions for Rebecca's reprieve. Sir William Harcourt, now once again the Liberal Home Secretary, was so moved by their appeal that he made a personal visit to Millbank Prison to ask after Rebecca's health and had her moved to a warmer cell.

Josephine kept in touch with Rebecca through Mr Merrick, the chaplain at Millbank Prison, and she visited her once a month, writing to Miss Priestman, 'Rebecca begs us not to fret about her as she is "well & happy" – brave soul! The Chaplain . . . has conceived such a good opinion of Rebecca that he says he will take her as his own housekeeper when she is released, if I don't want her, but I *do* want her'.[75] In fact, *thirty-eight* clergymen had written to Merrick, asking to have Rebecca. She left Millbank Prison at 8 a.m. on 10 April 1886, with 7*s.* 6*d.* 'good conduct money' in her purse and 'no end of parcels' from lady well-wishers, including six shawls and four rugs.

Josephine was then in Cannes nursing George, but Florence Booth was there to meet Rebecca in a cab. Stead had wanted to treat her to a celebration breakfast so that all her friends could welcome her home, 'but I felt I could not stand it', she said, and Florence Booth wisely took her to a quiet restaurant in the Strand where they had a cup of tea together.[76]

Josephine was unconvinced that Rebecca was fit for the excitement of active work, but Rebecca herself argued that she could only withstand temptation if she was engaged in responsible work. She rested for some months in private lodgings in Clapton, near the Salvation Army barracks there, her rent and washing paid for, it seems, by Josephine.[77] Josephine then asked her down to Winchester for a short stay, but her visit was enough to incense a mob to attack Josephine and some Salvation Army women afterwards. That night, Sunday 28 June 1886, Josephine wrote Bramwell Booth an account of the extraordinary goings-on. With the aid of three policemen she had been delivered safely to her door, but the crowd refused to leave and continued their howling. This brought out the Dean and the other canons who, she said, were angry with her for being the cause of 'such a disgraceful scene within the sacred precincts of the Close'.[78] George, mercifully, slept through it all, but Georgie, who happened to be visiting his parents, was just returning to the Close after his evening walk, and, hearing his mother insulted, 'he lost his temper, I grieve to say, and knocked down the foremost man'. She had not been at all afraid, she told Bramwell, but she was worried that Georgie would be charged with assault, and the Dean made much of her son's 'brawling in the Close'. Georgie was unrepentant: 'Well, it's rather hard to see one's Mother insulted by several 100s of roughs'.

Shortly after her release from prison Rebecca Jarrett sailed for Toronto as a Salvation Army rescue worker in the company of her first Army friend, Captain Jones, but the mission was a personal failure for Rebecca, who returned to England in late February 1887. Josephine was still sending her sums of money as late as December 1888.[79] She was then staying at a large home in Edinburgh that offered refuge to over a hundred women, and where she went under the pseudonym 'Mary Grey'.[80] It is an anonymous enough name, but since it was also the name of Josephine's grandmother, and we know that Josephine herself had used her maiden name as a disguise in the past, it is possible that it was she who suggested it to Rebecca. Josephine and Amélie both corresponded with her under that name. Only the 'head gentleman' and the matron, Jane Milne, knew Rebecca's true identity. Rebecca did return to the Salvation Army shortly after this, and she did good work for them until her death in 1928.

14

India

'Slavery under the British Flag'

THE CONSERVATIVE GOVERNMENT which had taken office in July 1885 and passed the Criminal Law Amendment Act, came out of the November 1885 general election as a minority government. In the run-up to this election, Josephine had published *A Woman's Appeal to the Electors*, in which she urged candidates to state whether they would support a public inquiry into Stead's prosecution, and made a forceful plea for female suffrage and 'a share in making laws' by which they were governed.[1] Among the MPs returned were 261 repealers, only twenty of them Conservatives.[2] The minority government lasted only until February 1886 when for a few months the Liberals again took office. James Stansfeld took the opportunity to introduce a bill for the repeal of the CD Acts, which, despite attempts to block it by Cavendish-Bentinck, was passed and given the Royal Assent on 15 April 1886.

When the news of repeal came through Josephine was abroad, just as she had been the previous year when the Criminal Law Amendment Act was passed. In early February, both Josephine and George were in 'a very shakey condition', and only waited for the imminent marriage of Stanley and his cousin Rhoda before heading off for Cannes, in order to recuperate before the Federation Congress at Easter which was to be held that year in Naples. The Butlers would not return to England for another ten months, and by then Rhoda's baby, their first grandchild, had been christened. They named her Josephine after her grandmother. It was Margaret Tanner who wrote to Josephine about the state of euphoria in the Ladies' Gallery when Stansfeld's preliminary 16

March motion that the CD Acts should be repealed was agreed unopposed. Stansfeld, Stuart and Wilson raced up to the ladies 'to receive our congratulations and share our joy – their faces were radiant'.[3] In Naples, Josephine and George received telegrams from Stuart and from Stansfeld, and wrote home to Stanley and Rhoda on Easter Sunday:

> Stansfeld telegraphed to us last thing at Naples, 'Queen's Assent Given'. That means to the repeal bill. It was done on my birthday, the 13th. So *that* abomination is dead & *buried.* Praise the Lord! I feel inclined to do as Cromwell did when he saw poor King Charles lying dead. He just took hold of the head & shook it a little, to be quite sure that it was loose from the body![4]

In fact, Royal Assent was given on 15 April, which was, as her ally Benjamin Scott pointed out, *his* 'natal day'.

For the remainder of the year, Josephine was largely lost to the cause while she was preoccupied with her husband's illness. They had begun the year with an ambitious schedule of travel. George was an indefatigable tourist and was known to set off on three sightseeing trips a day. There was also the excitement of meeting some illustrious fellow travellers. On the station at Cannes he was favoured by the notice of the Prince of Wales while their train was being made ready. The Prince was 'smoking and chatting like anybody else', noted George, and 'did not look a bit more distinguished than anybody else'.[5] At Genoa they were in time for the Carnival, and at Naples they were Hatty's guests at the Palazzo Caprioli. Josephine was not so fortunate in her sightseeing: while the gentlemen took George off to visit Pompeii, she was enlisted by the womenfolk to help organize a hospital bazaar! There were plenty of entertainments, though, including an evening dinner and fancy dress *conversazione* hosted by the Meuricoffres. Then, without warning, George came down with a malarial fever. In the middle of the night Josephine scribbled a terrified message to her eldest son. The following night she and Hatty sat up until 3 a.m., but George's condition did not worsen: 'He can keep nothing in his stomach, not even a spoonful of beef tea, and was very restless . . . I woke again at 6 & have been in his room ever since. Amelia brought him a cup of tea, which he has not *yet* thrown up! I brushed his hair & washed his hands for him'.[6]

George recovered enough to make the journey to Bad Homburg near Frankfurt, where they were joined by James Stuart and Stanley.

There was little for Stanley to do, in fact, other than 'saunter about with father's coat and air cushion' and escort George to the baths each day, where he would read him the paper and 'see that his head does not go under water and so drown him'.[7] Both George and Josephine were tetchy at times: 'Father fidgets & can't sleep. Mother frets & can't eat', but Stanley felt it his duty to stay with his parents until they were more settled. The Prince of Wales arrived there on 15 August, 'drinking away and looking very corpulent', according to Stanley, and he also met a friend of Stuart's, the widower of George Eliot, John Cross ('ever such a swell').[8] His father was well enough to take note of the several society beauties visiting Homburg, and asked Stanley to convey a message to Rhoda to the effect that 'with a long purse and no babies, you could easily cut them out'.

Stanley was able to return to Winchester by the end of the month, by which time his father had recovered sufficiently to travel on to Frankfurt, where George was once again to rub shoulders with royalty, at a splendid reception given by the local 'wine prince', Mauskoff. Josephine spied George 'hobnobbing with Princess Christian' (this was Queen Victoria's third daughter, Helena): George and the Princess 'stood side by side, sipping away'.[9] Still a convalescent, however, George abstained from sampling the best wines. To Stanley and Rhoda, Josephine sent back an excited account:

> Father gave one little sigh as he passed them, but refrained. He just tasted some white wine diluted deliciously somehow and flavoured with pineapple – some invention of the gods! . . . And O! Dody, the cakes, & the lovely goodies, & the rich ripe fruit festooned about, just ready to drop into your mouth! I was so bewildered that I ended by taking nothing.

Stanley was back in Winchester for the birth of his daughter, Josephine, on 23 September 1886, but a month later was recalled to Switzerland, where his father was much worse. By the autumn, Josephine was in a fireless *pension* at Muri, on the outskirts of Berne, nursing an ageing husband who, the doctors told her, was face to face with death. Their temporary lodgings were wholly unsuitable for an invalid in George's condition, or indeed for Josephine, who sat up night after night with *several* hot water bottles: 'I could see his breath go up like a vapour . . . his chest fluttering with his heart's rapid breathing . . . I used not to take my clothes off for nights & nights'.[10] When she went to her own room to pray for George, the tears froze on her cheeks.

Josephine later detailed his sufferings: pericarditus (inflammation of the membranous sac enclosing the heart), 'inflammation also of the valves of the heart, pleurisy of both lungs, & extensive inflammation of the lungs'. All three sons arrived in Berne, and came out to Muri daily, but it was not until the end of October that they were able to move George to a hotel in the town, Charles carrying his father in his arms. In early November they heard from Rhoda, who offered to come out with her baby in order to cheer George. She did the next best thing and sent George a photograph of herself with the baby on her lap.

The Bernerhoff was rather too grand for their always limited finances, but Hatty thoughtfully made a gift of cooking apparatus. 'At first', Josephine wrote to her Bristol friend, Mary Estlin, 'I burnt my hands & made sad messes, but now I can make beautiful cocoa & beef tea and several other things – an immense saving'.[11] She was soon spared the anxiety of such economies, however, when a friend lent her the services of a maid, and they received a gift, or rather a grant, of £100 from the Clifton LNA. Emily Ford, the daughter of a Quaker friend Hannah Ford who had died earlier that year, sent a similar sum. She declined Emily's further offer of an English male nurse, but she confessed her despair at not having the right things for George: 'They don't know what calf's foot jelly is here. They send you flabby stuff'.[12] As it was, Georgie thought to bring some from London.

Mrs Sumner, their friend from Winchester, visited them and was able to report that George was moving about, and was able to join the ladies downstairs briefly for luncheon. From Geneva, she sent Emily Ford a moving description of Josephine herself:

> What a wonderful face she has, and the look in it and on it which makes it so rare, is intensified I'm sure by all she has gone through . . . I never felt more quickly drawn to anyone, and I felt, above all, that she had *something* so few have: *such an understanding of God* . . . Her atmosphere was lovely to me. I felt at home in it . . . Then I went to her little room and we spoke to our Lord . . . I can never forget that bit of mortal time . . . How delightful her originality and all absence of conventionality is.[13]

Since the announcement of the repeal of the Contagious Diseases Acts, Josephine had been in frequent contact with the Priestman sisters as together they planned a conference to celebrate. Astonishingly, at the same time as she was looking after her ill husband she took upon herself its organization, even down to booking London hotel rooms for Federation members from the Continent! Seeking only the advice of Mary Priestman in Bristol, she was trying to meet their diverse requirements, and had also to consider social distinctions. They were expecting aristocratic ladies, 'a few Countesses etc.', and they needed equal consideration: 'I *am* republican. Still I think one must a little consult *habits*'.[14]

Now that repeal was achieved, for Josephine the crucial question was the future of the LNA.[15] She shared the anxiety of the Priestmans that it must 'never turn into a mere rescue society'.[16] Nor should they let it be absorbed into a purity movement, such as the Vigilance Association. From the *pension* at Muri, she wrote a circular urging that the organization remain in existence for at least a year. She drew attention to the wrongs of Indian and Chinese women, who were suffering from continued application of the CD Acts to British-governed territories abroad, saying that 'Mr Stuart has made my blood boil again with quite youthful wrath by what he has told me'.[17] Josephine was more than ready to take up the cause elsewhere, pointing out that, 'For twenty years Indian women have been oppressed and outraged even as women in Paris have not been'.

Frustration with the European work of the Federation had built up. The European campaign was too dependent upon the efforts of a few individuals, and it was becoming increasingly burdensome. With Josephine out of action for much of 1886, Humbert sent her anxious letters, reporting that the work of the Federation was effectively paralysed without her. Unable to rest during the Channel crossing in December 1886, Josephine began composing a long letter to the Priestmans which she finished at Winchester on Christmas Eve. Its subject was India and the Crown Colonies. Characteristically, she had conceived the new campaign entirely independently, and was to be its driving force. She began working on it with James Stuart, and on 29 December the two of them wrote out a plan of action, proposing that the LNA should make clear its continued existence as distinctly a women's society, and its determination 'to avenge the wrongs of our sister women in India and other countries'.[18]

By 1887 it was clear that India was the great problem. Although there was a division of the British government called the India Office, with a Secretary of State responsible to Parliament, all laws in India were made by the Governor-General and his Council who were very reluctant to repeal the CD Acts as they operated there. Yet the British

Parliament, as James Stuart demonstrated, did have constitutional power to interfere in Indian affairs, and could therefore insist upon repeal.

Stuart proposed to sound out Sir R.A. Cross and the Honourable Edward Stanhope, Secretaries of State for India and for the Colonies respectively, and then either Stansfeld or himself would ask the House how long it would be before repeal was extended to British territories. This, noted Josephine, would give Stuart 'the opportunity of telling the House some of the enormities which we learn from the Indian Blue Book, so as to horrify our good MPs', and would provoke discussion.[19] The ladies of the LNA would be reminded that they still had friends in Parliament, and that MPs should be 'bombarded' with petitions and memorials. Josephine also thought of getting to work on any missionaries about to depart for India: 'I think we ought to get hold of them, and stir them up'. At this very time, the *Pall Mall Gazette* published the MP, William Caine's exposé of the Contagious Diseases Acts in Egypt, and Stead wrote to Josephine, confirming that the colonies were the new crusade. As she told the Priestman sisters, 'Mr Stead writes to me that "this is the first shot fired, and he believes it means a great battle coming on" . . . It ought to stir us all up. We who are old cannot run about as we did, but at any rate we can think and advise'.[20]

Josephine's position on India was both Christian and political. She felt that her English ladies needed to be reminded that God gave His son to the *whole* world, and that the native women of India, too, were created in the image of their Divine Maker yet were being 'morally murdered' by their imperial masters.[21] Not only were they women oppressed by men, but 'women of a conquered race oppressed by their conquerers'.[22] Far from spreading the tenets of Christian civilization throughout the Empire, British imperialism was spreading moral darkness under a cruel and despotic rule.

Josephine's Christian pleading and her political reasoning were rather compromised by lurid anecdotes of female victimization and martyrdom. In the December 1886 number of the *Sentinel*, Josephine told her readers that when the CD Acts (or 'British State Harlotry', in Josephine's phrase) were first instituted in Bombay, hundreds of poor women had fled, many never to be heard of again: 'some perished in the forests; others were found dead at the bottom of wells, having committed suicide to escape an infamy which they could not endure even to contemplate'.[23] She commented ironically that it was sometimes boasted that the sun never set upon the British flag, but that it was also true 'that it never sets upon the institution of legalised impurity under British rule'. When she addressed a special Federation meeting on the Indian Question at Exeter Hall on 20 May 1887, she told the story of a Chinese woman in Hong Kong who had sold her little son into slavery to meet a fine imposed under the CD regulations, and who, in an attempt to escape the 'bloodhounds of debauchery', the brothel police, fell from a rooftop to her death.[24] Josephine took her as a symbol of the system: 'The blood of that forlorn woman cries from the grave to us to save her sisters from a similar doom'.

Josephine had written of her 'quite youthful wrath' over the brutal subjection of native women, but she was no longer able to carry on a new campaign personally. Attendance at Federation conferences in Europe each summer was only a possibility if Josephine and George could spend the best part of the year recuperating in the south of France or Italy. She was now fifty-eight, and it was out of the question that she could suddenly set off to tour America, as she was repeatedly asked to do at this time, or extend her personal ministry to India. When, as late as spring 1888 no further progress had been made in India, English repealers sent out the publisher Alfred Dyer and his wife, Helen, to conduct their own investigations.

Besides her own delicate health, there was now the well-being of her husband to consider. It must have been an odd period of adjustment for Josephine, especially after their recent parliamentary triumph, yet whatever frustrations she may have felt at being unable to lead this new crusade, she expressed them only rarely. There was, for example, her unease with the manner in which Alfred Dyer conducted his investigations throughout India. Josephine praised Dyer, writing of his special gifts for the task ahead, but earlier that year she had written to the Priestman sisters that she was very troubled by his *aggressive* character: 'For denunciation, and as a scourge, he is a well chosen instrument; but I daresay you feel as I do that there is a note wanting (and a sad want it is), and that is the note of compassion for our poor sisters and tormented sisters of India. I can discern not a trace of pity for them. His expressions are those of disgust and reprobation only.'[25] She felt that the necessary compassion was wanting, not in Dyer's case only, but too often among their male friends in Parliament. Josephine set up her own little penny-paper, the *Dawn*, at this time, partly to aid the campaign over India, as she tried to arouse her readers' interest with the stories of individual suffering.[26] The strength of the appeal for an expansion of sympathy and charity which she made in the very first issue of the *Dawn* suggests how much more difficult it was to elicit sympathy for anonymous Indian women than for ruined maids at home.

The campaign for India was given a fortuitous beginning when a private communication from the Quartermaster-General to the officers commanding divisions and districts was intercepted by Dyer and sent to Stuart in London. In Josephine's view it exceeded 'in horror and wickedness anything we have ever read'.[27] The 'Infamous Memorandum', as it was known, referred to complaints from the soldiers regarding the *quality* of the prostitutes they were being supplied with, and ordered that the women be 'sufficiently attractive'. It was advised that recruiting sergeants 'scour the country in search of young and "attractive" women', and that the government pay three rupees a head for every girl brought in.[28] James Stuart also wrote in the *Dawn* that Dyer had gained access to the 1885 Annual Report of the lock hospital at Umballa which suggested that recruiting matrons 'might be employed in importing younger and more prepossessing women at a small capitation grant'.[29]

This was the breakthrough: the shocking revelation that the British government in India actively sought to supply women for the use of the British troops was seized upon by the repeal movement. The Federation was quick to send out copies of the 'Infamous Memorandum' to all MPs. Angry petitioners, from W.H. Smith to the Bishop of Bombay, demanded to know why the military forces in India were exempted from recognizing the repeal of the ordinances, and Josephine reported to Margaret Tanner her observations, from the Ladies' Gallery of the House of Commons, of the government's discomfort: 'when Sir John Gorst [the Under-Secretary for India] had to confess that the ghastly story from India was true'.[30] Repealers were able to argue that only *absolute* repeal of the pernicious system in India would guarantee that such immoral practices never be repeated. The question was debated in the Commons on 5 June 1888, and the motion for repeal moved by Walter McLaren was carried without a single dissenting voice. This was a remarkable sign of the dramatic shift in the opinion of the House.

The Indian government was ordered to rescind the Acts, but General Sir Frederick Sleigh Roberts, Commander-in-Chief of the British Army in India, temporized and procrastinated, and over the next few years a system of regulation would be more or less maintained.

Josephine herself wrote to Roberts on 4 May 1888, asking whether he was able to deny the recent revelations, and printed his reply from Simla in the *Dawn*.[31] In his reply, Roberts acknowledged the 'awful colour' put on things by the leaking of the Quartermaster-General's circular, but he assured Josephine that the army's original conception of the CD Acts derived solely from concern for the health of British soldiers, 'who are surrounded in this country by far greater temptation than people in England have any idea of'.[32] He cautioned Josephine against making a too simple comparison between British or European women and their native sisters: 'Prostitution is a trade amongst the natives which is practised all over India; shame, in a European sense, does not attach to it. Mothers bring up their daughters to the vocation they have followed themselves'. Josephine's response was furious. She threatened Roberts with a second Indian Mutiny, telling him, 'nothing so surely produces a spirit of rebellion as the *trampling on the womanhood of a subject race by their conquerers*'.[33]

In 1889 the Abolitionists' campaign became centred upon the case of a fourteen-year-old Indian girl in Patna, west of Calcutta, a child-widow who had been sold into prostitution, Musamnat Luchmin. In many ways, this was a typical *cause sensationelle* for Josephine Butler, with echoes of the 'Maiden Tribute' campaign. Although Josephine refrained from reproducing other pieces on India from Dyer's *Sentinel*, she gave this particular story prominence. Three and a half pages from the *Bombay Guardian*, now being edited by Dyer, were reprinted in the February 1889 issue of the *Dawn*, and readers were kept informed of shocking developments in the case in subsequent issues.

Luchmin's case required little exaggeration. She had been already married and widowed at the age of eleven when she was returned to her mother, who later sold her to a man of her caste called Radakissin. She joined his house as a member of a growing harem consisting of Luchmin, one other widow aged twenty-six, and a prostitute. The two widows became converts to Christianity, and one evening in mid-October 1888 ran away to a Christian mission. The magistrates' court at Patna had ruled that Luchmin should be returned to Radakissin as her lawful protector. To the Abolitionists, the British magistrate was returning her to prostitution, and they took up the cause of the fourteen-year-old Christian convert as one which would both stir the consciences of English people at home and embarrass the British Parliament. Alfred Dyer bombarded the Viceroy of India with telegrams about the case, and also Sir John Gorst, the Under-Secretary of

State for India, sympathetic MPs and newspaper editors, including, of course, W.T. Stead, who could be relied upon to publicize the case. On 10 December, Stuart brought the matter before Gorst in the Commons, but Gorst showed little interest in its particulars. Presumably he saw no reason for the administration to interfere in a minor, isolated *native* affair, but the case played its part in making the government's stance on India an unpopular one.

At the twelfth Federation Congress, held at Geneva from 10 to 14 September 1889, Stuart talked confidently in his closing address of the wonderful progress of the Abolition movement in India, pronouncing the system in India 'under sentence of death'.[34] Yet the Indian government was currently putting the finishing touches to a major new piece of legislation that would effectively restore the Contagious Diseases Acts. On 21 December 1889, a year after Luchmin received her sentence in the Patna court, the government passed a new Cantonment Act, which 'permitted' the reintroduction of every single measure providing for the prevention, containment and cure of syphilis under the original Acts. Josephine's editorial in the *Dawn* was entitled 'A Call to Battle'. It was, she said, a battle against 'the tyranny of the lust and greed of Englishmen', a war 'against the most corrupt of corrupt officialism, against military oppression, materialism in high places, and vested interests of a kind which will not bear looking into'.[35]

In March 1891 Josephine wrote an address for the Conference and General Meeting of the London branch of the LNA. She was in Switzerland at the time, and her speech was delivered by Mrs Eva McLaren. It made an impassioned call for women to take the leading role in this campaign, insisting that 'in this lies the only hope of the future of our poor humanity, so far as this question of justice and moral purity is concerned'.[36] At the annual meeting of the LNA held on 29 May that year, which Josephine was able to preside over, she would again argue for the importance of prominent *women* workers in this cause, making a specific plea for younger women to take over the movement, in what she termed an 'Apostolic Succession'; but they must be young women possessing her own 'faith unto death'.

Two younger women were to step forward, women who would travel extensively in India, collecting evidence of the administration of the CD Acts and talking to the common people about their experience of regulated vice, just as Josephine had undertaken her personal crusade to Europe nearly two decades before. Their names were Dr

Kate Bushnell, and Mrs Elizabeth Andrews, the widow of a Methodist minister. They were American and both were leading members of the World's Women's Christian Temperance Union (WWCTU).

Elizabeth Andrews had read and been inspired by Stead's biographical sketch of Josephine, and had no doubt communicated this to Kate Bushnell, of the Social Purity Department of the WWCTU. In 1887, Dr Bushnell had investigated the lumbermen's camps in Wisconsin and upper Michigan, where she had found young women imprisoned in compounds and forced to be prostitutes, either lured to the camps by false advertisements or actually abducted. She was unsure of her precise calling, however, and spent many months in prayer, asking for divine direction. On a hot summer's day in 1890, she threw herself down on her couch: 'I said to the Lord that I was so stupid in understanding His guidance, that I thought He might have to send me the instructions I needed through a dream'. She fell asleep immediately, 'and dreamed that I felt myself tossed on the billows of the Atlantic on my way to England to see Josephine Butler'.[37] She wrote to Josephine at once, asking how she could be of service. Josephine was weak and exhausted from nursing her husband and she at first put the letter to one side, but, prompted, she felt, by God, she wrote to Dr Bushnell asking her to come to England at once. Elizabeth Andrews was due to travel the world in the role of a missionary for the WWCTU early in 1891, and the two headed straight for England and Josephine. They called on her in early March, and impressed Josephine with their quiet and steady demeanour and their 'deep and strong convictions'. 'I am much struck with them, & think you will be also,' she wrote to the Priestmans.[38] They wanted to go out to India as representatives of the Ladies' National Association, and 'at their own expense'!

They arrived in Calcutta in December 1891, on what Josephine considered 'one of the most difficult and even perilous missions ever undertaken in the course of our great crusade'.[39] At first they spoke to British officials, but were met with denials that CD regulation continued to exist. They decided to speak only to native Indians and immediately the system of regulation was revealed to them. They visited ten cantonments along the North-West Frontier, and found, in each of them, prostitutes maintained for the use of British soldiers. At Lucknow up to 200 prostitutes were housed in a large *chakla*, a building in which rooms were set aside for their use; at Peshawar there were a number of brothels in a single street; and at Rawalpindi they found several smaller *chakla* which were allotted to individual regiments, including one for the native troops. Only the women set apart for British troops were obliged to go to the lock hospital for regular examinations.[40]

A majority of the girls were widows, sold to the British Army by their husbands' families, and they found that many of them had been brought in by poverty or by fraud. Many of the prostitutes were children, some of them, like Luchmin, married and widowed while still very young. They were housed in wretched conditions in the *chakla*, and lived in fear of the brutality of the soldiers, especially when drunk. Most of all, Bushnell and Andrews found in these women a hatred of the humiliating physical examinations they were forced to undergo. Their greatest wish was for these examinations to be stopped. Pitifully, they clung to a belief that Queen Victoria would not countenance it, 'for she has daughters of her own; and she cares for her daughters in India also'.[41]

One woman at Lahore provided them with indisputable evidence of the continuance of compulsory examination in India: the ticket registering her as a prostitute, which bore her name, her caste, the date of her initial registration, her registration number, and a personal description. It was signed by the cantonment magistrate. On the reverse was a table listing her fortnightly inspections together with the comments of the medical officer. She had submitted to her most recent examination just two days before.

Before entering each new cantonment the American women were careful to post their latest reports back to England by registered mail, and when their situation looked particularly dangerous they took to writing on very thin notepaper which they sewed into the hems of their petticoats every night. They also sent their so-called secret report ahead of them when they left for England. Josephine thought the report wonderful, and said that there would have to be 'a searching light thrown upon all that it reveals to *us* privately'.[42] By the time they arrived back in England early in April 1893, the report had already been published as *A Statement of Facts* by Stuart and Stansfeld. The government set up a committee, of which Henry Wilson was a member, to investigate their findings. It was to take evidence from Dr Bushnell and Mrs Andrews, and also from Lord Roberts and the now retired Quartermaster-General, Chapman, who had been responsible for circulating the 'Infamous Memorandum'.

The Committee began sitting on 11 April, and Dr Bushnell and Mrs

Andrews were called to begin giving evidence that day. Sir James Stansfeld was determined that the British Abolitionists should not let the two women testify without large-scale support. The agitation had to begin at once, and Josephine was called upon to compose an appeal to be sent to all the religious papers: 'A large order!' Josephine exclaimed to Stanley.[43] She was at that time lodging with her sister, Emmy, on the Wandsworth Road. On the Sunday morning Emmy set the drawing-room table to rights, pushed it in front of the fire, marshalled in her stepdaughter with her 'type-writing machine', and before lunch Josephine had dictated a dozen letters.

Lord Roberts arrived in London in early May, and, in an interview with W. T. Stead for the *Review of Reviews*, promptly made a very public denial of the charges made. He 'abused us rather', Josephine noted. He said that the Contagious Diseases Acts had been withdrawn in 1888 and that no such regulation was in operation in any of the cantonments under his jurisdiction; further, as Commander-in-Chief, he professed absolute ignorance of such immoral practices as had been suggested by the Quartermaster-General's circular, the 'Infamous Memorandum'. This he continued to assert to members of the investigative Committee when he appeared before them on 4, 7 and 8 August. He was forced to make a complete retraction, however, on 11 August when Chapman revealed to the Committee that the system of regulation *was* operating in India, and that Roberts knew of it and had ordered him to prepare the circular which had become known as the 'Infamous Memorandum'. Indeed, he had 'read it over and entirely approved it'. Roberts immediately apologized to the two women whose report he had impugned, saying that it was in ignorance of the facts that he 'spoke against their veracity in public'.[44]

Strangely, Josephine, who was not present, and whose account of the proceedings of the Committee was derived from Henry Wilson's, was outraged not at Lord Roberts but at Chapman. Roberts she saw as merely '*very* careless', but Chapman, whom in her letter to Stanley she repeatedly calls 'a devil', as a religious hypocrite and a traitor to his commanding officer. Her bias against him, which included a hostile, Dickensian description of a man she had never seen, was astonishing. Chapman was apparently 'a dark evil-looking man . . . expressionless, with a mouth of a peculiar form, thin, mechanical, which slowly opens like a steel trap, to emit the lies he speaks with a face of black night and imperturbable impertinence, and then shuts again like a skeleton's mouth'.[45]

Thanks to the efforts of the two American women, victory was theirs, and it was sweet. The Departmental Committee were plainly shocked by Roberts's dishonourable testimony, and, as some recompense, they recommended that the government reimburse the Federation to the tune of £700 or £800 to pay for Dr Bushnell's and Mrs Andrews's expenses: 'So we have fought them with their own money!' There was some justice in this. Stuart had marvelled at the women's '*honestly economical*' accounts, noting that a *gentleman* agent sent out to India by the Federation had asked for more than double their expenses. Before the Committee had even made their recommendation, the Federation determined to make over a gift of £100 each to the ladies as a sign of their thanks.[46]

The Cantonment Act of 1889 was finally amended by the India Act No.V, which prohibited the registration and periodical examination of prostitutes. The new Act received the assent of the Viceroy on 8 February 1895.

15

The Death of George

'May God send us many such men'

JOSEPHINE'S ELDEST SON would in later years reproach her for his father's death, saying that, even when advanced in years and enfeebled in health, George 'took part in her work & her journeying to & fro, ungrudgingly giving his time & help to smooth her way; even to the fatal sea journey from Copenhagen when he took the dangerous chill'.[1] George himself had delivered a speech at the Federation conference, held at Copenhagen from 29 August to 1 September 1888, reporting on the significant recent progress of the Abolitionist cause in the Anglican Church. Josephine later pencilled on the envelope containing his speech, 'He was not well, and his voice was not strong. But he was listened to in deep silence'.[2]

Josephine's letters home to Stanley and Rhoda reveal little anxiety for her husband's health. Copenhagen was an exciting prospect for both of them: George had been commissioned by the *Contemporary Review* to write a piece on the famous Thorvaldsen sculptures,[3] and for Josephine it was a particularly thrilling Congress in terms of the women's interest it excited, interest that would serve as an encouraging example to the flagging effort among women back in England. The Danish women were quite unabashed when asked to speak in public, and even demanded a meeting of their own since one had not been included in the official programme: 'it was a great crowded meeting of working women and ladies such as one might have in Halifax or Leeds. Such a crush . . . It would have done your hearts good to see the rush of women wherever we went'.[4]

Josephine and a small party of ladies were invited to Sweden, and they took the steamer over to Malmö, where men were permitted to attend what had been planned as a women-only meeting. There was a touching incident on the night steamer back to Copenhagen. The head stewardess was curious about what the party of foreign ladies had been doing in Sweden. Miss Ida Willhaven, the only Danish speaker among them, explained, and, in Josephine's words, the stewardess 'looked round on us all, as if we had been messengers of deliverance and peace, and then flew to bring us out the best she had in her cupboard by way of refreshment. We drank our midnight tea with thankful hearts, as our little steamer ploughed through the Baltic waves.'[5] Josephine was also honoured with a personal invitation to call on the Crown Princess of Denmark (the daughter of the King of Sweden, who had married the eldest son of the King of Denmark), and found her surprisingly well informed about the progress of the Indian campaign: 'She was very nice, the Princess, and we had a long talk in her little room'. Their talk was sufficiently intimate for the Princess to reveal to Josephine that 'she does not like her brother-in-law, the Prince of Wales'.[6]

The Copenhagen Congress was significant for two very important, yet widely different, tributes to Josephine. The inaugural address was given by a self-styled disciple of hers, a Mr Pierson of Holland, who compared her to Joan of Arc, 'subjugating by the intensity and fervour of her faith the people who followed her'. He said that it was impossible for him to disobey the woman who, more than any other, 'has charged us with the heavy task of carrying on this war against patented vice'.[7] The tribute of George's speech was rather more unexpected, and its timing is of particular interest in what it reveals about the difficulty of Josephine's position during this period. She was the unquestioned leader of the Abolition movement, and had embarked upon the new campaign over India, yet she was increasingly hampered by George's declining health. Josephine felt very strongly that colleagues did not appreciate how much she was needed to nurse her aged husband. She described extensively in her biography of her husband how she was forced to refuse 'all invitations to attend meetings, in London or elsewhere – sometimes, I fear, to the surprise as well as regret of my fellow workers in public matters'. She felt that during their married life George had borne her frequent absences without complaint, and now that he was seriously ill she could not leave him. She did leave him for a short time when her sister Fanny survived a major stroke in July 1888, and 'Even on that occasion I was told by those at home that he seemed to feel my absence sadly, and that at the sound of a footstep or wheels on the drive, he would go to the window to see if by any chance it was his wife who had returned, though he knew that it was scarcely possible'.[8]

While Josephine felt a need to defend her absences from various committee meetings and conferences, George anticipated criticism of his wife from quite another quarter, from those who felt she wasn't being wife enough. To the audience at Copenhagen he firmly defended her against such a charge:

> It is sometimes said that women who take up a great cause for the benefit of their fellow creatures are in danger of neglecting the sacred duties of home. I know that such need not be the case; I may tell you that had it not been for the constant and devoted care which my wife bestowed on me, during a very long and serious illness, I should not be standing here to speak to you to-day.[9]

As always, Josephine was 'dead tired' by the end of the conference.[10] She and George both longed to get back to simple, wholesome English cooking. The food in Denmark was so rich it made Josephine bilious – and the tea was bad! Most of all, they were anxious to return in time for the birth of their second grandchild, Stanley and Rhoda's son, Andrew Stanley George Butler, known always as 'Bobby', who was born at the Close on 23 September.

They had a rough crossing on the homeward journey, and George, who had been pacing about on deck, caught the severe chill regretted so much by their eldest son. The London physician they consulted told Josephine that her husband might live only a matter of weeks or months. By the beginning of November, Josephine thought his time was come, and sent a desperate postcard to the Priestmans' niece, Helen Clark, in which she scribbled down her fear: 'I am full of anxiety about my husband. I should like so much to be permitted to go with him, if he has to go, out of this world. We have been so long together. He gets no better.'[11]

George was suffering from a bad attack of jaundice. A week later he was out of danger and sufficiently recovered to dine on a parcel of game sent by Georgie: 'It was excellent. Tender, well hung, and cooked to a T. Many thanks for your kind provision for my captious stomach'; he was so cheered that he thought he might even teach Stanley's wife Rhoda backgammon.[12] His bouts of rapid decline and equally rapid recovery would form a pattern over the next eighteen months.

In December 1888, George was ordered by his doctors to seek the warmth of southern France or Italy. On 8 January 1889, their thirty-seventh wedding anniversary, George made out his will, in which, having made over gifts of books and money to his sons and nephews (he left his breech loading gun and old muzzle holder to Stanley, and his trout rod and fly book to his brother Arty's son, Harold), the remainder of his estate, valued at nearly £9,000, was left to 'my dear wife'. Later that month, 'We old birds', as George described himself and Josephine, departed for Cannes and would not return to Winchester until April. Josephine was very aware how serious her husband's condition was, and closed her diary of their stay there, written for Stanley, which she entitled 'Journal of our quiet life at Le Cannet', by saying that it would serve 'to remind me of this time with father, the memory of which may some time be very precious'.[13] George was plagued by sleeplessness and attacks of diarrhoea. A manservant was hired, in whom they both had absolute trust, but even so, Josephine rarely left her husband's side. It was indeed a 'quiet life': each day began with breakfast in their rooms at 8 a.m., followed by devotional reading. A fellow hotel guest, Sir Mark Collett, the Governor of the Bank of England, lent the Butlers a copy of Henri Laresse's French translation of the Gospels which they read alongside the English. Josephine described to Stanley how, one Sunday morning, 'father read aloud to me the first chapter of Genesis, and then rendered it back into Hebrew – a great part of it – aloud, without any Hebrew Bible here, or any help. It sounds very fine. I thought it a sign that his memory is not impaired, at any rate'.

They were visited by Mrs Gladstone, who was sent up to the Butlers' apartment in the hotel lift 'which she must have nearly filled, for she is large', observed Josephine. A detailed description of Mrs Gladstone's attire was enclosed for the benefit of Rhoda: she was 'handsomely dressed in rich black velvet made with a plain skirt with a train (or demi-train), a cloak trimmed with sable all down and about it, and a very handsome bonnet, purple and black, her veil fastened with jewels'. Gladstone had pressed his wife to find out as much as she could about George's condition. His concern pleased Josephine, as did the Gladstones' enthusiasm for Hatty and Tell: they had got to know them in Naples and it had 'added much to their enjoyment of Italy'.

Josephine and George returned home in the spring, but this did not mean that Josephine could return to active duty. She made her apologies to the Executive Committee of the LNA for not attending the twelfth Federation Congress which was to be staged that year in Geneva, and, indeed, for taking no part in organizing it. This was the first Federation Congress at which Josephine had not been present since her founding of the organization in 1875. It was not simply her love for her husband that prompted her to stay at home, she claimed, but her sense of what she *owed* George: 'the dictate of my own heart is to remain by his side every hour, so long as he needs me. I am the more impelled to do this because of the generous and magnanimous way in which he gave me up to our cause for so many years, though he keenly felt the blank in his home through my enforced absences'.[14]

Josephine was able to preside over the annual LNA meeting at Exeter Hall on 24 July 1889. George, still in his own words 'the colour of autumn leaves',[15] had accompanied her to London, and had slipped into the hall unannounced, no doubt wanting to convey his personal thanks for the many messages of kindness he had received. Josephine was not unhappy that he had come since his need of care would be apparent to everyone: 'people will perhaps not so often write expressing a desire that I should do something more in public and hoping that he is now *quite well.* The London doctors gave us little hope of recovery'.[16]

Rhoda, who was then visiting with little Josephine and Bobby, sent accounts of Uncle George's condition back to Stanley in St Andrews. The children were the greatest comfort to Josephine, she said. 'They are just like her own children again', and 'have taken her quite out of herself', but Rhoda saw little of George. He was too weak to have people around him, '& he loves to have Aunt Josey to himself'. She would only see him at mealtimes, and then after dinner she would creep up to her own room, while 'the parents read & pray together'.[17]

They left Winchester on the doctors' advice. Their immediate destination was Scarborough, although Josephine was concerned about its rumoured expensiveness compared with foreign resorts. There was also the added financial burden of hiring a night nurse as well as the cost of George's manservant. Such anxieties had to be carefully concealed from the invalid: 'I try that my husband shall never see me look anxious or even know the causes. He seems to have grown much weaker in the last fortnight. He cannot dress himself at all, nor sit down nor rise up without help'.[18]

There was never any attempt to deceive herself that George was not dying, but the lengthy anticipation of his death was an appalling strain: 'I seem to have been maintaining such a long fight with death, and to be slowly getting beaten. Its power seems inexorable. And yet we have had such great blessings, and have been so one in heart and sympathy for forty years.' Even now, though, Josephine did not give herself up entirely to the care of George. She took with her the material for the next *Dawn*, and vowed never to cease to do what work she could. In fact, the move to Scarborough was a disaster: it was Josephine herself who broke down and had to be confined to her bed, suffering from fever and from congestion of the lungs.

While the Butlers were in Scarborough, the Federation Congress was in progress. Although she could not be there in person, Josephine was determined to address the assembly, and she wrote out no fewer than three separate speeches to be delivered by friends. The first speech was addressed to one of the women's meetings, in which she urged women to take heart from the examples of Elizabeth, the mother of John the Baptist, and the Virgin Mary, as models of female courage and strength of faith: 'Please never give way to weak thoughts about how little women can do'.[19] Josephine's second speech was delivered by Aimé Humbert. Its subject: the forthcoming centenary celebrations of the 1789 Declaration of the Rights of Man. Josephine reminded Federation members that the 'Rights of Man' had never been extended to *women* and suggested that the Geneva Congress adopt a resolution declaring the Declaration of 1789 to be one-sided and incomplete, and demanding that it should be superseded by a 'Declaration of the Rights of the human being', advocating the political equality of men and women.[20]

Mrs Richardson of York read out Josephine's third address which was a touching tribute to her husband. It would have been impossible for her to have done anything for the cause, she said, 'if God had not given me such a companion. In my whole life's work I have been sustained by his sympathy, and not only by his sympathy, but by his calmness and wisdom and the unfailing soundness of his judgement.'[21] It was a counterpart to George's tribute to his wife at the Copenhagen Congress the summer before, but it was also a tribute 'to my husband, now laid aside by illness', that served to silence the critics who might feel that Josephine was not pulling her weight.

After the briefest rest back at Winchester, George and Josephine were off again, this time to Naples at the invitation of Hatty and Tell. With the dangerous crossing from Copenhagen a year earlier in mind, Georgie decided to kit his father out in a new fur coat from the Hudson's Bay Fur Store, and sent a man over with half a dozen samples to the Grosvenor Hotel, where George and Josephine were staying prior to crossing the Channel. His father's sprightly response suggests that the Canon still very much had his wits about him. Although he was taken aback at first by the gift of such a fine coat, George reasoned, 'But if the proposition of such a garment will not only improve my chances of longevity, and give me a personal air of respectability, not to say distinction, and recall to my mind your affection and dutiful regard, I gladly accept'.[22]

George continued to write weekly bulletins to Georgie in a firm hand. In November he wrote from Naples that he had had a front tooth removed and a denture fitted ('which looks very well'), but to this letter Josephine privately added a postscript: 'We have been rather anxious about the dear Dad. He was so shaken by the loss of blood, and the doctor warned us that it is not a favourable symptom in his state'.[23] He was, however, strong enough to travel on to Amalfi, where they spent Christmas and the New Year, George enthusing about the local wines, before they began their long homeward journey on the coastal railway back to Naples, and then to Genoa, where assorted Grey sisters and nieces assembled to meet them. By early March they reached Cannes, with Josephine worn out and refusing visitors. George wrote home, 'Your mother and I cough too much to be pleasant'.[24]

George now consulted his doctor in Cannes, Dr Frank, about whether he thought him fit to resume his duties at Winchester; but George was told to put such thoughts behind him. He made no protest, but Josephine observed his eyes fill with tears of regret that he had been able to achieve so little during his broken ministry at the Cathedral. Dr Agnes MacLaren also tended George, making frequent calls. When Josephine asked her what to expect, and how long her husband had to live, she was told that Dr Frank advised them to risk moving George as soon as it became warmer: 'It is his own wish to go home, and his wish should now be your guide'.[25] Meanwhile, Josephine suffered many dark, sleepless nights, disturbed by visions of a lonely widowhood, 'but when the morning came his bright "Good morning, darling! I am pretty well. How are you?" used to dispel all clouds, and I could again rejoice, seeing his manly fortitude and cheerful spirit'.[26] From Cannes, on 9 March 1890, Josephine privately informed the Dean of Winchester that the doctors had pronounced George to be dying, and that it was his wish to return home to his family ('even though the journey is a risk').

Georgie came out at once to assist with the journey, and George seems to have been greatly comforted by his son's presence, trusting all arrangements to him, and still sporting the costly fur coat. They arrived at their London hotel at about 7.30 p.m. on 13 March 1890. George's brothers, Spencer, Arthur, Monty, and his sister, Louisa, were all there with Stanley. Charlie was in South Africa. George was only dimly conscious of their presence, and fell into a deep sleep. He died the next day in the presence of Josephine, Georgie and Stanley.

> About four o'clock in the afternoon, just before the end, appearing to feel that he was starting on a long journey, he turned his head to me and took my hand, and said rather anxiously, 'You will go with me, beloved, will you not? you will go with me?' The appeal went to my heart; I saw his mind wandered a little. I answered without hesitation, 'Yes I will! *I will go with you*'. For I knew that my heart would follow him whither he was going, and would dwell with him there.[27]

Poor Georgie had one final sad duty to perform. When Josephine later made preparations for her own death, she wrote a very special thank-you to her eldest son for all the loving support and practical help he had given George and herself over the years. Finally, she recalled his 'going out at night to that mournful mortuary chapel, and bringing back to me a lock of the dear grey hair. I have had that lock of hair with me in a case which I carry constantly'.[28] George was buried at Winchester. From South Africa Charlie sent a wreath of white immortelles.

Mr Gladstone himself wrote a gracious letter of condolence on 18 March:

> It is a solid pleasure to me, let me assure you, to have been permitted to do an act which acknowledged his services and character, and also I am glad to learn contributed something to his comfort and your own.
>
> I rejoice also to think with how much comfort you can look back upon a career no less blameless than useful and distinguished, and how recollection must aid in reviving you under bereavement and increasing your stock of courage for the work which doubtless God has got in store for you to do.[29]

Josephine stayed on at the Close until the end of the month, when she and Georgie began looking for a house in London. Her sister Emily came from Wandsworth to keep her company until they found one that suited them and slept in her room every night: 'when I awake with a dreadful feeling of loss and oppression she speaks to me, and makes some light and sometimes gives me a cup of tea, and so the night seems not so bad . . . I feel *best* when I see anyone who cares to talk about my beloved husband'.[30] To her elder sister, Tully, Josephine wrote, reproaching herself for any impatient words she might have said to George at the end, and she recalled Fanny's similar grief, 'half crying over her mistakes with her husband, how she might have estranged him by reproaches, and yet how he sometimes was most faulty towards her'.[31] George's dog, Carlo, was missing him, too. Searching the house for his master, he kept shutting himself in the lavatory, and had to bark to be let out: 'Every day used to be heard a muffled bark in the downstairs WC! His poor master used to have to frequent that corner *so much*, and Carlo used to wait at the door!'

Josephine and Georgie eventually found a house at 8 North View, Wimbledon Common, a slim four-storey semi-detached house with nearby stables, and there she did her best to live in quiet retirement, chiefly getting the house 'in nice order for my kind son'.[32] In England she could never be left in peace. 'You can imagine,' she wrote to the Misses Priestman, 'that such work is impossible for me where the doorbell rings all day.'[33] Yet it was Josephine herself who had put her address on the back page of the *Dawn* in October of that year. Unequal to replying personally to all the letters of condolence she had received, Josephine wrote an open letter to her friends in which she described the charms of her new home by the Common: 'There is perfect freedom to walk out at all times, without "dressing up", and in a few minutes one can find oneself in a retreat surrounded by purple heather and bracken, with a few scattered birch trees, where the solitude and silence towards evening make it difficult to realize that one is so near London'.[34]

By the autumn, though, she felt that she wanted to begin work again, in a quiet way, and spoke to the Priestmans about getting away by herself to Switzerland. Her departure, although it involved painful solitude and rigorous economy, was in fact a rational decision, and a highly natural choice: the people and the landscapes of Switzerland were familiar to her. The mountain range visible from her room at Serrières was 'the exact line which his dear hand so often traced', and the isolation, although darkened by 'the most heartfelt longing for that dear voice which is silent to me now', enabled Josephine to give herself up to the project before her, that of writing a memoir of her late husband.[35] Her three sons, she said, 'begged me' to write 'recollections of their father. It is a most sweet task'.[36]

Josephine went to Switzerland in 1890 in order to grieve for her husband in private, but the year would close with yet another family death. Her decision to settle near Neuchâtel had been prompted by her desire to see her niece Adela, who was now dying of consumption. Adela was her brother Charles's last surviving daughter by his first marriage to Rhoda's aunt, Emily Bolton. Josephine found her niece 'a perfect skeleton – tho' not thinner than my dear husband was'.[37] Adela had never known her mother, and she seems to have regarded her Aunt Josey and Uncle George as her closest family. When the Butlers moved to Winchester she was an almost permanent house-guest and witnessed her own sister Contie's death there, also from consumption, in 1884. Her stepmother now wrote to Josephine, 'scorning the idea of Adela being ill, and saying that she expects to see her in Ireland again this summer'.[38] Josephine did not reply, telling Stanley: 'I write to Uncle Charlie'. Adela Grey died on 30 December. Josephine was too ill to attend the funeral, and Amélie Humbert was asked to lay a bouquet of pure white roses on the coffin.

Josephine had made reference to the biography of George being 'a little of *our* life's history', and in this she was encouraged by Georgie's advice to her: 'Do not fear, dear Mother, to make it something of an *autobiography*; you can hardly help doing so, because father's life and yours were *so completely one*'.[39] James Stuart also encouraged her to write the book, saying that he, Stansfeld and others thought it would be certain to be widely read: 'The two names together would proclaim a united life'.[40] Writing to the *Women's Herald*, the Women's Liberal Federation paper, in the hope that they would review the book, Josephine explained, 'Of course there is in it a record of the work my husband and I did together; and besides this, I hope the book may be useful in showing what a true marriage may produce, of strong, united work'.[41] Nonetheless, Josephine was sensitive to the degree to which the work she was engaged upon was 'in some degree, also an autobiography'.[42]

In this, she was being wholly accurate. In Chapter 8 she describes how she began taking in sick and destitute prostitutes from the streets of Liverpool. In Chapter 9, she tells of how she came to lead the campaign to repeal the Contagious Diseases Acts: the call to serve, her mental conflict and her husband's blessing of her work with, 'Go! And

God be with you.' 'I recall that attitude even at this distance of time with wonder and admiration. I think there are not many men who would have acted thus'.[43] Josephine did seek to do her husband justice in recording his unseen, unrecognized involvement in the cause, but it was, inescapably, the biography of the *husband* of Josephine Butler.

When Josephine left for Switzerland she had not begun to think about a likely publisher for the biography, but, on the train from Paris to Basle, she happened to meet W.T. Stead and his wife. The couple had much 'pleasant conversation' with Josephine over dinner and tea, which led to an extravagant proposition: Stead offered Josephine 'a *large sum of money*' to publish her autobiography. 'I would not do it for anything – not for £50,000,' she exclaimed to Rhoda. 'But I thanked him. I should like to make some money, but not by speaking of my own self'.[44] She reasserted her position in a letter to the Misses Priestman, saying, 'I absolutely decline to write my own pitiful life. I hate the very appearance of egotism, and I feel almost a *disgust* of speaking of myself.[45]

Josephine may have grandly rejected Stead's proposal, but she was well aware that none of the leading London publishing houses would be likely to risk association with the repeal cause or with her name. She also felt too weak to 'grapple' with publishers like John Murray and Longman's, because 'they make hard bargains & treat one almost with contempt'![46] Putnam, the first publisher to express any interest, seems to have been unaware of the significance of George's role in the Abolition movement, and would only publish if Josephine put up the money, while T. Fisher Unwin declined, not because of the accounts of her work with prostitutes and the campaign for the repeal of the Contagious Diseases Acts, but because 'he does not like to publish a book with so much Christianity in it!' Josephine protested that it was not at all a religious biography in the conventional sense: 'There is too much about Dogs in it for that! And about shooting and fishing'.

The Priestman sisters suggested to Josephine a Bristol publisher, J. W. Arrowsmith. She was relieved to find a sympathetic publisher, even if he was 'not at the top of the tree', but stipulated that she did need to earn money by the venture, and began making detailed enquiries about royalties. After many delays caused by severe illness, the biography was eventually brought out in October 1892. Stead reviewed the it as 'The Book of the Month' in the November issue of his paper, the *Review of Reviews*, under the heading, 'The Life of a Modern Saint: By His Wife. An Ideal Picture of Domestic Life'. Although the headline would not have been Josephine's choice, Stead thoroughly understood her motive in writing the biography of her husband, and he selected passages that described the Butlers' 'united life'. He closed his review by quoting Josephine's own words: 'Who is there who will not rise from reading her book uttering her prayer, "May God send us many such men upon the earth!" '[47]

Josephine was sixty-two when her husband died. To her elder sister, she wrote, 'O! Tully, *what* a trial it is to be alone!'[48] She was to outlive George by sixteen years.

16

Geneva and Rome

'A fresh blow-up'

JOSEPHINE REMAINED IN Switzerland until February 1891, but felt that her work there on behalf of the Federation was disregarded and that she was quickly forgotten by old colleagues at home. Stuart had not even sent a personal message to her in Switzerland, and his silence, particularly at such a time, was odd. For some time, she felt, he had been letting his Federation duties slip. The previous summer, 1890, Stuart, at the age of forty-seven, had married a Miss Laura Colman (of Colman's Mustard), whose father was the Liberal MP for Norwich, and it was Josephine's suspicion that Stuart's wife '*does not like our cause* and that she is a drag on him in this respect'.[1] She felt Stuart's neglect keenly, writing to Stanley, 'It does not seem quite fair – I am old, a widow, and I have served twenty-one years. They would not find anyone else who can hit so hard as I', and adding, 'I think the Federation should give me £100 for the blow-up I have caused here!'[2]

Josephine's 'blow-up' related to the sexual exploitation of young girls in Geneva. When she had arrived there in December 1890, Josephine had been shocked to learn of long queues forming nightly outside brothels when an international medical conference was held in Geneva.[3] The prostitutes, most of them mere girls aged between thirteen and eighteen, then crowded into the hospitals for their check-ups, 'like vessels for unclean use, thrown together to be cleansed, *in order* to be used again!' As we have seen, she had gone to Switzerland with the intention of taking up her work once again 'in a quiet way'. She believed that she might feel nearer to George if she tried to work.

Indeed, a pattern seems to develop in which Josephine responds to bereavement by renewed campaigning, a pattern which may originate in her response to Eva's death all those years before.[4] Confronted with this new case, she decided to put herself in God's hands yet again, and her prayers were answered at once: 'It was like a voice that came down the chimney which said "Geneva!" again and again!'[5]

In November 1890 a fifty-year-old citizen of Geneva, a gentleman named Cougnard, had kidnapped five working-class girls whom he attempted to violate. Cougnard's first victim was a fourteen-year-old apprentice to a laundry, who had called at the house with his linen. He successfully 'seduced' her, and apparently got her to procure even younger girls for him. These children managed to escape with little more than torn clothes, and the children's parents went straight to the police.

Cougnard was well known to the working people of Geneva, who gave his house the nickname, 'The Geneva School of Morals'. He had been under investigation eighteen months earlier for the abduction and violation of seven little girls The present case against him came before a single magistrate, a *juge d'instruction*, who had exclusive authority to convict or declare a 'Non Lieu' ('Not Guilty'). The magistrate ruled that there was no case to answer: firstly, the case of the laundry-maid was set aside because at fourteen she was no longer a minor; secondly, the Geneva statutes made provision only for '*habitual* excitement to debauchery', yet the children claimed to have visited his house on just one occasion; and finally, although they had identified Cougnard, they had done so tentatively. The magistrate's verdict of 'Non Lieu' was announced on the day Josephine arrived in Geneva. Josephine, 'sick with shame and anger', wished for the youth and strength 'to stir up a fierce spirit of rebellion' among the working people of the city. No longer young, no longer strong, it was Josephine herself who was called to do so. The social iniquity of a gentleman preying on working-class children was, she said, 'too much for me, and, as my dear Stanley says, "Mother saw the devil triumphant and she *went for him*!" Yes, I did. The whole town was roused!'[6]

M. Merz, the father of one of the girls, a porter who worked for a printer's office, appealed for help to the Federation Bureau in Geneva. There was, however, no legal case to pursue, since the false entrapment of a minor with *intent* to seduce was not a crime, but Josephine could promise publicity to Merz: 'I will help you to make a little noise'.[7] In England she published an article in the April issue of the

Dawn, and in Geneva she began holding meetings to publicize the case, meetings which soon grew to two or three a day and attracted a wide following: male and female university students, working people, 'a few ladies of the higher class', and, according to the *Dawn*, 'an anarchist or two'.[8] Josephine did all that was within her power to do: she instilled in the working people a sense of the *legal* injustices of the Cougnard case, and a Committee for the Reform of the Legal Status of Women established itself to agitate for changes in the law. On her way home to England, passing through Neuchâtel, Josephine wrote to Mary Priestman, 'I am *much* encouraged, but *much* exhausted, and begin to question whether I dare go on, working at all in this way . . . I do feel so old sometimes'.[9]

Josephine did have one other reason for leaving Geneva. Merz had independently circulated a leaflet from his printing office, a plea to his 'fellow citizens, legislators, and fathers of families', attacking a state of affairs in 'civilized Geneva' in which a rich man could entangle the daughters of the poor 'for the satisfaction of his own monstrous vice', and be abetted, apparently, by the judicial system.[10] At the time it was circulated, public feeling was at its highest, and Josephine was not alone in her fear that a lynch mob might execute justice in the name of the poor children. The authorities were understandably suspicious of the provenance of Merz's leaflet. He was questioned about the authorship of the document, but no formal prosecution went forward. Then Josephine herself was summoned to appear, and she promptly left the city.

This experience did not distract Josephine from the important work she had to do in Neuchâtel, where she was to address two women's meetings arranged by Amélie Humbert. Her addresses demonstrate her continuing interest in a broad range of women's issues. Indeed, the work seemed to invigorate her. Armed with innumerable documents from Elizabeth Wolstoneholme, Josephine spoke of her interest in the Married Women's Property Act, but she spoke with equal authority on the clauses relating to child custody in the various Swiss cantons and on legal injustices affecting women which 'must be rooted up from our laws'.[11] Amélie testified to the extraordinary effect she had there: 'No words can describe *what* she has been – it seemed to me she has never spoken out so boldly and yet so tenderly. Her last bereavement and great sorrow has given her a special *halo* if I may say so. She *is* a saint on earth, our precious Mrs Butler! The warrior spirit has been greatly revived in her'.[12]

Josephine's sense that she had been forgotten in England was confirmed when, on her return, she organized the annual meeting of the LNA, which was held in Exeter Hall on 23 April 1891. She sent out four hundred invitations, but only thirty people attended: 'It was the coldest meeting I ever was at, and left quite a painful impression on me for days,' she told the Misses Priestman.[13] They took the hint and rallied old colleagues from around the country to hold a surprise meeting, '*as a welcome back to life for me, & as a reverent expression of remembrance of dear father*':

> The platform had been carpeted, & all along the front was a row of beautiful wreaths & roses & pots, & in front of my seat an offering in the shape of a lovely basket full of stephanotis & white azalias, & the handle drest with dark purple pansies . . .
>
> The most touching speech was by rough Henry Wilson MP. I think everybody was crying! There was no flattery, nor exaggerated compliments, but such a tone of affection for a kind old worker – a leader, as they said, never to be forgotten.[14]

To Josephine it seemed 'like a resurrection from the dead', although it does have more the appearance of a farewell.

Family claims were reasserting themselves. When Josephine returned to England she was needed to nurse her granddaughter, Josephine. At the New Year, soon after the death of her niece, Adela, Josephine had received word from St Andrews to say that her 'precious little Josephine', who was just three years old, had been unconscious for four days with a rheumatic fever which had left her paralysed. 'That darling is dearer to me than I can express,' wrote Josephine. 'She seemed like Eva come back to me.'[15] Rhoda and Stanley brought their daughter to see a specialist at Queen Anne Street, Cavendish Square, who said he could cure her if she was left under his care for eight weeks. When Josephine arrived home at Easter she was able to make regular visits to Cavendish Square, enabling Stanley to return to the university, and take with him a broken-down Rhoda, who had also to think about little Bobby back at St Andrews. Eva's death was very much on Josephine's mind: she wrote for Stanley some painful memories of that time which she had kept suppressed, and her own account of little Josephine as an earthly angel sounds uncomfortably close to earlier descriptions of Eva: 'It goes to my heart to see this sweet child. She is patient & cheerful, & lies night & day in one position'.[16] Against the noise of the roaring city, the patient would pipe up, 'There is a green hill far away', and when the Priestmans sent her a brightly coloured bouquet, little Josephine insisted that the flowers be divided and half be sent up to her mother in Scotland. By November, Josephine was able to report that the child was 'well & frisky. The darkest London fog has not the least effect on *that* bird's spirits',[17] and two years later, Josephine described how she and Stanley marched about with little Josephine on Tooting Common, now that she had grown out of her leg brace, 'with her warm gaiters & thick boots'.[18]

There were to be no more children for Stanley and Rhoda. In July 1893, the baby that they had prayed for was delivered prematurely. It was a very difficult confinement and the baby, a boy, was stillborn, 'as small as a wax doll but most beautifully formed & with a lovely face'. The nurse washed and dressed the tiny corpse and laid it in a box with flowers over it. Little Josephine and Bob were told, 'The baby has come dears, but it died on the journey.'[19]

Josephine was able to see more of Rhoda on her visits to London or when Josephine had holidays at St Andrews. Rhoda was of course her niece as well as her daughter-in-law, and seems to have been the grown-up daughter she had never had. She was an exceptional beauty,[20] and a stylish dresser, who liked to keep up with the latest fashions even from the distance of St Andrews. She seems to have depended for her fashion information to a large degree upon Josephine, who responded in full measure. Josephine had suppressed this harmless interest in dress for a good twenty years. In a letter to Rhoda from Cannes in early 1889, she had written a detailed description of the wardrobe of the MP Thomasson's daughter, Beatrice, complete with illustrations, even though she was ashamed of her 'horrid' diagram.[21]

> The material was a fine cashmere . . . of a most lovely *lavender* blue – not quite blue but bluer than lavender! The collar wh comes all the way down to the ground makes the dress *look* like an *over* dress with a skirt & waistcoat under (but they are all one) was made of a rich black watered silk, cuffs & narrow collar the same, & then . . . the collar . . . is drawn *across* the chest sideways. I admire that crossing the chest fashion. It is so elegantly done . . . & makes the chest look full . . . I feel very shabby among the smart people here.

Rhoda determined to deliver her aunt from accusations of shabbiness and took her in hand whenever she was down in London.

Josephine wrote to Anna Priestman praising Rhoda's 'good taste', saying that she had been '*clothing* me most kindly, as I am all in rags!' and finding it 'amusing & sweet to be domineered over by the young people as to my dress . . . If there is a question of expense, about a cloak or a dress, then George intervenes, & says, "hang the expense! Get her the very best thing you can, Rhoda. We will all subscribe!" '[22] She liked to show Rhoda off to her friends, and one day hired 'a nice little coupé' for the afternoon, with a 'sporting looking driver'. They called on a number of people, including the Galtons, the Spencer Butlers and the Stuarts: 'We were out about 3 hours, & Rhoda looked so nice in her pretty, large hat, & black dress, & she enjoyed leaning back in the coupé instead of rattling in a cab'.[23]

Josephine also became reacquainted with her brother George's orphaned granddaughter, Mia, who came to visit at Wimbledon Common in 1892. Mia's mother, Jane, had asked Josephine to stand as Mia's godmother in 1868, but after Jane's death in 1881 her father, Sir Horace St Paul, had never let his daughter know the Butlers, presumably from a horror of Josephine's campaigning life. On his death, Horace St Paul's trustees appear to have thrust Mia upon her remaining Grey relations, and Mia now sought out her godmother Josephine. She was an 'orphan heiress', like a heroine of a novel, as Josephine described her: 'Her father was a cousin to the late Earl Dudley, & like him very rich & rather cracked . . . Her father left heavy debts, & she is economising till all are paid. Yesterday only she sold at Christie's a portrait of her grandmother by Gainsborough for *5,000 guineas*, but she still has £50,000 of her father's debts to pay![24] She inherited the family seat, Ewart Park, five miles from Milfield, but the estate was heavily mortgaged and yielded very little rental.

Josephine declared Mia 'a dear nice girl', and was overwhelmed that she had 'taken an enormous love for me!' Mia also laughed at her cousin Georgie's jokes, and they soon fell in love. George was forty, Mia twenty-four. They were married on 19 January 1893 and made the Wimbledon house their home. Josephine, ordered to Cannes for her health, could not be at the wedding, but she was represented at the ceremony by her elder sister Tully, and she sent Mia a wedding present of 'a necklace of Swiss "black diamonds" '.[25]

Josephine now needed to find a new home for herself and moved to Balham, which was still then largely unbuilt. She found 'a wee house' at 29 Tooting Bec Road, and the house and its setting was everything she desired, which was '*not to be in London*, wh I could not endure . . . & to *see* some trees or something wh is not chimney pots'. She was pleased to have 'a dear little study', with her papers and books in order around her, and now felt as if she could write '*several* books'. The study looked out on to 'a meadow, with a few large elms in it, & in that meadow there is an Alderney cow, & when it is fine & I have my window open, I can hear the quiet munching of that Alderney cow, & nothing else'.[26]

A near neighbour, at 33 Childebert Road, Balham, was Miss Fanny Forsaith, the young Secretary of the British Committee of the Federation. Fanny was a deeply spiritual woman with whom Josephine felt able to converse intimately, and her letters to Fanny demonstrate Josephine's impressive knowledge of the Scriptures. Aside from her long and deep friendship with the Priestman sisters, to whom Josephine continued to write about Abolition matters and family news, and with whom she continued to exchange gifts (every Christmas she would receive a knitted shawl from Clifton), this new, late friendship was to be a sustaining one for Josephine. She praised Fanny's 'sweet manner', but also her 'stately presence'.[27] Miss Forsaith was an excellent worker (Josephine described her to Stanley as 'a vigilant politician')[28] and she proved a match for the rough-mannered Henry Wilson, who at first took objection to her because she received a salary for her work as Secretary.

Her maid Annie Shield came with her to Balham and helped Josephine run a strictly economical household. Just how the two women were economizing is indicated by a letter Josephine wrote to Rhoda in preparation for a visit from her two grandchildren with their nurse. She wanted to know whether the nurse would put up with meat just once a day: 'indeed, we often have no meat in the day, but I think nurse *needs* it, as well as the children, & wine also. I have no wine in the house but could get some, or beer if it is as good for her . . . And I will make a point of having *good* milk wh we can get from Furze Down'. When Charlie came to stay with his mother in spring 1895, she could hardly afford to put him up. He had gone to Africa as a gold miner in 1891, working for Cecil Rhodes's Chartered Company in Mashonaland (in what was to become Rhodesia), although 'There seems to be more fever to be got there than gold at present'.[29] He turned up in Balham in nothing but his mining clothes: 'high boots, & flannel shirts [and] he had to be set up with new clothes etc.'. 'My income which is *abundant* for me, is hardly enough to include a *man*. Men need more things – at least he is big & wants more food than I do'.[30] Josephine also lent money to her sister Emily and to Emily's husband's family, telling Rhoda, Emily's daughter, that 'the boys & Emmie' had been so nice to her and were making great efforts to pay her back, but that she now refused to accept further repayments: 'God will make it up to me, & I shall get set afloat again'.[31]

Her sister Tully died on 30 April 1893. Her death was evidently unexpected and a terrible shock to Josephine, who could not sleep for two nights, 'thinking of my dear sister'.[32] For some years now it had been Fanny's death that she had been anticipating. Fanny's condition was quite serious. She had survived a very serious stroke in 1888, but it left her nearly blind and practically immobile, and she began to show signs of senile dementia in spring 1892. A year later, her condition was unchanged, except that she had 'less *mind*', and Josephine herself began to 'have a great dread now of a very solitary old age'.[33]

In the autumn of 1893 Josephine turned her mind to Italy and began to make plans for a campaign in Rome, 'to get our "cause" there out of the *hole* it has fallen into'.[34] Earlier campaigns had been successful to a limited degree. In the early 1880s a commission of inquiry had found against the system of regulation but its report had been suppressed. In 1888 the report had resurfaced and state control of prostitution had been abolished by decree of the Italian Parliament, but, as in India, this decree had been largely ignored and the system continued to operate throughout Italy.[35]

It could not have been a more ill judged time to preach the evils of regulated prostitution. The Italy Josephine went out to in December 1893 was a country in the midst of a financial crisis. In the short time she had rested at Florence before coming on to Rome three banks there collapsed. In Rome she had not set eyes on a silver or gold coin: 'There is nothing but the poor little dirty pieces of paper from fifty lire (francs) down to one lire'.[36] Yet when Josephine met Professor Celli, chief of the Sanitary Office and Professor of Hygiene at Rome University, and a deputy, it was his view that they should press for the immediate suspension of the compulsory system of regulation and the abolition of the Polizia dei Costumi, because 'the country is on the verge of bankruptcy and *this* service is very costly'.[37]

Despite the possibility that Celli's plan might be adopted by the government, Josephine was uncharacteristically pessimistic, and felt that she personally was achieving little. Abolition was very much a party political question in Italy, and only those politicians on the extreme Left, the Radicals, would touch the subject. Josephine, however, set herself a more personal mission, to speak privately to individual politicians, and particularly, churchmen, to persuade them to take up the question. She had been advised that for the Pope to pronounce against regulation a supportive body of opinion had first to be established. She longed to convert the King of Italy ('I wish I could get at him!!'),[38] and had originally hoped for an audience with the Pope himself.

The more she learned of the Vatican, the less she wanted to speak with the Pope personally, and instead prepared a statement that a sympathetic cardinal could deliver on her behalf. She wrote to George and Stanley: 'Many ladies try to get an audience with the Pope. You have to be dressed according to order – all in black, no bonnet, but with a long black veil from head to foot – no gloves!'[39] She had been instructed that one was required to kneel at the door as one entered, then again in the middle of the room, and a third time at the Pope's feet, 'when you kiss the sapphire ring on his finger. Now, I confess to a moral objection to practising this subserviency. I like nice old gentlemen but I never want to kneel to any'. Nevertheless, she urged that the Pope use his spiritual authority to condemn regulation and she wrote to Theodore Minod at the Federation Bureau in Geneva asking him to write to the Vatican assuring the Pope of the support of the Catholic world on this matter. She also asked him to find an Italian copy of her pamphlet *Una Voce del Deserto* (originally published in French) to send to the Pope (her remaining spare copy was too shabby), 'for tho' I am a heretic & a woman, the Pope has wit enough to know & acknowledge the *truth* in it'.[40] A year later she was pleased to be sent word that the Pope had been moved by her appeal and was willing to issue a public statement of his support for Abolition. She thanked God that the Pope had proved himself 'a true & humble Christian, *altho'* a Pope'.[41]

Josephine was now becoming something of a liability to the Abolition movement. Her campaign in Italy was cut short by illness. She had conducted her first crusade to Europe nearly twenty years earlier, and was now aged sixty-five, easily tired, physically frail, and susceptible to disease. For two months out of the five that she was abroad, Josephine lay seriously ill in Rome with a 'malignant malaria'. At the New Year, she was rendered unconscious by the fever, 'so suddenly that I was deprived almost of sense and volition', and experienced what she came to believe was the Devil's wrath.[42]

At first she questioned, '*Why* the God of Love *allows* a child of His to be so knocked down and stamped upon for such a long time'. At dawn one day, when her nurse had slipped out of the room to attend early mass, Josephine felt drawn to articulate her reproaches and to confess her sins. She managed to raise herself up in bed, and to speak to God 'aloud, with a wonderful heart-eloquence which astonished myself'. God answered her that He was '*all pity*', and that He was angry to see her suffering. At noon she announced to the nurse that she wished to get out of bed, and to get dressed. The terrible inflammation of her throat, stomach and bowels had miraculously vanished. Fanny Forsaith was one of the few friends to whom Josephine felt that she could 'testify' about this cure. Fanny was permitted to show the letter to one or two 'bosom friends', but was asked to 'then keep it in some quiet drawer'.[43]

To his credit, Stuart forwarded two cheques amounting to £75 as soon as he learned of Josephine's inability to pay her medical bills. It was money that she suspected came from his own pocket, yet even this was barely enough to cover her bills in Rome: 'As it is I shall just be able to shove on,' she wrote to Stanley. The Priestman sisters and other friends helped her with further sums of money. In April she was able to travel on to Neuchâtel to call on Aimé Humbert, who burst into tears upon seeing her. He had suffered a minor stroke in 1892, which had aged him a good deal. Now quite helpless, he was looked after by Amélie and her married sister Marie. He had been excitedly waiting for Josephine's visit, and on the day she was due to arrive he 'awoke rather *dazed*, and wished his daughters a Happy New Year. They told him his mistake, and he replied, '"But it is a *feste*. What day is it?" Amélie said, "This is the day that Mrs Butler is coming you know", & he replied, "Ah yes, that is it. Thanks be to God".'[44]

On her return to England at the end of April 1894, Josephine was met with 'heavy news' concerning Georgie, who had been almost killed by being thrown from his horse in Richmond Park, and was still lying unconscious at his home in Wimbledon. His skull was fractured and one eardrum was broken. When he regained consciousness he became violent, and it needed two male nurses to hold him. Mia, who was then pregnant, was not allowed near him, and when Stanley arrived his brother assaulted him, striking him such a violent blow in the chest that he staggered and had to leave. He was greatly distressed about Georgie, but Josephine was later to recall his words of comfort for her: 'after all, Christ & George's *mother* are more than a match for all the diseases and devils in the world. It is not likely that God would have changed his *opinion* of you so suddenly'.[45]

Josephine took a room just around the corner from North View, at 14 West Place, in order to look after Mia, who said that 'up to now she had dwelt in a haven of *perfect peace* with him, & had never heard an impatient word from him, & that he had taught *her* so much self control'.[46] Worse was to follow. Her 'dearest George, who all his life has had such wonderful self control, so calm, so wise, so gentle – is now quite changed. He tries to throw himself out of the window, & has broken everything in his attempts at self-destruction. He does not in the least know what he is doing'.[47]

By August, Mia and George were able to take a holiday in Germany, leaving Josephine in possession of Ewart Park to get on with writing her *Reminiscences of a Great Crusade*, as it was to be called. She was assisted in this by the volumes of correspondence, documents and newspaper clippings carefully assembled by Aimé Humbert. In addition, 'This place is very favourable to it', she wrote to Mary Priestman. 'A library 43 feet long, softly carpeted, with 2 fireplaces, seven writing tables, & the walls lined with books of all ages, languages & subjects'.[48] She moved back to her house in Balham in the autumn, and asked Fanny Forsaith to help her in taking dictation, for she found writing the book involved a great deal of effort, 'to an old person'. She had written up the first ten years of the campaign and was absolutely exhausted: 'I suppose I must go on writing 6 hours a day till I die. I have written 15 things for publication lately wh people insist on having, & my thoughts are getting quite thin & worthless'.[49] She was anxious to 'avoid dryness, & the mere *report* style', and brightened up at Stuart's praise of the chapters he had seen so far, which he told her were 'far more interesting than any novel'.[50]

Josephine spent Christmas at Ewart. George was now much recovered and prepared to return to work, but at the end of February Mia had a miscarriage, or, as Josephine delicately expressed it, 'She was expecting a baby, & has had a disappointment, poor darling'.[51] Mia remained in bed for weeks, and George feared that he would lose her, knowing as he did that Mia's mother also 'went into decline' after a difficult pregnancy.

Charlie returned home from South Africa briefly in the spring of 1895, and promptly got engaged at the age of thirty-eight to 'a good dear young woman' named Margaret Talbot, who at twenty-eight was 'not too young'.[52] Josephine was delighted to have Charlie home and delighted to hear of his awakened political consciousness: 'He has come home from Africa, very *Radical*, & thinks "one man is as good as another, & better too!" '[53] He was about to take up a second contract with a mining company in Western Australia, and was posted to a spot called Bamboo Creek, 'far in the tropics'. He had promised Maggie that they would be married within a year but, according to Josephine, he was 'a prisoner' of his contract and could not return to England until July 1897, when he was sent straight to St Thomas's Hospital, a 'skeleton', with a typhoidal condition of the bowels. Charlie and Maggie were married on 31 August 1897 at St Margaret's, Westminster, and moved into furnished lodgings at Holborn. Josephine was struck by her youngest son's humble domestic arrangements. The newly-weds had very little to live on: it had been a '*plain little wedding*', and they made do with their 'two rooms & a tiny kitchen. They have no servant. Maggie cooks & together they make the bed & sweep the floor! I think it is nice of them! They look "merry as sandpipers" '.[54]

In the autumn of 1895, Josephine left her lodgings in Balham. She had begun to feel that it was a wretched 'Jerry house', and now many of her neighbours were leaving because the trees opposite had been cut down, '& a row of tall brick houses is built up close to my little study window, blocking out air & light. Not a blade of grass to be seen'.[55] Her grand piano and remaining pieces of furniture were packed off to Ewart and to St Andrews. She was with Hatty at La Gordanne in September when a telegram arrived with news of their sister Fanny's death, at the age of seventy-two, on 27 September. 'I had lost a *child*, who leaned on me, as well as a sister', Josephine wrote.[56] Fanny's grave lies close to Eva's in Leckhampton Churchyard at Cheltenham and bears the simple inscription, 'With Christ which is far better'. In her will she left a sum of money to the LNA. Josephine came back to England to help her sister Emmy with the disposal of Fanny's little property.

She had been persuaded to sit for the portrait painter George Frederick Watts as one of 'the people who have "made the century", whatever that may mean'.[57] Josephine was the only woman chosen for this honour. By the summer of 1895, Watts had completed twenty or so portraits. He and his young wife had built a house at Limner's Lease, near Guildford in Surrey, and Josephine was invited to stay with them for a week in October. Mia went with her for company, to read to her while she sat: 'I get so dazed and sleepy, I want to get free, but I try and behave'.[58] Josephine found Watts even more exhausted by the sittings than she was. He was nearly eighty, and she had many pleasant chats with him while he rested, lying on a sofa. She was not at all sure that he knew the extent of her public work, but one day, when the two of them were alone, Watts reproached himself for not having done more for the poor: 'what would I not give to be able to look back upon such a life as yours!' he exclaimed.[59] When Josephine left Limner's Lease, she went to kiss Mrs Watts to thank her for her kindness, 'and Mr Watts held up his old face so meekly to be kissed also, very much as dear father used to do. Indeed, in many old man ways, he reminded me of father'.[60]

Josephine said of the finished portrait that she had no doubt it would convey an idea of her hard life's work. It is a shockingly grim study, stark and spare, and Josephine seems to have aged rapidly from the Elliott & Fry photograph taken after George's death. Indeed, her face has the pallor and rigidity of a corpse, and stands out from a darkly obscure background. Her folded hands are faintly suggested by broad brush strokes, and her heavy mourning dress is offset only by a simple strip of white lace pinned to the head and falling upon her shoulders. Josephine took it calmly, but warned Stanley that it was 'not at all pretty, and the jaw and head are too strong and gaunt. I don't think my friends will like it . . . They say his pictures are seldom liked at first, but that they grow on people, on account of the power in them'.[61] The power of Watts's portrait is unarguable. It seems that Josephine's two single-handed European crusades in the early 1890s, and difficulties she had been having with the Federation had their effect upon her. Interestingly, Josephine herself recognized marks of suffering dating back to her crisis of faith at the age of eighteen, and wrote to Watts what she had found difficult to say to him, which was that when she saw the finished portrait, she had been inclined to burst into tears:

> I felt so sorry for her. Your power has brought up, out of the depths of the past, the record of a conflict which no one but God knows of. It is written in the eyes and whole face. There were years in which my revolt was, not against man, but against God; my soul went down to hell, and dwelt there.[62]

Yet Josephine vowed that she was 'ready to go down to Hades again, if it were necessary for the deliverance of [my] fellow creatures. But

God does not require that descent more than once. I could not say all this aloud'.

After an eventful autumn, Josephine and her maid Annie returned to Switzerland with the intention of spending a quiet winter in Territet, near Montreux, but by the middle of January she had returned to Geneva to fight her final battle there, the outcome of the earlier agitation she had played such a part in over the Cougnard case. Petitions demanding a change in the law had been organized and regulation was to be put to a referendum on 22 March 1896. Josephine was asked to help to 'stir up the women'.[63]

Abolitionists were attacked in the press, their meetings were attacked by organized gangs, and their posters were torn down, but this only served to rouse to action significant numbers of university men, doctors and clergy, and in particular women of all classes. When official venues for public meetings were denied the Federation, Amélie Humbert addressed a '*fiery*' speech to an all-women meeting in a local brasserie, where she 'denounced evil Governments as if she did not care if her head were cut off for it the next minute'.[64] The anger of the brothel keepers was such that extraordinary riots broke out on the night of the election. A mob marched through the streets, stormed a church, '& had a consecration service to the Devil . . . swearing & singing songs of the utmost blasphemy & obscenity'.[65] Threats were made to the lives of Federation workers and sympathizers and the Federation office was besieged.

The referendum was lost by 8,000 votes to 4,000. Many people had abstained from voting, and many had been confused by the way in which the alternative referendum proposals, for and against regulation, were put to them.

The Abolitionists' reaction to their defeat was remarkable. Josephine talked to them, not of defeat but of resurrection, and they immediately began to organize for the future. The campaign continued. In Lausanne, a Federation petition with the signatures of 6,000 women was presented to the Grand Council of the Canton de Vaud by 'women of the people' and a commission was appointed as a result. The women returned 'with radiant faces' because they had acted as 'citizens who had something to say to the Government' and had said it![66]

The lawless atmosphere in Geneva must have been terrifying, and the reports Josephine sent home convey the thrill of the battle. 'Shakey friends' were uneasy about rousing the mob, but the experience had borne out well Josephine's view that it was 'only by the force of awakened consciences *outside* Governments as well as inside them, that real reforms can be accomplished'.[67] Josephine assured her children that she was not in any danger personally, but she evidently got a stiff letter back from Stanley, who seems to have felt that the time had come for her to cease campaigning. He asked his mother whether she could really justify risking her safety and 'taking so much trouble about such a vile hole & corner place as Geneva when there are such large countries before us as Africa & Australia'.[68] Josephine replied that she was too old to begin work in other parts of the world, but that throughout Switzerland she and the Federation had experience and influence.

Josephine's record of the Abolition movement, *Personal Reminiscences of a Great Crusade*, was published that summer. It was an account of events she could recall clearly, and, above all, a statement of the movement's principles. Early sales were not good, even though there were some strong reviews in the national press. W.T. Stead again helped with publicity, advertising *Reminiscences* as his 'Book of the Month' in the *Review of Reviews* for October 1896. Josephine dreaded so much 'his style and what he might say' that she wrote imploring him to publish a simple review.[69] Yet, she granted that it was '*not so bad as it might have been*'. Thankfully, she wrote,

> One thing he has grasped & expressed & I am glad, for few people see it; I mean that the cause for wh I have worked is *not* a 'Purity Crusade' nor a Morality Crusade. These crusades are needed; but they are *educational*, slow & gradual, beginning in the nursery & the schoolroom; our Federation movement is quite another thing. It was & is a revolt against & an aggressive opposition to a gross political & illegal tyranny.[70]

Josephine had great difficulty with the 'Purity' movements which had grown out of the repeal campaign, such as the National Vigilance Association with which Stead was associated and which was formed in 1885 as an organization to ensure that the Criminal Law Amendment Act was being carried out throughout the country. Many repealers joined the NVA, and Henry Wilson was its Treasurer, but its punitive, repressive nature soon became apparent to Josephine and the LNA. There were 'purity crusades' and campaigns to clear the streets of prostitutes, as well as attacks on what was seen as obscenity in literature and entertainments like the music halls, and on public figures involved in sexual scandals. Josephine was to write protesting against the purity campaigners and their 'coercive and degrading treatment' of prostitutes, 'in the fatuous belief that you can oblige human beings to be moral by *force*'.[71]

For Josephine prostitution was a social and economic question, and in particular a question of the legal and political position of women. It could not be put right by punishment and repression, but only by fundamental changes to the status of women in society. It was not a question of 'purity'! Josephine's responses to such questions were always personal, and sometimes unpredictable, but rarely dogmatic. In the last years of the nineteenth century there were a number of sexual scandals involving public men in which she took a close interest, but about which she was rarely judgmental. She did collaborate with Stead in an attack on the Prince of Wales's conduct,[72] avoiding direct reference to his alleged sexual misbehaviour but alluding to a gambling scandal in which he had been involved, but she had distanced herself from the 'leaders of the war against impurity . . . the so-called "Stead party"', over the issue of the Irish leader, Charles Stewart Parnell's adultery.[73] For the sake of the fight for justice in Ireland she wanted him to retire from public life, but she urged compassion for the man. Similarly, when Charles Dilke, whose career as a Liberal MP had ended when he was named as co-respondent in an 1885–86 divorce case, stood again for Parliament in 1892, Josephine felt the purity campaign and petition mounted against him to be repugnant.[74]

There were also several notorious homosexual scandals in which Josephine either had or took an interest. It is clear from her correspondence with her son Stanley that she was acquainted with the personal histories of many upper-class gentlemen, and what is interesting here, too, is that while Josephine was horrified at the crime (she was a woman of her time in that respect), she was full of sympathy for the individuals whose lives were ruined by it. One involved a second cousin of Josephine's, Edmund Gurney, who seems to have committed suicide in a Brighton hotel in mysterious circumstances, although a verdict of accidental death was recorded. She was sure that the man to blame for his 'corruption' was Frederick Myers, who had been George's pupil at Cheltenham and who had worked with her in the campaign for female higher education in the late 1860s.[75]

More notorious was the 1895 scandal involving Oscar Wilde. This shocked Josephine, but, she wrote to Stanley,

> I am so sorry for him . . . I don't know how he will bear hard labour, and I hope they will treat him mercifully. As you say, there are others worse

than he, and 'society' seems to have been lately very badly diseased in this way. So it is well there should be a sharp awakening. But O! I pity the criminal on whose head society's vials of wrath are poured.[76]

Not content with pitying him in private, Josephine considered the idea of converting Wilde to Christianity (goodness only knows what Wilde would have made of such overtures). She told Stanley, 'I long to be allowed to send him a letter in prison. I suppose he must not receive letters'. She prayed 'for him constantly – that God will tell him that *He* does not despise him'.

Since Kate Bushnell and Elizabeth Andrews's mission in India on behalf of the LNA, strong ties had developed between the Purity Department of their organization, the World's Women's Christian Temperance Union, and the British Federation. Josephine was very much admired by the American women, and they honoured her with the rather grand title of 'World's Superintendent' of the Purity Department. British Abolitionists at first welcomed this collaboration, but it soon became clear that the purity members of the WWCTU did not have a sound understanding of the founding principles of the repeal movement. Very serious problems would develop when the leader of the British branch of the Christian Temperance Union, Lady Henry Somerset, began publicly recommending repressive legislative measures to regulate prostitution.

Josephine's first allusion to her difficulties with the WWCTU was made in a letter to the Priestmans in November 1893.[77] She was anxious to talk the matter over with them privately before she left for Italy. Her own modest winter campaign was rather overshadowed by the grand 'purity' tour then in preparation which was to be conducted by Frances Willard, President of the WWCTU and Lady Henry Somerset, who was having a private steamer built for the venture. The ladies' tour was to take in Italy, a country of which Josephine was convinced they knew nothing. She described an incident at Hatty's in Naples in March 1894 when Tell Meuricoffre came in to dinner one evening with one of the Roman newspapers which carried an advertisement for Lady Henry and Miss Willard's world cruise, announcing that they would visit the King of Italy, and the Pope in Rome. Hatty was furious that if the Pope and the King gave them a favourable reception, they would have all the credit and triumph, when it was Josephine who had sown the seed, and nearly died over it. Josephine had taken the news rather more calmly, saying that she had no objection to their 'carrying flags & blowing trumpets', but she thought she should write a report for the ladies, giving them a detailed account of the position in Italy, as well as reminding them of the work she had done there. She wrote in December 1893, and received from Lady Henry a patronizing reply 'to *their* "brave pioneer in Italy" – *hush*!'[78]

It was not until the spring of 1895 that she expanded upon her difficulties with the American purity campaigners, in a letter to Helen Clark, in which she advised Helen and her aunts 'to tell them frankly where we disagree with them'.[79] That April she had advised Lady Henry Somerset and Miss Willard that their members were 'going sadly wrong on account of ignorance of the abolitionist question'.[80] She felt she had a right to protest, 'since they insist on my remaining "World's Superintendent" for Purity'.[81] Purity workers from their organization had actually signed a letter *defending* the regulation of prostitution.

The defection of large numbers of Federation women followed, with Norwegian women calling for regulation to be reinstated in Norway, and a German-Scandinavian alliance emerged, supporting the compulsory examination of prostitutes as well as penal measures against them. New Zealand women, too – in 1893 the first in the British Empire to gain the suffrage – had passed a resolution in favour of the CD Acts.[82] There seemed to be a worldwide movement away from the position Josephine had fought for for most of her life. This came at a time when Josephine was completing her history of the repeal movement. She admitted that, for the first time, 'My book is beginning to be a great *burden* to me'.[83]

Josephine felt ousted, and suddenly her supporters seemed to be terribly few, consisting of the Priestman sisters, Fanny Forsaith, James Stuart, and her son, Stanley, who was, she believed, 'the only person who, now & then, holds up a lamp to me, to show that I am still in the old way, the right way, & that the principles we preach stand out pure and clear'.[84] Recent members of the Federation in Europe seemed not to know who Josephine was, regarding her as an eccentric old lady on the fringes of the movement. German men, in particular, treated her rudely. In their eyes, she was no longer the leader of a movement, but a rebel within: 'They regard me as an inconvenient unmanageable *intruder* into the Federation, an old woman who sets her own opinion against the whole of German male wisdom. I wish someone would tell them that I *founded* the Federation in 1875!!'[85]

Josephine finally severed all connections with Lady Henry

Somerset in 1897, over the latter's public declaration in support of regulation. On 13 November 1896, hundreds of Abolition workers from the early days of the repeal movement, 'many whose existence we had forgotten – some whom we thought had passed away', met in Birmingham to protest against the threatened revival of the CD Acts in India.[86] Josephine was adamant that Lady Henry should not be asked to speak: 'this is no time to speak eloquent generalities about Purity. We want an aggressive, war-like note'.[87] She was sick of hearing the Christian Temperance Union talk of their two questions as 'twin movements': as she reminded Fanny Forsaith, *they* were fighting *slavery*. Although Josephine was unable to attend the Birmingham meeting, Miss Priestman told her that she was remembered in prayers of thanksgiving to God who had spared her so long to them: 'It was really moving, to look round at all the assembled delegates from all parts,' she wrote to Josephine, and to see that 'the perennial life of truth in them & the burning hatred of injustice appeared to give them a strong confidence & determination'.[88] In the middle of the platform a chair had been left empty, whether on purpose or not Miss Priestman did not know, but to her, and to others too she thought, 'there was in that seat a vision of you'.

Unmoved by the atmosphere at Birmingham, Lady Henry proceeded to write a letter to the editor of *The Times*. Published on 21 April 1897, it outlined her six propositions for the reintroduction in India of a form of regulation even more repressive than the original CD Acts. Lady Henry was sufficiently concerned about the periodical examination of prostitutes to recommend the appointment of *women* doctors to carry out the examinations, and it was her wish to see the soldiers subjected to as much scrutiny as the women they consorted with: soldiers, too, were to undergo a periodical examination, every visit they made to a prostitute was to be recorded, and they were 'liable to severe penalty' if they attempted to visit prostitutes outside the government *chakla*. To Josephine's eyes, Lady Henry was proposing 'to drill them into debauchery': she called her '*grossly ignorant*', and her idea 'a pitiful hybrid monster'.[89]

Josephine was prepared to respond in the strongest terms. Her immediate action was to write a twenty-four-page pamphlet, *Truth before Everything*, which she issued on her sole responsibility, but as soon as Stuart heard of it he forwarded her a cheque for £20 to cover the cost of printing 9,000 copies. He felt it was crucial that Josephine was seen to be speaking for the Federation, and she was understandably gratified. The boldest gesture of her pamphlet was to cast off the purity movement from the Abolitionist cause, saying, 'It is a beautiful word that of Purity; but . . . how often even has it proved to be an encumbrance to the central principle which we were appointed to proclaim!', and advising Abolitionists to '*Beware of "purity workers" as allies in our warfare!*'[90]

The closest she came to naming Lady Henry Somerset was to refer to the author of the six points as 'the distinguished lady', but her colleagues in the Abolition movement were warned 'never to covet the adhesion to our cause of distinguished and influential persons, or persons bearing great names . . . until their clearness of conviction on the central principles we defend has been fully proved'.[91] For as well as the shock of seeing for the first time *women* betray the principles of the Abolitionists, Josephine was very disturbed by the class nature of these latest developments. Titled ladies were presuming to recommend legislation affecting the lives of poor women. For Josephine this remained a question of justice for women, and of social justice.

Her next action was to resign from her position as 'World's Superintendent' of the Purity Department of the WWCTU, asking what purity could be maintained if the state and the law take it upon themselves to regulate 'down to the smallest details . . . a disgusting and deadly vice, a vice which is the scourge of the world, the curse of the nations?'[92] As she had written to Stanley from Switzerland in 1896, '"Faithful unto death", & it shall be so to the end'.[93]

17

Final Years

'I think I may have to die'

In the last years of the century, Josephine moved about between a number of temporary addresses: she rented rooms in West Ealing, stayed with her sister Emmy in Wandsworth, and visited the families of all three sons. Unable or unwilling to settle, though often lonely, she led an almost independent life.

Josephine continued to be active in the cause. From January 1898 to July 1900 she edited a little monthly paper of her own which she called the *Storm-Bell*, in which she continued to assert the principles of the repeal movement. 'It will be so simple, so ABC in its character & so familiar in its style that the learned will despise it,' she told Fanny Forsaith.[1] She addressed the *Storm-Bell* to the humbler classes, to whom she intended the paper to be distributed free of charge. She prayed for a printer and for funds and got both. The Newcastle printers Mawson & Swann ('strong abolitionists') offered her their services for very little money, '& wish to do it *with heart*'.[2] Four thousand copies of the first number of her 'humble little periodical' were printed, but there was such an overwhelming demand for Josephine's paper that a further 11,000 were distributed. Josephine wrote to Stanley that soldiers at the Gibraltar garrison, 'from General Biddolphe downwards', had put in orders![3]

The chief attraction of the *Storm-Bell* for Josephine was that she would be left 'perfectly *free* as editor'.[4] Chiefly, the paper was used to make continued appeals to *women* to involve themselves in the Abolition movement. Josephine recalled episodes from the past thirty years' agitation and wrote biographical accounts of many of its leaders, men such as James Stansfeld and Yves Guyot. There was nothing very startling about the *Storm-Bell.* The same cannot be said for her major publication of these years, *Native Races and the War*, of 1900, in which she shocked her Abolitionist friends by supporting the British in the Boer War. There was strong anti-imperialist feeling in the circles in which Josephine moved, feeling which she had strongly shared in relation to Ireland and to India. She acknowledged that for the past century or more 'the great blot' on the expansion of the British people to other parts of the world was their 'displacement of native tribes by force and violence'.[5] Yet, influenced over the years, perhaps, by her cousin Sir Charles Grey, who had been Governor of the Cape Province in the 1850s, and by her own son Charles who had recently returned from South Africa, she seemed to be supporting an imperialist war. In fact, *Native Races and the War* is a typically well-researched account of the British presence in South Africa, of relations between the British and the Boers, and of both with the indigenous people of South Africa. This was the point for Josephine. She saw similarities between the way Africans were treated by the Boers, and the slavery which had been abolished in the southern states of America. She was not at all naïve about the link between British imperialism and commercial interests, but she did believe that the British would be a good deal more enlightened rulers in South Africa than the Boers had been. Where the Boers had enslaved, the British must make up for their neglect of duty and take upon them 'the claims of the millions of inhabitants of Africa who are God's creatures'.[6] She abhorred the way the Boers contemptuously referred to all Africans as 'kaffirs' and, even more, the English calling all Africans and Indians 'niggers'. 'Race prejudice is a poison which will have to be cast out,' she declared.[7]

Josephine closed her book by stating, 'I have here spoken for myself alone'. She was only too aware that some of her oldest and most valued friends and colleagues in the Abolition movement were 'absolutely opposed' to the views she had expressed on the native question, but said simply: 'I value friendship, and I love my old friends. But I love truth more'.[8] Henry Wilson banned the reprinting in the *Shield* of any of Josephine's speeches and writings of the past, saying that it would be dangerous to bring her name before the public at such a time. He sought to impress upon Fanny Forsaith 'the *intensity* of feeling amongst a great many (I should say the bulk), of the friends and supporters of the British Committee', who let him know that they were '*astounded*' at the line Mrs Butler was taking.[9] Millicent Fawcett was soon the only colleague with whom Josephine could discuss the war. To her she confided that she could count on the fingers of one hand those few Abolition friends in England who were '*not* strong pro-Boers'.[10]

The new century began ominously. In addition to her increasing political isolation, Josephine lost some of her dearest companions. As Josephine put it, 'My path seems strewn with the graves of friends and relatives'.[11] The first loss was Tell Meuricoffre, who died in his sleep in March 1900. Hatty survived him by just six months. Josephine had spent August and September at La Gordanne, and the sisters made plans for Hatty to return the visit the following year. Waiting at the station, 'The last thing she said was, "Will May be too early for me to come to England?" I replied, "You cannot come too early, my beloved", and she smiled and waved her hand'. Writing later to Federation friends, Josephine described how, on arriving in Dover two days later, she had received from Hatty's children 'that dreadful telegram. "Mother has passed away"'.[12] Thekla and her brothers begged Josephine to write a memorial of their mother, drawing upon the sisters' voluminous correspondence, and this she set about at once. Thekla read the first few pages of the proof sheets 'through her tears, but tears partly of gratitude and joy'.[13]

By January 1901, Josephine was battling against increasing pain and insomnia, so much so that she began to doubt whether her Life of Hatty would ever be completed: 'I know no one who could write the book to the end but myself, and I pray God to keep me alive to finish'.[14] As it was, the biography had, so far, taken her only four months to assemble, and would have been completed even earlier but for the interference of a maidservant at her Ealing lodgings. She explained to Rhoda that the housemaid had been taking her manuscripts about Hatty and lighting fires with them: 'the servant who slept with her says she used to take them up & read them, & then burn them. I have just paid £16 to my shorthand writer, & this is to be done over again'.[15] Perhaps the greatest charm of the biography was to demonstrate how her sister had adopted their father's Christian humility in devoting his life to the service of others, how, despite being 'obliged to be a good deal in Society & at the Court . . . she preserved her humble Christian character all thro',' and was always ready 'for hard work to help the suffering'.[16]

Then, on Tuesday, 22 January at 6.30 p.m., Queen Victoria died.

The nation woke to the news the following morning, and Josephine wrote at once to Stanley and Rhoda of the extraordinary outpouring of grief throughout the nation and the British Empire:

> I am sure our hearts are all *one* today in thinking of our dear, dear Mother Queen, the mother of her people, dutiful, faithful, courageous. One feels as if one had lost a dear friend. Everybody is crying, & people's blinds are drawn down. It is a real, *personal* grief. They cannot understand, I am sure, on the Continent, the sorrow we feel, but how wonderful is this electric thrill of love & sorrow thro' her whole Empire.[17]

Interestingly, the once republican Josephine had developed rather a sentimentalized attitude to the Queen, whom she thought 'an example to all women'. She wrote to Fanny Forsaith of 'the constant outflowing of [Victoria's] sympathy for all her people, of all classes, high & low', and of how the Queen had 'visited the hospitals speaking to every individual wounded & sick soldier'. She thought that it was far better for a country to have a good queen to reign than a king, because of the chivalrous feeling it stirred in men: 'It melts away some of their roughness & contempt of women. Quote this if you like & can'.[18]

In the spring of 1901, Josephine was to lose yet another family member. Her daughter-in-law, Mia, had become pregnant in the summer of 1900. A fragment of a letter survives from Josephine to Rhoda, carrying the exclamation: 'I think it is possible Mia will have twins! What a business!'[19] As the winter advanced, however, Mia was unable to get about, and George informed his mother that Mia had had such awful pain that Dr Walker had injected morphia as much as he dared, 'to save her reason or her life': '[he] thinks she is carrying the baby in some strange way, and is evidently very anxious'. Meanwhile, Josephine remained seriously ill herself, and told the Priestman sisters of 'several days of constant heart attacks'.[20] Mia saw out the difficult pregnancy, giving birth to a healthy baby girl, Irene Maria, on 18 March, but she died on 24 April. Josephine had not been to see her. Nor could she attend the funeral.

The day after Mia's death, she was writing to her St Andrews grandchildren, Bob and Josephine, thanking them for their prayers for Mia, and providing grandmotherly consolation ('She is now in heaven, face to face with Jesus, and with Grandpapa who will be so pleased to see her').[21] And although she warned them, 'uncle George's heart seems broken', it was her own mortality that seems most to have concerned her: 'I am very weak but I hope I shall live to see you all again, but I think it will not be for long'. When she did travel up to Ewart, she confided in George's housekeeper, Jane Grey, what she had not told her own son, that when she had been warned that Mia was dying, she was in bed with fever and so weak that she could not stand.[22] Delicacy had prevented her from adding to George's grief, but 'I think I made a mistake perhaps not to tell him; for he may have thought it strange that I came north so slowly. I have had an attack of gravel* and other things, and have bad fainting fits. I hope I shall not be a trouble to him and an anxiety'. Distracted by his grief for Mia, George seems not to have known how ill his mother was, and never did forgive her for not coming to his wife's bedside. The rift between them continued until Josephine's death.

Charlie, however, did realize his mother's condition, and he acted promptly to remove her from continued active involvement in the Federation she had founded a quarter of a century earlier. He wrote to James Stuart, urging an end to Josephine's ceaseless interviews and meetings with workers from around the country and from the Continent: 'Now, if my Mother was too ill to go to see her dying daughter-in-law, of whom she was *very* fond, and to be present with and condole her eldest son, it is not likely she is either able or willing just now to receive visitors . . . her condition has been – one might say – almost desperate'. He said that it was the feeling of Josephine's family 'that she has *done* her great life's work, and now deserves a complete rest from her labours for her remaining years', 'and that we . . . have the first claim to her society, for every year or even month which we can still save to her is precious to *us*'.[23]

Josephine's letter of resignation, in which she requested 'that her name be removed from the headings of letter paper and all printed documents', was sent to Henry Wilson, as chairman of the British Committee, on 11 May. 'She desires this in order that papers and letters may cease to be sent to her, which she is no longer able to read or reply to . . . This request and decision above expressed must be considered as absolute and final'.[24] For some time, of course, Josephine had not been altogether actively involved in the Federation work, and she had recognized that it was extremely unlikely that she would travel again to the Continent. Yet even this February, when Josephine was 'too weak even to sit up in bed', she had been sought out personally

---

*A build-up of urinary crystals which cause the sufferer to experience difficulty in passing urine.

by a German pastor, who asked her to forward 300 francs owed to a brothel by a young woman desperate to enter a refuge but by law compelled to work out her debt. This familiar appeal affected Josephine no less than had those from the prostitutes of Liverpool some thirty-five years earlier. She could not spare the money herself, but she requested Fanny Forsaith to lend the sum from Federation funds: 'O! please, for my sake and Christ's sake, try to get help . . . This girl seems to be standing by my bedside praying to me'.[25]

The tension between Josephine's public and private roles was never satisfactorily resolved in the minds of George or Charlie, nor, it would seem, in her own mind. The '*rather* ricketty' old writing desk which she had sent to Ewart along with other furniture when she moved from Balham in 1894, might suggest as much. Five years later, in spring 1900, Josephine wrote to Mia requesting either that the drawers be emptied and the contents sent in a packing case down to Ealing for her to sort, or that they move the desk to a safe corner until she was able to come up to Ewart herself to look through it. In it there were papers 'precious & unprecious', so hopelessly muddled that only she knew how to separate them. The drawers were apparently stuffed full of papers: plenty of official stationery and foolscap which she could still use, as well as printed pamphlets, and 'besides these things there are put away among them some dear old treasures, some faded writings, recording the childhood of my sons, memories of Eva, little pictures & relics wh I should like to have & put together'.[26] Josephine instructed Mia to break open the drawers if they were found to be locked, 'for where the little key is gone I know not!'

In the autumn of 1901, Josephine chose to revisit her own past, her own ghosts, starting from St Andrew's Parish Church in Corbridge, the church from which she and all her sisters had been married, and where the graves of her mother and father lay. She 'read reverentially the inscriptions',[27] but was disappointed that the graves were too much in shadow for her to make a satisfactory sketch, or to take a photograph. She then went on to her beloved Dilston, although the house itself was no more: 'I had to close my eyes to try to call up the dear house wh we lived in'. The new house that had been built in its stead was much larger, and three storeys high. It was, wrote Josephine, 'a huge mistake'. She was thankful that Mia and George would have seen her old home when they visited, some eight or so years previously, and that George had his father's drawing of Dilston hanging in the gallery at Ewart.

Her long account of this visit, and of the family memories it aroused, was written in the form of a special letter to George. Josephine chose not to return permanently to Ewart, however. On George's marriage to Mia in 1893, and their removal to Mia's family seat, Ewart Park, Josephine had sent with them numerous items of furniture, books, her husband's watercolours, and her piano, which she gave to Mia. Some of these things George paid for, but most certainly became part of the Ewart furniture rather than being put into storage, very much as if Josephine, or her children, intended that she should make Ewart her home. Ewart Park was the style of residence she belonged to by birth, with its high-walled wooded grounds, its stables and its turreted tower. It also had a library, a gallery and 'My Lady's Room', as well as a study, which Mia 'so kindly call[ed] mine',[28] but it represented a life of privilege Josephine had effectively renounced when she married George Butler, and perhaps felt unwilling to adopt now. She had lent money to Stanley, was saving up a further sum for Charles's voyage to South Africa, and admitted to Fanny Forsaith, 'I must economize strictly just now', adding, 'But I *like* humble life, and *muddling*, so long as I can have a good fire, and a bed *not* of iron!'[29]

By Christmas 1901, Josephine was installed in comfortable, and somewhat perverse, isolation in lodgings in Cheltenham where she now knew no one. Even though Charles had secured his mother's retirement from public duties, the puzzle of where she would live and be cared for now preoccupied her children. Rhoda suggested a Quaker home for the elderly and infirm, but Josephine clung to her independence: 'I don't think I should care to go to a Home or Retreat, so long as I can take care of myself. A little house *of my own*, however humble, is what I still hope to find'.[30] To the Misses Priestman she declared that she had made her mind up for solitude for a time, but in truth she missed her family terribly, and lamented that 'deep snow drifts have kept my northern children's letters back . . . so the postman passes and passes, with no letter for me'.[31] She pressed Stanley in particular for a Christmas message, and the day before Christmas Eve wrote to tell him that Charles's wife 'Maggie is sending me a little plum pudding of her own making. You will send me a thought on Christmas Day, won't you? I shall be quite alone'. She wished to know the dates of the Christmas tree, the servants' supper party, the children's ball, and Rhoda's dance, 'so that I might think of you each time'.[32]

Josephine's choice of Cheltenham was understandable because of the many family associations the town held: Fanny and little Eva were buried in pretty Leckhampton Cemetery, Eliza had had her first school there, and Edith had been married from there. Charles, Maggie and their little daughter Rosalind saw her settled in at Cheltenham, staying for three weeks and leaving just before Christmas. One fine frosty day they hired a carriage to take them to the cemetery, and placed a wreath of white immortelles on Eva's grave. Josephine's standing order of twenty shillings to the keeper had not bought care for the grave. The stone itself was in sad disrepair, the inscription almost worn away and Munro's medallion coated with black lichen. She ordered the stone to be cleaned, and put the grave under the care of a local gardening firm, Messrs Pates & Sharp, for the same yearly fee. The presence of Rosalind did much to dispel the sadness of the occasion: 'it was touching to see the dear little thing all drest in snow-white furs, trotting round among the graves, and chatting'. When Josephine asked the little girl what she was to her, she replied, 'Osalind grannie's *jabberbox*', and when they left, Josephine admitted, 'I miss her terribly, and the *silence* is sometimes dreadful'.[33] She had been delighted with their stay: 'It is so cheerful to hear their voices', she had written, 'and to see little dollies and untidy bits of pictures and toys lying about, instead of a tidy room with writing paper and pens and ink'.[34] Charles's and Maggie's second child, John, was born in June 1902 and Josephine stayed a few days with them at Malvern, taking her turn to give the baby his bottle: 'When he was well filled up, he used to look at me, & smile with that wide-mouthed toothless smile of a young baby wh is so bewitching'.[35]

Josephine claimed that she had 'retired from all public work',[36] but at Cheltenham she was again called to action. It so happened that her lodging house, 39 Clarence Square, was shared by a high-class prostitute, a foreigner who, according to Josephine, 'seemed at first all right', but who was suspected by the landlady and told to leave. 'I watched the gay, graceful slave of vice from my window as she left, & my heart bled for her. I was too ill to go to her, but we followed her up, & found her afterwards in a house of ill fame, patronised by *gentlemen*, and as fenced & protected by someone, perhaps some of [the] municipality, as much as a "maison tolerée" abroad. Such an atmosphere of French vice, & this is not the *only house* here of the kind'.[37] She discovered that high- and low-class brothels were well known to the local police 'in this Godly town', and there were also 'slums wh would be a disgrace to London or New York'. There was drunkenness in the back streets, families of twelve or thirteen living in a single room, and 'girls of 15, carrying their *own babies* in their arms, bundles of *rags*, & openly confessing themselves to be mothers'. What really pained and angered her was the professed ignorance of all this of the good citizens of Cheltenham: 'These correct Evangelical protestants! They don't *mean* to know of it'. She observed that they held conferences 'from wh they come away gorged with spiritual sweet stuff', yet they left 'this *seething* hell around them as bad as ever'. She was 'longing for dynamite'!

In March 1903 Josephine sat for her last portrait, a drawing in chalk by her young friend, Emily Ford. She wrote at once to Stanley to say that it was '*much* better than what Watts did. Perhaps that is not saying much; but it is really artistic, & I think like, with all its thinness & wrinkles'.[38] Three years later, however, she confided in Millicent Fawcett that she had been very ill at the time, 'full of pain, with a pained expression', and had actually fainted from having to sit in a fixed position for so long.[39] Josephine now professed not to like the picture at all, although it seems to have been Stuart's opinion that swayed her, complaining as he had that 'the face was so hard & stern & conveyed no idea of a person who was able to speak a word of hope or courage, tho' old'.[40]

Privately, Josephine dwelt with morbid satisfaction upon her increasingly frail appearance, writing to Fanny Forsaith, 'If you could see me unclothed down to my waist, I think you would weep! I really do. I was always thin, but now I have no flesh on my bones. You can count every rib . . . the bones of my right side are so sore, and almost raw, that I have to pad them with cotton wool'.[41] She had been suffering from a number of complaints: her eyesight was failing badly, she had emphysema, and ulceration of the stomach which caused sickness and required a milky diet. She had also had frightening 'paroxysms' of internal pain. Much against her will, she agreed to see 'a great specialist', a Dr Ferguson, who talked of '*internal cancer*, & necessary operations. I decided I would rather die than suffer this'.[42] She told Ferguson that God could heal her and He alone. Friends reassured her with tales of miraculous cures, and her own sons said, 'bother the expert! What does *he* know about it'.

George and Stanley finally persuaded their mother to come to them in the north. She was made comfortable at a house on George's estate, called Galewood, and a nurse was hired to attend her. It was just a few miles from her birthplace, and it was a blessed retreat to Josephine; here she could look out of her window and watch sheepdogs at work in the fields. She also delighted in the visits of her grandchildren, writing very sweetly about the baby, Irene: 'The darling is very loving to me; throws her arms round my neck, and almost stifles me with kisses . . . externally, one would think there was little to attract a child in a faded skeleton old grannie'.[43] She had, too, the unexpected pleasure of being recognized by local people, both as a national celebrity and as a Grey. During a brief visit to Newcastle, Josephine happened to order some writing paper at the stationers' Mawson & Swann, '& their man came to my room with his hair on end to ask if I was really Mrs Josephine Butler (Miss Grey!)'.[44] Similarly, one day at Galewood, the grocer from Wooler, a man named Lilico, called with his van to take their order in person. Not realizing that it was the grocer himself, Josephine instructed her maid to give the man a shilling for his trouble, '& in Wooler they now tell me that he said to his wife, "I will buy a new purse, and put that shilling in it, & *never part with it*"'.[45] Apparently her son Stanley had had an encounter with Mr Lilico a few years before, and reported humorously to his mother that Lilico had grasped his hand over the shop counter, saying, '"O Sir, you are the son of Mrs Josephine, allow me to shake your hand", & then, said Stanley, he wept, & his tears made a river all among the sugar & flour & rice on the counter!'

At Galewood, though, Josephine suffered such agonies of prolonged pain from her illness that she 'cried to God to preserve my brain' and guard her against thoughts of suicide: 'It would be so easy to take an overdose of chloral, & the longing to *separate oneself* from the tortured flesh is so strong'.[46] Yet, in her quieter moments, she was able to regard pain objectively as 'a *crucible*': 'The Refiner is standing over it & watching all the time, till He sees the least bit of the *Reflection* of His own tender face in it', and although her 'bodily heart beats like a steam-hammer', she considered her spiritual heart 'at rest'.[47] The nights were the worst, when she was kept awake by what she called her 'obsessions', memories of George or Eva, or thoughts of some 'sin & error & badness of my own in the past'. At such times she would say to herself, '"hang these pillows", & I thump them with a very unwholly [*sic*] energy', but lately, she told Fanny, 'I have begun to light my lamp, & I sit up in bed, & I raise my poor old skeleton hand to heaven, & I boldly say, "In Thy name, O! *Jehovah* Jesus, I defy this torment; *Joyfully*, I defy the Evil One"'.[48] She declared that it was worth the months of extreme pain 'to have been brought out of the life I had hitherto led (a *Christian* life, but not the highest), to the life where I am nothing, humbled to the dust, *emptied* & filled with *His* spirit'.[49] 'Now I have *no* physician except Christ', she declared.[50]

On 17 March 1905, one of her oldest colleagues, Margaret Tanner, died. She had remained as Treasurer of the LNA to the end. Josephine wrote this touching and generous memorial for Margaret's sisters, the Priestmans:

> We have always worked in perfect harmony, although differing markedly in natural character. To speak honestly, as one conscious of faults, . . . I was too impetuous, impulsive and sometimes rash. The keen sense of injustice which possessed both her and me, was apt at times to fill me with bitterness of soul. She, on the contrary, was always calm, steady, equal, gentle – a true representative of the Society of Friends . . . With all her gentleness, she had the utmost firmness, never wavering in the least in principle . . . She would say she owed much to me. Few people guess how much I owed to her, to that firm, quiet individuality.[51]

Like her own mother before her, Josephine was determined to die 'without any *fuss*!', but like her friend Margaret, she was also resolved 'to "die fighting" – if I *am* to die'.[52] Despite being forbidden all visitors, including her own sons, Josephine continued to get out of bed every morning and dress, even though it caused faintness: 'But O! the trial of dressing! I feel impatient with the *pins*'.[53] She would then lie on her sofa and begin to answer the many correspondents who wrote asking for money or for advice, 'as if I was a strong young woman'.[54] Her colleagues Fanny Forsaith and James Stuart were astonished to learn of the volume of work she still managed to get through. In 1905 she was spending five to seven shillings a week on postage alone: 'My maid is appalled, who writes a letter perhaps twice in the year'.[55] The mental occupation appears to have given her the strength to bear her terrible physical suffering, and prevented her from becoming, in her words, 'a mere old rheumatic croker'.[56]

Josephine was not being provided with adequate funds to meet these expenses. While she could joke to Fanny that she had 'not yet resorted to the Pawnshop',[57] Wilson and Stuart nit-picked over what to allow her: 'She is not a person one can reckon very exactly with'.[58] Stuart finally settled upon a cheque for £18 to cover past and present expenses. A year later, in March 1906, Millicent Fawcett (a vice-president of the LNA) offered a far more generous financial gift from the LNA, even though the gesture was a little late to benefit Josephine now that she was, in her words, 'a great invalid'.[59] A testimonial fund of £884 was collected, and an album was presented to Josephine. It contained three hundred or so signatures, and was covered in grey velvet and lined with white satin, its pages held together with white ribbon. Josephine was overwhelmed at the tribute, and she accepted the magnanimous gift with the now familiar proviso that she could never have entered upon her life's work without the support and collaboration of her husband and sons: 'I repeat that I prefer to use the word "we" rather than "I"'.[60]

She decided to respond to the LNA's gift with a printed message for easy circulation, and asked Millicent Fawcett to arrange that a photograph be attached to it. Emily Ford's portrait was selected, and paid for, but when she heard of this Josephine made known her preference for the last photograph taken by Elliott & Fry, which 'has at least a calm, good old face'.[61] Since Mrs Fawcett was in Naples, Josephine wrote directly to poor Emily, explaining why her portrait had been 'suppressed', and rather bluntly informing her that her it 'is not liked, for it is too deathlike & rather terrible. It surprises people, for I am really *not* like that at all times, tho' I am old'.[62] She offered to pay her for the now unwanted reproductions.

It was at this time that her son George's resentment over Josephine's apparent neglect of Mia resurfaced. He began to berate his mother for choosing to live 'so severely and independently *alone*' after his father's death: 'And Mia and I wanting and wanting and wanting to get you to come and live with us, and settle down among those who loved you as a mother and kinswoman, and not merely (though that as well) as a noble public worker'. He told her frankly, 'I feel I have lost a mother as well as a wife'.[63] George acknowledged that Mia may have been jealous of her mother-in-law, which was certainly Josephine's feeling, and that she was perhaps wise not to live with them permanently, but he totted up his mother's ever decreasing visits in what seems like obsessive detail: 'she was 13 weeks at Ewart in 1898 [presumably for the birth of George and Mia's son Horace], 8 weeks in 1899, 3 weeks in 1900, & in 1901 she only came after her "daughter" was no longer there to welcome her'.[64] He recognized that this tendency to isolate herself and her 'intense love of independence' was characteristic of the Greys and was 'a source of power', but argued that 'it is hard to make it work in harmony with open-hearted affectionate love'.[65]

This was but part of George's continuing resentment that she had put her public work before her family. In a bitter letter of recrimination, dated 17 June 1905, of which he kept a summarized record,

George noted that he had: 'Signed myself (1) as one of the public admiringly; (2) as father's eldest son'.[66] George's most serious accusation against his mother was that she had brought on his father's death:

> I said how 'freedom to serve' had been secured to her by father's daily toil as schoolmaster, earning livelihood for her & his children & how he also took part in her work & her journeying to & fro, ungrudgingly giving his time & help to smooth her way; even to the fatal sea journey from Copenhagen when he took the dangerous chill.

A week later he wrote again, comparing his eight years of marriage, with its 'few mementoes', to her thirty-eight years![67]

To Fanny Forsaith, Josephine spoke of the 'displacement' of her son's brain following the death of his wife,[68] but it is equally likely that George's behaviour towards his mother can be put down to the head injury and subsequent breakdown he suffered in 1894, 'which to some extent shook his brain', as Josephine put it to Monty, and again to Fanny, saying that he 'was for years *under a cloud*, sad, depressed, sometimes *warped* and strange in judgment'.[69] Josephine sought to make what amends were within her power. As her own death approached and she made notes for the advice of her three sons about the disposal of her property, she wrote out a special memorial of Eva addressed to George. In it she thanked him again for his strength and consolation at that time, 'and as I think of the past, instances of your kindness to me (and to father) crowd upon me'.[70] In a later list of 'Directions for my sons' written six months before her death, Josephine wrote of her special regard for Mia, who had always been 'a very loyal and affectionate daughter, and I mourn her loss. Her husband's sorrow pierced my heart'.[71] Her final words, addressed to all three sons, are a plea for forgiveness for 'the many faults and shortcomings towards you, of which I am deeply conscious'.

On 13 April 1906, Josephine spent her seventy-eighth birthday alone, since George's children had all gone down with whooping cough. 'Still *alive*!' she wrote triumphantly, to Fanny Forsaith.[72] She was having a restful spring: 'I am ordered to *bed* for *weeks*! Not to move, not to write, not to have *any* visits & O! what a relief it is to me . . . Florence Nightingale is still alive, & she has been in bed for seven weeks!'[73] In March she had been moved into new lodgings at 2 Victoria Villas, in Wooler itself. Her window looked out on to the hills, she had an excellent nurse, Mary Cockburn, and her landlady, Miss Moodie, was a good cook, 'with resources!' 'In fact, she almost *over feeds* me, & I feel greedy when I see her nice dinners come up. But I am a skeleton still – only bones – & I sometimes instinctively ask, "O Lord, can these bones live?" '[74] She was relieved that her recovery was so gradual: 'I am naturally so buoyant & *frivolous*, that if I were quite well all at once, I fear I might be apt to "get my head out" too much, & begin to plan & be too busy'.[75]

In the autumn, she had to undergo an operation to remove an upper molar so that a false plate could be fitted, '& then I shall have lovely artificial teeth to *smile* with!'[76] but the dentist was alarmed that Josephine had been bleeding from an ear and insisted that she consult a physician. There was no physician to be had in Wooler: 'Dr Dey is only a "surgeon *accoucheur*", & I don't want the *latter* person at the age of 80! So here is an *impasse*!'[77] She still relied upon the advice of Dr Carter in Liverpool, and she telegraphed his assistant to come up on the train. Yet she 'got through the worst & most dreaded hauling out of teeth' with no pain at all: a supreme act of faith, according to Josephine.[78]

She was amused that Mrs Terrel, with whom she had stayed in Ealing, expected her to look forward to a speedy death, 'as if she wanted to see me soon "safe in port" . . . as if it would be so blessed for me to go soon, as if just passing into the next room! & one sentimental friend writes, "how I must be *longing* to be taken into the rest of Heaven"! No! not a bit!!'[79] She was delighted that her own grandchildren continued to make plans for future holidays with her: ' "You are not to die yet, grannie", they say'.[80] But by the end of the year she knew that death was near. Throughout November and December Josephine was unable to leave her bed, and could move only 'with my nurse's strong arm to help me'.[81] She was just able to hold a pen to scribble a final note to her best-loved son, Stanley,

> Beloved ones, my Stanley, I think I may have to die. Don't mourn too much. Remember I shall be loving you all the more & nearer you than ever – & *come to me* in the presence of Jesus, & your darlings with you.
>
> The fever fell suddenly without warning.[82]

At 5 a.m. on Sunday, 30 December Josephine awoke and experienced difficulty in breathing. She refused to send for a doctor, and was able to drink a cup of tea. Miss Moodie and the nurse, Mary, were by her bedside. She thanked them for their tender care of her, whispered a final prayer, and then two hours later, quite peacefully, she died. Dr Dey certified the cause of death as 'Senile Debility', although he seems to have told George Butler that she had suffered from 'a rupture of the heart, [a] result of her great age and of the diminution of her vitality'.[83]

What followed was, in the words of Fanny Forsaith, 'most extraordinary – and I am tempted to add, hardly decent'.[84] Since Stanley Butler was suffering from influenza and was unable to leave his bed in St Andrews, and Charles and his family had emigrated to Canada, the sole responsibility for the funeral arrangements lay with Josephine's eldest son, George. His bitterness over his mother's readiness to sacrifice to her work her ties with her children and grandchildren evidently determined George to reclaim Josephine for her family after her death, and to make sure that the funeral was a private family affair, or rather *his* private affair, since the only other member of the Butler family able to attend the funeral besides George and his children was Stanley's eighteen-year-old son, Andrew.

The funeral was held at the tiny church of Kirknewton on the morning of Thursday, 3 January 1907. This was where Josephine's eldest brother George and her grandparents, George and Mary Grey, were buried (her grandparents' tombstone is situated just outside the entrance to the church), yet it was not where Josephine herself desired to be buried. She had made clear to her sons that it was their father's wish, and hers, 'that I should be laid by his side in the cemetery at Winchester'.[85] George did not telegraph Henry Wilson to tell him the date of the funeral until 8.37 p.m. the night before, which meant that neither the Wilsons nor their wreath would be present. James Stuart was not even honoured with a telegram. He received notification of Josephine's death by post on 2 January, while Fanny Forsaith only learned of her death through a postcard from Josephine's printer, Burfoot, the day *after* the funeral, and then an hour later saw the obituary in the *Daily News*. She wrote to Wilson in bewilderment at the way George had treated them all: 'The only excuse I can find for the sons is, that they may be carrying out Mrs Butler's wishes as to a very quiet funeral . . . but it could never have been her wish that her dearest friends should be pained as so many will have been by these proceedings'.[86] It was in fact Josephine's wish that her funeral 'be of the very simplest kind, & without any show of deep mourning. The more simple it is, the more will it be in accordance with my wishes'.[87]

The letters of condolence received by George, without exception, while expressing conventional sympathy for the grieving family, considered first what a loss Josephine's death was to the nation, and to the world. The social reformer Canon Samuel Barnett wrote of Josephine, 'she is one of the women who stand for England – a lady – a brave woman – she is hardly more than her work'.[88] Wilfred Powell, the godfather of one of George's daughters, offered his 'deepest and warmest sympathies in your loss and the loss of England'.[89] To her colleagues on the Continent, Josephine was the 'Mère de la Fédération', her 'great heart was sufficient to enclose us all'.[90] In view of George's resentment of his mother's sacrifice, it must have been particularly difficult for him to receive a letter from his uncle, Arty Butler, rejoicing in the fact that the papers all recognized her life's work and truly appreciated her achievements: 'other things about her are completely subordinate to this her great work'.[91]

Obituaries appeared in all the national newspapers, which were also taken up with the death of the great philanthropist, Angela Burdett Coutts. The *Daily News* commented how fitting it was that these 'two last heroic figures of the nineteenth century should have entered into their rest together'.[92] Angela Burdett Coutts's funeral, held on Saturday, 5 January, was very different to Josephine's interment at Kirknewton two days earlier. She was buried with full honours in Philanthropists' Corner at Westminster Abbey; the *Daily Telegraph* offered its readers photographs of the tomb and lengthy descriptions of the eminent guests who attended the ceremony. Although there were to be no public demonstrations of mourning for the death of Josephine Butler, the significance of her life's work was fully recognized:

> Mrs Butler's name will always rank amongst the noblest of those social reformers the fruit of whose labours is the highest inheritance that we have. She fought with enormous courage and self-sacrifice in a battlefield where she was subjected to the fiercest antagonism and the most distressing aspects of life that a delicately nurtured woman could be brought into contact with. She never faltered in her task, and it is to her in supreme that the English statute book owes the removal of one of the grossest blots that ever defaced it. Her victory marked one of the greatest stages in the progress of woman to that equality of treatment which is the final test of a nation's civilization.[93]

George Butler's final act of reclamation was in his choice of a portrait of his mother to be reproduced in one of the stained-glass windows at the back of the Lady Chapel, consecrated in 1910, in the new Anglican Cathedral in Liverpool. A series of windows of 'Noble

Women' was donated by the Liverpool Diocesan Girls' Friendly Society. Josephine is represented in the first atrium window beneath Elizabeth Fry and alongside Queen Victoria, Anne Clough, Catherine Gladstone, Christina Rossetti and Elizabeth Barrett Browning. The Bishop of Liverpool wrote to George asking for a suitable photograph of his mother, but instead George proposed that the George Richmond portrait of 1851 be used as a model. It was a very deliberate choice, since practically all the photographic studies of Josephine were official portraits for the use of the cause. The Richmond drawing was, on the contrary, a privately commissioned portrait, recording Josephine's last months of maidenhood before her wedding in January 1852. Years before Josephine took up any public work, she appears as a beautiful young woman, her heart light, on the threshold of private, personal and domestic fulfilment.

Notes

ABBREVIATIONS

BJG	Private Collection of Beverley Josephine Grey
BL	British Library
BLL	Brotherton Library, University of Leeds*
FL	The Women's Library (formerly the Fawcett Library), Josephine Butler Collection
George Butler	JEB, *Recollections of George Butler*, Bristol: J. W. Arrowsmith, 1892
Harriet Meuricoffre	JEB, *In Memoriam: Harriet Meuricoffre*, London: Horace Marshall & Son, 1901
JEB	Josephine Elizabeth Butler
JEG	Josephine Elizabeth Grey
John Grey	JEB, *Memoir of John Grey of Dilston*, Edinburgh: Edmondson & Douglas, 1869
Johnson	*Josephine E.Butler: An Autobiographical Memoir*, ed. George W. Johnson and Lucy A. Johnson, London: J. W. Arrowsmith, 1909
LUL	Liverpool University Library**
McHugh	Paul McHugh, *Prostitution and Victorian Social Reform*, London: Croom Helm, 1980
NRO	Northumberland Record Office
Petrie	Glen Petrie, *A Singular Iniquity: The Campaigns of Josephine Butler*, New York: Viking Press, 1971
Portrait	A. S. G. Butler, *Portrait of Josephine Butler*, London: Faber & Faber, 1954

*Copies of these letters form part of the Josephine Butler Collection at the Women's Library, London.

**Copies of letters ending in (I) form part of the Women's Library's collection.

PRO	Public Record Office
Reminiscences	JEB, *Personal Reminiscences of a Great Crusade*, London: Horace Marshall & Son, 1896
RIBA	British Architectural Library, Royal Institute of British Architects
SA	Salvation Army International Heritage Centre
Scott	Benjamin Scott, *A State Iniquity: Its Rise and Overthrow* (1894), New York: Augustus M. Kelley, 1968
St AUL	St Andrews University Library

INTRODUCTION

1. Tribute by Professor James Stuart (dated 14 January 1907), *Shield*, January 1907, p.1.
2. Millicent G. Fawcett and E. M. Turner, *Josephine Butler: Her Work and Principles, and Their Meaning for the Twentieth Century*, London: Association for Moral and Social Hygiene, 1927, p.1.
3. *Shield*, May 1907, p.34.
4. FL, JEB to Joseph Edmondson, 28 March 1872.
5. JEB, *Sursum Corda; Annual Address to the Ladies' National Association*, Liverpool: T. Brakell, 1871, p.14.
6. FL, LNA circular by JEB, 11 December 1877.
7. Ibid., MS speech by JEB, delivered to the Social Science Congress in Plymouth, September 1872. (In her manuscript of this particular speech, Josephine crossed out 'rightfully' and put 'wisely' in its place.)
8. JEB, *Paper on the Moral Reclaimability of Prostitutes, read by Mrs Butler at a Conference of Delegates from Associations and Committees Formed in Various Towns for Promoting the Repeal of the Contagious Diseases Acts, Held at the Freemasons' Tavern, 5 and 6 May, 1870*, London: Ladies' National Association, 1870, p.4.
9. LUL, JB 1/1, 1905/04/00 (I), JEB to Fanny Forsaith.
10. Ibid., 1903/03/05 (I).
11. Ibid., 1869/07/01 (I), JEB to Mlle Nad. Stassoff; PRO, *Report of the Select Committee of the House of Commons on the Administration and Operation of the Contagious Diseases Acts, 1880*, 1882 (340), IX.1, Q.5276.
12. The east window is situated in the Parish Chapel to the left of the altar at St Olave's Church, 8 Hart Street. The choice of subject for the new window was the inspiration of the Reverend Augustus Powell Miller, who became the new incumbent in 1943. Powell Miller had come from the parish of Crosby in Liverpool and knew of the windows commemorating 'Noble Women' in the Lady Chapel of the Anglican Cathedral.
13. *Shield*, January 1907, p.1; Scott, p.111.
14. Obituary in *Newcastle Chronicle*, reprinted in the *Shield*, January 1907, p.11.
15. Her colleague, Dr Baxter Langley, announced at one public meeting, 'since the days, and before the days of Joan of Arc, there never lived a nobler woman than Mrs Josephine Butler of Liverpool', *National League Journal*, 1 December 1875, p.4.

16. JEB, *Catherine of Siena: A Biography*, London: Dyer Brothers, 1878, pp.331–2.
17. JEB, *Reminiscences*, p.77.
18. FL, JEB to 'Kind Friends', n.d. [*c.* winter 1904–5].
19. LUL, JB 1/1, 1890/11/04 (I), JEB to her daughter-in-law, Rhoda Butler; FL, JEB to the Misses Priestman, 4 January 1891.
20. LUL, JB 1/1, 1903/03/05 (I), JEB to Fanny Forsaith.

CHAPTER ONE

1. LUL, JB 1/1 1903/08/11 (I), JEB to Fanny Forsaith.
2. I have accounted for ten children born to John and Hannah Grey, yet in a letter to her friend Albert Rutson, dated 1868, Josephine referred to her mother bearing twelve children (FL, 22 February 1868). When Mrs Grey died, Josephine described how she found relics of the children we know to have died, John and Ellen, yet she does not allude to any other bereavements. Josephine wrote to her husband, 'We have spent many hours in mamma's room, looking over letters and papers. Oh, that locked cabinet – what revelations of our darling mother's careful love has it not revealed! endless relics of her dear ones which she has preserved, remembrances of John and Ellen who died, and all our letters since we were children and which she has stored up' (*George Butler*, pp.150–1).
3. *John Grey*, pp.288–9.
4. Ibid., p.207.
5. Ibid., p.291.
6. Charles Grey Grey, *Sequel to the Story of My Official Life*, privately printed, 1907, p.2.
7. LUL, JB 1/1 1905/02/26 (I), JEB to Fanny Forsaith and Harriet Allen.
8. Ibid.
9. *Harriet Meuricoffre*, p.8.
10. Grey Grey, *Sequel* p.2. Christian Ignatius Latrobe (1758–1836) held a number of posts connected with the Moravian Church and two of his sons trained as ministers.
11. LUL, JB 1/1 1904/01/22 (I), JEB to her granddaughter, Josephine Butler.
12. *Harriet Meuricoffre*, p.293.
13. LUL, JB 1/1 1904/01/22 (I), JEB to her granddaughter, Josephine Butler.
14. Private collection of Beverley Josephine Grey, 'Written for my dear Sisters and Nieces. Remembrances of our dear Father and extracts from letters connected with his life and interests. Beginning in 1860, by his daughter, Frances Hardy Smyttan', typed transcript, Book One, p.15.
15. *John Grey*, p.147.
16. Grey Grey, *Sequel*, p.3.
17. Ibid., p.2.
18. *John Grey*, pp.293, 296.
19. Ibid., p.294.
20. LUL, JB 1/1 1906/10/07 (I), JEB to Fanny Forsaith. Her brother Charles

made a similar tribute to their father, writing that John Grey 'taught us to love truth and honesty, and impressed us with the rights of individuals in a free country' *(Sequel* p.2).

21. FL, Typescript draft of speech prepared by JEB, read on her behalf at the Jubilee Conference of the Federation by Fanny Forsaith, September 1905.
22. *John Grey*, pp.112–13.
23. FL, Typescript draft of speech prepared by JEB, read on her behalf at the Jubilee Conference of the Federation by Fanny Forsaith, September 1905.
24. Grey Grey, *Sequel*, p.3.
25. *John Grey*, p.127.
26. Ibid., p.71.
27. Ibid., p.126.
28. Ibid., p.162.
29. Ibid., p.142.
30. Ibid., pp.296–7.
31. Ibid., p.297.
32. Ibid., p.133.
33. Ibid., p.179.
34. Ibid., p.14.
35. LUL, JB 1/1 1903/08/11 (I), JEB to Fanny Forsaith.
36. *John Grey*, pp.205–6.
37. Sir George Grey (1799–1882), grandson of the first Earl Grey, was the MP for Devonport, 1832–47, North Northumberland, 1847–52, and Morpeth, 1853–74. From 1834 to 1839, he served as Under-Secretary for the Colonies.
38. *John Grey*, p.162.
39. FL, JEB to Miss Priestman, [*c.* June 1890].
40. *John Grey*, p.294.
41. LUL, JB 1/1 1904/02/11 (I), JEB to her granddaughter, Josephine Butler.
42. *John Grey*, p.263.
43. *Harriet Meuricoffre*, p.2.
44. *John Grey*, pp.297–8.
45. FL, JEB to Albert Rutson, 5 March 1868.
46. *Portrait*, p.37.
47. *Harriet Meuricoffre*, p.9.
48. JEB, 'Emancipation as I Learned it', *Storm-Bell*, January 1900, No.19, p.258. Fanny's diary records one Sunday in the summer of 1861, during a visit from Sir George and Lady Grey, when the family attended the morning service at Hexham Church, and then an afternoon service at St Andrew's (BJG, typed transcript of Fanny Smyttan's Diary, Book One, p.25)
49. *John Grey*, p.89. Virtually all the last remaining restrictions on Catholics were abolished under the 1829 Act, which removed the bar on Catholics taking seats in Parliament and holding public office (with the exception of Regent, Lord Lieutenant and Lord Chancellor).
50. This was presumably the children's nurse, Jane Cranston, whom

Josephine refers to elsewhere as poorly educated, yet very Christianly (*John Grey*, p.164). Fanny recalled that it was Jane Cranston who stayed behind with the younger children at Milfield while the house at Dilston was being completed. However, she also mentions a Miss Hunt, 'formerly a governess in the family, and our Mother's companion', who visited John Grey in the summer of 1862, before he retired from Dilston (BJG, typed transcript of Fanny Smyttan's Diary, Book Two, p. 82). Miss Hunt appears to have returned to Milfield to look after George Annett Grey's children.

51. LUL, JB 1/1 1904/10/08 (I), JEB to Fanny Forsaith.
52. FL, JEB to Miss Priestman, 17 January 1883. Josephine's three sons inherited their mother's antipathy to the Church of England. She wrote, '*All* my sons have almost given up going to Church, & have been denounced as "heathen men & publicans" in consequence. But it has really been because of high ritualistic tendencies in churches to which they have access, or on the other hand *narrow* Protestant hellfire preaching. I had rather they stayed away from Church than that they went to Church for mere respectability & form's sake' (LUL, JB 1/1 1904/11/06 (I), JEB to Fanny Forsaith and Harriet Allen). At the end of her life, Josephine advised all three not to regard church-going as 'synonymous with spiritual life', writing that 'a moribund condition attracts nothing, quickens nothing. There may be periodically a "noise & a shaking" among the dry bones, but they will not become living men, "an exceeding great army", except by the irresistible "Breath of God"' (*'The Morning Cometh': A Letter to My Children*, by 'Philates' [JEB], Newcastle: T. M. Grierson, Printer, 1903, p.49).
53. LUL, JB 1/1 1902/03/16 (I), JEB to Maurice Gregory.
54. Alec R. Vidler, *The Church in an Age of Revolution: 1789 to the Present Day*, Harmondsworth: Penguin Books, 1961, p.66. Irving's following continued to grow after his death, and took the title, 'the Catholic Apostolic Church', although its followers were popularly known as the Irvingites.
55. LUL, JB 1/1 1905/03/03 (I), JEB to Stanley Butler.
56. Ibid., JB 1/1 1902/03/16 (I), JEB to Maurice Gregory.
57. *Storm-Bell*, January 1900, No.19, p.258.
58. Earl Grey sent him a number of circulars to do with emigration, as a solution to the latter, but Josephine's father dismissed this out of hand, 'so long as Ireland has its thousands of starving and unprovided wretches to pour in upon us to fill up the vacancy', *John Grey*, pp.159–60.
59. Josephine's account of the famine in Ireland is taken from her pamphlet, *Our Christianity Tested by the Irish Question*, London: T. Fisher Unwin, 1887, p.44.
60. LUL, JB 1/1 1905/02/16 (I), JEB to Fanny Forsaith; FL, Typescript draft speech by JEB for the Jubilee Conference of the Federation, 1905.
61. *Storm-Bell*, January 1900, No.19, p.259.
62. FL, JEB to Fanny Forsaith and Harriet Allen, 31 January 1905.
63. LUL, JB 1/1 1905/04/26 (I), JEB to her son Stanley Butler and his wife, Rhoda.

64. FL, JEB to Professor Benjamin Jowett, n.d. (*c.*1860–70).
65. Ibid.
66. *John Grey*, p.165.
67. LUL, 1/1 1894/06/21 (I), JEB to Stanley Butler.
68. NRO, ZBU.E3/C1, JEB to Eliza Morrison, 12 April [1851].
69. LUL, JB 1/1 1894/06/21 (I), JEB to Stanley Butler.
70. Ibid.
71. Grey Grey, *Sequel*, p.35.
72. Beverley Grey has a photograph of this portrait in her private collection.
73. *John Grey*, pp.166–7.
74. FL, JEB to Henry J. Wilson, 1 June 1873.
75. Charles Grey Grey, *The Story of His Official Life: For His Children,* privately printed, 1906, p.1.

CHAPTER TWO

1. LUL, JB 1/1 1902/12/18 (I), JEB to her grandson, 'Bob', A. S. G. Butler.
2. Francis Galton FRS, *Memories of My Life*, London: Methuen, 1908, p.158.
3. Quoted in *George Butler*, p.31.
4. Ibid., pp.65–6.
5. Ibid., p.138.
6. Ibid., p.126.
7. Ibid., pp.59, 58.
8. George spelt Josephine's nickname 'Josie'. For simplicity, I have adopted the spelling used by Hatty, Fanny and their father, who all spelt her name 'Josey'.
9. NRO, ZBU.E2/12, George Butler, 'The Early Morn', Dilston, 13 October 1850, transcribed in Book of Poems, 8 January 1861, inscribed 'To my dear wife'.
10. NRO, ZBU.E3/B 1, George Butler to JEG, n.d. [*c.* summer] 1851.
11. Josephine always regarded their life together as beginning in 1851, rather than the date of their marriage in 1852. This seems to be borne out by George's gift to her in 1861, on the tenth anniversary of their engagement, of a bound copy of his courtship poems which he had carefully transcribed.
12. *George Butler*, pp.57, 56.
13. Ibid., p.58.
14. NRO, ZBU.E3/C1, JEG to Eliza Morrison, 15 March [1851].
15. Ibid.
16. Ibid.
17. Ibid.
18. Ibid., 12 April [1851].
19. Ibid., 15 March [1851].
20. *George Butler*, p.62. The Tractarians were so called because of the series *Tracts for the Times* which they published, re-examining the meaning behind all aspects of Church doctrine. It was not until the 1840s that the Oxford

Movement became synonymous with the term 'ritualism' through its investment of symbolic meaning in ceremony that was closer to Catholicism. It was generally feared that ritualism was an attempt to romanize the Church of England, a suspicion that seemed to be confirmed by the notable secessions to the Catholic Church by John Henry Newman in 1845 and Henry Manning in 1851. Two of George's closest friends, William Thomson and Max Muller, were of a like mind. In 1861 William Thomson published a counterblast to the Tractarians' *Essays and Reviews*, entitled *Aids to Faith*. He regarded ritualism as abhorrent if taken to excess, and a 'denial both of law and reason' (H. Kirk-Smith, *William Thomson, Archbishop of York: His Life and Times*, London: SPCK, 1958, p.39). The orientalist Max Muller was shocked, when he came to Oxford in 1848, to find learned scholars disputing 'purely ecclesiastic questions' that seemed to him 'simply childish': 'Nothing but discussions on vestments, on private confession, on candles on the altar, whether they were wanted or not, on the altar being made of stone or wood', and so on (Friedrich Max Muller, *My Autobiography. A Fragment*, London: Longmans, Green, 1901, pp. 280–1).

21. Quoted in *George Butler*, p.64.
22. NRO, ZBU.E3/C1, JEG to Eliza Morrison, 15 March [1851].
23. Raymond Lister, *George Richmond: A Critical Biography*, London: Robin Garton, 1981. Richmond's account book shows that he was requested to produce a copy of Josephine's portrait in 1852, and that she sat for a new portrait in 1853 (in 1868, Arty Butler commissioned Richmond to paint his official portrait as headmaster of Haileybury).
24. NRO, ZBU.E3/C1, JEG to Eliza Morrison, 22 June [1851].
25. Ibid., Harriet Jane Grey to Eliza Morrison, 12 August [1851].
26. Ibid., ZBU.E3/B1, George Butler to JEG, n.d. [*c.* summer] 1851.
27. LUL, JB 1/1 1901/10/12 (II), JEB to George Grey Butler.
28. Reprinted in *George Butler*, pp.72–3.
29. Reprinted ibid., pp.73–4.
30. NRO, ZBU.E3/C1, Harriet Jane Grey to Eliza Morrison, 12 August [1851].
31. *George Butler*, p.67.
32. NRO, ZBU.E3/A1, Typescript of Harriet Jane Grey's Diary, December 1851–January 1853.
33. Ibid., ZBU.E3/C1, Harriet Jane Grey to Eliza Morrison, 19 September [1851].
34. Ibid., ZBU.E2/4, Copy of marriage settlement, 1851.
35. Ibid., ZBU.E3/A1, Typescript of Harriet Jane Grey's Diary, December 1851–January 1853.

CHAPTER THREE

1. *Portrait*, p.42.
2. FL, Arthur Butler to George Grey Butler, 4 January 1907.

3. NRO, ZBU.E3/A1, Transcript of the Diary of Harriet Jane Grey, Saturday, 14 February 1852.
4. George Butler later pioneered Geography as a subject to be taken seriously in public schools: Liverpool College, where he became headmaster, was noted for its success in teaching Geography, and when he died, tributes were paid to his influence in this field by the Royal Geographical Society, and by learned institutions abroad.
5. FL, JEB to Albert Rutson, 22 May 1868.
6. NRO, ZBU.E3/A1, Transcript of the Diary of Harriet Jane Grey.
7. Ibid., ZBU.E3/C8, JEB to Spencer, Arthur and Montagu Butler, n.d.
8. *George Butler*, p.86.
9. Ibid., p.91.
10. FL, JEB to Albert Rutson, 5 March 1868.
11. Max Muller, *My Autobiography. A Fragment*, London: Longmans, Green, 1901, p.237.
12. LUL, JB 1/1 1904/09/16 (I), JEB to Stanley Butler. Josephine's grandson, A. S. G. Butler, writes that this piano was a gift from a rich Grey uncle (*Portrait*, p.42), yet in her letter to Stanley, Josephine remembered the piano being 'given to me by old uncle Hardy *before I was married*'.
13. *George Butler*, p.90.
14. Ibid., p.87.
15. Ibid., p.103.
16. RIBA, BuFam/2/5/2, George Grey Butler to Rhoda Butler, 8 November 1886.
17. LUL, JB 1/1 1853/12/00 (I), JEB to John Grey.
18. E. C. Rickards, *Zoe Thomson of Bishopthorne and her Friends*, London: John Murray, 1916, p.46.
19. LUL, JB 1/1 1853/12/00 (I), JEB to John Grey.
20. *George Butler*, p.63. Josephine added, 'To the end of this life, however, his character continued to be essentially that of a layman. He never had a cure of souls'.
21. Ibid., p.105.
22. NRO, ZBU.E2/7, JEB to Revd George Butler, n.d. [*c.* July] 1854.
23. Ibid., ZBU.E3/B1, Revd George Butler to JEB, n.d. 1854.
24. *John Grey*, p.248.
25. *Harriet Meuricoffre*, p.30.
26. *George Butler*, p.197.
27. RIBA, BuFam/2/3/15, JEB to Rhoda Butler, n.d. [*c.*1894–96].
28. NRO, ZBU.E3/B1, Revd George Butler to JEB, n.d. 1856.
29. LUL, JB 1/1 1905/03/03 (I), JEB to Stanley Butler. Josephine repeated such sentiments in a letter she wrote to her sons a few years before her death (which she had printed in the form of a pamphlet): 'God is equally the Creator of the Natural and the Spiritual. It was only to man's narrow vision that they seemed to be opposed', *'The Morning Cometh': A Letter to my Children*, printed for private circulation, Newcastle: T. M. Grierson,

1903, p.51. Josephine taught her boys to revere science as a study of the Creation. In the letter referred to above, Josephine reminded Stanley that when he was just five she demonstrated to him the pull of a magnet upon some needles which jumped up and clung to it: 'You opened your eyes wide, & gave a sigh, and said, "O! Mama, how wonderful God is!"'

30. It seems to have been the practice for subscribers to indicate their preference of subject, although Josephine's lily design was probably supplanted by the sketches of lilies offered by Lady Trevelyan, whose husband's patronage was assiduously courted by the architects, Deane and Woodward. Lady Trevelyan donated two capitals, while her husband, the naturalist Sir Walter Trevelyan, paid for five complete pillars at a total cost of £50. Lady Trevelyan's sketches of the white and the scarlet 'Martagon' lily are referred to several times in the Oxford Museum Archives, box 2, folder 6.
31. The poem itself was reworked and republished many times, but Rossetti did not begin to work on his painting of *The Blessed Damozel* until the 1870s.
32. This 1850 version of 'The Blessed Damozel' is taken from *Victorian Prose and Poetry*, ed. Lionel Trilling and Harold Bloom, London: Oxford University Press, 1973, p.620 (lines 7, 11 and 5).
33. FL, Alexander Munro to Revd George Butler, 11 October 1865.
34. LUL, JB 1/1 1868/06/00 (II), JEB to Mrs Ryley.
35. Thomas Woolner to Lady Trevelyan, 10 February 1857, quoted in *The Walker Gallery*, London: Scala Publications, 1994, p.166.
36. *George Butler*, p.94.
37. FL, JEB's letter of thanks to the Ladies' National Association for their testimonial, dated March 1906.
38. LUL, JB 1/1 1906/10/07 (I), JEB to Fanny Forsaith.
39. *George Butler*, p.99.
40. FL, JEB to Benjamin Jowett, n.d. [*c.*1860–70].
41. *George Butler*, p.96.
42. Ibid.
43. Ibid.
44. Ibid., p.98.
45. Ibid., p.102.
46. NRO, ZBU.E3/A2, JEB, 'Private Thoughts 1856–1865', December 1856, pp.11, 12.
47. *George Butler*, p.97. When, in the 1870s, Josephine published the case histories of some of the prostitutes she had rescued, she was brave enough to include the story of one young woman (not yet a prostitute), who was deserted by her gentleman seducer, and who, in her fury and despair, had suffocated their three-month-old baby son. Josephine questioned whether this girl, Margaret, was the real murderer of her child, and suggested instead that 'the irresponsibility of fathers of illegitimate children is one grand cause of the murder of babes'. She called it 'wickedness' that the shame and the burden of caring for such a child should fall upon the

mother alone, and she declared that 'When the hue and cry after the murderer of an infant comes my way, I look on; nor will I, by word or act, aid the discovery of the guilty mother', *National League Journal*, 1 June 1877, p.14. It would have been unthinkable for Josephine to have uttered such opinions in company in the Oxford of the 1850s.

48. PRO, 'Report from the Royal Commission on the Administration and Operation of the Contagious Diseases Acts 1866–69 (1871)', PP, 1871 (C.408–I), XIX, Q.12,842.
49. Vincent Quinn and John Prest (eds), *Dear Miss Nightingale*, Oxford: Clarendon Press, 1987, p.179.
50. NRO, ZBU.E3/A2, JEB, 'Private Thoughts 1856–1865', p.11.
51. Unfortunately, just one student has been recorded as a resident of Butler Hall in the Register of Private Halls which dates from 1855. The same student, a Henry B. Davis, is also mentioned in a letter in George's hand, confirming that Davis paid the statutable university fees for the Michaelmas and Trinity terms, 1856 (OU, WPL/56/1 and NEP/B/15c).
52. *George Butler*, p.128.
53. FL, JEB to Albert Rutson, 22 February 1868.
54. NRO, ZBU.E3/A2. JEB, 'Private Thoughts 1856–1865', p.16. Josephine made a further allusion to this spiritual crisis in a letter to a friend, written two years before her death: 'no one knows, that when they were all children, I, one night, was *forced* spiritually to rise from my bed, & I went to an empty room, & for hours I prayed that I might enter into a solemn covenant with God for their salvation. I have a record of it in a little old book' (LUL, JB 1/1 1905/01/05 (I), JEB to Fanny Forsaith).
55. NRO, ZBU.E3/A2, JEB, 'Private Thoughts 1856–1865', p.16.
56. *George Butler*, p.129.
57. On reaching Freetown, Catherine Butler died after giving birth to a stillborn baby boy on 4 August 1858. Her husband, the Bishop, was then ill with 'African fever' in the next room, but he crawled into her room and was able to talk to her before she died, 'sweetly resigned'. He wrote personally to 'My dear brother' George and Josephine, 'I have received and opened Josephine's and your letters to my Catherine. Alas! how I felt what you said, and what she would have read aloud to me had she been there' (reprinted in *George Butler*, p.146). Dr Bowen died within a few months of his wife and was buried next to her.

CHAPTER FOUR

1. *George Butler*, p.135.
2. Oliver Bradbury, 'A History of "The Priory", Cheltenham', *Cheltenham Local History Society Journal*, 16, 2000, p.27.
3. LUL, JB 1/1 1867/03/08 (II), JEB to Edith Leupold.
4. Josephine was still suffering discomfort from this injury when in her seventies (she described it as leaving 'painful results after many years of inactivity', FL, JEB to Helen Clark, 9 May 1906). It is absolutely unthink-

able that she and George used any contraceptive device ('mechanical contrivances', she called them). In 1888, Josephine told Gladstone's daughter, Mary Drew, that her instincts were 'absolutely against the idea of any artificial restraints to check the results of sexual intercourse', a view which stemmed from her fear of both the moral and physiological consequences of going against God's law (BL Manuscripts Room, JEB to Mary Drew, 17 November 1888). Neither does she appear to have suffered any miscarriages after the birth of Eva. In the early 1890s, Josephine's two daughters-in-law, Mia and Rhoda, suffered miscarriages, yet she made no allusion to having had such an experience herself.

5. NRO, ZBU.E2/18, George Grey Butler to Revd George Butler, n.d.
6. BJG, Transcription of Fanny Smyttan's Diary, Book Six, p. 104.
7. NRO, ZBU.E3/A3, Journal kept by Josephine and George Butler on a trip to Boulogne, April 1861.
8. *John Grey*, p.254.
9. BJG, Transcription of Fanny Smyttan's Diary, Book One, p.5 (presumably, Fanny was told this by Josephine herself). The stained-glass windows at St Andrew's Church, Corbridge, date from the 1860s onwards, when the seventh-century church was restored. The Puginesque great east window was donated by the Grey sisters and their daughters as a memorial to Hannah and John Grey who are buried together outside the east window.
10. FL, George Grey Butler to JEB, n.d. [*c.* May 1859].
11. BJG, Transcription of Fanny Smyttan's Diary, Book One, p.4.
12. While not wanting to draw too many conclusions from Fanny's oblique allusions to her private troubles, the impression that she was separated from her husband at this time is strengthened by a comment made later by Josephine, writing to their elder sister, Tully. In 1890, Josephine recalled how Fanny had cried 'over her mistakes with her husband, how she might have estranged him by reproaches, and yet how he sometimes was most faulty towards her' (NRO, ZBU.E3/C1, JEB to Mary Ann 'Tully' Garston, n.d. [*c.* late March 1901]). However, Fanny's gravestone in Leckhampton churchyard, Cheltenham, does bear the inscription, 'In Memory of Frances Hardy Smyttan, Widow of the Revd G. H. Smyttan'.
13. BJG, Transcription of Fanny Smyttan's Diary, Book One, pp.18, 17.
14. Information about Revd George Hunt Smyttan's church posts and about his death comes from the family researches of A. R. C. Bolton, *The Six Brides of Dilston*, Bognor Regis: New Horizon, 1984, pp.67–8.
15. BJG, Transcription of Fanny Smyttan's Diary, Book One, pp.54, 70.
16. The letter to Eliza is transcribed ibid., Book Two, p.84.
17. Ibid., Book Four, p.258.
18. Ibid., Book Six, pp.101, 104.
19. Ibid., p.102.
20. Ibid., p.106.
21. Ibid., p.112.
22. *George Butler*, pp.152–3.

23. *Portrait*, p.53.
24. LUL, JB 1/1, 1891/06/03 (I), JEB to Stanley Butler.
25. *George Butler*, p.153.
26. FL, Arthur Butler to George Grey Butler, 4 January 1907.
27. NRO, ZBU.E3/A10, JEB to George Grey Butler. It is suggested that Josephine wrote the two accounts in this file around 1903–4, just a few years before her death. A more likely date is December 1895. Perhaps prompted by her sister Tully's death in May 1893, Josephine made her will that June. Another sister, Fanny, then died in September 1895, and it was during the winter of 1895 that Josephine wrote out further instructions for her sons about the disposal of her property. She told Stanley, 'I am going to write some directions and some thoughts to be opened after my death; nothing in particular, but things which may be some help or comfort to my sons', LUL, JB 1/1 1895/12/04 (I).
28. NRO, ZBU.E3/A10, JEB to George Grey Butler.
29. *George Butler*, pp.154–5.
30. Ibid.
31. 'Melancholy Incident at Priory House', *Cheltenham Mercury*, Saturday, 27 August 1864, p.4.
32. St AUL, Butler Autograph Album, MS 30,069, John Brown to JEB, 30 August 1864.
33. *George Butler*, pp.155–6.
34. FL, Transcript of JEB's letter to the editor of the *Review of Reviews*, October 1891.
35. FL, JEB to Harriet Meuricoffre, 18 October 1882.
36. *George Butler*, p.164.
37. LUL, JB 1/1 1901/12/23 (I), JEB to Stanley Butler.
38. NRO, ZBU.E3/C4.5, 'Some additional notes for the guidance of my sons'.
39. *George Butler*, p.155.
40. Ibid. p.156.
41. NRO, ZBU.E3/A10, JEB to George Grey Butler, n.d. [*c.*1895].
42. FL, 'My Prayer for my Husband', 25 September 1864.
43. NRO, ZBU.E3/A10, JEB to George Grey Butler, n.d. [*c.*1895].
44. Ibid., 'Child of Sorrow' (JEB's account of Charles's grief at the loss of Eva, written for her eldest son, George), n.d. [*c.*1895].
45. Ibid.
46. Ibid., JEB to George Grey Butler, 11 December [no year].
47. Ibid. ZBU.E3/C1, JEB to Emily and Gertrude Butler, 19 May 1894.
48. *George Butler*, p.159.
49. *Harriet Meuricoffre*, p.101.
50. *John Grey*, p.148.
51. *Harriet Meuricoffre*, p.104.
52. Conversation with Dr Jean Hugh-Jones, Honorary Secretary of the Liverpool Medical History Society, April 1998.

53. Hatty's detailed account, written for her niece Edith, is reprinted in *Harriet Meuricoffre*, pp.106–7.
54. NRO, ZBU.E3/A2, JEB, 'Private Thoughts 1856–1865', pp. 23, 24.
55. Ibid., p.37.
56. Ibid., pp.24, 37.

CHAPTER FIVE

1. *George Butler*, pp.182–3.
2. FL, JEB to Fanny Smyttan, 27 February 1867.
3. *George Butler*, p.184.
4 FL, JEB to 'Dearest A[lan Raper]', 7 March 1867.
5. *George Butler*, p. 188.
6. LUL, JB 1/4/1, Undated statement to sons.
7. *Harriet Meuricoffre*, p.181.
8. FL, JEB to 'My dear A.', n.d.
9. Ibid., JEB to Mrs Myers, 26 February [1867].
10. Ibid., JEB to Miss Priestman, 24 January 1873.
11. Ibid.
12. Ibid., MS of article submitted to the editor of the *Torch*, 1868.
13. LUL, JB 1/1 1867/03/08 (II), JEB to Edith Leupold.
14. FL, JEB to 'Dearest A.', 7 March 1867.
15. LUL, JB 1/1 1867/03/08 (II), JEB to Edith Leupold.
16. *George Butler*, p.190.
17. LUL, JB 1/1 1905/04/00 (I), JEB to Fanny Forsaith (Miss Forsaith proposed to tell the story of Mary Lomax at the Jubilee celebrations of the Federation in 1905, and Josephine sent her suggestions for her speech).
18. Ibid.
19. FL, JEB to Fanny Smyttan, 12 February 1867.
20. Ibid., JEB to 'Dearest A.', 7 March 1867.
21. In her testimony before the 1871 Royal Commission, Josephine stated that she had 'had five living there at one time; not as servants, as friends and patients', PRO, 'Report from the Royal Commission on the Administration and Operation of the Contagious Diseases Acts 1866–69 (1871)', PP, 1871 (C.408–I), XIX, Q.12, 843.
22. LUL, JB 1/1 1905/04/00 (I), JEB to Fanny Forsaith.
23. Ibid.
24. FL, JEB to 'My Dear A.', n.d.
25. Ibid., Poem composed by Mary Lomax for JEB [*c.* March 1867].
26. Ibid., JEB to Mrs Myers, 26 February [1867].
27. LUL, JB 1/1 1867/03/08 (II), JEB to Edith Leupold.
28. Ibid.
29. FL, JEB to Fanny Smyttan, 27 February 1867.
30. Ibid., 12 February 1867.
31. Ibid.

32. Ibid.
33. The 1871 census return for the Benediction House lists thirty-seven female inmates between the ages of fifteen and twenty-nine although the most common age is seventeen. Many of the girls were from Liverpool but others had migrated to the city in search of work from as far afield as Scotland, Wales, Leicester, Bath, Woolwich and Dublin. Miss Cragg offered kindly advice to Josephine, and there was an easy exchange of inmates between their two houses, once Josephine had established her own House of Rest.
34. FL, JEB to Mrs Myers, 26 February [1867].
35. Ibid., JEB to 'Dearest A.', 7 March 1867.
36. Ibid., JEB to 'Dear A.', 27 February 1867.
37. Ibid., JEB to 'Dearest A.', 7 March 1867.
38. Ibid., JEB to Edith Leupold, n.d. February 1867.
39. Ibid., to 'Dearest A.', 7 March 1867.
40. Ibid.
41. Ibid., JEB to Mrs Myers, 26 February [1867].
42. JEB's Letter to The Worshipful the Mayor of Liverpool, March 1867, reprinted in Dale Spender (ed.), *The Education Papers: Women's Quest for Equality in Britain, 1850–1912*, London: Routledge & Kegan Paul, 1987, pp.91–2.
43. FL, JEB to 'Dearest A.', 7 March 1867.
44. LUL, JB 1/4/3, Order of Service, Prayers at the Opening of the Industrial Home by Revd George Butler.
45. FL, JEB to 'Dearest A.', 7 March 1867.
46. I have come across just one, very late, reference to her brother Charles's interest in her work. On 23 January 1894 Charles wrote to Miss Forsaith to thank her for sending him a copy of one of Josephine's letters describing her crusade in Rome. He added, 'I shall be much interested in reading other letters you may be kind enough to send me'.
47. FL, JEB to Fanny Smyttan, 27 February 1867.
48. Ibid., 12 February 1867.
49. Ibid., JEB to 'Dearest A.', 7 March 1867.
50. Ibid., JEB to Fanny Smyttan, 12 February 1867.
51. Ibid., JEB to Edith Leupold, n.d. February 1867.
52. Ibid., JEB to Fanny Smyttan, 27 February 1867.
53. Ibid., JEB reported Mrs Glayn's words to Mrs Myers, 26 February [1867].
54. Ibid., JEB reported Jane Cragg's praise to Fanny Smyttan, 12 February 1867.
55. Ibid.
56. Ibid.
57. Ibid., JEB to 'My dear A.', n.d.
58. Ibid., JEB to 'Dearest A.', 7 March 1867.
59. Ibid.
60. Ibid., JEB to Mrs Myers, 26 February [1867].

61. Recalled by Josephine in the *Storm-Bell*, June 1900, No.23, p.308.
62. FL, JEB to 'Dearest A.', 7 March 1867.
63. Ibid., JEB to Fanny Smyttan, 27 February 1867.
64. Ibid.
65. See Frances Finnegan, *Poverty and Prostitution: A Study of Victorian Prostitutes in York*, Cambridge: Cambridge University Press, 1979. Finnegan's study of the police records for York in the 1860s reveals a remarkable number of serial offenders for whom there was little hope of reclamation: unrepentant prostitutes who were repeatedly brought before the magistrates' court and fined or imprisoned for committing 'disorderly acts', that is for drunkenness or soliciting in the streets, as well as for thieving from their clients.
66. FL, JEB to Fanny Smyttan, 12 February 1867.
67. Ibid., 27 February 1867.
68. LUL, JB 1/1 1867/03/08 (II), JEB to Edith Leupold.
69. *George Butler*, p.191.
70. Ibid., p.193.
71. Ibid., p.192.

CHAPTER SIX

1. *George Butler*, pp. 174, 175.
2. Elizabeth Edwards, *Women in Teacher Training Colleges 1900–1960: A Culture of Femininity*, London: Routledge, 2001, pp.6, 17.
3. As a result of the Commission's findings girls' schools were included in the 1869 Endowed Schools Act. This meant that new secondary schools for girls could be founded, and existing schools expanded, using money secured from a number of endowment funds around the country, money that had previously been directed exclusively towards boys' schools.
4. NRO, ZBU.E2/17, Revd George Butler, 'The Higher Education of Women: An Inaugural Lecture', 1868, p.36.
5. James Stuart, *Reminiscences*, London: printed for private circulation at the Chiswick Press, 1911, p.232; LUL, JB 1/1 1906/06/07 (I), JEB to Fanny Forsaith and Harriet Allen.
6. Myers wrote an article advertising the University Extension Scheme for *Macmillan's Magazine* in December 1868, entitled 'Local Lectures for Women'.
7. Butler, 'The Higher Education of Women', pp.17–18.
8. Myers, 'Local Lectures for Women', p.163.
9. Blanche Athena Clough, *Memoir of Anne J. Clough*, London: Edward Arnold, 1897, p.119.
10. *John Grey*, p.291.
11. Ibid., pp.306–8.
12. FL, Mary Sommerville to JEB, 14 October 1869.
13. Ibid., JEB to Albert Rutson, 27 April 1868.
14. Ibid., 5 March 1868.

15. Ibid.
16. Ibid.
17. Ibid., 10 February 1868.
18. Ibid., 17 February 1868.
19. *John Grey*, p.90. Josephine quoted a local newspaper that boasted of her father's political influence: 'The Black Prince of the North he was sometimes called, in allusion to his swarthy but comely countenance'. 'Northumberland was then a genuine Tory county', but 'Mr Grey of Milfield was the man to obtain victory for his party, if victory for a Whig of the Grey school had been at that time practicable'.
20. FL, JEB to Albert Rutson, 9 May 1868.
21. In the late 1860s virtually every issue carried something on education. Anne Clough published 'Hints on the Organisation of Girls' Schools' in October 1866, and Millicent Garrett Fawcett wrote on 'The Education of Women of the Middle and Upper Classes' (largely publicizing the good efforts of the University Extension Scheme) in April 1868.
22. FL, JEB to Albert Rutson, 9 May 1868.
23. JEB, *The Education and Employment of Women*, Liverpool: T. Brakell, 1868, p.3.
24. Ibid., p.5.
25. Ibid, p.7.
26. FL, JEB to Albert Rutson, 7 May 1868.
27. Ibid., 12 May 1868.
28. In a long letter to Benjamin Jowett, Professor of Greek at Oxford, in which Josephine discusses her faith, she explained, 'I respect M. Comte greatly as a lover of his kind, but I fear I am guilty of opposing my inward feeling to his arguments', ibid., n.d. [*c.*1860–70].
29. Ibid., JEB to Frederick Harrison, 9 May 1868. A typescript copy of Josephine's letter to Harrison is held in the Fawcett Library; she appears not to have preserved Harrison's original letter to herself.
30. JEB, *The Education and Employment of Women*, p.16.
31. FL, JEB to Albert Rutson, 12 May 1868.
32. Ibid., JEB to Frederick Harrison, 9 May 1868.
33. Ibid., JEB to Albert Rutson, 12 May 1868.
34. Ibid., 22 May 1868.
35. Ibid.
36. Ibid., 23 May 1868.
37. Ibid., 2 June 1868.
38. Ibid., 28 May 1868.
39. Ibid., n.d. June 1868.
40. Ibid., 8 June 1868.
41. Quoted in Blanche Athena Clough, *Memoir of Anne J. Clough*, p.129.
42. JEB, 'Letter to Mr Bryce on Examinations for Governesses' (1868), in Dale Spender (ed.), *The Education Papers: Women's Quest for Equality in Britain 1850–1912*, London: Routledge & Kegan Paul, 1987, pp. 94–8.

43. On 17 February 1868, Josephine wrote to Albert Rutson that she had been invited to attend one of Emily Davies's meetings in London, at which Davies hoped to have Gladstone in the chair. Davies had pressed Josephine to be there, but she was then too ill to make the journey to London.
44. Davies believed that the Higher Examination would be offered to young women scholars as a (second-rate) substitute, and saw it as a compromise because it had no set standard and relied upon arbitrary judgement. Yet, in fact, the Cambridge Higher was recognized to be such a rigorous test of female students that in 1881, when women were formally admitted to sit for the Cambridge Tripos, they were allowed to take the Higher in lieu of some sections of the standard preliminary exam.
45. FL, JEB to Albert Rutson, 23 May 1868.
46. Merton Hall, which housed fourteen students, was one of the various Cambridge houses Clough took for her growing number of boarders. Anne Clough resigned as Secretary of the North of England Council for Promoting the Higher Education of Women in 1870 in order to pursue her work of establishing a women's college at Cambridge; she returned to the Council as its President from 1873 to 1874.
47. Stuart, *Reminiscences,* pp.162, 230.
48. Ibid., p.179.
49. FL, JEB to Anne Jemima Clough, 7 July 1869. Essentially, though, the differences between Newnham and Hitchin (which developed into Girton College in 1872) were rooted in the question of class. It was commonly said that Newnham was for governesses, and Hitchin for ladies. Miss Clough kept her fees far below those at Hitchin, and further significant reductions were offered as an encouragement to those young women intending to become teachers. In 1875 a Girton undergraduate could expect to pay £105 a year, while a trainee teacher at Newnham less than half that, at £45, plus six guineas for tuition (June Purvis, *A History of Women's Higher Education*, Milton Keynes: Open University Press, 1991, p.115).
50. FL, JEB to Anne Jemima Clough, 7 July 1869. A further and more significant division between Davies and Clough emerged when Anne Clough later approved a less onerous modern university curriculum for her Newnham students, to replace subjects like Latin and Greek. Emily Davies rejected the notion of a separate, and thus by implication inferior, education for women, and saw it as a position which accepted an inherent distinction between the intellectual capabilities of the sexes. She maintained that female students could prove their equality with men only by taking the same examinations, and submitting to the same criteria of judgement. She was adamant that female students should instead sit for the Cambridge Tripos, with its obligatory components, Latin, Greek and Mathematics, even though women would be at a significant disadvantage in having had no, or very little, schooling in these subjects.

51. LUL, JB 1/1 1869/01/11 (I), JEB to Sarah Maria Butler.
52. Ibid.
53. Ibid., 1869/02/00 (I).
54. Ibid.
55. Ibid., 1869/06/03 (I), JEB to Mme Troubnikoff.
56. John Stuart Mill, 'The Subjection of Women', in *On Liberty and Other Writings*, ed. Stephan Collini, Cambridge: Cambridge University Press, 1989, pp.199, 216.
57. Ibid., p. 196. The significance of Mill's thesis is in its ruthless examination of the legal position of married women under the system of 'Coverture', by which the wife exchanged her social and legal identity for her husband's protection. This goes some way towards explaining his failure to address the question of single women *not* provided for financially, who were of the greatest concern to Josephine Butler.
58. JEB (ed.), *Woman's Work and Woman's Culture*, London: Macmillan, 1869, p.ix.
59. Ibid., p.xvi.
60. Ibid., p.xxxi.
61. St AUL, Autograph Album compiled by Stanley Butler, MS 30,017, Princess Victoria Adelaide Mary Louisa, Empress Consort of Frederick, Emperor of Germany, and Princess Royal of Great Britain and Ireland, to JEB, 7 December 1868. She did, though, recognize that nurses required a more systematic and professional training. The Princess organized hospital care for the wounded during the 1866 Austro-Prussian conflict, and the 1870–71 Franco-German war, and was shocked at the poorly prepared nurses she had to work among. A nursing school was eventually named after her in Berlin.
62. Other subjects recommended for female study were Logic, Grammar, Mathematics, Anatomy, Physiology, Hygiene, and Chemistry; Ladies' Clubs, with their own tea-rooms and libraries, the Princess advocated as 'a great boon', even though the idea 'would be sure to startle the public' (ibid.).
63. St AUL, Autograph Album compiled by Stanley Butler, MS 30,018, Princess Louise Caroline Alberta, Duchess of Argyll to JEB, 27 March 1869. Josephine had in fact been examined by Dr Elizabeth Garrett about a year earlier, and had found the consultation very valuable, '*because* I was able to *tell* her so much more than I ever could or would tell to any *man*' (FL, JEB to Albert Rutson, 22 February 1868). However, the relationship between Butler and Garrett ceased when Garrett gave her very public support to the Contagious Diseases Acts.
64. Ibid., MS 30,071, John Stuart Mill to JEB, 22 March 1869.
65. LUL, JB 1/1 1869/04/00 (I), JEB to Mme Troubnikoff.
66. Maria Troubnikoff, born in Siberia in 1835, was the daughter of an exiled Decembrist. Stassoff, born in 1822, was the daughter of a court architect, and had pledged to devote her life to the poor (see Barbara Alpern Engel,

Mothers and Daughters: Women of the Intelligentsia in Nineteenth Century Russia, Cambridge: Cambridge University Press, 1983, pp. 56–61).

67. LUL, JB 1/1 1869/05/27 (I), JEB to Mme Troubnikoff.
68. Ibid., JB 1/3/2, Mlle Nad. Stassoff to JEB [*c.* June 1869].
69. Ibid., JB 1/1 1869/06/18 (I), JEB to Sarah Maria Butler.
70. The year 1871 is the date given by Josephine herself in the *Dawn*, January 1893, No.17, p.2. That year she presided over council meetings held in Liverpool on 23–24 June. In April, Josephine had some discussion with Professor Henry Sidgwick as to her successor as President of the North of England Council: she advised against nominating Anne Clough since she was too involved in her own Merton Hall scheme (see FL, JEB to Professor Henry Sidgwick, 9 April [1871]). However, Anne Clough's niece states that Josephine did not resign from the presidency until 1873, and that she continued to be involved in the progress of the Council, delivering a paper at one of their meetings in 1874 (see Blanche Athena Clough, *Memoir of Anne J. Clough*, p.135). The connection was certainly kept up: George Butler spoke at a council meeting in Leeds at the beginning of February 1877 (see *George Butler*, p.308).
71. FL, JEB to Mrs Maria Grey, 9 June [1871]. In early June 1871, Josephine had received a letter from Mrs Maria Grey (no relation), who with her sister Emily Shirreff, had recently set up the National Union for Improving Education. Maria's sister Emily was the first mistress of Girton College, and in 1872 they founded the Girls' Public Day School Company, which aimed to admit pupils from all social classes. Josephine pointed out to Mrs Grey that her work for the education of girls might suffer if her name was associated publicly with Josephine's own: 'I have always said to my friends, "Consider the bad odour in which I am with all persons who are in *good society*!" . . . for I am abhorred by every one above the middle class who happens to know anything about it'.
72. *Dawn*, January 1893, No.17, p.2.
73. Blanche Athena Clough, *Memoir of Anne J. Clough*, p. 121.
74. LUL, JB 1/1 1892/06/00 (I), JEB to Stanley Butler.

CHAPTER SEVEN

1. Scott, p.105.
2. FL, JEB to Charlotte Wilson, 25 November 1905.
3. Scott, p.106.
4. Ibid., p.107.
5. *George Butler*, p.218.
6. FL, JEB to Charlotte Wilson, 25 November 1905.
7. *George Butler*, p.217.
8. FL, JEB to Millicent Fawcett, 25 March 1906.
9. *George Butler*, p.219.
10. This account of 'The Call' was made by Josephine in a speech given in

Wigan on the evening of Friday, 20 May 1870, reprinted in the *Shield*, 13 June 1870, p.124.

11. *George Butler*, pp.219–20.
12. FL, JEB to Millicent Fawcett, 25 March 1906.
13. *Shield*, 18 July 1870, p.164. Josephine later republished this speech in the biography she wrote of her husband.
14. 'Obituary. Mrs Josephine Butler', *Daily Telegraph*, Wednesday, 2 January 1907, p.6.
15. The references to the *Saturday Review* and to Sir James Elphinstone are taken from Scott, pp.144, 143. Josephine reported Cavendish-Bentinck's remark in a letter she wrote to Henry Wilson, 23 September 1872, FL.
16. *Reminiscences*, p.8; LUL, JB 1/1 1895/01/17 (I), JEB to Rhoda Butler.
17. FL, Message sent by JEB on the occasion of the thirtieth anniversary of the Federation, meeting at Neuchâtel, September 1905, reprinted in Johnson, pp.226–7.
18. FL, JEB to Edith Leupold, n.d. [*c.* 9 April 1875]; JEB to the Misses Priestman, 17 February 1883.
19. Ibid., 3 March 1876; 28 April 1884.
20. Ibid., 28 April 1884.
21. *George Butler*, p.221.
22. FL, James Stuart to Henry J. Wilson, 28 June 1904.
23. Scott, p. 111.
24. *George Butler*, pp.225–6.
25. These letters were originally published in the same paper in September 1863, arguing against the then proposed legislation.
26. *Daily News*, Tuesday, 28 December 1869, p.6.
27. FL, JEB to Mrs Ford, 31 December 1869.
28. *Dawn*, 1 July 1893, No. 20, p.3.
29. *Reminiscences*, p.116.
30. LUL, JB 1/1 1870/01/03 (I), JEB to Sarah Maria Butler.
31. *George Butler*, p.251. These references to her mother-in-law's interest may in fact relate to the Butlers' *rescue* work rather than their repeal work, but Josephine does write about it within the context of the repeal campaign.
32. This account of the Liverpool meeting is taken from the *Shield*, 28 March 1870, pp.30–2.
33. Josephine's cousin was one of a group of Baptist and other Nonconformist ministers who had begun to protest to the government in 1860 when the policy of regulated prostitution was first instituted as a means to protect British troops in India.
34. *Shield*, 28 March 1870, p.27.
35. Ibid., p.33.
36. James Stuart, *Reminiscences*, London: printed for private circulation at the Chiswick Press, 1911, pp.230, 231.
37. Scott, p.108. An anonymous repeal pamphlet entitled, *Letter to My*

Countrywomen dwelling in the Farmsteads and Cottages of England (Manchester: A. Ireland & Co., 1871) gave a similar account of Josephine's extraordinary mission, concluding, 'I leave you to think how painful it must have been to a delicate and pure minded woman to speak on such a subject', p.8. (The pamphlet comprises two eleven-page 'letters'; the quotation is taken from the second of these.)

38. Scott, p.108.
39. Elizabeth Cady Stanton, *Eighty Years and More: Reminiscences 1815–1897*, Boston: Northeastern University Press, 1993, p.368.
40. Taken from Josephine's address to an audience of 700 working men in Birmingham on 21 April 1870, *Shield*, 9 May 1870, p.88. Josephine chose to reprint this passage in *George Butler*, p.230.
41. *Shield*, 13 June 1870, p.125.
42. Ibid., 3 December 1870, p.316.
43. *George Butler*, p.227.
44. NRO, ZBU.E3/A2, JEB's spiritual diary, 'Private Thoughts 1856–1865', p.25 (the entry dates from the summer of 1865).
45. John Woolman's phrase is quoted in the printed text of the speech Josephine gave at the County Hall, Carlisle, to an audience of 400 ladies on the morning of 25 November 1870, 'The Duty of Women' (Carlisle: Hudson & Scott & Sons, 1870, p.12). Garrison's statement is taken from her speech at an LNA meeting at the Priory Rooms, Birmingham, on the morning of Friday, 27 January 1871, reprinted in the *Shield*, 11 February 1871, p.385. Josephine slightly misquotes Garrison's 'Salutatory Address' in the *Liberator*, 1 January 1831 ('I am in earnest – I will not equivocate – I will not excuse – I will not retreat a single inch – and I will be heard!'). Garrison's son would take a great interest in the repeal movement in England and would become a firm friend of Josephine's.
46. FL, JEB to Fanny Forsaith, marked 'Private', n.d. [*c.*24 April 1897]. Josephine was reminded of the early days of the campaign when James Stuart attempted to moderate her uncompromising language in a manifesto she was writing at this time.
47. JEB, *Paper On the Moral Reclaimability of Prostitutes*, London: Ladies' National Association, 1870, p.7.
48. *Shield*, 23 May 1870, p. 91.
49. FL, Manuscript of JEB's account of 'The Garrison Towns of Kent', April 1870 (published in the *Shield* throughout April and May that year).
50. This letter, which bore the signatures of all the inmates of Mrs Hyde's home, was reprinted in the *Shield*, 18 April 1870, p.51.
51. *Shield*, 23 September 1871, p.661.
52. George's letters of 13 and 11 April 1870 are reprinted in *George Butler*, p.229.
53. Josephine's testimony before the Committee of Inquiry, 5 May 1882, reprinted in the *Shield*, 22 July 1882, p.141.
54. Ibid., 23 May 1870, p.91.

55. Judith R. Walkowitz mentions the case of a naval surgeon who died while making a private visit to Eliza Binney's brothel in Plymouth in 1869. Naval surgeons were, of course, the medical officials who performed the examinations on the registered prostitutes of Plymouth. See *Prostitution and Victorian Society*, Cambridge: Cambridge University Press, 1980, p. 172.
56. FL, Manuscript of JEB's account of 'The Garrison Towns of Kent', April 1870.
57. Dr J. J. Garth Wilkinson *The Forcible Introspection of Women for the Oligarchy Considered Physically,* London, 1870, p.33. Judith R. Walkowitz suggests that such shocking references to the internal examination were much publicized by Josephine Butler (*Prostitution and Victorian Society*, p.109; *City of Dreadful Delight: Narratives of Sexual Danger in Late-Victorian London*, London: Virago 1994 [1992], p.90). However, the two detailed references to the internal examination attributed to Josephine were in fact in private letters that she wrote to Dr Wilkinson, and were quoted by Wilkinson in his pamphlet.
58. Reprinted in Walkowitz, *Prostitution and Victorian Society*, p.202.
59. *Shield*, 2 May 1870, p.68.
60. Ibid., 23 May 1870, p.91.
61. Ibid., 3 June 1871, p.515.
62. BLL, Josephine Butler Papers, 'Letter from one of the Ladies who went to reside in one of the Subjected Districts, on purpose to watch the operation of the Acts, & rescue innocent victims', n.d. (This was presumably prior to the setting up of the Aid and Defence Association in the early summer of 1870.)
63. FL, JEB to Revd George Butler, 6 May [1870]. (Presumably she made a mistake about the date: she was writing on the first morning of the conference, 5 May.)
64. Ibid., JEB's letter of thanks to the LNA for their handsome testimonial, March 1906.
65. *George Butler*, p.231.
66. *Shield*, 6 June 1870, p.117.
67. Ibid., 2 May 1870, p.70.
68. Her father's cousin, Sir George Grey, had served as Governor of New Zealand in 1845–53 and 1861–67; in 1874 he was chosen as Superintendent of the province of Auckland and was briefly Prime Minister, from 1877 to 1879.
69. FL, Henry J. Wilson to JEB, 10 February 1873. Wilson wrote, 'I am like Baxter Langley & Madame Venturi in regarding you as my chief'.
70. This account of the election at Colchester is taken from the *Shield*, 12 November 1870, p.288.
71. This second account is taken from *Reminiscences*, p.27.
72. *Colchester Times*, Friday, 28 October 1870, p.3.
73. Scott, p.126.
74. *Reminiscences*, p.32. That this precaution was necessary is confirmed by a

letter relating to the election campaign at Pontefract two years later. Ursula Bright advised Henry Wilson, 'Remember in sending telegrams that they are in the hands of the Government & we know that at Colchester everything that passed was sent to headquarters', FL, 11 August 1872.

75. *Reminiscences*, p.29.
76. Ibid., p.30.
77. Ibid., p.31.
78. FL, JEB to Charlotte Wilson, 3 December 1870.
79. *Reminiscences*, p.26.
80. Comments from the press were reprinted in the *Shield*, 12 November 1870, p.292.
81. Ibid.. p.290.
82. JEB, *The Constitution Violated*, Edinburgh: Edmondson & Douglas, 1871, p.4.
83. *Shield*, 4 March 1871, pp.410–11.
84. JEB, *The Constitution Violated*, p.91.
85. Ibid., pp.39–40.
86. Ibid., pp.30, 64.
87. Ibid., p.7.
88. Ibid., p.36.
89. Ibid., p.57. The 1866 Act did provide for a woman to appeal against her detention in a hospital if she believed it wrongful, but it is unlikely that many women could afford to pay either an independent doctor to certify that she was 'clean', or a legal representative to bring her case before a magistrate. One matter that the 1866 Act was clear upon was that its officers should be given protection against charges of culpability in the carrying out of their duties. If a woman had a complaint against a particular policeman or doctor, she had to make it within three months 'after the Thing done' for her case to be heard at all. If she lost the case she would be liable for damages; if she won, the guilty police officer or surgeon was protected under the Act, and liable to pay the woman damages only 'if the Judge specifically certifies it' (Clause 42).
90. Ibid., pp.157–8.

CHAPTER EIGHT

1. *Shield*, 6 June 1870, p.118.
2. FL, JEB to Miss Priestman, 12 December [1871]. See 'Protest of the Associations against the Proposal of the Government to appoint a Royal Commission', *Shield*, 13 June 1870, p.127.
3. *George Butler*, p.234.
4. Ibid.
5. Ibid.
6. PRO, 'Report from the Royal Commission on the Administration and Operation of the Contagious Diseases Acts 1866–69 (1871)', PP, 1871 (C.408–I), XIX Q.12,841–13,115.

7. *George Butler*, pp.235–6, Frederick Pennington was chairman of the Finance Committee of the National Association and one of its chief benefactors.
8. FL, JEB to Margaret Tanner, 4 April 1871.
9. Ibid.
10. *Shield*, 8 April 1871, p.453.
11. FL, JEB to the Bristol Committee of the LNA, n.d. May 1871.
12. BLL, JEB to 'Dear Friends all over the Country', 8 July 1871.
13. Ibid., JEB to Hannah Ford, n.d. [*c.* January 1873].
14. The Report of the Royal Commission was printed in the *Shield*, 22 July 1871, pp.569–79.
15. Ibid., pp.574, 575.
16. Reprinted in the *Shield*, 13 May 1871, p.492.
17. Point 14 of the first dissenting report, reprinted ibid., Saturday, 22 July 1871, p.573.
18. FL, Anthony Mundella to Henry J. Wilson, n.d. [*c.* November 1872].
19. Ibid. This was recalled by Josephine in a letter to Margaret Tanner, 31 October 1896.
20. Ibid., JEB to Fanny Forsaith, n.d. [*c.* 4 September 1897].
21. *Shield*, 6 June 1870, p.120.
22. FL, JEB, 'A Few Words Addressed to True Hearted Women', 18 March 1872.
23. *Shield*, 3 June 1871, p.515 (this formed part of the evidence Daniel Cooper was prevented from delivering orally to the Royal Commission in 1871, but which he sent to the chairman as additional evidence).
24. FL, JEB, 'Letter on the Subject of Mr Bruce's Bill. Addressed to the Repealers of the CD Acts by Josephine E. Butler', 12 March 1872.
25. *Shield*, 3 June 1871, p.515.
26. FL, JEB to Henry J. Wilson, 26 August 1872.
27. BLL, JEB to 'Dear Friends all over the Country', 8 July 1871.
28. Ibid. James Stansfeld was President of the Poor Law Board in 1871 and was promoted to Secretary of the Treasury in 1872.
29. *Shield*, 22 July 1871, p.590.
30. FL, JEB to Revd George Butler, 21 July 1871.
31. Reprinted in the *Shield*, 22 July 1871, see pp.592–4.
32. JEB, *The New Era*, Liverpool: T. Brakell, 1872, p.6.
33. FL, JEB to Charlotte Wilson, n.d.
34. Ibid., JEB, 'A Letter on the Subject of Mr Bruce's Bill. Addressed to the Repealers of the CD Acts', 12 March 1872.
35. JEB, *The New Era*, p.48. The full title of the essay is 'The New Era; containing a retrospect of the regulation system in Berlin, of the repeated opposition directed against the system there, and the causes of the failure of that opposition; with an indication of the lessons to be learned from past failure, and of the source whence hope arises for the future'.
36. FL, JEB to Henry J. Wilson, 13 May 1872.

37. Ibid., JEB to Charlotte Wilson, (received) 25 May 1872.
38. Ibid. [*c.* 6 April 1872].
39. Ibid., JEB to Harriet Meuricoffre and Fanny Smyttan, n.d. [*c.* early June 1872].
40. LUL, JB 1/1 1897/04/26 (I), JEB to Fanny Forsaith.
41. Ibid.
42. See *Shield*, 29 June 1872, pp. 991, 999; ibid., 20 July 1872, p.1012.
43. Ibid., 20 July 1872, p.1011.
44. FL, Letter from JEB to the Members of the Purity Department of the Women's Christian Temperance Union, 27 September 1897. The principle of female suffrage was certainly prominent at public meetings held by the repealers, and in repeal literature throughout the long campaign. The *Shield* gave notice of suffrage meetings and reported suffrage debates in the House of Commons, because it was an 'allied question' (*Shield*, 1 April 1871, p.442). Judith Walkowitz provides a useful list of the various organizations in which leading members of the LNA were involved, and notes that seventeen out of thirty-three women were members of the National Society for Women's Suffrage (see Walkowitz, pp.126–7).
45. FL, JEB to Margaret Tanner and the Misses Priestman, 4 May 1874.
46. JEB, *Legislative Restrictions on the Industry of Women, Considered from the Women's Point of View*, London: Matthews & Sons, 1874, p.15. The pamphlet was signed by Josephine, Elizabeth Wolstoneholme, Emilie Venturi, and two factory workers, Ada Smith from Nottingham (Ada was the Honorary Secretary of the Nottingham branch of the LNA), and Dinah Goodall from Leeds.
47. Ibid., pp.3, 8. Eventually, though, Josephine came to admit the practical difficulties involved in mixing the two causes at repeal meetings.
48. Ibid.
49. FL, JEB to Charlotte Wilson, 12 November 1873. Sir George Otto Trevelyan (1838–1928) was the Liberal MP for Tynemouth (1865–68), and then for Border (Hawick) Burghs (1868–86).
50. FL, Ursula Bright to Henry J. Wilson, 11 August 1872.
51. *Reminiscences*, p.46.
52. FL, JEB (dictated to James Stuart) to Henry J. Wilson, 19 August 1872.
53. Josephine's account of the Pontefract election is taken from *Reminiscences,* p.48.
54. Ibid.
55. Ibid., p.49.
56. Ibid., p.50.
57. Ibid., p.48.
58. *Shield*, 31 August 1872, p.1065; ibid., 24 August 1872, p.1051.
59. Ibid., 17 August 1872, p.1043.
60. FL, JEB to Henry J. Wilson, 7 April 1873.
61. Ibid., Fragment of letter from JEB to Fanny Smyttan [*c.* 20 December 1872].

62. Ibid., JEB to Henry J. Wilson, 23 December 1872.
63. Ibid.
64. Ibid., n.d. [*c.* autumn 1872].
65. Ibid., 23 December 1872.
66. Ibid., JEB to William Clark, 6 July 1872.
67. Ibid., JEB to Henry J. Wilson, 16 October 1872.
68. Ibid., Revd George Butler to George Grey Butler, 27 October 1872. Josephine's three sons inherited a portion of their grandfather Grey's will. John Grey's legacy, which amounted to nearly £14,000, he divided amongst his children depending upon how many children they themselves had (John Grey had nearly thirty grandchildren at the time of his death). Under this scheme, Josephine received three shares for her three sons. (Since Fanny was childless and unsupported, her father bequeathed her a separate sum of £200 for her own use.)
69. Ibid., JEB to Henry J. Wilson, 1 April 1873.
70. Ibid., 24 September 1872.
71. Ibid., Postcard dated 31 October 1872. Josephine claimed that she often sent out '£1 worth *in postage* of printed matter in a day', BLL, JEB to Mrs Ford, 30 November 1872.
72. FL, JEB to Robert Martineau, 25 May 1873.
73. Ibid., Robert Martineau to Henry J. Wilson, 28 April 1873.
74. Ibid., 5 May 1873.
75. Ibid., JEB to Henry J. Wilson, 1 June 1873.

CHAPTER NINE

1. *Reminiscences,* p.61.
2. Ibid., pp.63–4.
3. Ibid., p.69.
4. FL, JEB to Revd George Butler, 13 December 1874; JEB to Sir James Stansfeld, 14 December 1874.
5. Ibid., JEB to Sir James Stansfeld, 16 December 1874.
6. Ibid., JEB to Revd George Butler, 13 December 1874.
7. *George Butler*, p.283.
8. FL, Fragment of letter from JEB to Sir James Stansfeld, 16 December 1874.
9. JEB, *The New Abolitionists*, London: Dyer Brothers, 1876, p.26.
10. *George Butler*, p.282.
11. Letter from JEB to Harriet Meuricoffre, 29 December 1874, reprinted in JEB, *The New Abolitionists*, p.26.
12. Letter from Harriet Meuricoffre, 31 December 1874, reprinted ibid., p.28.
13. A friend of the Butlers, Edward A. Cazalet, heard Josephine deliver her speech at the great Federation Congress in Geneva in 1877, and testified that she 'spoke in eloquent French' (FL, Edward A. Cazalet to George Grey Butler, 2 January 1907). Margaret Shaen, the daughter of William Shaen, chairman of the National Association, told Georgie Butler that

she heard his mother speak only once, and that was at Genoa, in Italian: the effect of Josephine's 'pathetic pleading voice . . . I shall never forget' (ibid., Margaret Shaen to George Grey Butler, 6 January 1907).

14. Ibid., JEB to Henry J. Wilson, 8 March 1875.
15. Letter from JEB to Harriet Meuricoffre, 29 January 1875, reprinted in JEB, *The New Abolitionists*, p.52.
16. Josephine had familiarized herself with the workings of the French system at the start of the English campaign to repeal the CD Acts. As early as March 1870 she had edited a translation of a French anti-regulation pamphlet, entitled *French Morality under the Regulation System* (trans. Madame Julie Daubie, Liverpool: T. Brakell).
17. FL, JEB to Sir James Stansfeld, 20–22 December 1874.
18. Reprinted in William Acton, *Prostitution*, ed. Peter Fryer, London: Macgibbon & Kee, 1968 (2nd edn 1870), pp.98–9.
19. FL, JEB to Sir James Stansfeld, 20–22 December 1874.
20. Acton, *Prostitution*, p.111.
21. Ibid., p.107. Acton was, however, writing from a position of authority within the system (he participated in at least fifty examinations one day at the Lourcine hospital, each examination, together with the required paperwork, taking no more than three minutes).
22. This account of Josephine's encounter with Lecour is taken from *Reminiscences*, p.71.
23. Ibid., pp.72–3.
24. FL, JEB to Sir James Stansfeld, 20–22 December 1874.
25. *Reminiscences*, p.79.
26. Ibid., p.77.
27. Ibid., p.78.
28. Ibid., p.80.
29. *Shield*, 4 April 1870, p.42. A bureau within the prison was later founded by Pauline de Grandpré with the aim of rescuing women once they had been released, and Josephine would visit her on subsequent visits to Paris. In her paper the *Storm-Bell*, Josephine recounted some of de Grandpré's experiences at St Lazare: 'She describes, in her diary, her visit to the *oubliettes* (places of forgetfulness) underneath the prison. She was let down into the outer darkness of these pestilential vaults, fearless of the horrible odours and poisonous air; the walls dripped with slime, the floors were deep in filth in which these noxious creatures crawled . . . She tells also how she was attracted by the sound of hammering to a remote part of the prison, and found there workmen engaged, privately, in flooring over with asphalt etc., a large vault filled with innumerable skeletons. "The skulls", she says, "were small, the teeth white and regular", showing the *youth* of the creatures whose despised corpses had been flung promiscuously there', *Storm-Bell*, February 1899, No.12, p.137.
30. *Reminiscences*, p.81.
31. FL, JEB to Sir James Stansfeld, 20–22 December 1874.

32. *Shield*, 1 February 1875, p.23; FL, JEB to Joseph Edmondson, 15 December 1874.
33. FL, JEB to Sir James Stansfeld, 20–22 December 1874.
34. Ibid., 16 December 1874.
35. Ibid., 20–22 December 1874.
36. Ibid.
37. Ibid., 14 December 1874.
38. Ibid., 20–22 December 1874.
39. Ibid.
40. Ibid., JEB to Revd George Butler, 13 December 1874.
41. Ibid., 16 December 1874.
42. Ibid., JEB to Harriet Meuricoffre, 29 December 1874.
43. *Shield*, 8 February 1875, p.34.
44. JEB, *The New Abolitionists*, p.32.
45. Mary Gibson, *Prostitution and the State in Italy, 1860–1915*, New Brunswick, NJ, and London: Rutgers University Press, 1986, p.190.
46. *Reminiscences*, p. 92.
47. FL, JEB to Henry J. Wilson, 25 July 1875.
48. BLL, JEB to Hannah Ford, 20 April 1875.
49. *Reminiscences*, p.89.
50. JEB, *The New Abolitionists*, p.28.
51. Ibid., p.33.
52. *Harriet Meuricoffre*, p.276.
53. FL, JEB to Harriet Meuricoffre, 21 January 1875.
54. Ibid., 5 February 1875.
55. Ibid.
56. JEB, *The New Abolitionists*, p.79.
57. Ibid., p.82.
58. Ibid., p.65.
59. FL, JEB to Harriet Meuricoffre, 5 February 1875.
60. *George Butler*, p.291.
61. FL, JEB to Harriet Meuricoffre, 5 February 1875.
62. Ibid., 19 February 1875.
63. Ibid., JEB's notes to her translation of Aimé Humbert's letter, dated 1 March 1875.
64. Ibid., JEB to Harriet Meuricoffre, 19 February 1875.
65. This is the version which appears in *The New Abolitionists*, pp.97–8.
66. FL, JEB to Harriet Meuricoffre, 19 February 1875.
67. Ibid., JEB to Revd George Butler, 13 February 1875.
68. Ibid., JEB to Harriet Meuricoffre, 19 February 1875.
69. *George Butler*, p.292.
70. FL, JEB to Harriet Meuricoffre, 19 February 1875.
71. *Shield*, 15 March 1875, p.69.
72. FL, JEB to Sir James Stansfeld, 20–22 December 1874.
73. Ibid., JEB to Harriet Meuricoffre, 5 February 1875.

74. Ibid., JEB to Henry J. Wilson, 28 February 1875.
75. Ibid., 22 February 1875.
76. *Shield*, 15 March 1875, p.78.
77. JEB to Joseph Edmondson and Friends, 15 February 1875, reprinted in *The New Abolitionists*, p.95.
78. FL, JEB to Henry J. Wilson, 8 March 1875.
79. Scott, pp.194–5.
80. Petrie, pp.183–4.

CHAPTER 10

1. FL, JEB to Edith Leupold, 9 April 1875.
2. Ibid.
3. *Daily Telegraph*, Wednesday, 5 May 1875, p.2.
4. Jenny Percy's statement as it appeared in the *National League Journal*, 1 August 1875, p.5.
5. FL: Mrs Percy's letter to the *Daily Telegraph* is reprinted in *Sheldrake's Aldershot and Sandhurst Military Gazette*, 3 April 1875.
6. McHugh, p.150.
7. FL, JEB to Edith Leupold, 9 April 1875. Josephine's first comment is doubly odd in that it seems to have been a play on the phrase learned by all musicians to help them memorize the ascending notes on the lines of the treble clef, 'Every Good Boy Deserves Favours'.
8. Ibid., JEB to Henry J. Wilson, 7 April 1875.
9. Ibid., JEB to Charlotte Wilson, 18 April 1875 (dictated to James Stuart). When Josephine suffered a nervous collapse in the second week of May, she asked the Wilsons if they could relieve her of Jenny for a fortnight, and requested that her lessons in writing and arithmetic be kept up.
10. Ibid., JEB to Henry J. Wilson, 19 April 1875.
11. *George Butler*, p.276.
12. Jenny Percy's statement, *National League Journal*, 1 August 1875, p.5. That last phrase, 'surely everybody ought to fight against [the Acts]', was cut by Josephine when she later reprinted the account in her biography of her husband.
13. FL, JEB to Henry J. Wilson, 22 April 1875.
14. Ibid., 9 April 1875.
15. Ibid., JEB to Henry J. Wilson, 15 April 1875. On 1 April 1875, the *Shield*, in its first account of the Percy case, reported the suicide of a young woman in Milan, who, lured to a brothel, poisoned herself with the phosphorous tips of Lucifer matches rather than become a prostitute.
16. Quoted in McHugh, pp.108–9.
17. FL, JEB to Henry J. Wilson, 12 May 1875.
18. Ibid., [*c.* 11] May 1875.
19. Ibid., James Stuart to Charlotte Wilson, 18 May 1875.
20. Ibid., JEB to Charlotte Wilson, 19 May 1875.
21. Ibid., Henry J. Wilson's circular, 20 May 1875.

22. Ibid., JEB to Albert Rutson, 22 May 1868.
23. Ibid., JEB to Joseph Edmondson, n.d. [*c.* mid-April 1875].
24. *Reminiscences*, p.188.
25. It was felt unnecessary to translate the essay into English, since the English campaign was so advanced; although Josephine certainly asked Wilson whether it *should* be circulated at home.
26. *The Voice of One Crying in the Wilderness*, trans. Osmund Airy, with an introduction by the Right Hon. James Stuart LLD, London: Simpkin, Marshall, Hamilton, Kent, 1913, p.16.
27. Ibid., pp.17, 31.
28. FL, Margaret Tanner to Henry J. Wilson, 23 May 1875.
29. Ibid., Jane Ord to Charlotte Wilson, 27 May 1875.
30. Ibid., Eliza McLaren to Charlotte Wilson, 27 May 1875.
31. Ibid., Joseph Edmondson to Charlotte Wilson, 26 May 1875.
32. Ibid., Dr Carter to Charlotte Wilson, 22 May 1875. (A rare reference to her husband's attendance is in one of James Stuart's progress reports for Mrs Wilson: 'She went with Mr B. to where the College boys were having their sports', ibid., James Stuart to Charlotte Wilson, 22 May 1875.)
33. Ibid., Revd George Butler to Henry J. Wilson, 31 May 1875.
34. Ibid., JEB to Mr and Mrs Wilson, 7 June 1875.
35. Ibid., James Stuart to Henry J. Wilson, 28 May 1875.
36. Ibid., JEB to Charlotte Wilson, 2 [or 3?] June 1875.
37. *National League Journal*, 1 August 1875, p.2.
38. FL, JEB to Henry J. Wilson, 22 April 1875.
39. Ibid., JEB to Miss Priestman, 19 September 1872.
40. Ibid.
41. NRO, ZBU.E3/B2, George Grey Butler to JEB, n.d.
42. FL, JEB to Mary Priestman, 4 July 1874.
43. Ibid., JEB to the Misses Priestman, 4 May 1874.
44. Ibid., JEB to Mary Priestman, 20 September 1874.
45. Ibid., JEB to Miss Priestman, 15 June 1875.
46. Ibid., 17 June 1875.
47. Ibid., JEB to Henry J. Wilson, 28 June 1875.
48. Ibid., 6 July 1875.
49. Ibid., 7 July 1875.
50. Ibid., 25 July 1875.
51. Ibid., 24 August 1875.
52. Ibid., JEB to Mary Priestman, [*c.*30] October 1875.
53. Ibid., JEB to Charlotte Wilson, [*c.*10] November 1875.
54. *Shield*, 1 December 1875, p.304. Sir Stephen Cave (1820–80) was Paymaster-General from 1874 to 1880, and Mr Gathorne-Hardy, later Viscount Cranbrook (1814–1906) was Secretary of State for War under Disraeli, from 1874 to 1878.
55. NRO, ZBU.E3/B4, Charles Butler to JEB, 22 July [no year].
56. Ibid., ZBU.E3/B3, Stanley Butler to JEB, n.d.

57. Ibid., ZBU.E3/B4, Charles Butler to JEB, n.d.
58. LUL, JB 1/1 1876/10/23 (I), JEB to Stanley Butler.
59. Ibid., 1878/09/15 (I).
60. J.L. Hammond and Barbara Hammond, *James Stansfeld: A Victorian Champion of Sex Equality*, London: Longmans, Green, 1932, p.206.
61. *Shield*, 3 November 1877, p.275.
62. E. Moberley Bell, *Josephine Butler: Flame of Fire*, London: Constable, 1962, p.141.
63. FL, JEB to Members of the Repeal Association, November 1877.
64. JEB, *The Hour before the Dawn: An Appeal to Men*, London: Trübner, 1876, p.35.
65. Ibid., p.95.
66. JEB, *Catherine of Siena. A Biography*, London: Dyer Brothers, 1878, pp.331, 328.
67. LUL, JB 1/1 1879/03/15 (II), JEB to Fanny Smyttan.
68. Ibid.
69. Ibid.
70. Ibid.
71. Ibid., 1879/07/11 (I), JEB to Stanley Butler.
72. Ibid., 1879/08/27 (I).
73. *Reminiscences*, p.197.
74. FL, JEB to Miss Priestman, 29 August 1879.
75. Ibid.
76. Ibid.
77. Ibid.
78. LUL, JB 1/1 1879/08/27 (I), JEB to Stanley Butler.
79. FL, JEB to Miss Priestman, 29 August 1879.
80. Ibid., JEB to Elizabeth Grey (her brother George's second wife), 27 December 1879.
81. It would appear that Eliza's new school was in Brighton. On 11 May 1876, Josephine wrote to George from London to say that she had been able to see her sister, who 'had come up from Brighton for the day on business', FL.

CHAPTER ELEVEN

1. FL, JEB, Circular directed to the Committee and Friends of the Federation, 11 January 1879. Significantly, Josephine chose to reprint this appeal at the very close of her autobiography, *Reminiscences*, pp.234–6.
2. The Friends' Association for Repeal financed the investigations of Dyer and Gillet and paid for the publication of their reports on the traffic in English girls to brothels on the Continent (see McHugh, pp.191–3).
3. Quoted in JEB, *A Letter to the Mothers of England: Commended also to the Attention of Fathers, Ministers of Religion, and Legislators*, April 1881, p.17.
4. Ibid., p.11.

5. Ibid., p.13.
6. Lenaers's statement was later recounted by Josephine in her paper, the *Storm-Bell*, May 1899, No.15, p.182.
7. *Shield*, 25 December 1880, p.169.
8. FL, JEB to Dr William Carter, 1 April 1880.
9. Alfred S. Dyer, *The European Slave Trade in English Girls. A Narrative of Facts*, London: Dyer Brothers, 1880, p.27.
10. FL, JEB to Dr William Carter, 1 April 1880.
11. *Reminiscences*, p. 229.
12. Dyer, *European Slave Trade in English Girls*, pp.19–20.
13. *George Butler*, p.344.
14. *Shield*, 2 February 1880, p.19.
15. Ibid., 1 May 1880, pp.63–5.
16. Ibid., 28 August 1880, p.138.
17. Ibid., 16 October 1880, p.144.
18. *George Butler*, pp.337–8.
19. *Reminiscences*, p.218.
20. Ibid., p.219.
21. *Shield*, 16 October 1880, p.142.
22. *Reminiscences*, p.216.
23. FL, JEB to Elizabeth Lundie, 2 November 1880.
24. Ibid., JEB to unknown recipient, n.d. [*c.* autumn 1880].
25. Ibid.
26. *Reminiscences*, p.222.
27. JEB, *A Letter to the Mothers of England*, pp.5–6.
28. Reported in the *Shield*, 19 February 1881, p.29.
29. *Reminiscences*, pp.230–1.
30. Ibid., p.231.
31. *Shield*, 25 December 1880, p.169.
32. Alfred Dyer, *Six Years' Labour and Sorrow: The Fourth Report of the London Committee for Suppressing the Traffic in British Girls for Purposes of Continental Prostitution*, London: Dyer Brothers, 1885, p.15.
33. Josephine responded, 'Such a remedy is *morally* inadmissible. It is impossible that a Christian government can consistently take part in any plan for permitting women to take upon themselves the trade of prostitution', quoted ibid., p.19.
34. FL, JEB, 'To the Ladies who signed the Memorial to Lord Granville', 27 May [1881].
35. PRO, *Report of the Select Committee of the House of Lords Appointed to Inquire into the State of the Law Related to the Protection of Young Girls* (1881–2) PP, (344) XIII.823, Q.1047. (Adeline's testimony was presented by Alfred Dyer.)
36. *Sentinel*, September 1881, pp.19, 21.
37. JEB, *A Letter to the Mothers of England*, p.15.
38. *Sentinel*, November 1881, p.55.

39. FL, JEB to Charlotte Wilson, 29 September 1881; ibid., 3 October 1881.
40. *Sentinel*, November 1881, p.55.
41. FL, JEB to Charlotte Wilson, 8 October 1881.
42. It was their suggestion that birth certificates issued at Somerset House to women between the ages of twenty and thirty should bear a conspicuous red stamp in French warning of fraudulent certificates.
43. *Sentinel*, August 1881, p.128.
44. The provisions of the Criminal Law Amendment Bill in its final state are reprinted ibid., September 1885, p.477.
45. G. S. Railton (ed.) *The Truth about the Armstrong Case and The Salvation Army*, London: Salvation Army Book Stores, 1885, p.7.

CHAPTER TWELVE

1. FL, JEB to Helen Clark, 29 April 1877.
2. Ibid., JEB to Robert Martineau, 22 May 1882.
3. Ibid.
4. RIBA, BuFam/2/3/1, JEB to Rhoda Bolton, 13 November [1881].
5. FL, JEB to Stanley Butler, 15 September 1878.
6. *George Butler*, p.309.
7. Ibid., p.356.
8. Ibid., p.346.
9. LUL, JB 1/1 1881/11/24 (I), JEB to Stanley Butler.
10. FL, JEB [to Miss Priestman?], n.d. [*c.* late summer 1879]; *George Butler*, p.338.
11. RIBA, BuFam/2/3/1, JEB to Rhoda Bolton, 13 November [1881].
12. This was evidently also a concern of George's, and on the advice of his brother, Spencer, he wrote to the manager of the Union Bank in early May, requesting that his railway bonds be entered in their joint names, so that in the case of his death Josephine would be able to dispose of them as she wished.
13. FL, Robert Martineau to Henry J. Wilson, 10 June 1882.
14. Ibid., 24 May 1882.
15. JEB to Robert Martineau, 22 May 1882.
16. Ibid., JEB to Revd George Butler, 17 August 1882.
17. Ibid., JEB to Robert Martineau, 22 May 1882.
18. *George Butler*, p.358.
19. Ibid. pp.356, 359.
20. Ibid., p.363.
21. FL, JEB to Miss Priestman, 22 June 1887.
22. BLL, Josephine Butler Collection, JEB to Hannah Ford, 8 October [no year]. It is likely that this letter dates from the Butlers' early years at Liverpool, since Josephine explains that she has 'now in my house, at this moment, two poor erring girls, waiting places, whom I have to clothe & feed'.
23. FL, JEB to Harriet Meuricoffre, 18 October 1882.

24. RIBA, BuFam/2/3/15, JEB to Rhoda Butler, n.d. [*c.*1893–95].
25. *George Butler*, p.375.
26. RIBA, BuFam/3/4/3, Rhoda Butler to Stanley Butler, 14 January n.d. [*c.* 1888].
27. *George Butler*, p.375.
28. FL, JEB to Miss Priestman, 12 May 1883.
29. Ibid., JEB to Harriet Meuricoffre, 18 October 1882.
30. LUL, JB 1/1 1882/07/09 (II), JEB to Charles Butler.
31. FL, JEB to Miss Priestman, 10 November 1882.
32. Ibid., 15 November 1882.
33. *George Butler*, p.402.
34. RIBA, BuFam/2/3/8, JEB to Rhoda Butler, n.d. [*c.* spring 1884].
35. FL, JEB to Miss Priestman, 9 July 1884.
36. Ibid.
37. 'Mrs Josephine Butler: Interview', *All the World*, January 1891, pp.49–50.
38. FL, JEB to Revd George Butler, [4] May 1882.
39. PRO, *Report of the Select Committee of the House of Commons on the Administration and Operation of the Contagious Diseases Acts, 1880*, 1882 (340), IX.1, Q.5412; Q.5414–15.
40. Ibid., Q.5431–2.
41. FL, JEB to Robert Martineau, 2 October 1882.
42. Ibid., JEB to Miss Priestman, 17 January 1883.
43. Ibid.
44. Ibid., n.d. [*c.* late January 1883]. Josephine wrote of Ursula Bright's agnosticism to her son, Stanley, 'That it seems is the fashionable name for an unbeliever', LUL, JB 1/1 1881/11/24 (I).
45. LUL, JB 1/1 1883/03/03 (I), JEB to Stanley Butler.
46. FL, JEB to Miss Priestman, n.d. [*c.* 21 February 1883].
47. Elizabeth Cady Stanton, *Eighty Years and More: Reminiscences 1815–1897*, Boston: Northeastern University Press, 1993, p.361.
48. FL, JEB to Miss Priestman [*c.* 21 February 1883].
49. FL, MS of JEB's circular to MPs, 'Ought Women to be in the Gallery of the House of Commons on the 27th? Letter to an MP', n.d. [*c.* 20 February 1883].
50. LUL, JB 1/1 1883/03/03 (I), JEB to Stanley Butler.
51. Ibid.
52. Ibid.
53. JEB to Stanley Butler, 28 February 1883, reprinted in Johnson, p.132.
54. LUL, JB 1/1883/03/03 (I), JEB to Stanley Butler.
55. Ibid.
56. Ibid.
57. Ibid.
58. Ibid., 1903/03/05 (I), JEB to Fanny Forsaith.
59. Ibid.
60. FL, Sir James Stansfeld to M. Emilie de Laveleye, 5 September 1883.

61. Scott, p.223.
62. *Shield*, 2 June 1883, p.168.
63. FL, Draft statement by JEB, dated 11 May 1883.
64. *Shield*, 2 June 1883, p.167.
65. FL, JEB to Mrs Hinde Smith, 20 August 1883.
66. *Shield*, 4 August 1883, p.238 (JEB was writing from Neuchâtel on 22 July 1883).
67. Ibid., 3 November 1883, p.258.
68. McHugh, p.225.

CHAPTER THIRTEEN

1. Since 1870, Josephine had shown a strong interest in the Salvation Army. She could recall driving over to Liverpool College one evening to pick up George, who, getting into the carriage beside her, 'laid upon my knee a poor little shabby newspaper, saying, "There, that will interest you"'. ('Friends and Helpers IX: A Fearless Champion. Mrs Josephine Butler', *All the World*, December 1895, p.366.). It was the first number of the Army's paper, *War Cry*. She took it up to her room as soon as they got home, 'and read every word of it, and thanked God'. As soon as members of the Salvation Army came to Liverpool she joined their meetings, and on visits to London she met with William and Catherine Booth, who became at once firm supporters of the repeal movement.
2. SA, 'Rebecca Jarrett', typed transcript, SA Heritage Centre, Queen Victoria Street, London, p.4. This transcript preserves Rebecca's spelling and makes no attempt to add any punctuation.
3. Rebecca's exact date of birth is given in an account of her life written by a Salvation Army officer after conversations with Rebecca. Rebecca herself seems only to have a vague idea of her age in the accounts she wrote of her early life.
4. JEB, *Rebecca Jarrett*, London: Morgan & Scott, 1886, p.21.
5. There are four different extant versions of Rebecca's autobiography in the Salvation Army Archives at Queen Victoria Street, all bearing the title 'Rebecca Jarrett'. The first is a handwritten memoir left by Rebecca; the second is a typed transcript of another memoir (which records some of the same events in slightly more or less detail); the third is a set of supplementary typed sheets; and the fourth is a typed account by a Salvation Army officer based upon conversations with Rebecca.
6. SA, 'Rebecca Jarrett', handwritten MS.
7. Ibid., Rebecca Jarrett to Florence Booth, 29 January [1885]. Both Josephine and George had taken a great interest in a House of Healing in north London, and she recommended it to her nephew, Tom Bolton. On the day of Josephine's visit, Lady Radstock's two daughters testified that 'they had been raised up in one hour from an infectious fever'. Josephine wrote to Stanley, 'There is such a crowd weekly that the hall can no longer hold them . . . There were grand people in carriages, & beggars in rags

... Mr Boardman, a venerable old American who is at the head of the work hauled me in thro' the crowd, to sit near him', LUL, JB 1/1 1884/03/26 (I).

8. JEB, *Rebecca Jarrett*, p.31.
9. SA, 'Rebecca Jarrett', typed transcript, pp.9–10; Rebecca Jarrett to Florence Booth, n.d. [*c.* February or March 1885].
10. Ibid., Rebecca Jarrett to Florence Booth, 2 ? 1885.
11. JEB, *Rebecca Jarrett*, p.31.
12. SA, JEB to Florence Booth, 26 March [1885].
13. SA, 'Rebecca Jarrett', typed transcript, p. 11.
14. JEB, *Rebecca Jarrett*, p.40.
15. SA, 'Rebecca Jarrett', handwritten MS.
16. JEB, *Rebecca Jarrett*, p.30.
17. SA 'Rebecca Jarrett', typed account from conversations with Rebecca Jarrett, p.9. This would seem to be confirmed by Rebecca's statement in the typed transcript of her memoirs. At Winchester, she says, 'my thoughts turned to others what I could do for them the first thing as I had got a little money I aimed to open a Home for some one else to break from the drink', p.8.
18. JEB, *Rebecca Jarrett*, pp.37–8.
19. SA, 'Rebecca Jarrett', typed account from conversations with Rebecca Jarrett, pp.10–11.
20. Reported in *Winchester Observer and County News*, Saturday, 29 August 1885, p.6. Rebecca was also a tender nurse to the terminally ill women she received. Josephine referred to a woman identified only as 'Mary', who seems to have been in the final stages of syphilis, 'one of those cases in which the sufferer becomes a mass of corruption before death' (JEB, *Rebecca Jarrett*, p.34). Neighbours protested at the stench, and even the doctor would not step beyond the front door, telling Rebecca to take the woman to the Winchester Workhouse infirmary. She was forced to do so, but she wrote a grim account of it, saying that 'directly I got there she cried bitterly for on the door she was taken into was written in large letters the *Pest House* she knew it was her last home', SA, 'Rebecca Jarrett', typed transcript, p.11. Mary died there two days later.
21. SA, Rebecca Jarrett to Florence Booth, n.d. [*c.* April 1885].
22. Ibid., 'Rebecca Jarrett', typed transcript, p.9.
23. Text of Florence Booth's address given at the Centenary Meeting held in honour of Josephine's birth, in the Westminster Central Hall, London, in April 1928, reprinted in the *Deliverer*, June 1928, p.29.
24. SA, JEB to Florence Booth, 26 March [1885].
25. *Deliverer*, June 1928, p.29.
26. LUL, JB 1/1 1879/03/15 (I), JEB to Fanny Smyttan.
27. G. S. Railton (ed.) *The Truth about the Armstrong Case and the Salvation Army*, London: Salvation Army Bookstores, 1885, p.8.
28. Ibid.

29. Ibid., p.7.
30. Josephine discussed the press handling of the Jeffries case in her pamphlet, *The Revival and Extension of the Abolitionist Cause. A Letter to the Members of the Ladies' National Association*, Winchester: John T. Doswell, 1887, p.11.
31. W. T. Stead's speech to the Federation Conference at Antwerp, 17 September 1885, reprinted in the *Shield*, 3 October 1885, p.144.
32. LUL, JB 1/1 1885/02/27 (I), JEB to Stanley Butler.
33. FL, JEB to Miss Priestman, 5 June 1885.
34. Railton, *The Truth about the Armstrong Case*, p.10.
35. SA, 'Rebecca Jarrett', handwritten MS.
36. Railton, *The Truth about the Armstrong Case*, p.10.
37. Ibid., p.13. (Of course, Stead was not present when the examination took place. Eliza may not have objected at the time, but at the subsequent trial she testified to her disgust at being interfered with by Madame Mourez.)
38. Josephine wrote that she 'disapproved from the first of that part in the proceedings. I was not cognisant of it till after the fact', JEB, *Rebecca Jarrett*, p.55.
39. Railton, *The Truth about the Armstrong Case*, p.14.
40. *Pall Mall Gazette*, 6 July 1885, p.1.
41. Ibid., p.3.
42. Ibid., 7 July 1885, p.4.
43. Ibid., 8 July 1885, p.5.
44. Ibid., 9 July 1885, p.3.
45. Railton, *The Truth about the Armstrong Case*, p.9.
46. *Methodist Times*, 23 July 1885, p.473.
47. *Pall Mall Gazette*, 21 July 1885, p.12. This resolution was passed at a crowded meeting convened by the Borough of Hackney branch of the Young Men's Christian Association; other meetings demanded that the age of consent be raised to eighteen.
48. The British retreat from the Sudan had weakened an already floundering government, and on 8 June 1885 Gladstone had resigned after losing an important vote on the budget.
49. FL, JEB to the Misses Priestman, 10 July 1885.
50. JEB, *Rebecca Jarrett*, p.11.
51. SA, Amélie Humbert to Rebecca Jarrett, 3 August 1885. Josephine opened a new 'Cottage Home' at another address in Winchester in the spring of 1887, explaining to the Priestman sisters that she was 'so continually fired into on all sides to help our poor unfortunate sisters when weak or out of health, or in circumstances of trouble . . . This work, as you understand, is almost inseparable – at least in my case – from the Federation work', FL, JEB to Margaret Tanner and her sisters, 24 March 1887.
52. LUL, JB 1/1 1885/07/00 (II), JEB to Stanley Butler.
53. Ibid.; SA, 'Rebecca Jarrett', typed transcript, p.13.

54. RIBA, BuFam/3/4/1, Rhoda Bolton to Stanley Butler, 16 July [1885].
55. FL, JEB to Arthur J. Naish, 26 July 1885.
56. JEB, Letter to the Editor, *Winchester Observer and County News*, 15 August 1885, p.5.
57. Estelle Stead, *My Father: Personal and Spiritual Reminiscences*, London: Thomas Nelson & Sons, 1918, p.146.
58. FL, Circular sent out by the London Committee of the LNA, August 1885. In later years, Josephine would admit to Miss Priestman that she had '*never* heartily sympathised with the work of the Vigilance Society'. It was her objection that 'there is a constant tendency towards *external* pressure, and inside that a tendency to let the pressure fall almost exclusively on women', FL, JEB to Mary Priestman, 5 November 1894. 'I continue to protest that I do not believe that any real reform will ever be reached by *outward repression* . . . The principle of the Federation has always been to let *individuals alone*, not to pursue them by any outward punishments, nor drive them *out of any place* so long as they behave decently – but to attack *organised prostitution*, that is when a third party, actuated by the desire of making money, sets up a house in wh women are sold to men, or keeps any place for his own gain wh is a market of vice'. Yves Guyot went further than Josephine's rather tame warning to LNA members in August 1885. He resigned from the Federation in September 1885, telling delegates at the Antwerp Conference that he had supported the Federation 'while I thought it was a movement in favour of liberty . . . events which have taken place in London prove to me that it has transformed itself into a movement in favour of repression . . . I cannot follow on that ground': reported in the *Shield*, 9 January 1886, pp.2–3.
59. 'The new order of chivalry' was the rallying cry of many of the Hyde Park speeches, and the *Pall Mall*'s leader for 19 October glorified Stead's role in improving the morality of the nation.
60. FL, LNA circular, August 1885.
61. Ibid., JEB to Miss Priestman, 6 October 1885. Josephine explained, 'Mr Hughes is printing as a leaflet an article I wrote for him in the *Methodist Times*. It is on Women's Suffrage & repeal. If you like, I will send you some'. Another letter she wrote to the *Christian* was reprinted in the *War Cry* on 7 October and was subsequently published separately: 'The *Christian* has printed 3,000 of my letter because so many people have asked for it. He will send 1,000 to you'.
62. FL, JEB to Margaret Tanner, 16 August 1885.
63. Ibid., George Grey Butler to JEB, 3 September 1885.
64. *Shield*, 3 October 1885, p.143.
65. *George Butler*, p.402.
66. JEB, *Rebecca Jarrett*, pp.19, 15–16.
67. RIBA, BuFam/2/2/12, Stanley Butler to Rhoda Bolton, 31 October [1885].
68. *Winchester Observer and County News*, 7 November 1885, p.6.

69. JEB, *Rebecca Jarrett*, p.49.
70. Ibid., p.54.
71. *George Butler*, p.405. William Booth was equally scathing about Stead, writing to his wife, Catherine, on 9 November, 'And here is Stead, abandons poor Rebecca, and said that the verdict is just, etc., etc., etc..' and he urged Catherine to join him in returning to their own work, in order to 'wipe out the very name of Eliza Armstrong'. When Stead's sentence was pronounced, the General spared him no pity, saying 'of course, it will *make him*' (Harold Begbie, *William Booth, Founder of the Salvation Army*, London: Macmillan, 1920, II, pp.50, 52).
72. FL, JEB to Miss Priestman, 17 December 1885.
73. William Booth to Catherine Booth, 10 November 1885, reprinted in Begbie, *William Booth*, II, p.52.
74. JEB, *Rebecca Jarrett*, p.6.
75. FL, JEB to Miss Priestman, 17 December 1885.
76. SA, 'Rebecca Jarrett', typed transcript, p.32.
77. Ibid. On 27 April 1886, Rebecca wrote to Florence Booth from Clapton, 'I do want you to ask Mrs Butler for some money for me for I have to pay for my lodging and my washing Capt [Jones] gives me my food with her lasses . . .'
78. Ibid., typed transcript of letter from JEB to Bramwell Booth, 28 June 1886.
79. Josephine sent her some money so that she could leave one unsatisfactory refuge (unsatisfactory because it was a Catholic institution and Rebecca refused to go to confession!) in order to travel to the Home in Edinburgh that she had heard about. Writing to Florence Booth on 28 March 1889, Rebecca explained, 'Mrs Butler sent me some money down when I left they would only give me a shilling', SA.
80. See letters in the Salvation Army International Heritage Centre between Rebecca Jarrett and Florence Booth, between March and May 1889. Rebecca was given a good character by the matron under the name of 'Mary Grey'. On 11 May 1889, Rebecca wrote to Mrs Booth, 'Mrs Josp Butler knows I am here I wrote to her she sent me a nice letter back also Miss Humbert'.

CHAPTER FOURTEEN

1. JEB, *A Woman's Appeal to the Electors* (1885), reprinted in Johnson, p.138.
2. This figure is from McHugh, p.227. Benjamin Scott has the figure at 257, Scott, p.224.
3. FL, Margaret Tanner to JEB (fragment), n.d. [*c.*16 March 1886].
4. LUL, JB 1/1 1886/04/25 (I), JEB to Georgie, Stanley and Rhoda Butler.
5. FL, Revd George Butler to George Grey Butler, 9 March 1886.
6. Ibid., JEB to George Grey Butler, 26 March 1886.
7. RIBA, BuFam/2/4/1, Stanley Butler to Rhoda Butler, 13 August [1886].
8. Ibid., BuFam/2/4/2, 15 August [1886].

9. LUL, JB 1/1 1886/08/29 (I), JEB to Stanley Butler.
10. FL, JEB to Emily Ford, 15 November 1886.
11. Ibid., JEB to Miss Estlin, 31 October 1886.
12. Ibid., JEB to Emily Ford, 15 November 1886.
13. Ibid., Mary Sumner to Emily Ford, 5 December 1886.
14. Ibid., JEB to Mary Priestman, 11 June 1886.
15. Josephine was disturbed to hear of the independent decision of two other prominent branches, the Dublin and the Birmingham ladies, who had announced that they had dissolved, and 'reconstituted the committee for future work – whatever that may mean', ibid., JEB to Mary Priestman, 6 June 1886.
16. Ibid., JEB to Mary Priestman, [*c.*7] May 1886.
17. Ibid., JEB to Friends, 19 October 1886.
18. Ibid., JEB and Professor Stuart to Margaret Tanner and Mary Priestman, 29 December 1886. Josephine was able to declare to the Lausanne conference of 1887 that progress had been made. Under instruction from Britain, the CD ordinances had been abolished in Trinidad, Jamaica and Barbados. Soon, with the exception of Fiji, all the Crown Colonies, that is those colonies directly governed from Britain through the Colonial Office, had followed suit. Hong Kong and the Straits Settlements had pleaded special circumstances, requesting to be allowed to maintain 'tolerated houses', and had been required to lay all their regulations relating to prostitution before the UK Parliament.
19. Ibid., JEB to the Misses Priestman, 4 January 1887.
20. Ibid., JEB to Friends, 29 January 1887.
21. *Dawn*, 1 May 1888, No.1, p.11.
22. FL, LNA circular by JEB, 11 March 1888.
23. *Sentinel*, December 1886, p.142.
24. Ibid., June 1887, p.67.
25. FL, JEB to the Misses Priestman, 27 February 1888.
26. The first number of the *Dawn*, 1 May 1888, promised to address recent complaints she had received that of all the English Abolition organs only the *Sentinel* afforded space for continental or colonial news, but by the second issue, published in August, Josephine had recognized the redundancy of merely repeating stories from Dyer's paper. Although important Indian items continued to be printed in the *Dawn*, it was mostly concerned with European news.
27. FL, JEB to George W. Johnson, 28 February 1888. Johnson was a late convert to the Abolitionist cause, becoming a member of the Federation in 1887.
28. Ibid., LNA circular by JEB, datelined Winchester, 11 March 1888.
29. Quoted in 'Professor Stuart's Report', *Dawn*, 1 November 1888, No.3, p.13.
30. FL, JEB to Mrs Tanner, 12 May 1888.
31. Roberts had devoted his life to service in the Indian Army, and among many honours, he had been awarded the Victoria Cross. Josephine was

already familiar with his name from hearing soldiers at the military hospital in Winchester, invalided home from India, praise their commander: 'deriving my impressions from their testimony, I had ever thought of him as a "good man", – for so his soldiers called him', JEB, *The Present Aspect of the Abolitionist Cause in Relation to British India: A Letter to my Friends*, London: British, Continental & General Federation, June 1893, p.6.

32. *Dawn*, 1 August 1888, No.2, p.17.
33. Ibid.
34. Ibid., 1 October 1889, No.7, p.7.
35. Ibid., 1 April 1890, No.8, p.2. The offending clause of the 1888 Cantonments Bill (Clause 24, Section 29) ran thus: 'The Governor General in Council may make rules providing for the removal and exclusion from a Cantonment of persons suffering or suspected to be suffering from any infectious contagious disorder, and the appointment and regulation of hospitals or other places within or without the cantonments for the reception and treatment of persons suffering from any disease' (reprinted ibid., 1 July 1889, No.6, p.16).
36. Ibid., 1 April 1891, No.12, p.18.
37. Elizabeth Andrews's and Kate Bushnell's accounts of their divine calling are reprinted in JEB, *The Present Aspect of the Abolitionist Cause*, pp.13–16.
38. FL, JEB to the Misses Priestman, 9 March 1891.
39. Elizabeth Andrews and Kate Bushnell, 'The Queen's Daughters in India' (1898), reprinted in *The Queen's Daughters: An Anthology of Victorian Feminist Writings on India, 1857–1900*, ed. Penelope Tuson, Reading, Berks: Ithaca Press, 1995, p.184.
40. Taken from Elizabeth Andrews's speech to the annual (public) meeting of the LNA, 24 May 1893, reported in the *Dawn*, 1 July 1893, p.13.
41. JEB, *The Present Aspect of the Abolitionist Cause*, p.26.
42. FL, JEB to George W. Johnson, 14 July 1892.
43. LUL, JB 1/1 1893/04/17 (I), JEB to Stanley Butler.
44. Ibid., JB 1/1 1893/08/24 (I).
45. Ibid.
46. FL, JEB to Miss Priestman, 17 April 1893.

CHAPTER FIFTEEN

1. NRO, ZBU.E3/B2, Summary of letter to his mother by George Grey Butler, 17 June 1905.
2. FL, Revd George Butler's speech, 'Progress of the Abolitionist Cause in the Anglican Church', dated August 1888.
3. Bertel Thorvaldsen (*c.*1768–1844) was a neoclassical sculptor born in Copenhagen who bequeathed all the works in his possession, and much of his fortune, to his country. Many of his sculptures can be seen in Copenhagen, including one of Thorvaldsen's most famous pieces, *Christ and the Twelve Apostles*.

4. LUL, JB 1/1 1888/09/04 (I), JEB to Stanley Butler; FL, JEB to Mary Priestman, 4 September 1888. The Thorvaldsen Museum opened in Copenhagen in 1848.
5. *Dawn*, 1 November 1888, No.3, p.6.
6. LUL, JB 1/1 1888/09/01 (I), JEB to Rhoda and Stanley.
7. *Dawn*, 1 November 1888, No.3, p.6.
8. *George Butler*, pp.447–8.
9. *Dawn*, 1 November 1888, No.3, p.4.
10. LUL, JB 1/1 1888/09/01 (I), JEB to Rhoda and Stanley.
11. FL, JEB to Mrs W. S. Clark, 10 November 1888.
12. Ibid., Revd George Butler to George Grey Butler, 16 November 1888.
13. LUL, JB 1/1 1889/02/17 (I), 'Journal of our quiet life at Le Cannet, Sunday 17 to Saturday 23 February 1889', addressed by JEB to Stanley Butler.
14. FL, JEB, Letter to the Executive Committee of the LNA, 29 July 1889.
15. *George Butler*, p.459.
16. FL, JEB to Miss Priestman, 26 July 1889.
17. RIBA, BuFam/3/4/9, Rhoda Butler to Stanley Butler, n.d. [*c.* summer 1889].
18. FL, JEB to the Misses Priestman, 25 August 1889.
19. These conference speeches were recorded in the *Dawn*, 1 October 1889, No.7, p. 10.
20. FL, JEB to Mary Priestman, 19 July 1889.
21. *Dawn*, 1 October 1889, No. 7, p.5.
22. FL, Revd George Butler to George Grey Butler, 9 October 1889.
23. Ibid. (with postscript by Josephine), 23 November 1889.
24. Ibid., 24 February 1890.
25. *George Butler*, p.472.
26. Ibid., p.474.
27. Ibid., p.478.
28. NRO, ZBU.E3/A10, 'Memory of a Child of Sorrow', letter from JEB to George Grey Butler [*c.*1903–4].
29. FL, William Ewart Gladstone to JEB, 18 March 1890.
30. Ibid., JEB to Mrs Margaret Tanner, 30 March 1890.
31. NRO, ZBU.E3/CI, JEB to Mary Ann Garston ('Tully), n.d. [*c.* late March 1890].
32. FL, JEB to the Misses Priestman, 18 October 1890.
33. Ibid., 4 January 1891.
34. *Dawn*, 1 October 1890, No.10, p.14.
35. LUL, JB 1/1 1890/11/04 (I), JEB to Rhoda Butler; FL, JEB to the Misses Priestman, 13 November 1890.
36. FL, JEB to Helen Clark, 23 June 1891.
37. Ibid., JEB to the Misses Priestman, 13 November 1890.
38. LUL, JB 1/1 1890/11/29 (I), JEB reported Mrs Grey's remarks in a letter to Stanley Butler.

39. FL, JEB to the Misses Priestman, 4 January 1891.
40. Ibid., JEB to Miss Priestman, 8 June 1892.
41. Ibid., JEB to the editor of the *Women's Herald*, 19 October 1892.
42. Ibid., JEB to George W. Johnson, 14 July 1892.
43. *George Butler*, p.220.
44. LUL, JB 1/1 1890/11/04 (I), JEB to Rhoda Butler.
45. FL, JEB to the Misses Priestman, 4 January 1891.
46. Ibid., JEB to Miss Priestman, 15 June 1892.
47. 'The Book of the Month', *Review of Reviews*, November 1892, p.501 (Stead quotes a letter from Josephine to Hatty, dated 14 August 1876, which is reprinted in *George Butler*, p.303).
48. NRO, ZBU.E3/C1, JEB to Mary Ann Garston ('Tully'), n.d. [*c.* late March 1890].

CHAPTER SIXTEEN

1. LUL, JB 1/1 1893/06/07 (I), JEB to Stanley Butler.
2. Ibid., 1891/02/03 (I).
3. FL, JEB to Mr and Mrs Thompson, 24 December 1890.
4. This is also observed in *Portrait*, p.154.
5. FL, JEB to the Misses Priestman, 4 February 1891.
6. Ibid.
7. 'Story of Outrage and Injustice', *Dawn*, 1 April 1891, No.12, p.8.
8. Ibid., p.16.
9. FL, JEB to Mary Priestman, 11 February 1891.
10. Reprinted in the *Dawn*, 1 April 1891, No.12, p.8.
11. Ibid., p.16. She continued, 'From the moment when woman comes to have interests which compete with those of men, the point of view is changed, and one sees that in fact the law has been made in the interests of the male sex . . . It is, perhaps, in marriage itself, that the injustice of the law is most conspicuous'.
12. FL, Amélie Humbert to Mary Priestman, 6 February 1891.
13. Ibid., JEB to the Misses Priestman, n.d. [*c.*26 April 1891].
14. LUL, JB 1/1 1891/06/03 (I), JEB to Stanley Butler.
15. FL, JEB to the Misses Priestman, 4 January 1891.
16. Ibid., JEB to Miss Priestman, n.d. [*c.* 1 May 1891].
17. LUL, JB 1/1 1891/11/16 (I), JEB to Stanley Butler.
18. FL, JEB to Miss Priestman, 27 November 1893.
19. Ibid., JEB to Mary Priestman, 18 July 1893.
20. Josephine was tickled to recall how Rhoda had once caught the fancy of Prince Eddy (the eldest son of the Prince of Wales who died in January 1892), who had rooms above Stuart's at Cambridge and was sometimes his smoking partner: 'in Chapel I remember how he looked hard at Rhoda over his prayer book', LUL, JB 1/1, 1892/01/15 (I), JEB to Stanley Butler.
21. Ibid., 1889/03/29 (I), JEB to Rhoda Butler.
22. FL, JEB to Miss Priestman, 29 July 1892.

23. LUL, JB 1/1 1893/06/07 (I), JEB to Stanley Butler.
24. FL, JEB to Miss Priestman, 29 July 1892.
25. LUL, JB 1/1 1903/1/22 (I), JEB to Stanley Butler.
26. FL, JEB to Mary Priestman, 18 July 1893.
27. LUL, JB 1/1, 1894/07/11 (I), JEB to Fanny Forsaith; ibid., 1897/01/28 (1), JEB to Stanley Butler.
28. Ibid., 1894/08/30 (I), JEB to Rhoda Butler.
29. Ibid.
30. FL, JEB to Mary Priestman, 2 March 1895.
31. LUL, JB 1/1, 1895/03/00 (I), JEB to Rhoda and Stanley Butler.
32. FL, JEB to Miss Priestman, 6 May 1893.
33. LUL, JB 1/1 1893/08/13 (I), JEB to Stanley Butler.
34. Ibid., 1893/09/09 (I).
35. See E. Moberley Bell, *Josephine Butler: Flame of Fire*, London: Constable, 1962, p.203; *Portrait*, p.154.
36. LUL, JB 1/1 1893/12/23 (I), JEB to her Sons ('Letter No.2').
37. Ibid., 1894/01/09 (I), JEB to Stanley Butler.
38. Ibid., 1893/12/06 (I), JEB to James Stuart.
39. Ibid., 1893/12/13 (I), JEB to her Sons ('Letter No.1'). She would later refer to her sister-in-law Gertrude Butler's conversion to Catholicism in January 1897, writing to Stanley to tell him that his aunt 'is now in Rome kissing the old Pope's toe', ibid., 1897/01/10 (I). She did, however, believe that it was 'much better she should be an honest Papist, than stand "shivering on the brink" of slippery Ritualism'.
40. Ibid., 1894/01/02 (I), JEB to M. Minod.
41. Ibid., 1895/03/00 (I), JEB to Rhoda and Stanley Butler.
42. Ibid., 1894/03/10 (I), JEB to Fanny Forsaith.
43. Ibid.
44. FL, JEB to the Misses Priestman, 21 April 1894.
45. This was later recalled by Josephine in a letter to Fanny Forsaith, LUL, JB 1/1 1896/08/03 (I).
46. NRO, ZBU.E3/CI, JEB to Emily and Gertrude Butler, 19 May 1894.
47. FL, JEB to the Misses Priestman, 7 May 1894.
48. Ibid., JEB to Mary Priestman, 20 September 1894.
49. Ibid., JEB to Helen Clark, 18 April 1894.
50. Ibid., JEB to the Misses Priestman, 24 December 1894.
51. Ibid., 3 May 1895.
52. Ibid.
53. Ibid., JEB to Mary Priestman, 2 March 1895.
54. Ibid., 19 August 1897; JEB to the Misses Priestman, 10 November 1897.
55. LUL, JB 1/1 1895/01/29 (I), JEB to Rhoda Butler; FL, JEB to Mary Priestman, 27 October 1895.
56. FL, JEB to Mary Priestman, 2 October 1895.
57. LUL, JB 1/1 1895/10/04 (I), JEB to Rhoda Butler.
58. Ibid.

59. Ibid., 1895/10/10 (I), JEB to Stanley Butler.
60. Ibid., 1895/10/14 (I).
61. Ibid.
62. LUL, JB 3/4/6; quoted in a letter to the editor of *The Times* by Winifred Coombe Tennant, 4 July 1928.
63. LUL, JB 1/1 1896/01/17 (I), JEB to Rhoda Butler.
64. FL, JEB to the Misses Priestman, 7 April 1896 ('Letter V').
65. Ibid., 23 March 1896; FL, JEB, 'Dear Miss Forsaith and all our Friends', 25 March 1896 ('Letter IV').
66. Bell, *Josephine Butler*, p.233.
67. FL, JEB to the Misses Priestman, 7 April 1896 ('Letter V').
68. LUL, JB 1/1 1896/03/28 (I), JEB to Stanley Butler.
69. Ibid., 1896/10/00 (I), JEB to Rhoda and Stanley Butler.
70. Ibid.
71. JEB, *Truth before Everything*, Liverpool: Pewtress, 1897, p.8.
72. 'Character Sketch', *Review of Reviews*, July 1891, p.30. Josephine informed Helen Clark, 'It was concocted in our little drawing-room here; I gave Mr Stead ideas I had had for some time about him [Prince Albert Edward]. It was originally more severe, but Mr Gladstone read it in proof and wrote an earnest letter of nine pages, approving it, but begging it might be less strong, as he would be sorry to think of its having some influence prematurely in weakening the monarchy. The spirit and motive of it are *very* serious. The *style* is Mr Stead's', FL, JEB to Helen Clark, 15 July 1891.
73. Parnell was cited as co-respondent in the divorce trial of his fellow Irish MP, Captain Willie O'Shea and his wife Katherine, which opened on Saturday, 15 November 1890. O'Shea was granted a decree nisi on Monday the 17th and details of the case were now circulated in the press: Parnell had conducted an adulterous affair with Mrs O'Shea dating from the autumn of 1880, and Mrs O'Shea had borne him two surviving daughters, Clare, in 1883, and Katie, in 1884. The fact of Parnell's adultery, Josephine said, 'cut my heart like a knife', and she wanted him to retire from the Home Rule movement to limit the political damage his actions had caused.
74. She told Miss Priestman that her advice to Stead was that 'The personal element both in this and Parnell's case weakens the cause when pushed too far – and to many it appears like relentless persecution. I should be glad to see the question shake itself free of persons', FL, 6 April 1891.
75. LUL, JB 1/1 1895/04/25 (1), JEB to Stanley Butler. According to Josephine, Edmund was not Myers's only conquest: she had 'long ago heard a dreadful account of Lord Battersea'. She was later to hope that he 'had got a fright' from the Wilde revelations.
76. Ibid., 1895/06/04 (I).
77. FL, JEB to the Misses Priestman, 6 November 1893.
78. LUL, JB 1/1 1893/12/27 (I), JEB to Fanny Forsaith.

79. FL, JEB to Helen Clark, 6 May 1895.
80. Ibid., JEB to the Misses Priestman, 4 April 1895.
81. Ibid., JEB to Mary Priestman, 26 July 1895.
82. JEB wrote to Mary Priestman that they recognized the Acts 'as a benefit to posterity & a protection to married women in unfortunate circumstances' (ibid.).
83. Ibid., JEB to Miss Priestman, 9 April 1895.
84. LUL, JB 1/1, 1895/08/10 (I), JEB to Stanley Butler.
85. FL, JEB to the Misses Priestman, 3 May 1895.
86. Ibid., Miss Priestman to JEB, 15 November 1896.
87. LUL, JB 1/1 1896/10/27 (I), JEB to Fanny Forsaith.
88. FL, Miss Priestman to JEB, 15 November 1896.
89. JEB, *Truth before Everything*, Liverpool: Pewtress, 1897, p.13; FL, JEB to the Misses Priestman, 28 July 1897; LUL, JB 1/1 1897/04/26 (I), JEB to Fanny Forsaith.
90. JEB, *Truth before Everything*, pp.7, 8.
91. Ibid., pp.1, 8. In private letters to Fanny Forsaith, Josephine described Lady Henry's supporters as 'vulgar sycophants', 'wretched flatterers & blinded worshippers', writing, 'It is rather humiliating to think that any great number of English women should be so infatuated about a person like Lady H.S., because of her title & winning manner. Happily not *all* the BWCTU are so silly' (FL, JEB to Fanny Forsaith, 18 February 1898; 16 February 1898).
92. FL, JEB's letter of resignation from the Purity Department of the WWCTU, 27 September 1897.
93. LUL, JB 1/1 1896/03/28 (I), JEB to Stanley Butler.

CHAPTER SEVENTEEN

1. FL, JEB to Fanny Forsaith, 13 December 1897.
2. Ibid., JEB to Margaret Tanner, 8 December 1897.
3. Ibid., JEB to Stanley Butler, 9 February 1898.
4. Ibid., JEB to Fanny Forsaith, 15 December 1898.
5. JEB, *Native Races and the War*, Newcastle upon Tyne: Mawson, Swann & Morgan, 1900, p.140.
6. Ibid., p.143.
7. Ibid., p.152.
8. Ibid., p.154.
9. FL, Henry J. Wilson to Fanny Forsaith, 7 January 1901.
10. Ibid., JEB to Millicent Fawcett, 20 June 1900. Millicent Fawcett was the leader of the ladies' commission of inquiry into the Boer concentration camps in South Africa in 1901.
11. Ibid., JEB to Mary Priestman, 2 November 1901.
12. Ibid., Personal newsletter from JEB, 'addressed only to a certain number of kind friends who have been my fellow workers in the past', March 1901; LUL, JB 1/1 1902/03/24 (II), JEB to Mr Dawson.
13. FL, JEB to the Misses Priestman, 14 February 1901.

14. LUL, JB 1/1 1901/01/24 (I), JEB to Fanny Forsaith.
15. Ibid., 1901/01/29 (I), JEB to Rhoda Butler.
16. Ibid., 1902/03/24 (II), JEB to Mr Dawson.
17. Ibid., 1901/01/23 (I), JEB to Stanley and Rhoda. Later that week she commented, 'the *whole world* is mourning, except a few wretched French people', ibid., 1901/01/29 (I), JEB to Rhoda Butler.
18. Ibid., 1901/01/24 (I), JEB to Fanny Forsaith.
19. Ibid., 1901/01/31 (I), JEB to Rhoda Butler.
20. FL, JEB to the Misses Priestman, 14 February 1901.
21. LUL, JB 1/1 1901/04/27 (I), JEB to her grandchildren, A.S.G. ('Bob') and Josephine Butler.
22. NRO, ZBU.E3/B2, JEB to Mrs Jane Grey, housekeeper, n.d. 1901.
23. FL, Charles Butler to James Stuart, 7 May 1901.
24. Ibid., JEB to the chairman of the Committee of the Federation, 11 May 1901.
25. Ibid., JEB to Fanny Forsaith, 19 February 1901.
26. LUL, JB 1/1 1900/04/30 (II), JEB to Mia Butler.
27. Ibid., 1901/10/12 (II), JEB to George Grey Butler.
28. Ibid., 1898/09/29 (II), JEB to Mia Butler.
29. FL, JEB to Fanny Forsaith, 20 September 1901.
30. LUL, JB 1/1 1901/10/30 (I), JEB to Rhoda Butler.
31. FL, JEB to the Misses Priestman, 21 December 1901.
32. LUL, JB 1/1 1901/12/23 (I), JEB to Stanley Butler.
33. FL, JEB to the Misses Priestman, 21 December 1901.
34. Ibid., 8 December 1901.
35. LUL, JB 1/1 1902/08/05 (I), JEB to Fanny Forsaith.
36. Ibid., 1902/03/24 (II), JEB to Mr Dawson.
37. Ibid., 1902/12/13 (I), JEB to Fanny Forsaith.
38. Ibid., 1903/03/02 (I), JEB to Stanley Butler.
39. FL, JEB to Millicent Fawcett, 9 April 1906.
40. Ibid.
41. LUL, JB 1/1 1903/08/11 (I), JEB to Fanny Forsaith.
42. Ibid., 1903/06/25 (I).
43. NRO, ZBU.E3/C8, JEB to Henry Montagu Butler, 31 December 1903.
44. She wrote to Fanny Forsaith, 'the *firm* are ready to receive papers & instructions from me, & get petitions signed and – no, not quite to die for me!!', LUL, JB 1/1 1905/00 (I).
45. Ibid., 1904/10/08 (I).
46. Ibid., 1904/04/05 (I).
47. Ibid., 1905/07/09 (I); ibid., 1/2/12 [*c.*26 February 1906?].
48. Ibid., 1905/07/09 (I); ibid., 1906/03/18 (I).
49. Ibid., 1906/06/25 (I).
50. Ibid., 1906/10/03 (I).
51. Quoted in E. Moberley Bell, *Josephine Butler: Flame of Fire*, London: Constable, 1962, p.249.

52. LUL, JB 1/1 1902/10/07 (I), JEB to Fanny Forsaith; ibid., 1904/05/28 (I).
53. Ibid., 1905/07/05 (I).
54. Ibid., 1906/01/06 (I).
55. FL, JEB to Fanny Forsaith, 10 March 1905.
56. LUL, JB 1/1 1906/10/07 (I), JEB to Fanny Forsaith.
57. Ibid., 1904/10/00 (I).
58. FL, James Stuart to Henry J. Wilson, 21 March 1905.
59. Ibid., JEB to Emily Ford, 14 April 1906. After her death, Josephine's estate was valued at £1,753 5*s.* 7*d.*
60. Ibid., Printed letter of thanks to the LNA by JEB, dated March 1906.
61. JEB to Millicent Fawcett, 9 April 1906.
62. JEB to Emily Ford, 14 April 1906. Emily was staggered to receive this, since, as she told Mrs Fawcett, Josephine had always told her that her portrait was 'best!', and she was hurt that Josephine was so out of touch with Emily's recent work. She signed herself, 'a little sorrowfully, Emily Ford' (ibid., 31 July 1906).
63. NRO, ZBU.E3/B2, George Grey Butler to JEB, 15 June 1905.
64. Ibid., Summary by George Grey Butler of a letter he wrote to JEB, 17 June 1905.
65. Ibid., George Grey Butler to JEB, 15 June 1905.
66. Ibid., Summary by George Grey Butler, 17 June 1905.
67. Ibid., George Grey Butler to JEB, 24 June 1905.
68. LUL, JB 1/1 1903/11/21 (I), JEB to Fanny Forsaith.
69. NRO, ZBU.E3/C8, JEB to Henry Montagu Butler, 14 June 1901; LUL, JB 1/1 1906/02/18 (I), JEB to Fanny Forsaith.
70. NRO, ZBU.E3/A10, JEB to George Grey Butler, n.d. [*c.*1903–4].
71. NRO, ZBU.E3/C4, 'Directions for my sons *to be read after my death*', endorsed May 1906.
72. LUL, JB 1/1 1906/04/02 (I), JEB to Fanny Forsaith.
73. Ibid., 1906/02/01 (I).
74. Ibid., 1906/04/05 (I).
75. Ibid., 1906/03/18 (I).
76. Ibid., 1906/10/05 (I).
77. Ibid., 1906/10/03 (I).
78. Ibid., 1906/10/05 (I).
79. Ibid., 1906/09/00 (I).
80. FL, Printed letter of thanks to the LNA from JEB, dated March 1906.
81. LUL, JB 1/1 1906/12/27 (I), JEB's last letter to Mrs Terrell (dated New Year's Eve, but written several days earlier, probably on 27 December).
82. Ibid., 1906/12/28 (I), JEB to Stanley Butler.
83. FL, Henry J. Wilson's translation of a circular issued by the Geneva Office of the Federation dated 2 January 1907.
84. Ibid., Fanny Forsaith to Henry J. Wilson, 5 January 1907.
85. NRO, ZBU/C4, 'Directions for my sons *to be read after my death*'.

86. FL, Fanny Forsaith to Henry J. Wilson, 5 January 1907.
87. NRO, ZBU/C4, 'Directions for my sons *to be read after my death*'.
88. FL, Canon Samuel A. Barnett to George Grey Butler, 7 January 1907.
89. Ibid., Wilfred Powell, HBM's Consulate, Philadelphia, to George Grey Butler, 18 January 1907.
90. Ibid., E. Pieczynska and H. von Muller to George Grey Butler, 6 January 1907.
91. Ibid., Arthur Gray Butler to George Grey Butler, 4 January 1907.
92. 'A Noble Woman', *Daily News*, Wednesday, 2 January 1907, p.6.
93. Ibid.

Bibliography

WORKS BY JOSEPHINE BUTLER

Address at the Annual Public Meeting of the Ladies' National Association, held in London, 11 June 1896, Bristol: Ladies' National Association, 1896

Address delivered at Craigie Hall, Edinburgh, 24 February 1871, by Josephine E. Butler, Manchester: A. Ireland, 1871

Address delivered at Croydon, 3 July 1871, by Josephine E. Butler, London: National Association, 1871

An Appeal to the People of England on the Recognition and Superintendence of Prostitution by Governments, Nottingham: Frederick Banks, 1870

A Call to Action: being a Letter to the Ladies of Birmingham, Supplementary to an Address given in Birmingham. November 1881, by Josephine E. Butler, Birmingham: Hudson & Son, 1881

By Whom in Future Are We To Be Governed?, London: Offices of 'The Christian', October 1885

Catherine of Siena. A Biography, London: Dyer Brothers, 1878

'The Constitutional Iniquity of the Contagious Diseases Acts of 1866 and 1869', Speech given at Bradford, 27 January 1871

The Constitution Violated, Edinburgh: Edmondson & Douglas, 1871

The Duty of Women in relation to our Great Social Evil, and Recent Legislation thereupon, being an Address delivered by Mrs Josephine E. Butler, in the County Hall, Carlisle, on the Morning of 25 November 1870, Nearly 400 Ladies Present, Carlisle: Hudson Scott & Sons, 1870

The Education and Employment of Women, Liverpool: Thomas Brakell and London: Macmillan, 1868

A Few Words Addressed to True-Hearted Women, Liverpool: T. Brakell, 1872

Government by Police, London: Dyer Brothers, 1879

The Hour before the Dawn. An Appeal to Men, London: Trübner, 1876

In Memoriam: Harriet Meuricoffre, London: Horace Marshall & Son, 1901

The Lady of Shumen, London: Horace Marshall, 1894

Legislative Restrictions on the Industry of Women, Considered from the Woman's Point of View, London: Matthews & Sons, 1874
'Letter to Mr Bryce on Examinations for Governesses' (1868) in Dale Spender (ed.), *The Education Papers: Women's Quest for Equality in Britain 1850–1912*, London: Routledge & Kegan Paul, 1987
A Letter to the Mothers of England: Commended also to the Attention of Fathers, Ministers of Religion and Legislators, April 1881
Life of Jean Frederic Oberlin, Pastor of the Ban de la Roche, London: Religious Tract Society, 1882
Memoir of John Grey of Dilston, Edinburgh: Edmondson & Douglas, 1869
The Moral Reclaimability of Prostitutes, read by Mrs Butler at a Conference of Delegates from Associations and Committees Formed in Various Towns for Promoting the Repeal of the Contagious Diseases Acts, Held at the Freemasons' Tavern, 5 & 6 May 1870, London: Ladies' National Association, 1870
'The Morning Cometh'. A Letter to my Children, printed for private circulation, Newcastle: T. M. Grierson, 1903
Native Races and the War, Newcastle upon Tyne: Mawson, Swann & Morgan, 1900
The New Abolitionists, London: Dyer Brothers, 1876
The New Era; containing a retrospect of the regulation system in Berlin, of the repeated opposition directed against the system there, and the causes of the failure of that opposition; with an indication of the lessons to be learned from past failure, and of the source whence hope arises for the future, Liverpool: T. Brakell, 1872
The New Godiva: A Dialogue, London: W. Isbister, 1883
Our Christianity Tested by the Irish Question, London: T. Fisher Unwin, 1887
Personal Reminiscences of a Great Crusade, London: Horace, Marshall & Son, 1896
Portion of an Address given by Mrs Josephine E. Butler. at a Conference of Women held in Geneva, on 16 August 1881, London: Hazell, Watson & Viney, 1881
The Present Aspect of the Abolitionist Cause in Relation to British India, A Letter to my Friends, London: British Continental & General Federation, June 1893
The Principles of the Abolitionists. An Address delivered at Exeter Hall, 20 February 1885, by Mrs Josephine E. Butler, London: Dyer Brothers, 1885
Rebecca Jarrett, London: Morgan & Scott, 1886
Recollections of George Butler, London: Simpkin, Marshall, Hamilton & Kent, and Bristol: J. W. Arrowsmith, 1892
The Revival and Extension of the Abolitionist Cause. A Letter to the Members of the Ladies' National Association, Winchester: John T. Doswell, 1887
The Salvation Army in Switzerland, London: Dyer Brothers, 1883
Social Purity, London: Morgan & Scott, 1879
Some Thoughts on the Present Aspect of the Crusade against the State Regulation of Vice, Liverpool: T. Brakell, 1874
Speech delivered by Mrs Josephine E. Butler at the Fourth Annual Meeting of the 'Vigilance Association for the Defence of Personal Rights', held at Bristol, 15 October 1874, London: Vigilance Association, 1874

'State Regulation of Vice', speech given to a Meeting of Ladies in the Friends' Meeting House, Hull, 29 September 1876

Sursum Corda: Annual Address to the Ladies' National Association, by Josephine E. Butler, Liverpool: T. Brakell, 1871

'To the Worshipful the Mayor of Liverpool' (March 1867) in Dale Spender (ed.), *The Education Papers: Women's Quest for Equality in Britain 1850–1912*, London: Routledge & Kegan Paul, 1987

Truth before Everything, Liverpool: Pewtress, 1897

The Voice of One Crying in the Wilderness. Being her first appeal made in 1874–5, to continental nations against the system of regulated vice. Now first translated into English by Osmund Airy, Bristol: J. W. Arrowsmith, 1913

Vox Populi, Liverpool: T. Brakell, 1871

Woman's Work and Woman's Culture, ed. Josephine Butler, London: Macmillan, 1869

SECONDARY SOURCES

Acton, William, *Prostitution* (1857), ed. with introduction and notes by Peter Fryer, London: Macgibbon & Kee, 1968

'An Irish Christian', *Rejection of Home Rule. Our Christianity Defended. A Reply to Mrs Butler's 'Our Christianity Tested'*, London: J. Kensit, 1887

Anon., *Letter to my Countrywomen dwelling in the Farmsteads and Cottages of England*, Manchester: A. Ireland, 1871

Ballhatchet, Kenneth, *Race, Sex and Class under the Raj: Imperial Attitudes and Policies and Their Critics 1793–1905*, London: Weidenfeld & Nicolson, 1980

Begbie, Harold, *William Booth, Founder of the Salvation Army*, London: Macmillan, 1920

Bell, E. Moberley, *Josephine Butler: Flame of Fire*, London: Constable, 1962

Bland, Lucy and Doan, Laura, *Sexology Uncensored: The Documents of Social Science*, Cambridge: Polity Press, 1998

Bolton, A. R. C., *The Six Brides of Dilston*, Bognor Regis: New Horizon, 1984

Bolton, Jasper, *Quickly Ripened: or, Recollections of the Late Jasper Bolton*, London: John F. Shaw, 1872

Boyd, Nancy, *Josephine Butler, Octavia Hill, Florence Nightingale: Three Women Who Changed Their World*, London: Macmillan, 1982

Bradbury, Oliver, 'A History of "The Priory"', *Cheltenham Local History Society Journal*, 16, 2000

Brock, M. G. and Curthoys, M. C. (eds), *The History of the University of Oxford, Vol. VI, Nineteenth-Century Oxford. Part 1*, Oxford: Clarendon Press, 1997

Bryant, Margaret, *The Unexpected Revolution: A Study in the History of Education of Women & Girls in the Nineteenth Century*, London: University of London Institute of Education, 1979

Burton, Antoinette, *Burdens of History: British Feminists, Indian Women, and Imperial Culture, 1865–1915*, London: University of North Carolina Press, 1994

Butler, A. S. G., *Portrait of Josephine Butler*, London: Faber & Faber, 1954

Butler, George, 'The Higher Education of Women: An Inaugural Lecture', 1868

Caine, Barbara, *Victorian Feminists*, Oxford: Oxford University Press, 1993

Clough, Blanche Athena, *Memoir of Anne J. Clough*, London: Edward Arnold, 1897

Crozier, Ivan, 'William Acton and the History of Sexuality: the Medical and Professional Context', *Journal of Victorian Culture*, 5.1, Spring 2000, pp.1–27.

Daubie, Julie (trans.), *French Morality under the Regulation System*, foreword by Josephine Butler, Liverpool: T. Brakell, 1870

Deacon, Richard, *The Private Life of Mr Gladstone*, London: Frederick Muller, 1965

Drenth, Annemieke van and Haan, Francisca de, *The Rise of Caring Power: Elizabeth Fry and Josephine Butler in Britain and the Netherlands*, Amsterdam: Amsterdam University Press, 1999

Dyer, Alfred S., *The European Slave Trade in English Girls. A Narrative of Facts*, London: Dyer Brothers, 1880

—*Six Years' Labour and Sorrow: The Fourth Report of the London Committee for Suppressing the Traffic in British Girls for Purposes of Continental Prostitution*, London: Dyer Brothers, 1885

Dyhouse, Carol, *Girls Growing Up in Late Victorian and Edwardian England*, London: Routledge & Kegan Paul, 1981

Edwards, Elizabeth, *Women in Teacher Training Colleges 1900–1960: A Culture of Femininity*, London: Routledge, 2001

Engel, Barbara Alpern, *Mothers and Daughters: Women of the Intelligentsia in Nineteenth-Century Russia*, Cambridge: Cambridge University Press, 1983

Fawcett, Millicent G. and Turner, E.M., *Josephine Butler: Her Work and Principles, and Their Meaning for the Twentieth Century*, London: Association for Moral and Social Hygiene, 1927

Finnegan, Frances, *Poverty and Prostitution: A Study of Victorian Prostitutes in York*, Cambridge: Cambridge University Press, 1979

Forster, Margaret, *Significant Sisters: The Grassroots of Active Feminism 1839–1939*, London: Secker & Warburg, 1984

Fowler, W. S., *A Study in Radicalism and Dissent: The Life and Times of Henry Joseph Wilson, 1833–1914*, London: The Epworth Press, 1961

Galton, Francis, *Memories of my Life*, London: Methuen, 1908

Gibson, Mary, *Prostitution and the State in Italy, 1860–1915*, New Brunswick, NJ and London: Rutgers University Press, 1986

Grey, Beverley, 'Mrs Josephine Butler: Unusual Domestic Snapshots of a Fiery 19th-Century Feminist', *Cheltenham Local History Society Journal*, 16, 2000

Grey, Charles Grey, *The Story of His Official Life: For His Children*, London: privately printed, 1906

—*Sequel to the Story of My Official Life*, London: privately printed, 1907

Hall, Trevor H., *The Strange Case of Edmund Gurney*, London: Gerald Duckworth, 1964

Hammond, J. L. and Hammond, Barbara, *James Stansfeld: A Victorian Champion of Sex Equality*, London: Longmans, Green, 1932

Harsin, Jill, *Policing Prostitution in Nineteenth Century Paris*, Princeton: Princeton University Press, 1985
Holcombe, Lee, *Wives and Property: Reform of the Married Women's Property Law in Nineteenth-Century England*, Toronto: University of Toronto Press, 1983
Holmes, Marion, 'Josephine Butler: A Cameo Life-Sketch' (1910), London: The Women's Freedom League, 1928
Holton, Sandra Stanley, 'Free Love and Victorian Feminism: The Divers Matrimonials of Elizabeth Wolstoneholme and Ben Elmy', *Victorian Studies*, 37, Winter 1994, pp.199–221
Hunt, John Dixon, *The Wider Sea: A Life of John Ruskin*, London: J. M. Dent, 1982
Jeffries, Sheila, *The Sexuality Debates*, London: Routledge & Kegan Paul, 1987
Jenkins, Roy, *Dilke: A Victorian Tragedy* (1958), London: Papermac, 1996
—*Gladstone*, London: Macmillan, 1995
Johnson, George W. and Johnson, Lucy A. (eds), *Josephine E. Butler: An Autobiographical Memoir*, London: J. W. Arrowsmith, 1909
Key, Robert, *The Laurel and the Ivy: The Story of Charles Stewart Parnell and Irish Nationalism*, London: Penguin Books, 1994
Kirk-Smith, Harold, *William Thomson, Archbishop of York. His Life and Times*, London: SPCK, 1958
Lerner, Laurence, *Angels and Absences: Child Deaths in the Nineteenth Century*, London: Vanderbilt University Press, 1997
Levine, Philippa, *Victorian Feminism 1850–1900*, London: Hutchinson, 1987
Lister, Raymond, *George Richmond: A Critical Biography*, London: Robin Garton, 1981
Longford, Elizabeth, *Eminent Victorian Women*, London: Weidenfeld & Nicolson, 1981
Longford, Elizabeth (ed.), *Darling Loosy: Letters to Princess Louise 1856–1939*, London: Weidenfeld & Nicolson, 1991
Lyons, F. S. L., *Charles Stewart Parnell*, London: William Collins Sons, 1977
Mahood, Linda, *The Magdalenes: Prostitution in the Nineteenth Century*, London: Routledge, 1990
Mason, Michael, *The Making of Victorian Sexuality*, Oxford: Oxford University Press, 1995
McHugh, Paul, *Prostitution and Victorian Social Reform*, London: Croom Helm, 1980
Midgley, Clare, *Women against Slavery: The British Campaigns, 1780–1870*, London: Routledge, 1992
Mill, John Stuart, *On Liberty and Other Writings*, ed. Stephan Collini, Cambridge: Cambridge University Press, 1989
Müller, Frederick Max, *My Autobiography: A Fragment*, London: Longmans, Green, 1901
Myers, F. W. H., 'Local Lectures for Women', *Macmillan's Magazine*, December 1868

—*Fragments of an Inner Life: An Autobiographical Sketch*, London: Society for Psychical Research, privately printed, July 1893

Nead, Linda, *Myths of Sexuality: Representations of Women in Victorian Britain*, Oxford: Basil Blackwell, 1988

O'Dwyer, Frederick, *The Architecture of Deane and Woodward*, Cork: Cork University Press, 1997

Pearson, Michael, *The Age of Consent: Victorian Prostitution and its Enemies*, Newton Abbot: David & Charles, 1972

Petrie, Glen, *A Singular Iniquity: The Campaigns of Josephine Butler*, New York: Viking Press, 1971

Plowden, Alison, *The Case of Eliza Armstrong: A Child of Thirteen Bought for £5*, London: BBC Books, 1974

Purvis, June, *A History of Women's Higher Education*, Milton Keynes: Open University Press, 1991

Quinn, Vincent and Prest, John (eds), *Dear Miss Nightingale*, Oxford: Clarendon Press, 1987

Railton, G. S. (ed.), *The Truth about the Armstrong Case and the Salvation Army*, London: Salvation Army Bookstores, 1885

Report from the Royal Commission on the Administration and Operation of the Contagious Diseases Acts 1866–69 (1871), PP, 1871 (C.408-I), XIX

Report of the Select Committee of the House of Commons on the Administration and Operation of the Contagious Diseases Acts, 1880, 1882 (340), IX.1

Report of the Select Committee of the House of Lords Appointed to Inquire into the State of the Law Related to the Protection of Young Girls (1881–82) PP, (344) XIII.823

Rickards, E.C., *Zoe Thomson of Bishopthorne and her Friends*, London: John Murray, 1916

Schults, Raymond L., *Crusader in Babylon: W. T. Stead and the Pall Mall Gazette*, Lincoln: University of Nebraska Press, 1972

Scott, Benjamin, *A State Iniquity: Its Rise and Overthrow* (1894), New York: Augustus M. Kelley, 1968

Shepherd, John A., *A History of the Liverpool Medical Institution*, Liverpool: Liverpool Medical Institution, 1979

Simey, Margaret, *Charity Discovered: A Study of Philanthropic Effort in Nineteenth Century Liverpool* (1951), Liverpool: Liverpool University Press, 1992

Spender Dale (ed.), *The Education Papers: Women's Quest for Equality in Britain 1850–1912*, London: Routledge & Kegan Paul, 1987

Stanton, Elizabeth Cady, *Eighty Years and More: Reminiscences 1815–1897*, Boston: Northeastern University Press, 1993

Stead, Estelle, *My Father: Personal and Spiritual Reminiscences*, London: Thomas Nelson & Sons, 1918

Stead, W. T., *My First Imprisonment*, London: E. Marlborough, 1886

—*Josephine Butler: A Life Sketch*, London: Morgan & Scott, 1887

Stuart, James, *Reminiscences*, London: printed for private circulation at the Chiswick Press, 1911

Sturge, Elizabeth, *Reminiscences of My Life and Some Account of the Children of William and Charlotte Sturge and of the Sturge Family of Bristol*, printed for private circulation, Bristol, 1928

Sturt, Mary, *The Education of the People: A History of Primary Education in England and Wales in the Nineteenth Century*, London: Routledge & Kegan Paul, 1967

Summers, Anne, '*The Constitution Violated*: the Female Body and the Female Subject in the Campaigns of Josephine Butler', *History Workshop Journal*, Autumn 1999, 48

Thomas, Henry Elwyn, *The Martyrs of Hell's Highway. A Novel with a Purpose*, London: H. R. Allenson, 1896, with a preface by Josephine Butler

Townsend, Charles, *Political Violence in Ireland: Government and Resistance since 1848*, Oxford: Clarendon Press, 1983

Tuson, Penelope (ed.), *The Queen's Daughters: An Anthology of Victorian Feminist Writings on India, 1857–1900*, Reading, Berks.: Ithaca Press, 1995

Uglow, Jenny, 'Josephine Butler: From Sympathy to Theory', in Dale Spender (ed.), *Feminist Theorists: Three Centuries of Women's Intellectual Traditions*, London: The Women's Press, 1983

Vidler, Alec R., *The Church in an Age of Revolution: 1789 to the Present Day*, Harmondsworth: Penguin Books, 1961

Wainwright, David, *Liverpool Gentlemen: A History of Liverpool College, an Independent Day School, from 1840*, London: Faber & Faber, 1960

Walkowitz, Judith R., *Prostitution and Victorian Society: Women, Class and the State*, Cambridge: Cambridge University Press, 1980

—*City of Dreadful Delight: Narratives of Sexual Danger in Late-Victorian London* (1992), London: Virago Press, 1994

Ware, Vron, *Beyond the Pale: White Women, Racism and History*, London: Verso, 1992

Wilkinson, J. J. Garth, *The Forcible Inspection of Women for the Oligarchy Considered Physically*, London, 1870

Williamson, Joseph, *Josephine Butler: The Forgotten Saint*, Leighton Buzzard: The Faith Press, 1977

Wilson, A. N., *Eminent Victorians*, London: BBC Books, 1989

Wilson, Henry J., *A Rough Record of Events and Incidents Connected with the Repeal of the 'Contagious Diseases Acts 1864–1869' in the United Kingdom. And of the Movement against State Regulation of Vice in India and the Colonies 1858–1906*, printed for private circulation, Sheffield: Parker Brothers, 1907

Yanni, Carla, *Nature's Museums: Victorian Science and the Architecture of Display*, London: Athlone Press, 1999

Index